Principles of Operations Management

Amitabh S. Raturi
University of Cincinnati

James R. Evans
University of Cincinnati

Australia · Canada · Mexico · Singapore · Spain · United Kingdom · United States

THOMSON
SOUTH-WESTERN

Principles of Operations Management
Amitabh S. Raturi and James R. Evans

VP/Editorial Director:
Jack W. Calhoun

VP/Editor-in-Chief:
George Werthman

Sr. Acquisitions Editor:
Charles McCormick, Jr.

Sr. Developmental Editor:
Alice Denny

Sr. Marketing Manager:
Larry Qualls

Production Editor:
Amy McGuire

Media Developmental Editor:
Chris Wittmer

Sr. Media Production Editor:
Amy Wilson

Manufacturing Coordinator:
Diane Lohman

Production House:
Argosy Publishing

Printer:
Thomson/West
Eagan, MN

Design Project Manager:
Bethany Casey

Internal Designer:
Bethany Casey

Cover Designer:
Bethany Casey

Cover Images:
©Digital Vision Ltd.

For permission to use material from this text or product, submit request online at: http://www.thomsonrights.com

For more information contact South-Western, 5191 Natorp Boulevard, Mason, Ohio 45040. Or you can visit our Internet site at: http://www.swlearning.com

Brief Contents

Contents

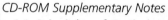

CHAPTER 10

Projects in Contemporary Organizations 283

CHAPTER 11

Emerging Challenges in Operations Management 318

TOOLS AND TECHNIQUES IN OPERATIONS MANAGEMENT

Preface

Principles of Operations Management provides an introduction to fundamental concepts of operations management in a meaningful and concise fashion. The text is designed to meet the needs of MBA students and mature students in other disciplines, such as engineering programs, and to support shorter, modular courses for which comprehensive texts are not feasible. A great deal of flexibility has been built into this package, however, through the student CD-ROM with "Bonus Materials" that provide additional notes and discussions, a comprehensive set of quantitative tools supplements, and cross-references to recommended published cases. This book may be used effectively for short five- or six-week modules or for full quarter- or semester-long courses.

This book focuses on presenting the most important principles of OM that drive business success. It highlights practical applications in various organizations through short vignettes. The book is organized into 11 chapters including one on emerging issues.

- Chapter 1, The Scope and Language of Operations Management, sets the stage by introducing basic ideas, language, and terminology of OM, its role in business, the concept of a value chain for goods and services, and the key focus areas that are addressed in subsequent chapters.

- Chapter 2, Operations Strategy and Performance Measurement, discusses the role of OM in strategic business planning and how OM can leverage operational capabilities to achieve competitive advantage. It also introduces performance measurement systems and metrics by which operations performance can be evaluated.

- Chapter 3, Product and Service Design and Development, focuses on the strategic importance of product and service concepts, approaches for ensuring the design and development of products and services that meet customer needs, and methods for ensuring successful development efforts.

- Chapter 4, Process Design and Improvement, addresses the strategic importance of process decisions, process thinking and technology, high-performance work systems, and related topics including time performance measurement, process variability, facility design, and process improvement.

- Chapter 5, Facilities and Capacity Planning, takes a broad look at the role of facilities in supporting operational capability, facility charters, and capacity planning.

- Chapter 6, Quality Management, provides a succinct yet comprehensive overview of quality management, focusing on key principles of total quality, contemporary frameworks such as Baldrige, ISO 9000, and Six Sigma, and systems for quality control and improvement.

○ · Chapter 7, Supply Chain Management, addresses the role of integrated supply chain management, strategic roles of inventory, measurement and evaluation of supply chain performance, the "bullwhip" effect, and coordination issues in managing supply chains.

○ Chapter 8, Inventory Management and Enterprise Planning Systems, traces the evolution of material planning systems from traditional reorder-point systems to modern ERP. Aggregate planning, MRP, manufacturing resource planning, and operations scheduling are described.

○ Chapter 9, Lean Thinking and Just-in-Time Operations, addresses concepts of lean thinking and lean production, principles of just-in-time, constraint management, and the integration of lean principles into modern Six Sigma initiatives.

○ Chapter 10, Projects in Contemporary Organizations, focuses on project management methodology and scheduling, including resource management, and cost control.

○ Chapter 11, Emerging Challenges in Operations Management, takes a reflective look at the topics discussed in the book and presents some perspectives on emerging issues that students will likely face in dealing with OM in the future.

Unique features of this book include Internet Projects in each chapter, designed to enrich students' understanding and knowledge of practice, and Experience OM exercises—hands-on, experiential exercises designed to make many of the principles "real" and facilitate classroom discussion. In addition, the Tools and Techniques supplements on the CD-ROM present a wide variety of quantitative methods that support functional OM topics. These materials provide instructors with the flexibility to introduce additional topics or emphasize modeling and problem solving.

Throughout *Principles of Operations Management,* the Web sites of many companies and organizations are presented as examples. Mention of URLs is also often part of the Internet Projects and other exercises. To allow readers to avoid the problem of dead links, all of the actual URLs can be found on the text's Web site, **http://raturi_evans.swlearning.com.** The URLs listed on the text's Web site will be continually corrected and updated as necessary.

ANCILLARIES

Author Amit Raturi has prepared instructor materials for each of the text chapters. These include guidelines and short answers for discussion questions, answers to problems, exercise debriefs, cross-references to recommended published cases, and suggestions about pedagogical strategy including a summary of principles. Solutions provided for the problems in the Tools and Techniques supplements and PowerPoint slides to enhance classroom presentations were prepared by author Jim Evans.

The instructor support materials are on a CD-ROM that is available to adopters through your South-Western publisher's representative, the Academic Resource Center at 800-423-0563, or **http://www.swlearning.com**. Ask for ISBN 0-324-00897-X.

ACKNOWLEDGMENTS

We express our appreciation to the following individuals who provided insightful comments during the preparation of this book:

Linda Angell
Victoria University of Wellington

Al Ansari
Seattle University

Philip Frye
Boise State University

Wendell Gilland
University of North Carolina Chapel Hill

Yunus Kathawala
Eastern Illinois University

Nicholas Petruzzi
University of Illinois

James Pope
Valdosta State University

Robert Schlesinger
San Diego State University

William Tallon
Northern Illinois University

Finally, we wish to thank Senior Acquisitions Editor Charles McCormick, Jr., and Senior Developmental Editor Alice Denny of South-Western for their support and assistance throughout the preparation and production of this book.

Please feel free to contact us with comments and suggestions for improvement. Again, recall that the instructor's materials are available to adopters by calling 800-423-0563 and requesting ISBN 0-324-00897-X.

AMITABH S. RATURI
Amit.Raturi@UC.edu

JAMES R. EVANS
James.Evans@UC.edu

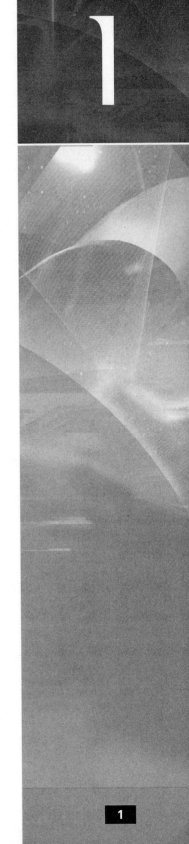

The Scope and Language of Operations Management

Operations management (OM) is concerned with the design, implementation, and maintenance of the operations function in manufacturing and service organizations—the activity that is responsible for acquiring such resources as materials, technology, and skilled employees, and configuring processes to create and distribute goods and services for consumers. Over the course of modern history, the operations function has emerged as a principal driver of competitive advantage for many firms. Specifically, the operations function has contributed to significant improvements in the cost, quality, timeliness, and availability of products and services—the four key metrics on which operations performance is measured. Thus, it plays as important a role as finance, marketing, and other traditional business functions.

This chapter develops the scope and language of operations management—the key concepts and terminology that you will need to understand the fundamental principles of OM. Specifically, we address:

- The definition of OM (*Section 1.1*).
- The importance of OM in achieving competitive advantage (*Section 1.2*).
- The differences between goods and services, the concept of a process, and the role of supply chains (*Section 1.3*).
- The key focus areas of OM and its role within the broader scope of business (*Section 1.4*).
- The evolution of OM and the challenges it faces (*Section 1.5*).

Material on the CD-ROM discusses some useful tools and techniques for operations management.

1. The Role of Quantitative Methods in OM

1.1 WHAT IS OPERATIONS MANAGEMENT?

Operations management (OM) is the business activity that involves the design, development, and maintenance of systems and processes that transform resources, such as raw materials, technology, and labor, into goods and services that meet customers' needs. For example, a manufacturing plant takes raw materials in the form of parts, components, and subassemblies and transforms them into manufactured products such as automobiles or bicycles, using resources such as labor, capital, and energy. As another example, a hospital uses diagnostic tests, medicines, consultations, and processes such as surgery and radiology to transform sick patients into healthy individuals. Specifically, OM focuses on principles and approaches used for the following:

- Designing the system of value-adding processes (called the **value chain**) for manufacturing goods and delivering services.

- Designing and managing processes that support the value chain; for example, product design, purchasing and materials management, storage and transportation, customer support, technology development, and work systems.

- Controlling and improving the value chain and support processes to achieve and sustain high levels of business and organizational performance.

- Managing the interface with other functional areas of business such as marketing, finance, and human resources in a way that enables the organization to derive competitive leverage from the operations function.

How important is OM? Consider that the original IBM personal computer, with 64 kilobytes of internal memory, a clock speed of 4.77 KHz, and one 360K floppy drive, sold for about $2,500 in the early 1980s—more than $5,000 in today's dollars. Today, you can purchase a system with at least 256 megabytes of internal memory, clock speeds of over 2 GHz, and a hard drive with a capacity of 40 GB or more for approximately $1,000. Many other products, including automobiles, consumer electronics, and appliances, show similar improvements in performance and quality, coupled with lower prices in real dollars.

> ## OM PRINCIPLE
>
> Significant improvements in product and service performance would not be possible without dramatic increases in productivity resulting from better technology and product design, more efficient manufacturing and service processes, enhanced information management, and superior systems integration—all of which characterize OM.

Throughout this book we will highlight many *OM Principles*—the most essential "takeaways" you should gain from this book. These are relevant to *all* business students, regardless of their area of study. In addition, we present numerous examples of *OM Practice*; the first one—"OM in the Workplace"—describes how some of our former graduates in various disciplines are using OM knowledge in their daily work.

OM PRACTICE

OM in the Workplace
OM principles apply in every business discipline.

Teresa Louis, an accounting major in college, now works at Chiquita Brands in a division that produces and sells fruit ingredients such as banana puree, frozen sliced bananas, and other fruit products. Although her primary job is an accountant, Teresa uses OM skills to support her work. Part of her responsibility is to look at the monthly profit-versus-cost analysis by product to calculate a net contribution. She examines the product costs at the plant level to find more efficient and cost-effective methods of production, such as reducing plant downtimes to increase efficiency and thus profitability. Part of the closing process is to reconcile the Inventory Movement because inventory is the principal driver of the fruit commodity business. Having accurate inventory balances and levels is very important because the percentage of sales is based on these figures. Teresa is also involved in ensuring inventory accuracy at the company's distribution centers.

Tom James, an information technology and management major in college, now works as a senior software developer for a small software development company that creates sales proposal automation software. Tom uses OM skills in dealing with quality and customer service issues related to the software products he is developing. He is also extensively involved in project management activities, including identifying tasks, assigning developers to tasks, estimating the time and cost to complete projects, and studying the variance between the estimated and actual time it took to complete a project. In addition, he is involved in continuous improvement projects that seek to reduce development time and increase the efficiency of the development team.

1.2 OPERATIONS MANAGEMENT AND COMPETITIVENESS

OM PRINCIPLE

The primary purpose of the OM function is to support the organization's business strategy and help create and sustain competitive advantage. Operations managers must work in harmony with all other business functions.

Why is OM important for every business student? The answer is simple: OM is fundamental to an organization's achievement of its mission and competitive goals. OM is directly responsible for producing and delivering goods and services. Without goods and services, there would be no customers. Without customers, there would be no revenue. We think you get the picture!

Well-designed manufacturing and service operations exploit a company's **distinctive competencies**—the strengths unique to that company—to meet these needs. Such strengths might be a particularly skilled or creative workforce, strong distribution networks, or the ability to rapidly develop new products or quickly change production-output rates (see the *OM Practice* box on BMW). Many other firms have excelled at operations to improve their competitive position, including FedEx, Wal-Mart, IBM, Bombardier, Harley-Davidson, Toyota, Walt Disney, Avis, SSM Health Care, and Southwest Airlines.

OM PRACTICE

BMW
BMW's competitive advantage revolves around basic OM principles.

The banner "Customers Drive Our Future" greets visitors to BMW's Spartanburg, South Carolina plant, which produces Z3 roadsters and its new SUV, the X5. BMW operates one of the cleanest and quietest assembly plants in the industry, with three distinctive competencies: speed, flexibility, and quality. BMW's approach to meeting its cost challenges is to speed things up. The plant was launched in 23 months. The X5 was developed in 35 months, and the company has an aggressive target of reducing new product development cycles by 30 percent. The way to customize every car to meet an individual customer's needs is to have "efficient flexibility." With 22 color options

for the Z3 (since replaced by the Z4), 123 center consoles, and 26 wheel options, BMW has become a master at logistics. Its flexibility extends to management and people; it is introducing two 10-hour shifts to accommodate the growth of the X5. Finally, its commitment to quality, exemplified by consistent fit and finish tolerances and elimination of tolerance "stack-up" with a new door-hanging technology, is imperative to meet the needs of its demanding customer base.

These attributes are in stark contrast to the traditional German style of operations, which is essentially to engineer until it can't be engineered any more. Instead, embracing a concept called *accelerated learning*, BMW has been a beta test site for SAP's R3 Enterprise Resource Planning software and learned more efficient methods of setting up a factory from Honda plant engineers.[1]

OM is linked directly with many initiatives that firms use to sustain and revitalize competitiveness. These include such approaches as rapid product development, process improvement and total quality, lean production, and supply chain management. As the workplace becomes more flexible, as information technology (IT) and e-commerce permit new and innovative work arrangements, and as customers become more demanding, OM will continue to play a significant role from a strategic business perspective. In Chapter 2 we will focus on the key components of operations strategy and their relationship to overall business strategy.

In addition, a firm's success or failure can depend on how it manages operations on a daily basis. For example, Jeff Bezos's original concept for Amazon.com was to have no warehouses or inventory, but he quickly learned that he needed his own warehouses so that he could control a transaction from start to finish. With warehouses came a whole host of issues that required a high level of OM expertise, such as conveyor technology, picking algorithms, and productivity improvement. Between 1999 and 2003, improved designs and OM tripled the volume that Amazon's warehouses can handle and reduced costs from nearly 20 percent of revenues to less than 10 percent. While most other dot-coms failed, Amazon has begun to thrive and now has an operating profit margin approaching Wal-Mart's.[2]

Many firms have focused on revamping OM practices as a strategic initiative (see the *OM Practice* box about NUMMI, which illustrates typical actions taken by operations managers to deliver products and services better, faster, and cheaper than competitors). After German auto manufacturer Porsche saw its 1992 sales drop to one-fourth of its 1986 peak and incurred a $133 million loss, CEO Wendelin Wiedeking hired two Japanese efficiency experts. With their help, the company tackled a wasteful parts inventory, cut layers of management, negotiated more flexible work rules, reduced product development time from seven to three years, trimmed parts suppliers from 1,000 to 300, reduced defects by a factor of 10 through rigorous quality control, and revamped the assembly process to produce new 911s in 60 versus 120 hours for its predecessor.[3]

OM PRACTICE

New United Motor Manufacturing (NUMMI)

Better management, not technology investment, transforms an inefficient GM auto plant.

New United Motor Manufacturing, Inc. (NUMMI) is a joint venture between General Motors (GM) and Toyota. In setting up the company, Toyota transformed an antiquated California assembly plant into GM's most efficient factory. Before GM closed its old plant in 1982, it was a battleground between inflexible managers and workers with an absenteeism rate of 20 percent. Toyota quickly turned the plant around by hiring the best of the former workers and replacing GM's 100 job classifications with teams of multiskilled workers. Absenteeism dropped to less than 2 percent.

Productivity at the plant rose to twice the average level at other GM plants. The Toyota managers achieved this improvement without adding special technology. Instead, they focused on five areas:

1. New products are designed for easy assembly and easy modification.
2. Production layout is organized by product needs, not by function.
3. Production flow is managed so carefully that inventories are almost nonexistent.
4. Workers share responsibility for quality.
5. Employees participate in nearly all decisions.

The beauty of the system is not in the individual elements, but in how the elements are integrated into a coherent operations strategy. Even without much automation, each worker was producing 63 cars a year by 1989, more than in any other U.S. plant and 40 percent above the average at that time. Unfortunately, GM was not able to fully integrate these principles into its other traditional operations.

Today, NUMMI continues to flourish as a company of 5,000 team members who produce the Toyota Corolla, Toyota Tacoma, and Pontiac Vibe. Recently, it began to produce a right-hand drive Toyota, the Voltz, for export to Japan.[4] For a thorough description of NUMMI's production system, assembly operations, and quality assurance processes, see the text Web site at **http:// raturi_evans.swlearning.com**.

Today, the need to sustain and improve operations' performance is greater than ever. Consider Ford Motor Company, which, according to *Fortune*, "used to brag 'Quality is Job One' [and] now produces vehicles with more defects than any of its six largest competitors, according to a survey by J.D. Power & Associates." An anonymous Wall Street analyst added that "costs are up, productivity is down, and the value of the brands is sinking." Various recalls on popular vehicles and the Firestone tire fiasco have further tarnished the company's image.[5] Former CEO Jac Nasser admitted that quality problems and production delays cost the company over $1 billion in lost profits in 2000 and was removed from office by the Ford family in October 2001. It is somewhat ironic that Ford, which radically transformed Jaguar's manufacturing processes from one of the worst in quality to one of the best, experienced such problems in its own operations.

Operations management is as critical to service firms as it is to manufacturing. Take Nordstrom, for example, which achieved legendary status as a premier customer service organization. In recent years, the company has seen its sales, earnings, and stock price plummet. Its customer service is not the distinctive competency it once was as competitors have improved their service and products. Though Nordstrom has always tried to offer superior service with great marketing and store designs, it has stumbled on basic OM issues such as inventory management and consistency in execution. As late as 2001, Nordstrom had not fully installed its first computerized inventory system in all 123 stores and was still depending partly on handwritten notes compiled in loose-leaf binders by sales clerks to manage inventory.[6] In this book we shall provide a balanced treatment of both manufacturing and service issues in operations.

OM principles also play a critical role in such nonmanufacturing activities as auditing, marketing, entertainment, and investment banking. "Better, faster, cheaper" defines the heart and soul of OM, and suggests that OM principles and tools can benefit all functional managers.

OM PRINCIPLE

The OM function in any organization—profit or nonprofit, service or manufacturing—contributes to the organization's ability to satisfy customers and achieve competitive advantage through *lower costs, ever-improving quality, shorter time, and increased responsiveness.*

1.3 PRODUCTS, PROCESSES, AND SUPPLY CHAINS

Operations are focused on goods and services, collectively referred to as **products. Goods** are tangible items that can be transferred from one place to another and can be stored for purchase by a consumer at a later time. For example, automobiles, home appliances, and packaged foods are usually produced in one location and purchased in another. **Services,** such as providing financial advice or a vacation experience, take place in direct contact between a customer and representatives of the service function. *Customer contact* is a key characteristic of services. A high level of customer service is vital to retaining current customers as well as for attracting new ones. Examples of service organizations include hotels, hospitals, law offices, educational institutions, financial institutions, transportation organizations, and public utilities. They provide such services as a restful and satisfying vacation, responsive health care, legal defense, knowledge enhancement, accurate check processing, safe transport, and reliable electric power. In addition to activities that involve direct customer contact, services also include "back office" support for internal customers of an organization, such as IT support, training, and legal services.

Services now dominate the economies of most industrialized nations. In the United States, they generate nearly three-fourths of the gross domestic product and account for almost 80 percent of all jobs. Customer service is playing a more prominent role, and IT is a dramatic new force in all kinds of industries and businesses (see the *OM Practice* box on the Ritz-Carlton). Many of the scientific and behavioral management approaches originally developed for manufacturing operations are being widely applied in services. Note, however, that although manufacturing employs a declining share of the U.S. working population, manufacturing is still a vital part of the U.S. economy. The value of U.S.-manufactured goods is more than 50 percent higher than the value of the goods turned out by Japan and a third larger than the combined output of France, Germany, and Britain; furthermore, productivity has increased steadily for over 20 years.[7]

OM PRACTICE

Ladies and Gentlemen at the Ritz-Carlton

The Ritz-Carlton Motto is "We Are Ladies and Gentlemen Serving Ladies and Gentlemen."

Faced with consumers looking for reliability, timely delivery, and value, the hotel industry is a very competitive business. The Ritz-Carlton focuses on the principal concerns of its main customers and strives to provide them with highly personalized, caring service. Attention to employee performance and information technology are two of the company's many strengths that have helped it to achieve superior performance.

The Ritz-Carlton operates from an easy-to-understand definition of service quality that is aggressively communicated and internalized at all levels of the organization. Its "Three Steps of Service, Motto, Employee Promise, Credo, and Basics"—collectively known as the Gold Standards—are instilled in all employees through extensive training. The standards allow employees to think and act independently and innovate for the benefit of both the customer and the company.

The Ritz-Carlton uses many sources of information to learn what its customers want. These sources include travel partners such as airlines and credit card companies; focus groups; customer-satisfaction and performance data, which are gathered daily; complaints, claims, and feedback from the sales force; customer interviews; travel industry publications and studies; and even special psychological studies to interpret what customers mean, not just what they say, and to determine what language will best appeal to them. Information systems involve every employee and provide critical, responsive data on guest preferences, the quantity of error-free products and services provided, and opportunities for improvement. Each production and support process is assigned an "executive owner" at the corporate office and a "working owner" at the hotel level. The "owners" are responsible for developing and improving the processes; they have the authority to define the measurements and determine the resources needed to manage them. The Ritz-Carlton even has a process to overcome cultural resistance to change: stress the importance of the change, express confidence that it can be made, provide a reason why people as a group should make the change, and allow time for them to accommodate to the change.[8]

Many goods and services that were transacted on a pay-on-delivery basis are now evolving into **contracts.** Contracts are business exchanges in which neither services nor goods are transferred; instead, there is an implicit understanding between the customer and the provider that goods and services will be provided on an "as needed" basis. With a contract, the customer pays a fee and then is entitled to a manufactured good or a service; indeed, the customer may or may not exercise this option. Historically, firms in the insurance industry have operated on contracts—today, increasingly, health-care providers, Internet and applications service providers (ASPs), and many other businesses are moving to contract-based transactions.

Table 1.1 summarizes some key differences and operational consequences among goods, services, and contracts across several factors that shape operational decisions in organizations. With a manufactured good, the customer walks off with

OM PRINCIPLE

The differences between goods, services, and contracts significantly affect the way an operations function should be managed.

most of the "output" when it is purchased. In contrast, services and contracts are intangible. For example, much service work is knowledge based and performed by people, making it far less exact and consistent than manufacturing. Generally, people cannot treat each customer precisely the same from one day to the next. Human interaction during the delivery of the service—in the form of "customer contacts" or "moments of truth"—becomes the focus of attention. Service occurs in the presence of the service provider, making it difficult to manage capacity and control quality since inventory cannot be stored and inspected prior to the

TABLE 1.1	*Some Comparisons among Goods, Services, and Contracts*		
Operations Factors	**Goods**	**Services**	**Contracts**
Value	Value is provided by physical processing during manufacturing.	Value is provided by availability of the service, leading to sensory or psychological satisfaction.	Value is provided by the promise (guarantee) of availability of a product or service when the contract is exercised.
Tangibility	Goods are tangible; specifications are easily defined; and goods can be inspected for quality.	Services are intangible; operational characteristics are difficult to specify; and services cannot be inspected for quality prior to consumption.	Intangibility is often accompanied by an absence of customer presence for long periods of time.
Process design	Manufacturing can be isolated from the customer and designed for efficiency.	The service process must be designed to occur in the presence of the customer.	The process must be designed to accommodate batches and surges in demand.
Inventory	Products can be stored for later consumption.	Services are consumed as they are created.	Many operations can be conducted "off-line," or not in the presence of the customer.
Capacity	Manufacturing capacity can be designed for average demand.	Capacity must be designed for maximum demand.	Capacity must be flexible to accommodate periods of low and high demand.
Quality	Manufacturing processes can achieve a high level of precision and repeatability.	Consistency of human performance is more difficult to maintain; customer perceptions are subjective.	Quality is perceived only when the option is exercised, and may be influenced by time and availability.
Location	Facilities can be located to minimize operations and transportation costs.	Service facilities must be located near the customer.	Centralization and economies of scale are more likely.

service encounter. A manufacturing defect can always be reworked before shipping; if a service worker makes an error in the presence of a customer, it is too late. Transactions via contracts are even more complicated because all customers may choose to exercise their options (their entitlement) at the same time. An exercise at the end of the chapter allows you to explore the operational challenges faced by the health-care industry as it shifts from a fee-for-service system to a "capitation" fee-based system in which health maintenance organizations contract with customers to provide health service on a "when needed" basis.

Today, the landscape of operations—particularly in manufacturing—is changing significantly, and distinctions among goods, services, and contracts are becoming muddled. For example, Xerox, in its strategy to be the "Document Company," redefined its product as facilitating communications rather than just selling copy machines.[9] It now offers products that can copy handwritten documents, convert them to electronic form, and e-mail them. Such products have allowed Xerox to increase the services related to document management in its output bundle. Recent thinking suggests that most manufacturing firms are better off thinking of their output in terms of the service bundle they provide to the customer.[10] Hilton hotels have automated the process of delivering goods and services (keys and directions) at kiosks by using "smart cards" that store customer information, allowing the hotel to assign rooms based on customer preferences (such as smoking versus non-smoking).[11] Mercedes is developing a system that will connect the car's software via the Internet to a customer assistance center, which will be able to diagnose any problems while the car is being driven and even download and repair the problem without the owner having to make a trip to the service center. Many other traditional manufacturing companies like check printers and wafer fabrication equipment firms are also refocusing their strategies around services. This transition creates significant challenges for OM.

> **OM PRINCIPLE**
>
> Pure manufacturing firms no longer exist; today, most firms produce a *bundle* of goods and services and are redefining their manufacturing capabilities within a service framework.

A firm's products and services may be *standard* in the sense that customers have no choice (the original IBM PC was produced in one standard configuration), or they may be *customized* to meet the needs of individual customers. For example, Dell computers may be configured online to meet customer specifications, and cell phones can be bought in a wide variety of colors and styles. **Customization** refers to a firm's ability to respond to a customer's individual needs, thereby making its products and services more attractive. In a common form of customization, customers can choose from various options when an order is placed. For example, the purchaser of a new car selects the type of transmission, body style, seats, and audio equipment that he or she prefers. Managing operations is more difficult with customization because it entails handling different product and service configurations, managing many more components, or dealing with more complex service procedures. The *OM Practice* box on Dell provides some insight into the role of operations in a customization environment.

Processes and Supply Chains

"How do we design a new product?" "How do we assemble it?" "How do we resolve a customer complaint?" These are only some of the many questions that confront operations managers every day. The answer to any "how" question can usually be found by describing the *process* used to accomplish the activity. A **process** is a set of linked activities that perform some manufacturing or service task that adds value (the amount buyers are willing to pay for what a firm provides)[12] to a good or service. A process is the basic unit for defining and managing key operations functions within the value chain.

Key processes include primary **value creation processes,** which produce benefit for customers and the organization by generating products and services, such as design, manufacturing, and service delivery, and **support processes,** which provide infrastructure, but generally do not add value directly to the product or service. For example, Merrill Lynch Credit Corporation identifies eight primary processes in its value chain: business development (design of credit products and services), marketing, client services, lending support services, underwriting, lending services, post closing/secondary marketing, and loan administration. Its

OM PRACTICE

Dell, Inc.
Operations is at the core of Dell's success.

Dell's business model is based on delivering quickly to customers the exact computer that they want. The manufacturing and service challenges it faces are enormous, however, because customers have an almost unlimited number of choices. For example, each machine can have any of a dozen or so microprocessors and any of two dozen network adapters. When you figure in memory, disk drives, video cards, storage devices, sound cards, and even monitors, the number of potential combinations quickly skyrockets—and that's not even including the types of software that Dell can install on each system. Nevertheless, Dell has emerged as the top seller of PCs in the United States, largely because of the way it designs and manages operations.

Before 1997, Dell had a standard assembly-line process for making servers and PCs. Computers were processed sequentially with one person after another adding a bolt here, a processor there. In this progressive-build system, it took up to 25 people to build one machine. To improve the speed of assembly and allow customized options, Dell had to find a way for the manufacturing teams to know they had all the parts and components needed to finish an order—whether it was for a single PC or for 200 of them—before they started building the first one. To handle all possible combinations, Dell instituted a system of baskets, racks and traffic signals, called the Pick-To-Light system, that is based on an up-to-the-minute database tied to inventory levels of components. The system keeps track of which materials need replenishing and makes sure the racks are filled with the proper components. This improves both order accuracy and speed of production.

After implementing this and other systems in its Metric 12 plant in Austin, Texas, Dell applied this approach to all of its manufacturing centers. It has increased its manufacturing speed and throughput by 150 percent, raised the uptime of its manufacturing lines by more than 95 percent, and reduced the repetitiveness of assembly-line jobs, thereby reducing employee turnover.[13]

support processes include technology information systems, human resources, administrative services, legal, business services such as quality assurance, and finance. A process such as order entry that might be a core process for one company (e.g., a direct-mail distributor) may be a support process for another (e.g., a custom manufacturer). In general, core processes are driven by external customer needs while support processes are driven by internal customer needs.

Generally, processes involve combinations of people, machines, tools, techniques, and materials in a systematic series of steps or actions. Figure 1.1 shows the role of processes in the overall value chain that extends from suppliers to customers. **Inputs** consist of the resources—materials, capital, equipment, personnel, information, and energy—used to produce the desired outputs. **Outputs** are the tangible goods or intangible services that result from the process. Inputs typically are selected by the operations function in cooperation with other functions. For example, the purchase of capital equipment such as machine tools involves working with the finance and purchasing functions, and product design processes often involve marketing and engineering personnel. The selection of appropriate inputs may depend on several factors:

○ **Market:** Changes in customer requirements for product features and services may require changes in an organization's mix of inputs. For example, widespread use of the Internet by home computer owners has led to the use of alternative microprocessors (e.g., Intel Celeron) than those typically used by "power users" (Intel Pentium).

○ **Technology:** Advances in technology often lead to changes in the inputs used in a process. For instance, the increased use of automation and advanced technology in production means that new hires must have more advanced skills and knowledge.

○ **Environmental Regulations:** Regulations on emissions have had significant effects on the mix of inputs used by power-generating firms.

FIGURE 1.1 | *A Process View of Operations Management*

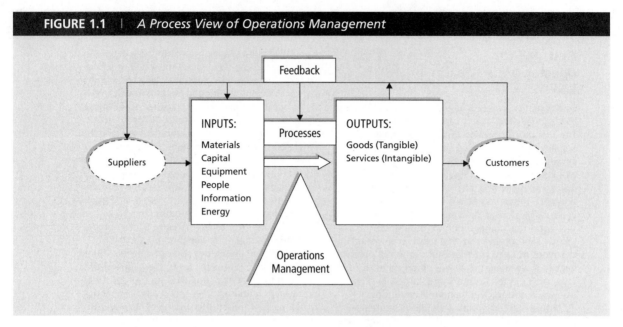

Suppliers provide inputs to a process. For example, an automobile engine plant may purchase steel from a steel company to produce engines. The steel company is a supplier to the engine plant. This is an example of an **external supplier.** A supplier may also be another department, function, or individual within the organization; we call these **internal suppliers.** Some examples are the tool clerk who provides tools to machinists or the hotel receptionist who provides information about new guests to housekeepers.

One critical decision that every firm makes is how many of the inputs to keep under its direct control. For example, a computer manufacturer might choose to produce its own circuit boards, disk drives, and other components; or it might decide to outsource the production of all components and simply assemble them.[14] Such decisions are called **make-or-buy decisions** and determine the **span of process**—the proportion of value-added operations controlled by an organization compared to the sum of all value-added operations needed to deliver the product or the service to the customer.

Acquiring inputs at a more primary stage, for instance, acquiring a supplier firm, is called **backward integration.** Delivering outputs in a more finished stage is **forward integration.** A manufacturing firm that opens its own retail outlets or initiates direct marketing to customers is integrating forward. Both forward and backward integration increase the span of process. The principal argument for increasing the span of process is to gain more control over supply or distribution. For instance, a computer manufacturer

> **OM PRINCIPLE**
>
> The wider the span of a process, the greater the control over the process, but also the more complex the task of OM.

with a larger span will be less dependent on suppliers that may not ship on time or have erratic quality, but it will need many more resources for component manufacturing, order processing, and delivery.

In contrast, many firms want to reduce their span of process by outsourcing some of their processes. The principal reasons are often the following:

1. The confusion and loss of focus created by an increased span of process are not worth the benefits of economies of scale and better control.

2. By outsourcing processes that are not critical for competitiveness, a firm may get better value as it can shop for the best provider of such services.

Customers receive the outputs of a process. Those who ultimately purchase a firm's final goods and services are usually called **consumers**. The recipients of goods and services from external suppliers are called **external customers,** while the recipients of goods and services from internal suppliers are called **internal customers.** Thus, the engine plant is an external customer of the steel company, and the machinist is an internal customer of the tool clerk. This distinction between consumers and (internal and external) customers is important for operations managers. The needs of each group are quite different and lead to different operations capabilities that must be met. For example, a consumer product company like Procter & Gamble must pay attention to consumers' needs for product quality and performance, as well as to external customers' (like Wal-Mart's) needs to supply the right products at the right time.

> ## OM PRINCIPLE
>
> The job of most employees is to meet the needs of their internal customers in order to satisfy the ultimate external customer, the consumer.

One view suggests that every customer's experience is determined by a company's order management cycle: every time the order is handled, the customer is handled, and every time it sits unattended, the customer sits unattended.[15]

The concept of internal customer has profoundly changed OM thinking. It helps employees understand how they fit into the system and how their work contributes to the final product, and it enables managers to view the organization as a system. For example, an illegible or incomplete order can result in the wrong pizza being delivered to the customer.

The role that consumers and other customers play in operations has changed in the past several decades. Previously, companies developed products that they thought consumers wanted without conducting extensive market research. Consumer input was not used in designing the product, nor was it sought to determine how well the product was liked. If the product did not sell, it was scrapped, and the company tried something else. Today, most organizations recognize that consumer input and feedback are essential in designing and redesigning products and processes to provide satisfaction, and every opportunity is taken to obtain such information. Nonetheless, some firms resist becoming "slaves to demographics, to market research, and to focus groups."[16] Chrysler, for instance, forged ahead with the original minivan despite research showing that people did not favor such an odd-looking vehicle. Firms in high-tech and research environments may tend toward incremental innovation (as opposed to radical innovation) if they pay too much attention to the consumer's immediate needs.

Most production systems consist of many "chains" of customers and suppliers, both internal and external. A **supply chain** is a network of facilities and distribution options that procures materials, transforms these materials into intermediate and finished products, and distributes these finished products to customers.[17] Most organizations are dedicating greater resources, technology, and brainpower to improving supply chain performance, an indication of the growing importance of supply chain management, which will be discussed fully in Chapter 7.

The configuration of a supply chain depends, to a great extent, on how the organization responds to customer demands. Two important types of processes are make-to-order and make-to-stock. With a **make-to-order** process, the customer has the ability to specify the nature of the product or when it is made. For example, manufacturers of jet engines produce only in response to orders from aircraft builders and allow the customers some flexibility in specifying the product to their needs. Many service firms, such as restaurants, have make-to-order processes because their services are highly customized or delivered on demand. With a **make-to-stock** process, the customer does not have this ability and must pick the product off the shelf. Manufacturers of radios and other small appliances build standard models and store them for future sale, so their processes are make-to-stock. A self-service cafeteria is another example of a make-to-stock process. Outputs from make-to-stock and make-to-order systems differ with respect to the variety and quantity of products made. It has been argued that firms producing functional, make-to-stock products with predictable demand should emphasize efficiency in designing their supply chain, whereas firms with innovative, made-to-order products should design their supply chain for responsiveness.[18]

> **OM PRINCIPLE**
>
> Because make-to-order processes typically produce a larger variety of products in smaller quantities than do make-to-stock processes, different transformation processes are appropriate for the two systems. Transformation processes for make-to-stock firms generally focus on efficiency while those for make-to-order firms focus on responsiveness and customization.

A key OM issue is how to manage a production process. Make-to-order systems typically operate as pull systems. In a **pull system,** the process happens only in response to a signal from an immediate, downstream user. The objective is to buy/make/receive/deliver/move exactly what is needed, when it is needed.[19] Dell, Inc. uses this concept in its manufacturing process so that its computers always incorporate the latest technology. The company stores virtually no inventory of key components; when an order is received, it triggers upstream orders for only those components that are needed. This implies that operations managers must coordinate all procurements from their suppliers quite closely. In contrast, a computer manufacturer such as Hewlett-Packard that produces standard products for sale in retail stores such as Circuit City and Radio Shack generally operates a **push system.** In this approach, a preplanned production schedule dictates the sequence and timing of the production process. Thus, the objective at HP would be to create an efficient schedule for planning receipt and use of materials.

> **OM PRINCIPLE**
>
> Pull systems trigger processes based on an immediate downstream demand, while push systems preplan the production and delivery of products and services.

However, a make-to-stock system may also operate as a pull system at the micro level. We will discuss this further in Chapter 9. In any case, the different systems require different approaches to managing operations.

1.4 KEY DECISIONS IN OPERATIONS MANAGEMENT

The scope of OM encompasses value creation and support processes and is best explained by examining the types of decisions that operations managers face. Table 1.2 summarizes these decisions, which can be put into three categories: *structure, infrastructure,* and *people and organization.* **Structural decisions** refer to the "hardware" of organizations; they are long-term decisions that require substantial capital investment and are difficult to reverse once they are in place. Examples are the number and size of facilities and the extent of process automation. **Infrastructural decisions,** or the "software" of operations, typically are more tactical in nature and facilitate the management of day-to-day issues. One example is the type of planning and control system used to ensure timely and efficient delivery of goods and services. Decisions about people and the organization of the operations function interact significantly with both structural and infrastructural decisions. Such issues are not unique to the operations function, however; they impact other functions such as marketing and finance and are

| TABLE 1.2 | *Key Decision Areas in Operations Management* |

Category	Decision Area	Typical Questions	Contemporary Challenges
Structure	Products **(What?)**	• Do we produce standard or custom products and services? • Do we make to order or make to stock?	• How do we design products and services that are easy to make? • How can we coordinate design teams that are scattered across the world?
	Processes **(How?)**	• What kind of equipment should we use? • How much of the process should be automated? • How should processes be configured?	• How do we exploit new IT developments such as the Internet for rapid and flexible response to customer needs?
	Capacity **(How much?)**	• How much is needed? • What type? • When should capacity be increased or decreased?	• How do we use flexible capacity options (such as temporary workers) and economies of scope for competitive advantage?
	Facilities **(Where?)**	• Where are they located? • What products should be produced in each?	• How do we manage and exploit global opportunities for locating facilities?
Infrastructure	Quality management **(How to improve?)**	• How do we prevent defects and errors? • How do we improve products and processes?	• How can we better learn from customers? • How can we improve quality to world-class standards?
	Inventory and supply chain management **(How to acquire and deliver?)**	• What products should we outsource? • How many suppliers should we use?	• How do we manage the supply chain for increased value to the customer? • What effect does the Internet have?
	Schedule management **(When?)**	• Should scheduling be centralized or decentralized? • How do we prioritize work and/or customer orders?	• How do we use available cost and financial information in scheduling? • How do we integrate enterprise resource planning systems into operations?
	Project management **(How to manage nonroutine tasks?)**	• How do we respond to customers' special needs? • What information do we need to effectively manage a project?	• How can we develop a learning organization in a geographically dispersed environment? • How can we best manage projects that cut across functional boundaries?

(continues)

TABLE 1.2	Key Decision Areas in Operations Management, continued

Category	Decision Area	Typical Questions	Contemporary Challenges
People and Organization	Workforce **(Who?)**	• What skill levels and training should employees have? • What types of compensation and reward systems are best?	• How can we develop truly "high-performance" work systems? • How can we better align work systems with long-range plans and objectives?
	Organization **(What structure?)**	• Is a hierarchical or team-based work structure better? • Should we train in-house or outsource?	• What structures are best suited for operations in different countries? • Should we "flatten" the organization?

Source: This categorization was first suggested by Robert Hayes and Steven Wheelwright, *Restoring Our Competitive Edge*, New York: John Wiley, 1984, pp. 30-33.

dealt with more effectively through the human resource management function. Thus, in this book, we restrict our attention to the eight decision areas in the structure and infrastructure categories. These decision areas address basic management questions such as what to produce, and how to do it, as outlined in Table 1.2.

It is important to understand the complex tradeoffs involved in operational decisions as well as how the different decision areas may be affected by such decisions. For example, quality of a product or service may improve with the procurement of more sophisticated process technology or with better supplier management programs. The decision to build a new facility may change how the firm needs to manage the supply chain. In addition, many of these activities require interaction with other functional areas of the firm such as finance, marketing, and accounting, as well as with external stakeholders such as suppliers and partners. As such, the operations function provides a unifying structure for coordinating different areas of an organization to meet its fundamental goal of satisfying all stakeholders—customers, employees, suppliers, owners, and society at large. This is what makes the task of managing operations challenging and fun.

OM PRINCIPLE

The eight decision areas in OM—products, capacity, facilities, processes, supply chain management, schedule management, quality management, and project management—are interrelated, and decisions in one category often influence another.

The decisions represented by these eight categories describe the operations strategy of an organization. Operations strategy is the portfolio of operations choices made in each of these categories to deliver competitive advantage to the organization. Developing an appropriate operations strategy involves ensuring that some operational decisions do not conflict with others. For example, a firm that takes pride in its ability to provide superior customer service and spends a lot of money and time ensuring that the quality of its service is outstanding may undo all its efforts by having inadequate capacity that results in long waiting times. We deal with issues related to the operations strategy of the firm in Chapter 2.

Structural Decisions

Structural decisions involve product and service design, process design and technology, capacity, and facilities. Because they typically require substantial capital investment, they usually are screened through the finance function—the capital budgeting process.

Product and Service Design

Product and service design drive many other business decisions. This function may be performed independently using engineering, marketing, or research and development (R&D) groups. However, many organizations integrate product design and development with process design and development, because decisions about product and service offerings are constrained by process capabilities and, in turn, affect the kind of process capabilities needed. Specifically, from an operations perspective, the following are important issues:

1. The nature of the product or service and how it affects the process.
2. Methods and systems for translating product and service needs to process requirements.
3. Innovative ways of product, service, and contract bundling that maximize process effectiveness.

Products and services range from those that are custom-made to those that are standardized and manufactured or delivered in large volumes. For instance, should sandwiches in a fast-food restaurant be made in response to customers' orders or made to a set of standard specifications and stored until customers demand them? Likewise, a grocery store must decide whether to use scanners or read prices manually. Custom products are unique, and cost is generally not an important issue. On-time delivery, quality, and the capability to design and manufacture different products can determine success. In contrast, firms that manufacture high-volume types of products usually benefit most from standardized designs, low cost and repetitiveness, and high availability of the product. Thus, it is important that managers understand the nature of the process and its implications for cost and productivity, quality, timeliness, and availability.

Some products, such as soft drinks and pizzas, have long product life cycles; others, such as electronics, have very short life cycles. Marketing strategies to renew or extend product life cycles often depend on introducing technological improvements in the product. Such strategies must be coordinated with operations for success. Product and service design issues are discussed further in Chapter 3.

Process Design and Technology

At least four process design choices have direct consequences on an organization's ability to respond to the market or to competitors:

1. The organization's resources (personnel and equipment) and their capabilities.
2. Its use of technology and automation.
3. The physical linkages within processes, including the layout of the facilities.
4. The linkages between process flow and information flow.

A make-to-order system employing general-purpose resources allows for flexibility in providing varying products and services. A make-to-stock system with special-purpose resources dedicated to one or a few tasks or products provides high volume and low unit costs. How a process is configured can make a significant difference in its effectiveness (see the *OM Practice* box).

Alexander Doll Company
Toyota's principles of process design improve doll assembly.

For over 75 years, the Alexander Doll Company has made collectible dolls modeled after fictional characters such as Cinderella and real people including Elizabeth Taylor; the dolls sell for $40 to $600. The daughter of a Russian immigrant founded the business in 1923. After being sold to two investors, however, it was headed for bankruptcy in 1995 when an investment group formed by TBM Consulting of North Carolina purchased it. The investors included manufacturing specialists who had studied Toyota's lean manufacturing system and taught it to dozens of U.S. manufacturers. Though making dolls is easier than making cars, it still requires considerable planning and coordination. The costumes may contain 20 or more separate items that go through as many as 30 production steps; fabric cannot be reordered; and 75 percent of the styles change each year. When the company was purchased, the plant had more than 90,000 dolls stored in partly finished condition, parts were stacked to the ceiling, and customers had to wait up to 16 weeks for delivery. When the new CEO tried to fill an order for 300 dolls, only 117 could be completed because so many pieces were missing. After reorganizing the factory using Toyota principles and organizing workers into seven- or eight-person teams responsible for completing doll or wardrobe assemblies, work in process has been cut by 96 percent and orders can now be filled in two weeks.[20]

Technology can often reduce unit costs and labor requirements, provide greater product variety and flexibility, increase quality, and improve a firm's ability to make and deliver products quickly. Technology decisions can be difficult and risky, however. For example, highly automated plants are very expensive. John Deere spent $500 million on its automated plant in Waterloo, Iowa, and General Electric spent over $300 million on automation improvements in its facility in Erie, Pennsylvania. Fabrication facilities for silicon chips ("fabs") may cost $1.5 billion or more.

Service organizations face similar issues. Many service processes are replacing traditional human interaction with self-service processes that are often computer or Internet based. For example, airlines are now allowing travelers to check in before flights on the Web or from kiosks located in the airport terminal. Nonetheless, implementing technology too quickly and without a rational basis can lead to disaster, as many firms discovered when they jumped on the e-commerce craze in the late 1990s, only to find that many traditional "bricks and mortar" strategies were more effective than "clicks and mortar." Process design and its effect on a firm's competitiveness are discussed in Chapters 4 and 9.

Capacity

Capacity is a measure of a system's output rate. At least three capacity choices have a direct impact on the ability of a firm to respond to customer demands:

1. The amount of capacity.
2. The timing of capacity expansion.
3. The type of capacity.

For example, what is the economic effect of expanding a facility versus building a new facility? What are the pros and cons of having one large facility versus several small ones? Are capacity decisions different for well-established products and new products? How does a firm make capacity decisions to cope with cyclic variations in demand? How does a firm best take advantage of economies of scale in planning capacity? Is having excess capacity necessarily bad?

Capacity decisions normally influence cost, quality, timeliness, and availability. Does a firm have the right kind of capacity? An airline might consider changing from large jets (which provide economies of scale) to smaller jets and more frequent flights (which provide a greater degree of customer service). Because no inventories are available to buffer demand, capacity defines the service organization's ability to meet demand. Too much capacity requires a high fixed-cost structure, while too little capacity can result in inadequate service delivery, resulting in the loss of (dissatisfied) customers. Capacity decisions are discussed in Chapter 5.

Facilities

The facilities strategy of an organization is closely related to its capacity decisions. Key facilities issues include the size of the facilities, their location, and their specialization. In the semiconductor industry, for example, small, low-volume plants are built for new products with considerable risk, whereas high-volume plants are used for stable, mature products. Managers must trade off economies associated with large, centralized production facilities with distribution costs and customer service.

Location decisions can be either global or local. What differences might a firm expect if it builds a facility in the United States, Mexico, or Singapore? At the local level, location is a critical strategic decision for many service organizations, such as restaurants and hotels. For instance, should a hotel locate in a downtown area or along an expressway? Oil companies often locate processing plants near supplies of crude oil to achieve economies of scale, while individual distribution outlets are located much closer to customers.

Decisions on how to structure product groups within plants, what types of processes to develop, and what volume to produce are important, especially in rapidly changing industries. Should a firm organize its facilities with a product charter (all plants make a product or a product line) or a process charter (plants focus on specific parts of the process)? Chapter 5 also addresses these issues.

Infrastructural Decisions

OM PRINCIPLE

The ability of the operations function to support an organization's business strategy and ensure that processes deliver the distinctive competencies an organization requires depends significantly on infrastructure.

Infrastructure refers to the management systems and policies associated with managing quality, schedules, inventory and the supply chain, and projects.

Quality

Quality is no longer viewed as simply "a good product or service." The contemporary notion of quality encompasses all aspects of a customer's relationship with an organization; thus, the quality infrastructure needs to be focused on delivering ever-improving value to customers that results in competitive advantage (the external view), as well as improving organizational performance and capabilities (the internal view). This can be done only by managing the entire enterprise, and all its components, from a systems perspective that is driven by customer needs and expectations. The behaviors found in high-performing organizations are reflected in a set of values that include visionary leadership, a customer-driven focus, organizational and personal learning, valuing employees and partners, agility, a focus on the future, managing for innovation, managing by fact, public responsibility and citizenship, focus on results and creating value, and a systems perspective. The design and operation of an effective quality management system are addressed in Chapter 6.

Inventory and Supply Chain

Competitive advantage derives from a streamlined flow of materials. Meeting demand requires timely and efficient delivery of goods. Supermarket chains operate their own distribution centers to better control the logistics of supply. A fast-food corporation may decide it should raise its own cattle rather than rely on external suppliers. While scheduling systems focus on effective use of resource capacity, the supply chain focuses on making the right materials available at the right time and the right place. "Lean production," as implemented and popularized by Toyota, stresses minimal inventories and just-in-time purchasing and production. The supply chain extends beyond the firm itself and generally includes suppliers. Some of the key questions that must be addressed are: Should we make components or purchase them from external suppliers? Should we acquire suppliers or merge with them? Should we use one or several suppliers? Increased integration of suppliers, or a "partnership strategy," requires more complex control by operations managers. Many companies work with only one or a few suppliers in an atmosphere of mutual dependence and trust. They help to train their suppliers in methods of quality assurance and improvement. In return, they expect 100 percent delivery of quality materials and components when needed. Issues related to supply chain management are addressed in Chapter 7, and other aspects of inventory management are discussed in Chapter 8.

Schedules

At least three aspects of a scheduling system have a direct impact on the flow of work through the organization: the extent of centralization in the creation of schedules and timetables for processing work, decision rules that adjust the level of work with variation in demand or prioritize work in a given fashion, and policies that govern the flow of work through the system.

For many service businesses, the most critical issue in achieving customer satisfaction may be reducing the time customers wait in line. Operating decisions that affect customer perceptions of waiting time and service quality are critical for long-term success. For instance, many managers of grocery and discount department stores are able to shift employees from such ancillary activities as stocking shelves to staffing checkout lines as demand increases.

How operations are planned and controlled affects the cost, quality, timeliness, and availability of products and services. While actual decisions made on a day-to-day basis may affect specific customer interactions, the policies in place for making such decisions have long-term effects. The evolution of enterprise resource planning (ERP) systems requires that workflow be coordinated with the flow of information across functional areas of the organization. This "tighter coupling" of work and information places unique demands on the organization. Chapters 8 and 9 focus on these topics and elaborate on the distinctions between push and pull systems, forward and backward scheduling, and alternative ways of scheduling work.

Project Management

So far, we have described structural and infrastructural decisions related to creating and maintaining a production and delivery system that focuses primarily on repetitive operations. **Projects**—structured sets of tasks that must be completed in a certain sequence, on time, and on budget and that often involve loose clusters of personnel from different departments or functions—are infrequent, sporadic activities designed to accomplish a specific purpose. Projects are often used to implement changes and improvements within an organization. Examples include reconfiguring a facility, implementing a new software package, or conducting an investigation into the causes of poor quality. In some functions, such as new product development, projects are used on a routine basis. Many organizations do only project work, for example, companies that conduct market research studies or clinical research trials for drug company clients. Project management principles and tools provide ways for project managers to best channel resources and accomplish project objectives. Chapter 10 emphasizes the importance of an effective project management system for leveraging the contributions of operations and other functions.

Internal and External Interfaces of the Operations Function

In many organizations, managers tend to view problems from the perspective of their own domain. Conflicts can arise, however, when operations are not viewed as a strategic component of the whole firm. In particular, the marketing function is often at odds with operations. Table 1.3 summarizes the key issues that often cause conflict between these two functions within our classification of structural and infrastructural decisions.

The issues and disagreements in Table 1.3 suggest that:

1. Either the firm does not have a clear agreement on such basic competitive parameters as the amount of product diversity, level of quality, customer service, capacity utilization, and lead-time, or

2. the firm evaluates performance by functional segregation, with marketing choosing such measures as new customers, market share growth, and customer service levels and operations selecting measures related to internal operations, such as utilization levels, inventory levels, reject rates, and costs.

This is not an unusual situation. Thus, it is important to recognize the roles that other functional areas, such as marketing or finance, play in influencing policies and objectives that affect the operations function. In the same manner, it is vital that all functional managers appreciate the role of the operations function.

The following briefly summarizes the role of key organizational functions and how they relate to operations:

○ **Finance:** Economic and financial decisions affect the choice of equipment, use of overtime, cost-control policies, and price-volume decisions. The practices and performance of the operations function are often dictated by economics of manufacturing and delivery, which are closely tied to the economics of the process (capital-labor ratios, investments in automation and inventories, etc.) It is thus imperative that finance personnel understand the nature of technology used in operations and the practice-performance gap in their organization. At the same time, knowledge of financial procedures, limits, and capabilities is vital for an operations manager.

○ **Marketing:** Marketing is responsible for understanding customer needs, generating and maintaining demand for the firm's products, ensuring customer satisfaction, and developing new markets and product potential. The firm's strategic positioning and its market segmentation decisions dictate much of manufacturing and operations strategy. Historically, the conflict between operations and marketing in most organizations has resulted from the lack of broad agreement on critical organizational decisions such as the width of the product line, the amount of time taken to deliver the product, and service or quality levels. The interface between these two functions offers wide leverage in most organizations: increased understanding and trust between operations and marketing propels many organizations to higher levels of effectiveness.[21]

○ **Accounting:** Accounting provides data on product and service costs that help managers evaluate operational performance. Further, the effectiveness of operational planning and

TABLE 1.3	Functional-Level Interactions of Marketing and Manufacturing		
Decision Area	**Problem Area**	**Typical Marketing Comment**	**Typical Manufacturing Comment**
Products	What types of products should we offer to customers and markets?	Our customers want many different features and customizable options.	If we broaden the product line too much, costs will skyrocket because we will be forced to use short, uneconomical production runs.
Processes	What should be the priorities in designing processes?	Production processes must be flexible to meet promised delivery dates made by the sales force.	We cannot meet every demand made by sales; this will create chaos and increase costs and make the system unmanageable.
Capacity	How much capacity do we need?	Our customers always have to wait; why can't we increase capacity?	We have plenty of capacity; the sales forecasts are always wrong, and we can't effectively use the capacity we have.
Facilities	How many facilities do we need, and where should they be located?	We need to be close to customers to give them the best possible service. Therefore, we need many smaller facilities.	We should consolidate facilities into large centralized operations to provide economies of scale.
Quality Management	What level of quality should we provide?	Our customers tell us that this is what they want and expect. Why can't you meet all their requirements?	The products and designs that marketing dictates are impossible to make with high quality with the technology we have. All the resources go to marketing efforts, not to production.
Inventory and Supply Chain	What products should we stock, and how much of each?	We can never supply the right products from our stock of inventory; there always seems to be a backorder.	We can't keep every possible item in stock; do you know how much that would cost?
Schedule Management	How do we schedule production runs?	We can't fulfill our promises to customers if you don't schedule what we need when we need it!	You can't keep giving us unrealistic lead-times that strain our resources!
Project Management	How do we roll out new products?	We have to continually make design changes to reflect the needs of our customers— and we need them tomorrow!	Design changes set our schedules back and increase our costs. Do you have any idea of how long it takes to change our production setups?

Source: Based on B. Shapiro, "Can Marketing and Manufacturing Coexist?" *Harvard Business Review*, 55(1997): 104–114.

budgeting is often driven by the accuracy of accounting data. A problem for many organizations is that accounting provides very detailed data on costs, but not on quality and delivery. As a result, managers may overemphasize cost at the expense of quality and delivery. Tracking performance in a balanced fashion requires that the firm develop common, objective platforms for performance evaluation. The use of multi-objective performance management systems is one way that accounting can facilitate the task of evaluating effectiveness.[22]

- **Design:** Product design and engineering determines product specifications to meet customer needs; process development and engineering subscribes the production methods necessary to make the products. These two functions are often housed in different functions (typically engineering and operations, respectively), but separating innovation (product design and development) from systematization (process engineering) invariably leads to organizational conflict. Shrinking product life cycles further exacerbate the demands on the product development process: launching more new products faster requires tight integration between these two functions. Initiatives such as simultaneous engineering and early supplier involvement in the product design process elevate the role of operations in the product and service concept design process.

- **Human Resources:** The human resource function includes recruiting and training employees, enhancing employee well-being and development, and fostering motivation. Operations' approaches such as continuous improvement and total quality rely on human energy. As firms rely more heavily on temporary workers and more employees work from home offices, flexibility in the design of operations becomes imperative. Similarly, as employees with children increasingly opt for "flextime," the operations function has to develop unique process configurations to accommodate them with minimum disruption in the flow of work. Work safety also has direct implications for process design. In services, the human resource focus is vital, as customers' perceptions of an organization are generally formed by their interaction with customer contact personnel, such as customer service representatives.

- **Information Systems:** Information systems provide the means for capturing, analyzing, and coordinating the information needs of all of the preceding areas as well as operations. The growth and evolution of planning systems have a direct impact on operations. The emergence of enterprise resource planning (ERP) systems that generate all relevant information for the organization based on operational plans makes the operations function a focal point in many organizations. The operations master schedule becomes the driver of all business planning including recruiting, cash flows, and marketing promotions. Evolution of IT permits the integration of "islands of automation" into computer-integrated manufacturing (CIM) systems. A synergistic assessment of operations (processes) and information systems to manage the processes is even more critical in service and contract businesses since much of the value is added through timely and effective information exchange. Much of the progress in IT is wasted if the operations function does not respond to the challenge created by the increased availability of information.

Other aspects of the external environment also have dramatic influences on the operations function. For example, competitors' pricing structures, new product introductions, and product features influence a company's strategy and its use of operations to compete. Laws and regulations dealing with employee safety, ergonomics, public risk, materials that may be used, and import restrictions constrain operations decisions. Technology, particularly new technology, always leads to questions of change and upgrade, with associated financial requirements to set up the technological infrastructure. Finally, the local community affects the availability of adequate labor, delivery of raw materials and components, and acceptance of company policies.

1.5 EVOLUTION AND CHALLENGES OF MODERN OPERATIONS MANAGEMENT

1.1

In the last century, OM has undergone more changes than any other functional area of business. See *Supplementary Notes 1.1* on the CD-ROM for a brief overview of the historical evolution of OM. Figure 1.2 shows a chronology of major changes in the scope of OM and the focal points on which businesses compete in the marketplace. OM has undergone three key shifts in emphasis:

1. From cost and efficiency to value creation.
2. From mass production to agility and customization.
3. From functional specialization to a systems approach to achieving high performance.

OM's early focus was internal: efficiency and cost reduction dominated management thinking. As customer needs have emerged as the principal driver of competitive success, OM's focus has become external—providing enhanced value through improved quality, better products, faster response, and lower prices. This has been facilitated by improvements in manufacturing systems—most notably, lean manufacturing—which have led to **mass customization** (the use of technology and management techniques to customize and produce smaller quantities of products at mass-production speeds to meet an individual customer's needs) and **agility** (the

OM PRINCIPLE

The benefits of lean manufacturing stem from making the product right the first time, continuous improvement, high quality, flexible production, low inventories, and minimizing all forms of waste.

FIGURE 1.2 | *Chronology of Operations Management Themes*

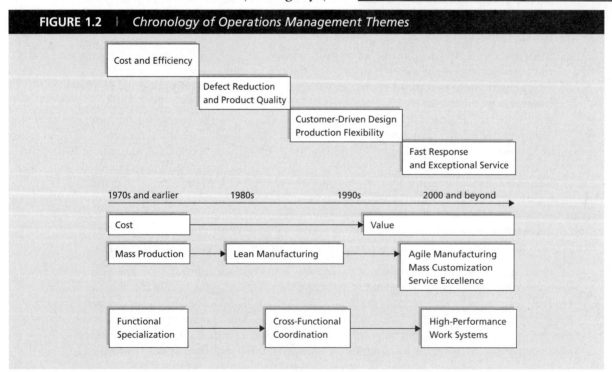

ability to respond quickly and flexibly to un-planned environmental and customer/market changes), as well as improvements in work systems.[23] **Lean manufacturing,** which was developed by Taiichi Ohno at Toyota Motor Company in the 1950s, is a streamlined production system that provides high levels of quality, productivity, and customer response. Today's lean production systems employ multiskilled workers, cross-functional teams, integrated communications, supplier partnerships, and highly flexible and increasingly automated technology to produce varieties of products. Such systems combine the best features of old-style craft production and early twentieth-century mass production: the ability to produce a variety of customized products with short lead-times.

> ## OM PRINCIPLE
>
> Inflexible mass-production methods, though very efficient and cost-effective, are inadequate for contemporary goals of increased product variety and continual product improvement.

Lean manufacturing is a prerequisite to agility because a company with large inventories, sluggish response, and poor quality cannot respond quickly to market changes. **Agile manufacturing,** which blends automation and computing technology, is the ability to economically produce a variety of products in any quantity with rapid changeovers. For instance, at an IBM plant in North Carolina, a 40-worker team simultaneously builds 12 different products ranging from bar-code scanners to fiber-optic connectors for mainframe computers and satellite communication devices for truck drivers. Each worker has a computer screen that displays a checklist of parts to install and guides the worker through the assembly steps if help is needed.

Lean and agile manufacturing have led to mass customization. For example, ChemStation, a 20-year-old industrial-detergent firm based in Dayton, Ohio, formulates cleaning products to meet an individual customer's specifications. When the customized product is ready for delivery, a ChemStation employee drives it to the customer's site and pumps the detergent into a reusable tank that has been installed in an accessible location. This "prescient delivery" system is a good example of mass customization—the customer doesn't even know the driver has been there. Of course, ChemStation monitors its customers' usage patterns closely; a salesperson periodically visits each site to see how much of the detergent is left. After a while a pattern emerges, and the salesperson doesn't have to check the levels any longer.

The focus on value has also forced many companies to rethink service. With the increasing importance of services, the emphasis of OM is changing even more. Service requires new types of workers: flexible, creative people who are able to work with minimal supervision to provide the exceptional service that today's consumers demand. If product quality cannot be economically improved and prices cannot be lowered, service may offer an opportunity for improvement, as in the case of Hewlett-Packard (HP). HP's Instrument Systems Division faced a problem when a key competitor cut its price for voltmeters. Should HP do nothing and risk losing sales, or should it lower its price to retain volume but lose revenues? HP chose a third alternative: it held its price steady, but increased its warranty from one to three years. The product was highly reliable, so the additional cost for the extra warranty was much less than the increase in profit. Also, rather than having customers wait for a failing unit to be repaired, HP changed its warranty policy to include shipment of a new unit within 24 hours. The perceived value of those additional services actually increased HP's market share and profitability.

Finally, organizational emphasis has shifted from functional efficiency to cross-functional coordination and high-performance work systems. **High-performance work systems** are characterized by flexibility, innovation, knowledge and skill sharing, alignment with organizational directions, customer focus, and rapid response to changing business needs and marketplace requirements. The design of these systems needs to be addressed at the individual, process, and organizational levels. At the individual level, work systems should enable work activities to be accomplished effectively and promote flexibility and individual initiative in managing and improving work processes. This requires extensive employee involvement, empowerment, and training and education. At the process level, cooperation, teamwork, and communication are key ingredients. At the organizational level, compensation, recognition, and attention to employee well-being through health, safety, and support services are major factors for outstanding performance.

The need to understand and coordinate these systems will continue to present interesting challenges to operations managers. In addition, a variety of other issues will affect the future of OM. One need only look at the automobile industry to understand this. Although the auto industry is

> **OM PRINCIPLE**
>
> The discipline of operations is highly dynamic, requiring organizations to continually learn and adapt to changing external and internal forces.

often referred to as "mature," dramatic changes in product and market leadership, technology, distribution channels, and even the geography of production have occurred in the past two decades and will continue in the future. A study from the U.S. Department of Commerce concluded that although operations will face numerous challenges in the future, the auto industry will continue to be viewed around the world as "the industry of industries" due not only to its sheer size in many nations' economies but also to its multidimensional complexity.[24] Table 1.4 summarizes these challenges using the structure and infrastructure classification that we introduced earlier.

A survey of CEOs by Louis Harris & Associates concluded that six major trends affect major U.S. companies: globalization, improving knowledge management, cost and cycle time reduction, improving supply chains globally, manufacturing at multiple locations in many countries, and managing the use of more part-time, temporary, and contract workers.[25] Echoing many of these factors, the American Society for Quality identified eight key forces that influence quality—and, we believe, OM in general:[26]

○ **Partnering:** Superior products and services will be delivered through partnering in all forms, including partnerships with competitors.

○ **Learning Systems:** Education systems for improved transfer of knowledge and skills will better equip individuals and organizations to compete.

○ **Adaptability and Speed of Change:** Adaptability and flexibility will be essential to compete and keep pace with the increasing velocity of change.

○ **Environmental Sustainability:** Environmental sustainability and accountability will be required to prevent the collapse of the global ecosystem.

○ **Globalization:** Globalization will continue to shape the economic and social environment.

○ **Knowledge Focus:** Knowledge will be the prime factor in competition and the creation of wealth.

○ **Customization and Differentiation:** Customization (lot size of one) and differentiation (quality of experience) will determine superior products and services.

○ **Shifting Demographics:** Shifting demographics (age and ethnicity) will continue to change societal values.

All of these critical business issues affect the management of operations; this clearly supports the strategic importance of OM. In this concluding section, we discuss three broad issues that are particularly important for OM and capture these trends: the challenges of a global economy, the role of IT in managing knowledge, and the increasing need for agility.

TABLE 1.4	*Future OM Challenges in the Automobile Industry*

Category	Decision Area	Challenges
Structure	Products **(What?)**	• New features such as global positioning and navigation systems • How to best use substitute fuels such as solar energy and electricity • Developing a "world car" using common platform designs but customized to regional consumer needs
	Processes **(How?)**	• Political pressures to make processes safer, more ergonomic, and more environment-friendly • Innovations, such as making processes "automation ready"
	Capacity **(How much?)**	• Exponential growth of demand and supply in developing countries • Flat demand in the developed world with numerous model and styles, creating the need for high levels of flexible capacity
	Facilities **(Where?)**	• Global sourcing of components creating pressures for finding best locations • More concentration in specific locations resulting from economics of development and supply chain costs • More dispersion of facilities because of market diffusion and radical shifts in technology (e.g., electric vehicles)
Infrastructure	Quality management **(How to improve?)**	• Dealing with government regulations forcing more quality and process standards • Improving quality capability and performance to compete with the best (e.g., Toyota) • Improving customer service and warranties
	Inventory and supply chain management **(How to acquire and deliver?)**	• Larger and more complex supply chains because of outsourcing • Increased use of Internet (e.g., auctions) for procurement
	Schedule management **(When?)**	• Increased coordination across multiple facilities • Improving speed and agility for faster delivery of custom vehicles
	Project management **(How to manage non-routine tasks?)**	• Pressures to invest in innovative projects (e.g., world car, alternative energy sources, reduced emissions) • Cooperation among nations
People and Organization	Workforce **(Who?)**	• Improved knowledge management and sustenance of intellectual assets • Better human relations and partnerships with unions
	Organization **(What Structure?)**	• Identification and implementation of best practices

Globalization

Most large organizations today are global. With advances in communications and transportation, we have passed from the era of huge regional factories with large labor forces and tight community ties to the era of the "borderless marketplace." No longer are "American" or "Japanese" products manufactured exclusively in the United States or Japan. The Mazda Miata, for example, was designed in California, financed in Tokyo and New York, tested in England, assembled in Michigan and Mexico, and built with components designed in New Jersey and produced in Japan. With mergers and acquisitions in the automotive industry, companies like Ford and General Motors have strong international presences, with Ford owning or partnering with Volvo, Jaguar, and Aston Martin in Europe and Mazda and Daewoo in Asia. Experts expect that the number of vehicle manufacturers will continue to dwindle and that such countries as Egypt, Iran, and North Korea will be top automotive growth centers.[27] Nations such as Korea, Taiwan, China, Singapore, Mexico, Brazil, and India also are rapidly becoming industrialized and competitive in major markets.

Global integration, which requires the coordination and balancing of global resources, is vital for competitiveness. Firms with a disconnected system of geographically scattered operations will lose precious economies of scale.

> **OM PRINCIPLE**
>
> Managers of global operations must understand and implement new ideas developed elsewhere and work within the cultural constraints of different countries.

Knowledge Management and Information Technology

In many organizations, similar activities are performed at different locations or at the same location by different people. Examples would be a manufacturer with plants spread out over the world, or a clinical research organization that performs research studies for drug companies in a project environment. Yet, in most organizations, knowledge is rarely, if ever, shared among employees performing similar jobs. A benchmarking study conducted by the American Productivity and Quality Center (APQC) reported that 79 percent of managers from the 70 responding companies felt that managing organizational knowledge was central to their organization's strategy, but 59 percent said that their firm was performing this management function poorly or not at all.[28] Although 88 percent believed that a climate of openness and trust was important for knowledge sharing, 32 percent of the respondents said that their organization did not have such a climate. In many companies, the gap was attributed to a lack of commitment to knowledge management on the part of top managers.

One of the indicators of a true learning organization is the ability to identify and transfer best practices within the organization, sometimes called **internal benchmarking** (see the *OM Practice* box on Royal Mail). The APQC notes that executives have long been frustrated by their inability to identify or transfer outstanding practices from one location or function to another. They know that some facilities have superior

> **OM PRINCIPLE**
>
> Most people have a natural desire to learn and to share their knowledge, but in many organizations, they are prevented from doing this by a variety of logistical, structural, and cultural hurdles. Operations managers need to understand and deal with these hurdles.

practices and processes, yet operations units continue to reinvent or ignore solutions and repeat mistakes.[29] The following are some of the reasons that knowledge may not be shared within an organization:

○ An organizational structure that promotes "silo" thinking in which locations, divisions, and functions focus on maximizing their own accomplishments and rewards.

○ A culture that values personal technical expertise and knowledge creation over knowledge sharing.

○ Lack of contact, relationships, and common perspectives among people who don't work side-by-side.

- Overreliance on transmitting "explicit" rather than "tacit" information—the information that people need to implement a practice that cannot be codified or written down.

- Not allowing people to take the time to learn and share and help each other outside their own small corporate village, or not rewarding them for doing so.

OM PRACTICE

Royal Mail
Royal Mail promotes an internal best practice learning process.

Royal Mail, the largest business unit within the Post Office Group in the United Kingdom, handles an average of 64 million letters per day using approximately 160,000 people at 1,900 operational sites. Each potential good practice (a term used to recognize that a practice may not be the best, but is good enough to provide significant performance gains) requires formal documentation including a description of the practice; names and telephone numbers of the contacts; the date; a process diagram; description of the major steps, who performs them, and what is needed to do the work; implementation resources; and risks and barriers. A panel then evaluates each practice to determine if it should be adopted by other parts of the business. If a practice is deemed *mandatory*, all units and staff are required to adopt it; if it is *recommended*, application is optional, depending on local conditions.

Royal Mail uses six measurements to evaluate its approach:

1. The number of potential national good practices reaching national process groups.
2. The proportion of national good practices becoming confirmed good practices.
3. The extent of implementation.
4. The cycle time from first submission to entry in the national database.
5. The benefit gained compared to the anticipated benefit.
6. Satisfaction of members of the national and business unit process groups.[30]

Information technology provides the principal avenue for managing and sharing knowledge. Three specific trends in IT pose challenges for operations managers in the future. First, the distributed processing environment and software for enterprise resource planning (ERP) allows organizations to make appropriate information available when needed. This dramatically improves the task of managing the process. Mapping process and information flows simultaneously to coordinate tasks and data for managing the tasks remains a challenge for many organizations. Second, advances in process automation allow firms to redefine their core processes and design better systems to accommodate the needs of product and service variety. Third, the emergence of e-commerce creates new demands for managing processes while also providing new opportunities for reconfiguring them. Shipping a product that you do not currently have in stock at the time of the order quickly to a customer requires extremely close coordination with suppliers. Internet brokers today offer many services related to searching, finding, and establishing a supplier base for manufacturing.

Maintaining and Enhancing Agility

Today's consumers have high expectations, which increase every day. They demand an increasing variety of products with new and improved features that meet their changing needs. They expect products that are defect-free, have high performance, are reliable and durable, and are easy to repair. They also expect rapid and excellent service for the products they buy. For the services they buy, customers expect short waiting and processing times, availability when needed, courteous treatment from employees, consistency, accessibility and convenience, accuracy, and responsiveness to unexpected problems.

Agile production and mass customization enable firms to make products better, cheaper, and faster than their competitors and facilitate innovation and increased product variety. Nonetheless, transforming operations from stable, rigid systems to operations that support agility will continue to be a difficult challenge.

OM PRINCIPLE

Incorporating product innovation with price, quality, and flexibility requires a coordinated effort among all facets of an organization, particularly marketing, finance, and operations.

Summary of Key Points

- Operations management (OM) is the business activity that involves the design, development, and maintenance of systems that transform resources, such as material, technology, and labor, into goods and services that meet customers' needs. It addresses manufacturing and service delivery; management of the value chain; the design, control, and improvement of the value chain; and the interface with other functional areas of business.

- Products—the output of operations—include goods, services, and contracts. Goods are tangible items that can be transferred from one place to another; service is a social act between a customer and the representatives of the service firm. Services differ from products in many ways and thus require different approaches to management.

- A process, which is a set of linked activities that perform some manufacturing or service task, involves people, machines, tools, techniques, and materials in a systematic series of steps or actions. Processes transform inputs into outputs that have added value. Operations must, therefore, be simultaneously concerned about suppliers, inputs, processes, outputs, customers (both external and internal), and the entire supply chain.

- Together, the processes that create value for customers are known as the value chain; it includes value creation processes and support processes.

- Operations managers face three types of decisions involving structure, infrastructure, and people and organization. Structural decisions involve products, capacity, facilities, and processes; infrastructural decisions involve supply chain management, schedule management, quality management, and project management; and people and organization decisions involve the workforce and type of work structure.

- Operations decisions must support overall business strategy by making decisions and tradeoffs among the structure, infrastructure, and people and organizations, all focused around an organization's distinctive competencies.

- Other functional areas of the firm, such as marketing, finance, human resources, accounting, design, and information systems, affect the operations function. All functions must work together as a system in order to be effective.

- Over the last century, the emphasis of OM has shifted from cost to value; from mass production to mass customization, agile manufacturing, and service excellence; and from functional specialization to cross-functional coordination and high-performance work systems. Future challenges include managing global operations, managing knowledge and information technology, and maintaining and enhancing agility to better meet customer needs.

Questions for Review and Discussion

1. What do you think are the distinctive competencies of McDonald's, Wal-Mart, Dell, Southwest Airlines, and Amazon? How do you think their OM activities and strategies support these competencies?

2. What are the distinctive competencies of the college where you are currently studying? Explain how operations decisions support (or might be needed to improve) these distinctive competencies.

3. What are the key differences between goods, services, and contracts? What implications do these differences have for OM?

4. Describe the key OM issues that would be associated with a pizza delivery franchise like Pizza Hut or Papa John's. Which are associated with goods (pizzas) and service (home delivery and other aspects of service)?

5. Provide some current examples of customized products and services. What OM issues would be important for the products and services you selected?

6. Provide an example of a customized product or service that was important to you. How well was the producer able to meet your needs?

7. Define a process and explain its key components. What challenges do operations managers face in managing processes?

8. What is a supply chain?

9. Explain the difference between make-to-order and make-to-stock processes.

10. What is the difference between a pull system and a push system?

11. Explain the concept of a value chain. How are processes typically classified in a value chain?

12. Explain the difference between structural and infrastructural decisions.

13. Explain the important issues associated with the eight key decision areas in OM. What are some of the current challenges that operations managers face in each decision area?

14. Explain how a national pizza chain like Pizza Hut or Papa John's might address each of the structural, infrastructural, and people and organization issues discussed in this chapter.

15. Why do conflicts often arise between manufacturing and marketing? How can such conflicts be resolved?

16. Describe how other business functions support operations.

17. Describe the elements of modern OM. How have these evolved?

18. Discuss how the conclusions of the U.S. Department of Commerce study of the automobile industry affect OM.

19. What issues do operations managers face today? What should companies be doing to address these issues?

20. From the current business literature, develop one or two *OM Practice* cases that address topics discussed in this chapter

Internet Projects

To find Web links to carry out each of the following projects, go to the text Web site at **http://raturi_evans.swlearning.com**.

1. Toyota is very proud of its OM function and its ability to leverage it for competitive advantage. Take a virtual tour of Toyota's production process. This tour has four parts: customers and products, the flow, assembling a car, and smoothing the flow. These are related to the eight operations areas described in this chapter as follows:

Segment	Structure and Infrastructure
Customers and products	Products and service concept
The flow	Supply chain management
Assembling a car	Process design, capacity, and facilities
Smoothing the flow	Planning and scheduling systems, quality and project management

Prepare a report summarizing how Toyota's operations relate to each operations area.

2. Over the last 30 years, Yamaha has established a strong presence in the musical instrument market, which is known for its finicky and demanding customers. Trumpets,

horns, clarinets, saxophones, and flutes are all wind instruments, but they need very different kinds of process expertise. Identify the commonalities and differences in the processes used to make these five instruments.

3. Through Ross Fink, you can take over 221 plant tours. Visit three facilities and discuss the critical operations challenges that each of them faces.

4. Westpark Healthcare center in Toronto is a local provider of complex, continuing, long-term care. Summarize the distinctive decisions that Westpark seems to have made in key operations areas (structure and infrastructure).

5. Take a virtual tour of BMW's facilities where the X5 and Z4 are produced. Summarize BMW's operations using the structure, infrastructure, and people and organization categories outlined in this chapter. You may not observe anything during this tour in some categories, such as the project management category.

EXPERIENCE OM

Operational Challenges in the Changing Health-Care Environment

Since 1988, when Allied Signal became the first major company to transfer all its self-insured employees to health maintenance organizations (HMOs), corporate America has embraces managed care. In the economics of managed care, three systems have emerged: on the extremes are *fee-for-service (FFS)* and *capitation*, while global fees for integrated episodes of care claim the middle ground.

This exercise allows you to evaluate the operational implications of the two extreme forms of health-care delivery—FFS and capitation. In FFS, patients receive health care from primary providers such as doctors and hospitals, which then bill the insurance company for the costs. Under capitation, the health-care provider receives a fixed capitation fee for every patient enrolled in the program and is responsible for providing medical services for that patient. In most states, Medicare payments, for example, are made in the form of capitation fees. Similarly, most HMOs receive a fixed payment per customer per year for all services provided. Thus, a health-care delivery system that switches from an FFS system to capitation (loosely interpreted here as managed care or HMO-provided care) must change significantly. Specifically, your task is to interpret the changes a health-care delivery system (say, a large hospital) must undergo as its revenue base changes from predominantly FFS to predominantly capitation payments.

Organize into teams of three students each and discuss the structural and infrastructural changes that a large urban hospital would foresee. In each decision area, summarize at least three key changes. Be sure to describe the existing "optimal" structure and the revised "optimal" structure. The following example allows you to generate some insights on "capacity management" while additional material is provided in *Supplementary Notes 1.2* on the CD-ROM to facilitate discussion in each category.

Example: Capacity Management with Capitation Systems

Traditional health care operated with the idea that the length of a hospital stay should depend only on the condition of the patient. This noble goal is challenged under capitation: because the health-care provider is compensated the same amount for every patient, profit maximization dictates reducing the length of stay to minimal required standards. Thus, every hospital must tighten its resource structure and patient schedules so that it simultaneously meets the objectives of efficiency and quality. In some sense the risk is now borne by the health-care provider. Under FFS, health-care providers were responsible only for quality while the insurance provider "indirectly" monitored efficiency and utilization.

With capitation, one would expect to see:

1. Hospital mergers and allowances as providers seek the benefits of economies of scale in efficiently delivering services.
2. A renewed emphasis on increased capacity utilization as the provider tries to control operating costs.
3. Careful appointment schedules and fees for breaking appointments because the provider can no longer pass on these costs to other parties in the value chain.
4. A focus on preventive care (lower cost per episode) in order to reduce expensive downstream maladies and an increase in secondary and tertiary care (higher cost per episode).
5. An "optimum" goal of increasing market size (number of patients provided care by the provider under an umbrella policy) as this increases the revenue base; at the same time a goal of reducing "health-care incidents" or illnesses as each such episode exposes the provider to the cost of care. The former translates to a hospital aligning with primary care providers in the vertical chain to feed it a larger number of customers; the latter translates to the hospital not wanting these providers to send any cases to it.
6. Capacity focus for specialty services such as lab work, and transcriptions.

 Use the template in the Bonus Materials folder on the CD-ROM to organize and report your answers.

Operations Strategy and Performance Measurement

The operational capabilities that enable an organization to pursue its long-term competitive business strategy are collectively called *operations strategy*. The structural and infrastructural decisions discussed in Chapter 1 provide the building blocks of operations strategy. The decisions made by the operations function are embedded within an organizational context, however, so we must consider the dynamics of the process for implementing strategy. In other words, turning plans into actions requires that managers understand the organizational ramifications. Implementing strategy successfully requires a comprehensive and effective performance measurement system as well as a keen understanding of the contextual and political environment in which a manager operates.

This chapter explores the scope of strategic planning with a particular focus on operations strategy and performance measurement. Specifically, we address:
- Fundamental concepts of strategic planning from an overall business perspective and the specific role of operations strategy (*Section 2.1*).
- Three distinct perspectives on operations strategy that also provide foundations for its effective implementation (*Sections 2.2–2.4*).
- Organizational approaches to implementing operations strategy (*Section 2.5*).
- The scope of an effective performance measurement system and the key metrics by which operations performance is assessed (*Section 2.6*).

2.1 STRATEGY AND STRATEGIC PLANNING

Every organization is concerned with its competitiveness and long-term growth. **Strategic planning** is the process of determining long-term goals, policies, and plans for an organization. Though *strategy* means different things to different people, James Brian Quinn has provided a useful definition:

> [Strategy is] a pattern or plan that integrates an organization's major goals, policies, and action sequences into a cohesive whole. A well-formulated strategy helps to marshal and allocate an organization's resources into a unique and viable posture based on its relative internal competencies and shortcomings, anticipated changes in the environment, and contingent moves by intelligent opponents.[1]

The two key ideas in this definition are *organizational resources* and *posture*. **Organizational resources** include such assets and capabilities as functional strengths, technology, product development, and process and market expertise. The **posture** of an organization describes its strategic focus—often referred to as *competitive priorities*—and how its resources are organized and deployed.

Competitive priorities might be low cost, high quality, exceptional service, or fast market response and should reflect customer needs and expectations. For example, low cost is clearly a competitive priority of Wal-Mart, whereas exceptional service might better characterize Nordstrom's. How operations are managed should support these competitive priorities, and we will discuss this later in the chapter.

Operational strengths and vulnerabilities are key inputs to strategic planning. They can be determined through an **environmental assessment,** which is often accompanied by a SWOT (Strengths, Weaknesses, Opportunities, Threats) analysis and helps identify *critical success factors* on which a strategy must focus. From the environmental assessment, an organization develops strategies and action plans. **Strategies** are broad statements that set the direction for the organization. A strategy might be directed toward becoming a preferred supplier, a low-cost producer, a market innovator, or a high-end or customized service provider. **Action plans** identify what an organization must do to meet its strategic objectives. Action plans often require significant changes in human resource requirements, such as redesigning the work organization or jobs to increase employee empowerment and decision making, promoting greater labor-management cooperation, modifying compensation and recognition systems, or developing new education and training initiatives. For example, to increase the number of patents, an organization's action plans might include hiring more engineers, developing a creativity training program, and changing its financial incentive approaches. Finally, organizations need performance measures and/or indicators for tracking progress relative to action plans.

> ## OM PRINCIPLE
>
> An effective strategic planning process usually begins with an environmental assessment of customer and market requirements and expectations; the competitive environment; financial, societal, and other risks; and human resource, operational, and supplier/partner capabilities.

Many Internet startups and other organizations have met their demise because of a mismatch between resources and posture and their operations consequences (see the *OM Practice* box "Wired for Failure"). Operations management (OM) plays a critical role in determining the appropriate mix of resources and using them effectively to successfully execute the chosen posture. This suggests that firms must have an operations strategy that is aligned with their overall business.

Essentially, an organization must address two questions that define its mission and vision, respectively: "Who are we?" and "What do we want to be?" The **mission** of a firm defines its reason for existence. It might include a definition of products and services the organization provides, technologies used to provide these products and services, types of markets, important customer needs, and distinctive competencies—the expertise that sets the firm apart from others. For example, the mission of Solectron, a global contract manufacturer for the electronics industry, is "to provide worldwide responsiveness to our customers by offering the highest quality, lowest total cost, customized integrated design, supply chain and manufacturing solutions through long-term partnerships based on integrity and ethical business practices." A firm's mission guides the development of strategies by different groups within the firm. It establishes the context within which daily operating decisions are made and sets limits on available strategic options. In addition, it governs the tradeoffs among the various performance measures and between short- and long-term goals. Finally, it can inspire employees to focus their efforts toward the overall purpose of the organization.

OM PRACTICE

Wired for Failure
A mismatch between resources and posture can lead to disaster.

Between Thanksgiving and Christmas in 1999, some 22 million shoppers spent more than $5 billion shopping online.[2] Traffic on sites like Yahoo and Kbkids.com grew by 500 percent. Outpost.com, a computer and electronics retailer, sold $2 million of merchandise in one day. Yet, while retailers were still rushing to exploit e-commerce, Internet message boards began to fill up with comments like "I'll never shop online again for Christmas." As Fortune magazine noted, "it takes much more than a logo and a Web site to run an e-tailing operation. Online retailers aren't so different from brick and mortar stores. They run out of stock, sell damaged merchandise, and hire rude sales help. . . . Hordes of companies flooded the market. Trouble is, many of them spent heavily to market and promote their brands but scrimped on infrastructure—the unglamorous side of the business, which focuses on delivering products to customers. The results were often disastrous." Amazon.com, for example, initially tried to have suppliers maintain inventory, but found that it needed to build traditional distribution centers around the country to improve customer service and control over the product.[3] In 2000, approximately 135 dot-com companies went out of business.

Many organizations are "wired for failure"; that is, their processes are not designed effectively or aligned with each other.[4] Airports, for example, face problems similar to those the e-tailers confronted. During a typical 4:15 to 4:30 p.m. time slot, 35 flights are scheduled to arrive in Atlanta, even though in optimal weather conditions the airport can handle only 25 arrivals in 15 minutes; with bad weather, this drops to 17. Another example is a company that celebrated its largest sales contract in history only to discover that all qualified suppliers for critical materials were at capacity. A clear understanding of the operational implications of strategic choices is vital to success.

The **vision** describes where the organization is headed; it is a statement of the future that would not happen by itself. It articulates the basic characteristics that shape the organization's strategy. A vision should be brief, focused, clear, and inspirational to an organization's employees. It should be linked to customers' needs and convey a general strategy for achieving the mission. Solectron Corporation's is simple: "Be the best and continuously improve." A mission and vision help an organization to understand the gap between its current resources and its desired posture and to realign its resources accordingly.

> ## OM PRINCIPLE
> Strategy is dynamic and must address gaps between current resources and posture, as well as temporal changes that may affect them. Figure 2.1 illustrates this principle.

The current posture in Figure 2.1 is best reflected by the articulation of goals, which is usually done in the organization's strategy. Current resources can be inventoried to assess whether they contribute to these goals or to possible future goals. Once the current resources have been inventoried, the organization may take one or more of the following steps:

1. *Achieving a strategic fit between current resources and current posture,* which frequently entails closing the gap between current resources and current posture and is facilitated by an assessment of current strengths and weaknesses through a SWOT analysis.

> ## OM PRINCIPLE
> The operations function can be used for delivering competitive advantage by (1) achieving a strategic fit between goals and resources, (2) redeployment of operations' resources, and/or (3) a strategic realignment.

2. *Redeployment,* which occurs when an organization redefines its current resources so that they protect the firm's future competitive position. Examples are shifts toward a more technologically adept workforce or more automated machines. Such preemptive resource moves may lead to the creation of barriers to entry for other firms.

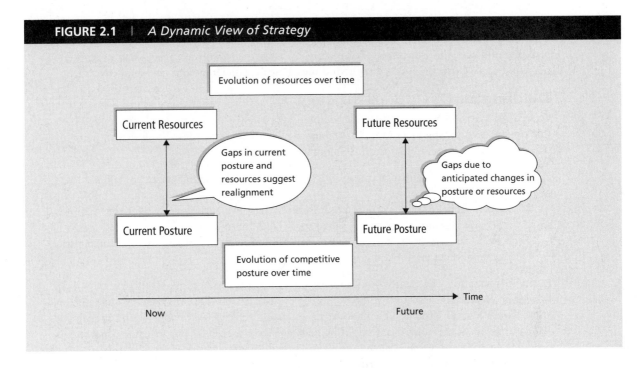

FIGURE 2.1 | *A Dynamic View of Strategy*

3. *Strategic realignment,* which occurs when an organization redefines its current posture based on anticipated shifts in technology, markets, the basis for competition, and the like.

An increasingly popular view of strategic planning comes from the "capability school" of writers such as Hamel and Prahalad.[5] Their emphasis is not so much on matching a company's strategy to current business conditions as on leveraging its resources to do new and different things and stretching what is available to achieve ambitious goals. This translates to linking the *current* resources to *future* posture in Figure 2.1. The focus is on building new sets of capabilities rapidly to deliver **competitive advantage**—a firm's ability to achieve market superiority over its competitors by offering better customer value.

One taxonomy for establishing the relative importance of competitive factors is to distinguish between *order qualifiers* and *order winners*. Order qualifiers are market attributes that are required for a product to even be considered by customers. Order winners are product or service attributes that directly contribute to winning business. Customers regard them as key reasons for purchasing the product, service, or contract. Thus, improving performance on an order-winning factor should improve the chances of gaining more business. We will consider these further in the next chapter in the context of product design. There are two major criticisms of using the order-winning and order-qualifying criteria for competitive assessment, however. First, order winners and qualifiers are based on how customers assess their decision when considering a single transaction. In reality, purchasing decisions and purchasing alliances with suppliers are often driven by a concern for long-term relationships. Some customers may accept occasional lapses in performance because they wish to preserve the long-term relationship with their supplier. In other words, the relationship itself becomes an order-winning criterion. Second, the concept is based on sales history and perceived benefits as customers interpret them. Perceptions change over time, and different customer segments have different needs and expectations. Thus, a strategy based on these criteria may not be sustainable in the long run.

Despite these shortcomings, making distinctions between order-winning and order-qualifying criteria helps an organization prioritize its objectives and improve its resource-planning and allocation decisions. For example, a firm that identifies price as an order winner will be driven toward achieving economies of scale, efficiency, and cost-reduction.

Defining an Operations Strategy

Operations strategy may be formally defined as the set of decisions across the value chain that supports the implementation of higher-level business strategies. To illustrate, consider three types of business strategies for a manufacturer:[6]

1. Produce a well-defined set of products in a fairly stable market environment as a low-cost leader.
2. Provide high product variety and customization in a turbulent market that requires innovative designs to meet customer-specific requirements.
3. Provide rapid response for constantly changing product lines in an unstable, uncertain, and unpredictable market.

In the first situation, the firm would be best served by emphasizing quality, productivity, and flexibility in production. This would require a well-balanced, synchronized manufacturing approach with small setup and changeover times, strong supplier involvement, and high work standardization. Some equipment might be dedicated to a particular product line or family of products. In this case, a *lean manufacturing system* would work well.

In the second situation, the firm would need to be able to operate at different levels of production volume while also achieving low cost and high quality. Product design would require constant innovation and short development cycles. Operations would need to be highly flexible in a make-to-order environment, with employees having high levels of knowledge and skills and diverse capabilities. An operations strategy based on *mass customization* would be appropriate.

Finally, in the third situation, the operations function would need to be highly responsive to unplanned change in a competitive environment. Product design might have to be more collaborative with customers and suppliers. Production processes would need to be highly flexible. The workforce would have to be entrepreneurial in a dynamic and flexible organizational structure. In this case, *agile manufacturing* would characterize the operations strategy.

Shouldice Hospital in Canada is one of the best-known examples of a focused strategy that is built around a distinctive competence. Built on a converted country estate that gives the hospital "a country club" appeal, Shouldice Hospital is widely known for one thing—hernia repair. This small, 190-bed hospital averages about 7,000 operations annually. Patients' ties to Shouldice do not end when they leave the hospital; every year the gala Hernia Reunion dinner (with complimentary hernia inspection) draws more than 1,000 former patients. Some have been attending the event for over 30 years. It is interesting to note that approximately 1 out of every 100 Shouldice patients is a medical doctor. The structural and infrastructural decisions that Shouldice makes contribute to its success (see the *OM Practice* box).

OM PRINCIPLE

An effective operations strategy requires the proper choices and tradeoffs for each of the eight structural and infrastructural decisions we introduced in Chapter 1.

OM PRACTICE

Shouldice Hospital

Shouldice Hospital's service strategy is focused on its distinctive competency.

- **Product and Service Design:** Shouldice accepts only patients with uncomplicated external hernias. Based on a preassessment, a small percentage of the patients who are overweight or otherwise represent an undue medical risk are refused treatment. Simplicity allows Shouldice to optimize on recovery time for the patients.

- **Process Design and Technology:** Shouldice uses a superior technique developed for this type of hernia by Dr. Shouldice during World War II. All patients undergo a screening exam and complete a diagnostic questionnaire (also available over the Internet) prior to their operation. Early ambulation is encouraged; patients literally walk off the operating table and engage in light exercise throughout their stay, which lasts only three days.

- **Capacity:** Shouldice's medical facilities consist of five operating rooms, a patient recovery room, a laboratory, and six examination rooms. Shouldice performs, on average, 150 operations per week. Although operations are performed only five days a week, the remainder of the hospital is in operation continuously to attend to recovering patients. It could easily (and profitably) increase capacity with weekend operations but feels that this would strain the staff.

- **Facilities:** The country club atmosphere, lush green lawns for walking, gregarious nursing staff, and built-in socializing make a surprisingly pleasant experience out of an inherently unpleasant medical problem. Regular times are set aside for socializing. For example, in the evening patients gather in the lounge area for tea and cookies. All patients are assigned a roommate with similar background and interests.

- **Quality Management:** Quality is ensured through standardization, patient feedback, and surveys. Shouldice's post-op rehabilitation program is designed to enable the patient to resume normal activities with minimal interruption and discomfort.

- **Schedule Management:** An operation at Shouldice is performed by one of the 12 full-time surgeons assisted by one of seven part-time assistant surgeons. Surgeons generally take about one hour to prepare for and perform each hernia operation, and they operate on four patients per day. The surgeons' day ends at 4 p.m., although they can expect to be on call every fourteenth night and every tenth weekend. Such schedules are very attractive to the surgeons as well as the staff.[7]

OM PRINCIPLE

Operations strategy should focus on the synergies among structural and infrastructural decisions from a systems perspective, because optimizing one decision area may degrade the performance of another.

In making structural and infrastructural decisions, however, a firm may face tradeoffs. For a manufacturer, locating closer to customers might improve responsiveness, but result in higher cost for obtaining materials and supplies. At Singapore Airlines, for instance, strategic choices include deciding what size of aircraft to purchase, what routes to fly, and what overall capacity utilization levels to target to balance customer service and profitability, as well as scheduling staff to flights. The scheduling of airline crews requires balancing the objectives of efficiently using staff resources with accommodating individual staff preferences and meeting safety regulations.

Perspectives on Operations Strategy

One can interpret tasks associated with developing and implementing operations strategy in three distinct ways: as *rational*, *organizational*, or *political* processes that accompany the development and implementation process (Table 2.1). No organization practices just one of the three perspectives in isolation, but they do allow us to better understand how different firms address strategy and match capabilities to postures.

TABLE 2.1	*Three Perspectives on Operations Strategy*		

	PERSPECTIVE		
	Rational	**Organizational**	**Political**
Basis for strategy	Rational choice	Organizational structures and processes	Political processes
View of organization	Rational person	Natural system	Bargaining table
Focus	Content	Process	Context
Key questions	How do firms modify *what* decisions are made?	How do firms modify *how* decisions are made?	How does distribution of power affect outcomes?
Operations strategy concept	Consistency between structure, infrastructure, and business strategy	The projects that an organization undertakes and the processes (teams, leadership, etc.) it uses to manage them	Role of operations in creating competitiveness and the balance of power between operations and other functional units

Source: Based on concepts in W. Richard Scott, *Organizations: Rational, Natural, and Open Systems,* Upper Saddle River, NJ: Prentice Hall, 1998.

The rational perspective assumes that organizations behave like rational individuals and that one can explain organizations' actions as cognitive processes. It is sometimes equated with the notion of an "economic person" who is "objectively rational" and has complete knowledge of the consequences that will follow from all possible alternatives. The essential feature of this perspective is the view that decisions are the product of rational and conscious choice.

The organizational perspective sees decisions not as the result of deliberate choice, but as outputs of organizational processes. From this perspective, organizational decisions are the result of standard operating procedures and programs. Thus, projects that are (and will be) supported by an organization are the ones that have "top management support" or a committed "champion" or that can withstand the formal scrutiny of the capital budgeting process. When the decision cannot be handled by such procedures, the search for solutions follows particular patterns that are influenced by well-established organizational routines. A champion who does not find initial support for a project may go through a routine of building coalitions and creating "buy-in" in the organization. Such organizational adaptations produce changes in structures and routines that subsequently affect decisions. For example, new leaders may emerge through this process that can influence the direction of decisions.

In the political perspective, decisions are seen as outcomes of internal and external political processes, for example, the political games one often observes within an organization. As a result, decisions are influenced by bargaining power among individuals. In explaining a decision within this model, one has to consider the players, their positions and preferences, and the game that resulted in a particular decision. For example, although the operations function frequently accounts for the majority of a firm's human and financial assets, organizations often overlook the role that this function can play in accomplishing corporate objectives. At other times, explicitly or otherwise, operations is relegated to a "reactive" role, responding to the marketing and financial needs of the firm. Wickham Skinner of the Harvard Business School has eloquently stated this:

> Top management unknowingly delegates a surprisingly large portion of basic policy decisions to lower levels in the operations area. Generally, this abdication of responsibility comes about more through a lack of concern than by intention. And it is partly the reason that many manufacturing policies and procedures developed at lower levels reflect assumptions about corporate strategy, which are incorrect or misconstrued.[8]

2.2 OPERATIONS STRATEGY AS RATIONAL CHOICE

OM PRINCIPLE

Different types of processes have different characteristics, require different skills and management approaches, and result in different levels of performance on cost, quality, time, and availability measures. Recognizing these differences is an important first step in ensuring that resources and capabilities are aligned with the product and market requirements of any organization.

Any operations strategy must ensure that appropriate processes are being used for the products and services they produce or deliver. The assumption here is that a fit between resources (processes) and posture (goals or market needs) will necessarily result in a more effective strategy. Three different models of operations strategy rely on this logic.

The Product–Process Matrix

We introduced the notion of a process in Chapter 1. Five major process types define most operations:

1. **Project processes** consist of a series of discrete and customized steps designed to produce a unique, one-of-a-kind product or service. Examples of projects include the launch of a new product, complicated surgeries, consulting or construction projects, deployment of the armed forces (military campaigns), and building customized products such as ships and airplanes
2. **Job shop processes** focus on creating a large variety of products or services, each produced in a relatively small volume, as opposed to projects, which produce one-of-a-kind products that may never again be repeated. Examples of job shops include general-purpose machine shops, most service-oriented businesses, repair facilities, and hospitals.
3. **Batch flow processes** also have jumbled flow of products and/or customers, but differ from job shops in that larger quantities are produced and most products or customers follow similar flow patterns. Examples of batch processes include bookbinderies, airlines, and many manufacturing firms.
4. **Line flow processes** produce very large volumes along a fixed flow pattern. The process is broken down into relatively simple operations, with resources specializing in a small number of tasks. The process is designed for uninterrupted operation by organizing and integrating all processes. Repetition and simplicity are essential features of each activity. Line flow processes are very conducive to automation because of the high level of standardization.[9] Examples of line flows can be found in automobile production, fast-food restaurants, and many consumer goods.
5. **Continuous flow processes** are similar to line flow processes with the distinction that they apply to a continuous flow of commodity products rather than discrete items such as automobiles or electronics. Examples include oil, steel, chemicals, and paper. Bottling and packaging lines are often designed for continuous flow with virtually no manual intervention.

Projects and job shops represent disconnected flow processes, where the next process to be performed is often predicated on a customer's unique requests. Batch, line, and continuous flow processes reflect the organization's desire to gain efficiency from operations by systematizing the flow. An organization may often contain elements of several major process types, however.

Selecting the appropriate process for a particular product is important. A continuous process, for example, because of its lack of flexibility, is unlikely to be especially effective in a market where customized, low-volume products are the norm, just as a job shop is unlikely to be the best way to produce a commodity item. The **product-process matrix,** shown in Figure 2.2, maps

OM PRINCIPLE

Different process types possess characteristics that make them more or less suitable for different competitive environments. No single process is likely to be appropriate in all circumstances. A large capital investment in the wrong process can be difficult to rectify.

product attributes against the major process types and can help a firm define its manufacturing strategy. Zone A, referred to as the *diagonal strategies* in Figure 2.2, suggests the most appro-

FIGURE 2.2 | *The Product-Process Matrix*

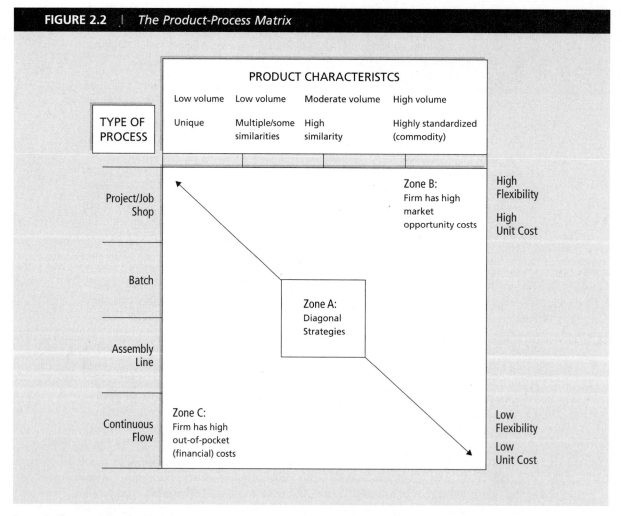

Source: Based on concepts introduced by Robert Hayes and Steven Wheelwright, *Restoring Our Competitive Edge: Competing Through Manufacturing,* New York: John Wiley & Sons, 1984, 208–221.

priate matchups. Thus, for example, a firm that produces low volumes of unique products is advised to use a job shop structure, whereas one that produces high volumes of commodity products would best use a continuous flow process.

So what happens if a firm decides to use a job shop process for a high-volume standard product? As shown in the figure, it is in Zone B, losing significant opportunities to increase market share or make more profit. Lacking process efficiency, such a firm will be incapable of competing with firms that have more efficient processes. Similarly if a firm sets up a line process for low-volume customized products (Zone C), it incurs significantly higher investments in processes, equipment, and methods than necessary.

The product-process matrix allows a firm to assess the "strategic fit" between its current posture and current resources. In choosing among alternative processes, managers must develop a detailed understanding of the available alternatives based on the following criteria:

1. What will each alternative cost in the short term and long term?
2. What will each alternative provide in terms of cost, quality, time, and availability of output?
3. What will each alternative require in terms of raw materials, energy, infrastructure, managerial talents, and other inputs?

In addition, the product-process matrix can also indicate how to shape operations strategy in the future. Consider a firm that has to design a future process for a product whose demand is going to increase substantially. The product-process matrix indicates that the firm should plan to redeploy its future resources toward more high-volume and low-cost processes—assembly lines, systematic automation of processes, greater process engineering expertise, more standard operating procedures (as opposed to customization), dedicated equipment, greater specialization, and the like. Similarly an organization, foreseeing the growth of the Internet and/or flexible resources (reprogrammable machines or automated teller machines), must change its strategic alignment from cost toward greater product variety and greater flexibility. Figure 2.3 suggests both these transitions.

One helpful way to think about operations strategy is to contrast the structural and infrastructural implications of being on the two ends of the diagonal strategies in a product-process matrix. This is summarized in Table 2.2. In developing the profile of resources and capabilities that a firm should build across various areas, an organization must constantly remind itself of its current, as well as its future, posture (see the *OM Practice* box on McDonald's).

Having selected a particular process strategy, managers must then identify the critical operational challenges. For job shops and jumbled flow processes, identifying and breaking bottlenecks, scheduling and loading the plant, and keeping quality at high levels are important. For line and continuous flow processes, meeting materials requirements, keeping capacity utilization high, and planning future facilities are the key management tasks. Clearly, in order to succeed management must be sensitive to the peculiar demands of the operating system, for that determines many of their subsequent responsibilities.

Strategic Dimensions of Services

OM PRINCIPLE

While the customer is buffered from the process by inventory in manufacturing, the presence of the customer in a service process creates unique challenges from a strategic perspective. A distinguishing feature of different types of service firms is the extent of customer contact.

The concept of the product-process matrix can also be applied to services, but with the additional element of customer contact. **Customer contact** refers to the physical presence of the customer in the system.[10] The extent of contact is the percentage of time the customer must be in the system relative to the total time it takes to serve him or her.[11] Systems in which the percentage is high

FIGURE 2.3 | *The Product-Process Matrix over Time*

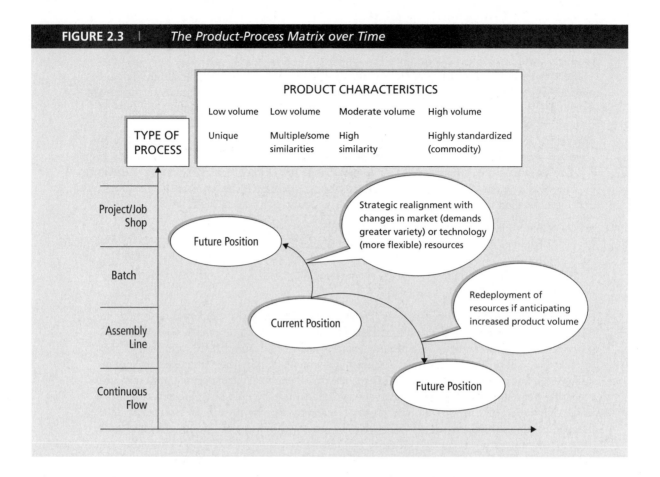

OM PRACTICE

McDonald's

McDonald's transitions from make-to-stock to make-to-order.

McDonald's used to make food to stock, storing sandwiches in a large tray used to fulfill customer orders. Although the company had about 25,000 restaurants, it had lost some of its competitive edge. Sales went flat in the mid-1990s, and independent market testing showed a widening gap with its competition in food quality. Worse, fast-food customers like variety, and when they switch foods, they switch restaurants. The make-to-stock system was not meeting these new demands.

After five years of lab and market testing, McDonald's rolled out its new Just for You system to create a make-to-order environment. This required a massive change in computer technology, food production equipment, and food preparation tables, as well as retraining all 600,000 plus of its domestic food production workers.

Unfortunately for McDonald's, the change has apparently backfired. Sales did not improve as expected, and customers complained about slow service. The new system doubled the average service time to 2 to 3 minutes per order, and 15-minute waits are not uncommon. McDonald's stock price has fallen, and rivals such as Wendy's have captured market share.[12]

TABLE 2.2	*Impact of the Product-Process Matrix on Structure and Infrastructure*

		TYPE OF PROCESS	
Category	**Decision Area**	**More like Job Shop Processes**	**More like Continuous Flow Processes**
Structural decisions	Products	Products often change as variety and innovation are the main competitive advantages; hence, design and development are very important.	Products are highly mature, and only incremental refinements are necessary.
	Processes	With a high variety of products, no one process dominates. Varied processes require mastery of multiple methods and technologies.	Process technology and design must support the ability to perform repetitive tasks very efficiently.
	Capacity	Capacity can be added in small, low-cost increments, allowing some flexibility to balance the risks of too much or too little capacity.	Large chunks of capacity are added at one time and at high capital costs.
	Facilities	Facilities can be configured in many different ways to accomplish the same purpose, allowing flexibility and rapid change.	Facilities are typically designed to capture economies of scale, are often physically massive, and have limited flexibility in how they can be configured and changed.
Infrastructural decisions	Quality management	Design quality is vital as customized products force attention to customers' requirements. Standards are difficult to develop because of the wide variety of products and processes used.	Continuous processes can be controlled easily by taking selected in-process measurements throughout the process to ensure conformance quality.
	Supply chain management	High in-process inventories are required because of the large variety of work and uncertain demand. This also makes it more difficult to coordinate with suppliers. Transportation of outbound goods must be carefully managed across the large customer base.	Material requirements are known with greater certainty, smoothing the flow of materials from suppliers. Formal relationships and long-term contracts can be established with suppliers. Finished goods can be shipped on a routine schedule.

(continues)

TABLE 2.2   *The Impact of the Product-Process Matrix on Structure and Infrastructure, continued*

		TYPE OF PROCESS	
Category	Decision Area	More like Job Shop Processes	More like Continuous Flow Processes
Infrastructural decisions *(cont.)*	Schedule management	Scheduling is very difficult because the high variety of jobs, quantities, and priorities requires that each order be managed independently on common machines and processes. Maintaining accurate status information over time is difficult.	Scheduling is simple because of a narrow product range, common process requirements, and generally stable demands.
	Project management	Ensuring completion of customer orders by promised dates is in essence a project and can be accomplished using project management principles and techniques.	Project focus is generally low and might involve installation or replacement of large capital equipment.

are called *high-contact systems*; those in which it is low are called *low-contact systems*. Many low-contact systems, such as check processing at a bank, can be treated as quasi-manufacturing systems, since most of the principles and concepts used in manufacturing apply. Service systems with high customer contact are more difficult to design and control. Table 2.3 lists areas of service strategy that have important implications in the design of the service delivery system in high-contact systems versus low-contact systems.

Haywood-Farmer extends the concept of contact along two other dimensions—service customization and labor intensity. The result is a segmentation of service organizations with important strategic implications.[13]

Examples of classifying service organizations according to these dimensions are shown in Table 2.4. Service businesses that are low in all three dimensions (contact, customization, and labor intensity) are similar to factories. Operations strategy for such services should be based on aspects such as facilities, process technology, and supplier integration. For example, some national pizza chains like Papa John's use small facilities to prepare pizzas for delivery while larger commissaries produce the ingredients to take advantage of economies of scale. The focus is on efficiency and quality. As customer contact increases, one must consider the impact of labor intensity. For services with low labor intensity, the customer's impression of physical

> **OM PRINCIPLE**
>
> In addition to customer contact, service organizations differ by the degree of *service customization* and the degree of *labor intensity*. Understanding these differences helps to develop a rational operations strategy.

TABLE 2.3   *Impact of Customer Contact on Structure and Infrastructure*

		IMPACT OF CUSTOMER CONTACT	
Category	Decision Area	High-Contact Systems	Low-Contact Systems
Structural decisions	Products	The service must consider environmental factors and the nature of customer interaction with service providers.	The service need not consider intangible factors associated with customer interactions or behavior of service providers.
	Capacity	The number of service providers must match peak demand; forecasting must take into account short-term time fluctuations in demand.	Capacity may be set at an average demand level; forecasting can focus on longer time horizons.
	Facilities	Locate operations close to the customer.	Locate operations close to suppliers, transportation access, or labor.
	Processes	Process designs have a direct impact on customer interaction and satisfaction and must include the customer's physical and psychological needs and expectations. Increased requirements for customization makes it difficult to set firm time standards.	Because the customer is not directly involved in the process, designs may focus on efficiency similar to pure manufacturing operations.
Infrastructural decisions	Quality management	Quality is more difficult to measure and control, and must focus on the customer-provider interactions and include significant behavioral training.	Quality standards may be defined more precisely in terms of easily measurable attributes such as accuracy and completeness.
	Inventory and supply chain management	Less relevant, because the service transaction involves the customer with little movement and flow of tangible products.	More relevant, because low-contact services may be supported by inventory-related activities; for example, check processing, which involves storage and transportation.
	Schedule management	To accommodate the customer, schedules must focus on the availability of service. Trying to smooth production flow will result in loss of business.	Because the customer is not involved in intermediate activities and is primarily concerned with completion dates, scheduling can focus on operational efficiency.
	Project management	Each customer transaction is unique, and the service can often be treated more like a project.	Because high volumes of repetitive services are processed, there is less similarity to projects.

Source: Modified from Richard B. Chase, "Where Does the Customer Fit in a Service Operation?" *Harvard Business Review*, November–December 1978, 137–142.

TABLE 2.4	*Three-Dimensional Classification of Service Systems*		
	Labor Intensity	**Customer Contact**	**Customization**
1. Utilities, transportation of goods	Low	Low	Low
2. Lecture teaching, postal services	High	Low	Low
3. Stock brokering, courier services	Low	Low	High
4. Repair services, wholesaling, retailing	High	Low	High
5. Computerized teaching, public transit	Low	High	Low
6. Fast food, live entertainment	High	High	Low
7. Charter services, hospitals	Low	High	High
8. Design services, advisory services	High	High	High

facilities and process technology are important. For high levels of labor intensity, more attention must be paid to human resources. As customization increases, the service product and process must be designed to fit the customer. Thus, issues of product and process technology become the principal strategic focus relative to the levels of labor intensity and customer contact. The customer contact model and the service process matrix provide good examples of rational models that allow organizations to reconcile resources and posture.

Many firms are repositioning their strategies. For example, by adopting kiosks and self-service checkouts, firms in the retail, banking, and airline industries are reducing contact and labor intensity and at the same time increasing the level of customization, as the next *OM Practice* box discusses.

OM PRACTICE

Self-Service Customer Strategies

Many service firms are refocusing their operations to marry technology and customer interaction to gain efficiency and enhance the customer experience.

Today's customers have little time to spare and will not tolerate waiting unnecessarily for service. To shorten the wait at check-in counters, Delta Air Lines is spending millions on self-service check-in kiosks at airports to provide customers with a hassle-free experience. These kiosks allow customers with an electronic ticket to check-in, check baggage, print boarding cards, select or change seats, request to stand by for upgrades, and change flights. The automated process takes 30 to 60 seconds for people with only carry-on baggage and less than 2 minutes for people checking bags. Using the kiosks saves the average customer 10 to 15 minutes. Delta also plans to modify the kiosks to that they can also handle check-ins for international

flights. The goal is to have half of all Delta customers checking in at the kiosks.

Retailers have long embraced the use of back-office technology to help them operate more efficiently. Advanced product-fulfillment systems allow grocery and apparel chains to automatically reorder items at the moment they are scanned—one box of macaroni sold, one box listed on order. More recently, these same merchants are putting technology onto the sales floor to increase customer interaction in the service process. Federated Department Stores is introducing computer kiosks where shoppers can order gifts from bridal registries, enter shipping information, and enter their credit card information with a swipe. The order is gift-wrapped and normally shipped within two days. Leading grocery retailers like Kroger, Meijer, and Thriftway are also installing self-checkout systems. U-Scan allows shoppers to ring up, bag, and pay for their own groceries in designated express lanes.[14]

2.3 OPERATIONS STRATEGY AS AN ORGANIZATIONAL PROCESS

The discussion of the product- and service-process matrixes has highlighted the importance of matching the product or service to the process and deriving the operations strategy based on this analysis. In many organizations, however, product and service decisions are driven by the marketing function and process decisions by the finance function. For example, many firms have launched Web-based ordering processes without paying adequate attention to the logistics tasks necessary to deliver the product to the customer.[15] The demise of the legendary dot-com venture Webvan tells an interesting story. In an industry with razor thin margins, Webvan was launched for Internet ordering and home delivery of groceries. Initial funding was substantial, or so it seemed. After two years, however, the firm found that the structure and infrastructure needed to support the business concept were larger than it had anticipated; a year later the firm ceased existence. Inadequate definition of operations strategy in the business plan caused its demise.

> **OM PRINCIPLE**
>
> Operations managers are often placed in the position of having to react to strategic plans that were developed from primarily financial and marketing perspectives. The lack of coordination can be disastrous. Thus, it is important that operations be involved in the process of implementing strategy.

As an organizational process, strategic planning consists of two key activities: *strategy development* and *strategy deployment*. In many firms, strategy development consists of a structured process that begins with an environmental and competitive assessment followed by the development of strategies, objectives, and action plans, along with resource allocation and metrics for tracking progress. Nonetheless, despite the prevalence of sophisticated and strategic planning processes, many organizations fail to execute strategy well. According to Patrick Schaefer of Ernst & Young, some key issues include the following:[16]

- Lack of understanding important causal relationships, such as business drivers and outcomes.

- The wrong information serving as the informational basis. Much of the knowledge that organizations create does not focus on real strategic needs.

- Inability to connect strategic objectives to everyday operating activities. One way of doing this is through performance measurement systems, which we address later in this chapter.

- Dormant learning processes. This often results from inadequate analytical tools, lack of employee inputs, and failure to define what gives the organization a dynamic character—that is, what differentiates it from others.

Hoshin Kanri

The Japanese introduced a process known as *hoshin kanri* (literally "pointing direction") for strategy deployment.[17] The idea is to point, or align, the entire organization in a common direction. A **hoshin** is a one-year plan for achieving quality, cost, delivery, morale, or other key organizational objectives (see the *OM Practice* box on Solectron). Many companies, including Florida Power and Light, Hewlett-Packard, and AT&T, have adopted this process (in the United States,

> **OM PRINCIPLE**
>
> Executing strategy successfully requires an effective methodology. Many firms employ a process known as *hoshin kanri*.

hoshin kanri is often referred to as **policy deployment** or **management by planning**).

With hoshin kanri, top management is responsible for developing and communicating a vision, then building organization-wide commitment to its achievement.[18] This vision is deployed through the development and execution of annual objectives and means to achieve them. For example, an objective might be "Decrease the new product development cycle from eight to four months by December 2006." The means to accomplish this goal might include establishing an effective product development process, requiring new documentation for product development, and streamlining the design process. At lower levels of the organization, progressively more detailed and concrete means to accomplish the objectives are determined. Here is where operations fits in. Hoshins developed at the operational level must be consistent with the corporate vision; similarly, those developed at the team- or front line-level must be consistent with the operations' objectives. A process occurs whereby objectives and resources that might be required to achieve those objectives are negotiated between hierarchical levels of the organization. The effectiveness of this process is in linking goals, actions, and resources at each level in the organizational hierarchy; thus, it is an effective process model for operations strategy deployment.

One characteristic of hoshin kanri is the development of performance measures that are used to indicate progress toward accomplishing the objectives. Management reviews these measures at specific checkpoints to ensure the effectiveness of individual elements of the strategy.

OM PRACTICE

Strategic Planning at Solectron Corporation

Solectron Corporation uses a three-pronged strategic planning process to keep pace with the rapidly changing electronic environment.

The strategic planning process at Solectron, a worldwide leader in electronic assembly, includes a three-year strategic plan that is updated annually, an annual operating plan, and an annual improvement plan that sets specific goals and stretch targets for all units and processes within the company. The first step in the strategic planning process is a review of the company's current projected performance; previous years' mission, vision, strategy, and plans; and long-range technological, economic, and societal trends and risks. This process is led by the CEO, Ko Nishimura, and includes site general managers, senior vice presidents, and the corporate staff. Their objective is to identify markets and services to be served, establish mid- to long-range financial targets, update the mission and vision as appropriate, and understand the company's capabilities.

The inputs to the goal-setting process for regions and sites include the corporate mission, vision, and strategy; the worldwide market and competitor trends; and customer requirements. The outputs of this process are the strategies, market targets, and financial targets for the regions and sites. Capability maps are also developed, and the mission, vision, and strategies for the regions and sites are aligned with those of the corporation as a whole. Three-year market plans are developed based on local and regional projections. Plans for all regions are reviewed for alignment, and plans to fill capability gaps are also finalized.

Solectron uses a hoshin planning process to deploy its strategic plan and define the annual improvement plan. Regional executives and the general managers at each production site determine their targets based on their knowledge of customer requirements. Individual plans for each account and each site support Solectron's strategic objectives; however, managers still have considerable freedom in determining how to achieve goals for financial performance, customer satisfaction, and employee satisfaction.[19]

Implementing Strategy Through Projects

A quick way of assessing a firm's operations strategy is to review its current projects. Often firms say that their strategy is something like "highest quality" and yet have no projects on hand for managing or improving quality. Projects give a "realistic" picture of an organization's real intentions. Often they are undertaken without a clear

OM PRINCIPLE

Projects undertaken by an organization reflect the true operations strategy of the organization and provide a means for strategy implementation and achieving targets.

strategic goal; for example, many firms are pursuing Web-enablement projects simply to follow the crowd. As resources are marshaled and work is accomplished on the projects, strategy gets defined more clearly, and the "emergent" strategy is often different from the "espoused" or "intended" strategy. Projects suggest a pattern in a set of actions an organization takes and reflect the actual behavior of the firm, not the way it says it behaves (espoused strategy) or the way it says it wants to behave (intended strategy).[20] An example of aligning projects to strategic improvement initiatives is provided in the *OM Practice* box on OMI.

OM PRACTICE

Operations Management International
Projects drive strategic improvements at OMI.

Operations Management International (OMI), headquartered in Greenwood Village, Colorado, runs more than 170 wastewater and drinking water treatment facilities in 29 states and eight other nations. Between 1998 and 2000, OMI's public customers realized first-year savings that averaged $325,000, their operating costs decreased more than 20 percent, and facility compliance with environmental requirements improved substantially.

Improvement initiatives in the company's strategic plan are selected and crafted so that each initiative contributes significantly to achieving one or more key strategic objectives and customer requirements. In a recent year, OMI had 26 improvement initiatives under way, each assigned to a team led by a high-level executive. All teams write charters that state their purpose, objectives, and timeline for completion. A team charter also specifies which of OMI's more than 150 critical processes are involved, the measures that will be used for evaluation, costs, required resources, and other information vital to the success of the initiative. Charters provide team members and company executives with the means for a quick and thorough analysis of progress toward planned goals.[21]

Strategic problems differ in their level of uncertainty and the experience that an organization has in addressing them.[22] Standard, routine initiatives with which the organization has much prior experience can be addressed using routine project approaches whereas more ambiguous initiatives with which the organization has little prior experience presents a significant challenge. Table 2.5 illustrates the differences among project activities in a continuum of strategic initiatives. Because the goals, experience, and conditions for each type of project are quite different, the charge (or **charter**) given to the team implementing the project must also differ. Known and easy projects require a task focus and action-oriented solutions. Known but difficult projects require a flexible approach and a project champion and sponsor to carry the project through difficult times. Known but unpredictable projects require mobilizing support on an organization-wide basis so that distractions and early failures do not lead to a loss of commitment by the project team. Finally, the unknown project charter requires managerial maturity to deal with the ambiguity inherent in such situations.

The project perspective on strategy requires that an organization balance its investment in all four kinds of projects. This allows the organization to optimize on action and innovate simultaneously. On the one hand, it can optimize current processes through known, action-oriented solutions; on the other, it can innovate using new technologies, altered processes, new global locations, or different management paradigms. It also sets the guidelines for specific implementation practices that would lead to effective deployment of strategy. For example, the project perspective on operations strategy deployment maintains that gaining *buy-in*, or endorsements from project members before starting a project, is pivotal for effective deployment of "unknown" projects because project members must deal a very high level of uncertainty.

TABLE 2.5	*Fitting Projects to Operations Strategy*			

	SCOPE OF STRATEGIC INITIATIVE			
	Known and Easy	**Known but Difficult**	**Known but Unpredictable**	**Unknown**
Example of an operations strategy initiative	Replace a piece of equipment the firm currently has with a new one	Buy a new model of the equipment with upgraded and expanded features	Buy a similar, but different, model from a new supplier	Buy next-generation equipment that uses untested technology
Key question	How do we make it happen?	What do we have to do differently to adapt?	How do we deal with uncertainties?	What impacts might this project have on the organization?
Goals	Clear	Clear	Known	Unknown
Experience with similar strategic initiatives	Considerable	Some	Very little	None
Conditions	Status quo	Different but predictable	Different and unpredictable	Generally unknown
Focus of project	Rapid implementation	Testing and integration	Exploration and knowledge acquisition	Organizational learning
Project characteristics	• Traditional planning and control approaches • Focus on results and meeting deadlines	• Focused learning and experimentation • More flexibility in managing the project • Increased focus on team cohesiveness	• Creativity in dealing with uncertainties • Higher flexibility in project management • Task and completion times more difficult to predict	• Project charter difficult to define • Lack of foreseeable termination may lead to frustration • Ambiguity creates conflict

2.4 OPERATIONS STRATEGY AS A POLITICAL PROCESS

As we noted earlier, operations is often at odds with marketing and finance; operations managers, who have little power in many organizations, often face substantial political barriers in trying to implement an effective operations strategy. Power and politics often dictate that the organization's strategy be driven by concerns other than operations.[23] In a common stereotype, an operations manager is viewed as a technical "caretaker" who typically dwells on the constraints of the system. Managers who view the operations function from this perspective think of it as essentially a control function and push finance and marketing perspectives of strategy. By helping other executives understand the true role of operations in business strategy, operations managers can diminish internal political games and help the organization focus on its true mission. Table 2.6 provides some classic perspectives of the continuum of operations strategy in both manufacturing and service organizations and the characteristics of typical firms in each stage. These stages represent the evolution from "caretaker" status to a

OM PRINCIPLE

The migration of firms from Stage 1 to Stage 4 requires significant changes in behavior and the political acceptance of operations. Within a Stage 4 classification, the operations function has a proactive or externally supportive role. Operations is seen as a critical contributor to a firm's competitiveness.

highly innovative and customer-focused organization, requiring an operations strategy that supports the organizational focus. They can move toward a more externally-supportive role by doing the following:

○ Identifying and nurturing the operational competencies that the firm possesses, such as volume, quality, low cost, or customer responsiveness.

○ Benchmarking performance with what others are doing in relation to market demands to identify and prioritize weaknesses and gaps.

○ Participating more actively and vigorously in the political debate that establishes an organization's strategy.

Political perspectives on development and deployment of effective strategy rely on methods such as moving the organization to higher levels of operations management maturity (as in Table 2.6), creating a critical mass of champions who understand and can apply OM effectively (as General Electric and others have done with Six Sigma), or influencing the organization to make significant investments in OM initiatives (such as implementing Enterprise Resource Planning systems).

TABLE 2.6	*Evolution of Operations in Business Strategy*		
Maturity Level	**Manufacturing Characteristics**	**Service Characteristics**	**Principal Focus**
1	Flexible but primarily reactive to marketing demands	Reactive to customers' needs; not particularly focused on performance and customer service	Management control systems for performance monitoring
2	Maintain consistency with competitors through similar technology	Meet customers' basic expectations through disciplined procedures and essential technology	Current industry practice and capital investments
3	Manufacturing investment and plant charters actively structured to guide decisions	Exceeding expectations on multiple dimensions through highly trained workforce and technology enhancements	Support the business strategy by aligning operations with key needs
4	Innovative and leading-edge manufacturing practices develop a competitive advantage.	Customer delight is a core value, supported by advanced and innovative technology and a highly empowered workforce.	Operations decisions on a par with marketing and financial decisions

Source: This perspective was introduced in Robert Hayes and Steven Wheelwright, *Restoring Our Competitive Edge,* New York: John Wiley & Sons, 1984, 396. Richard Chase extended it to services—see R. Chase, N. Aquilano, and F. R. Jacobs, *Production and Operations Management: Manufacturing and Service,* 8th ed., Boston: Irwin McGraw-Hill, 1998.

2.5 APPLYING THE PERSPECTIVES ON OPERATIONS STRATEGY

Perspectives on operations strategy—rational, process, and political—are useful because they offer concrete guidelines on how to address key tradeoffs and synergies in managing a firm's resources and defining its posture. Six key propositions offered for developing operations strategy (Table 2.7) can diffuse problems that might be encountered in operations strategy development and deployment. For example, in many firms, the operations and marketing functions constantly battle over product proliferation. The marketing perspective, rational in itself, argues for a wider product line in order to offer customers a wide range of choices. The operations perspective, driven by a need for efficiency and cost-effectiveness, argues the opposite. Frequent product changeovers lead to inefficient use of resources, and operations managers, aware of the cost of increased variety, are loathe to "make the product in every color, size, and shape possible." The propositions solve this dilemma by suggesting that the firm specify the breadth of the product line. This allows the operations function to acquire the appropriate technology and create the appropriate level of operational flexibility. It also allows the marketing function to strategically think through the "basket of goods" it must deliver to the market for competitive advantage. The strategy can be implemented through a simple dictum; if a new product is introduced, an old one must be discarded.

2.6 MEASURING OPERATIONS PERFORMANCE

Measurement is vital for assessing progress (see the *OM Practice* box on Boeing). The term **balanced scorecard** was coined by Robert Kaplan and David Norton of the Harvard Business School in response to the limitations of traditional accounting measures. Its purpose is "to translate strategy into measures that uniquely communicate your vision to the organization." Their version of the balanced scorecard consists of four perspectives:

- **Financial Perspective:** Measures the ultimate results that the business provides to its shareholders. This includes profitability, revenue growth, return on investment, economic value added (EVA), and shareholder value

- **Internal Perspective:** Focuses attention on the performance of the key internal processes that drive the business. This includes such measures as quality levels, productivity, cycle time, and cost.

- **Customer Perspective:** Focuses on customer needs and satisfaction as well as market share. This includes service levels, satisfaction ratings, and repeat business.

- **Innovation and Learning Perspective:** Directs attention to the basis of a future success—the organization's people and infrastructure. Key measures might include intellectual assets, employee satisfaction, market innovation, and skills development.

While the balanced scorecard provides a comprehensive approach to viewing the performance of a firm as a whole, operations managers use more specific criteria—cost, quality, time, availability—for measuring operations performance and assessing how well strategies are being accomplished. We might think of these criteria as a "balanced operations scorecard." What is important is that the measures used in operations be consistent and aligned with broader corporate measures. More importantly, the measurement system should provide the workforce with information enabling them to identify problems, develop solutions, and produce better results.

> ## OM PRINCIPLE
>
> Tradeoffs in operations strategy typically are guided by their impact on four principal performance criteria: cost (and productivity), quality, time, and availability (including flexibility).

| TABLE 2.7 | Key Propositions for Operations Strategy |

Proposition	Contemporary Organizational Perspective	Role of Operations
Firms can compete in many ways.	Operations has a role to play in supporting the firm's strategy, no matter what that strategy might be.	Establish and leverage all sources of competitiveness—cost, quality, time, flexibility.
Firms cannot be all things to all people.	The primary tradeoffs in any business are best assessed by a comprehensive evaluation of its operational capabilities.	Concentrate on the most important competitive priorities rather than trying to do everything exceptionally well.
Tradeoffs in structural and infrastructural operational decisions must be made.	In any complex system, operations is limited in its ability to perform in any specific dimension. For example, maximizing speed of delivery may have detrimental impacts on cost or quality.	Operations managers often are bearers of bad news and must take a political posture in educating the rest of the organization.
Operations strategy is defined by the pattern of decisions across many categories of structure and infrastructure: success is determined by the alignment of these decisions.	Synergy in structural and infrastructural choices, as well as policies and procedures, leverages the capabilities of the entire organization.	Communicate the level of consistency or inconsistency in structural and infrastructural choices, and propose policy and guidelines that resolve inconsistencies.
Operations strategy effectiveness depends on the match between the strategy, other functions, and the overall business.	An effective operations strategy integrates and reinforces the business strategy and other functional strategies. All managers see the operations function as a provider of distinctive competencies to achieve the firm's vision.	Operations managers participate proactively in political and strategic debates. This allows them to understand other functional strategies better as well as convey to the other functions the role of operations.
Over the longer term, an operations strategy succeeds as it guides the business in building capabilities essential to achieve the firm's chosen competitive advantage.	Capabilities such as low cost, high quality, quick delivery, and availability require distinct and differing approaches. Long-term competitive advantage is sustained through an effective and deployable operations strategy.	Proactively build capabilities that create long-term advantage in the marketplace.

Source: Propositions based on Kim B. Clark, "Competing through Manufacturing and the New Manufacturing Paradigm: Is Manufacturing Strategy Passé?" *Production and Operations Management Journal,* 5, no. 1 (Spring 1996): 42–58.

Cost and Productivity

Cost is one of the most popular measures of business performance, and one on which operations decisions can have significant influence. For example, producing high volumes of few products with long production runs and infrequent design changes is generally less costly than producing smaller volumes of newer products with short production runs and frequent design

OM PRACTICE

Boeing
Operational inefficiencies uncover a fundamental measurement problem.

In the early 1990s, Boeing's assembly lines were morasses of inefficiency. A manual numbering system dating back to World War II was used to keep track of an airplane's four million parts and 170 miles of wiring; changing a part on a 737's landing gear meant renumbering 464 pages of drawings. Factory floors were covered with huge tubs of spare parts worth millions of dollars. In an attempt to grab market share from rival Airbus, the company discounted planes deeply and was buried by an onslaught of orders. The attempt to double production rates, coupled with implementation of a new production control system, forced Boeing to shut down its 737 and 747 lines for 27 days in October 1997, leading to a $178 million loss and a shakeup of top management. Much of the blame focused on Boeing's financial practices and lack of real-time financial data. With a new CFO and finance team, the company created a "control panel" of vital measures such as material costs, inventory turns, overtime, and defects using a color-coded spreadsheet. For the first time, Boeing was able to generate a series of bar charts showing which of its programs were creating value and which were destroying it. The results were eye-opening and helped the company formulate a growth plan. As one manager noted, "The data will set you free."[24]

changes. Innovations in product design and process technology can also reduce the costs of production, as can efficiencies gained through meticulous attention to operations, such as using a pull system instead of a push system and delayed differentiation as discussed earlier. Typical operational cost measures include inventory investment, supplier costs, material costs, direct labor, scrap, and overtime. Two factors that influence the cost of any product or service are utilization (how resources are being used) and productivity (how effectively and efficiently they are being used).

Utilization—the ratio of the input used in creating some output to the amount of that input available for use—is a common surrogate for cost. It reflects how "busy" a resource is. An example is direct labor utilization. If 10 workers work an 8-hour shift, and 60 hours of labor are used to manufacture a product during the shift, then the direct labor utilization is 75 percent [60 hours/(10 × 8 hours) = 0.75]. Another common utilization measure is machine utilization, which measures the

OM PRINCIPLE

Higher resource utilization and productivity suggest lower product or service cost. Utilization measures input used to input available; higher utilization suggests, but does not necessarily imply, lower cost, as a resource may be busy working on non-value-added tasks.

percentage of time machinery is actively producing output. Low utilization signifies wasted dollars and opportunities for improvement. In service industries, high utilization may reduce costs, but degrade customer service, as occurs when insufficient staffing results in excessive customer waiting.

Productivity is the ratio of output of a production process to the input. It accounts for the methods used to produce a product or service. A process is more productive when the specific processes, people, and resources that it uses are designed to create more output with the same level of input. Table 2.8 illustrates some typical productivity differences between "lean" and "nonlean" automobile manufacturers. Japanese companies, led by Toyota, have demonstrated a much higher level of productivity than U.S. firms.

Productivity is usually expressed in one of three forms: total productivity, multifactor productivity, or partial-factor productivity. **Total productivity** is the ratio of total output to total input. Examples of total productivity ratios are tons of steel produced per dollar of input and dollar value of wheat produced per dollar of input. Total productivity measures do not show the interaction between each input and output separately, however, and thus are too broad to

TABLE 2.8	Output of Lean and Nonlean Automobile Manufacturers (units per employee per year), 1993–1999						

	NONLEAN COMPANIES			**LEAN COMPANIES**			
Year	**GM**	**Ford**	**Renault**	**Volkswagen**	**Toyota**	**Nissan**	**Honda**
1999	13.61	9.6	12.42	25.71	23.59	17.3	19.49
1998	9.05	9.7	14.05	15.13	20.73	17.89	14.67
1997	9.15	10.33	11.65	9.99	24.59	16.07	21.02
1996	8.51	10.38	10.81	10.63	24.53	20.22	13.67
1995	7.97	15.72	10.85	8.87	22.95	15.47	16.32
1994	7.94	11.92	11.62	9.1	22.95	13.91	16.32
1993	7.55	11.71	10.8	8.3	31.29	15.54	17.24

Source: M. Reza Vaghefi, "Creating Sustainable Competitive Advantage: The Toyota Philosophy and Its Effects," *Mastering Management Online,* issue 7, October 2001, http://www.ftmastering.com/mmo/index.htm; republished in FT.com, September 5, 2002.

OM PRINCIPLE

Operations managers generally use partial productivity measures, particularly labor-based measures, because the data are readily available and are easier to relate to specific processes and more directly reflect the operations view than total or multifactor measures. However, they may not provide complete information and must be used cautiously.

be used as a tool for improving specific areas of operations. **Multifactor productivity** is the ratio of total output to a subset of inputs. For example, a subset of inputs might consist of only labor and materials, or only labor and capital. The use of a multifactor measure as an index of productivity, however, may ignore important inputs and thus may not accurately reflect overall productivity. Finally, **partial-factor productivity** is the ratio of total output to a single input. The U.S. Bureau of Labor Statistics uses "total economic output per total worker-hours expended" as a measure of national productivity; in doing so, the bureau is computing a partial-factor productivity measure. See *Supplementary Notes 2.1* on the CD-ROM for further discussion and numerical examples of productivity measurement.

In many service organizations, productivity measures such as the number of letters sorted per employee, number of meals prepared per cook, or number of miles of roads treated with salt per dollar expended can be developed in the same way as their counterparts in manufacturing organizations. In other service organizations, however, especially those engaged in knowledge work with high customer contact such as consulting, legal services, or health care, productivity is generally more difficult to measure. For example, a common definition of nursing productivity is "hours per patient day." It ignores indirect nursing care, ancillary costs, and overhead. A better way of defining nursing productivity is the ratio of the total revenues generated by patients admitted to the unit to all resources consumed in treating the patient.

Quality

In the last half of the twentieth century, quality became one of the most important performance measures for both consumers and producers and a key element of an organization's strategy. Quality is a multifaceted concept and can be viewed in many different ways.

The **design quality** of a product relates to how well it meets customers' needs—often called **fitness for use.** Products of superior design that are appealing, reliable, easy to operate, and economical to service give a perception of quality to the consumer. If a poor-quality product leaves the factory, however, the impact can include time and cost responding to customer complaints, decreased customer satisfaction, and eventually a loss of business.

> **OM PRINCIPLE**
>
> The two key elements in understanding quality are
>   1. how well a product or process is designed (**design quality**), and
>   2. how well a product or process conforms to the standards established by the design (**conformance quality**).

Conformance quality depends on the design of an organization's processes and the ability to control them to specifications. For example, a machine may not be able to perform a certain operation, such as grinding a piece of metal to a certain smoothness because the required specifications are outside its range. Even if the machine is capable of producing to specifications, it may not be able to do so consistently because its operators are not trained properly or because of poor-quality materials. In services, human behavior is less consistent and much more difficult to control. Inattention to the quality of production or service processes can result in higher costs and lower productivity because of increased scrap, rework, yield losses resulting in lost capacity, downtime, additional testing, and lost time.

A focus on high design quality alone can create many problems if not properly coordinated with operations. For example, many years ago at BMW, product development was a lengthy process. The firm positioned itself as a leader in automotive innovation, and design engineers

> **OM PRINCIPLE**
>
> Good design quality does not necessarily mean good conformance quality.

would make last-minute changes to the product design to incorporate the latest and the best technologies. But these late changes meant that the operations function did not have enough time before product launch to make sure it had the right suppliers, equipment, and processes for making and assembling a car. Conformance quality (or launch quality as it is known in the automobile world), as a consequence, was not very good. By improving the design change process, launch quality improved substantially.

A popular measure of conformance quality is the number of **nonconformities (or defects) per unit.** In services, an analogous measure is *errors per opportunity*, as each customer transaction provides an opportunity for many different types of errors. FedEx, for instance, uses 10 different factors to measure its service quality. The weights reflect the relative importance of each failure. Losing a package, for instance, is more serious than delivering it a few minutes late. The index is reported weekly and summarized on a monthly basis.

Organizations also use many other specific indicators to measure conformance quality. These are generally classified into two groups: **attributes,** which are measurements obtained by counting; and **variables,** which are measures of some continuous dimension such as time, length, or volume. Table 2.9 gives some examples.

Time

Time is one of the most important sources of competitive advantage and is a key measure of operational performance.[25] Increased time in manufacturing and service processes often results in higher costs. For example, the health-care industry has started paying strict attention to the average length of hospital stays for two reasons. One is the desire of managed care organizations to improve resource (bed) productivity. The other is that as contracts (capitation fees) replace fee-for-service compensation systems, an extra day in the hospital for the patient does not mean additional revenues for the provider. Contract-based organizations, such as

| **TABLE 2.9** | *Examples of Attribute and Variable Measurements* |

Attributes	**Variables**
Percentage of accurate invoices	Time waiting for service
Number of lost parcels	Number of hours per week correcting documents
Number of complaints	Days from order receipt to shipment
Percentage of absentees	Time to process travel expense accounts
Mistakes per week	Cost of engineering changes per month
Errors per thousand lines of code	Cost of rush shipments
Percentage of shipments on time	Time between system crashes

those in the managed care industry, must pay a lot of attention to time-based metrics in order to use their resources effectively.

In operations, time is measured in several ways. The total time required to deliver a finished product that satisfies a customer's needs from the time the order is placed is referred to as the **product lead-time.** For a make-to-order firm, this includes time spent on design, engineering, purchasing, manufacturing, testing, packaging, and shipping. For a make-to-stock firm, it is the time to deliver the product from the warehouse (or wherever the product is stored) to the customer. In a service firm, the lead-time includes all preprocessing (such as diagnostic tests in health care), in-process activities (including waits and delays) and the postprocessing time (such as time for recovery in health care).

Lead-time is often characterized by the specific process in the design-production-delivery chain. For example, the time to develop and launch a new product or a service is referred to as the **product development lead-time.** For example, it typically takes between 18 and 36 months to develop and deliver a new model of an automobile. Product development lead-time can be a key driver of competitive advantage. Being the first to market a new product enables a firm to charge a higher price, at least until competitive products are offered. For example, when first introduced, Motorola's pocket-sized cellular telephone was 50 percent smaller

OM PRINCIPLE

Short product development lead-times enable companies to introduce new products and penetrate new markets more rapidly, and they also increase a company's flexibility in responding to changing customer needs.

than any competing Japanese product and sold for twice the price. Another advantage of short product development lead-times is that every month saved in development time may save a large company millions of dollars in expenses. Still another is that short product development lead-time reduces the need to forecast long-term sales, allowing more accurate production plans to be developed and reducing inventory.

Delivery lead-time is the time required to produce and deliver a product to a customer upon placing an order. In the extreme case, a product that is already in stock will have a zero manufacturing lead-time; the delivery lead-time will be simply the time to package and ship. Variability in processes induces departures from planned cycle times and manufacturing lead-times, creating some unique challenges for operations managers, particularly when salespeople make delivery commitments to customers. Making the finished goods inventory and work-in-process information available to sales and marketing is a critical first step in improving delivery reliability. Also needed are control systems that ensure that the sales function does not promise overly optimistic delivery dates just to get the customer order. Most firms establish minimum delivery time standards for this purpose. Closer coordination between the marketing and operations function is thus necessary for improved delivery lead-times.

Availability and Flexibility

Service and product variety have become important means of competitive differentiation. This means that firms must be able to make products or services available to customers *when* they want them, *where* they want them, and *in the form* they want them. From an operations perspective, this means paying more attention to availability and flexibility.

Availability refers to making a product or service available to a customer when and where it is needed. This often requires a firm to think about service in entirely new ways. For example, automated teller machines (ATMs) provide banking service at all hours of the day. The Internet has led to "after-hours" stock trading and other forms of e-commerce. **Flexibility** is the ability to make rapid changes to a production process, thereby providing a wide variety of products, highly customized products and services, or rapid response to changing market conditions. Henry Ford's logic ("they can have it in any color as long as it is black") does not work in today's society. For example, although Harley-Davidson's annual output is relatively small (around 40,000 bikes per year), it offers numerous models, accessories, and customized features that make almost every bike unique. This is possible because its manufacturing operations are built around programmable robots and other forms of flexible automation.[26] As another example, customers may easily configure and customize a computer at Dell's Web site.

Availability is measured in several ways. For a system that is either working or not, such as an ATM, **uptime** measures the percentage of time the system is working. For products stored in inventory, a common measure is the **service level,** which is the probability a customer will find the product available. When a product is not available, it is considered a **stockout.** Thus, the service level is one minus the probability of a stockout. When there is a stockout, a firm may issue a raincheck, thereby retaining the demand. If the customer agrees to wait until the product is available, the stockout is referred to as a **backorder.** If the customer decides to purchase it elsewhere, the stockout becomes a **lost sale. Outage quantity** refers to the amount of goods or services that are not available when the customer demands them.

The **fill rate** refers to the proportion of demand met by the system over some period of time. One could interpret this as

$$\text{Fill rate} = \text{sales/demand}$$

This is a tricky measure because one can claim that the real demand for any product or service is never really observed; what is observed is what was actually made available. This makes the above definition difficult, if not impossible, to operationalize. An example is the customer who drives away when he or she perceives a long wait at the drive-through window of a fast-food restaurant. Thus, a more practical definition is

$$\text{Fill rate} = (\text{sales})/(\text{sales} + \text{outage quantity})$$

Because we cannot observe the true demand, this measure is at best an upper limit of the true fill rate of the system.

Delivery reliability—the proportion of orders delivered on time—is one way of measuring the ability of a firm to meet its customer commitments. One confusing aspect of this measure is the meaning of "on time." For a company like FedEx, this might be a clear specification: next-day delivery by 10:30 a.m. The U.S. Postal Service, however, defines Priority Mail delivery as "2–3 days," which might lead to different customers having different perceptions of on-time delivery. Often, delivery dates are negotiated with the customer. Many services now promise delivery within a certain lead-time or the service is free. Delivery reliability is essentially an availability metric; not having the producer deliver on time implies that the product or service was not available when needed.

Many organizations create higher availability by making themselves more flexible. Flexibility is just another way to cope with uncertainty. Not finding a bank loan officer when a customer wants to apply for a loan results in dissatisfaction; if the employees at the bank are flexible, however, an investment adviser might be able to perform the task.

Flexibility can be viewed in several ways.[27] **Volume flexibility** is the ability of a firm to quickly adapt to changes in product or service demand. One measure of volume flexibility is the change in cost when volume changes. A firm is more flexible if this change is small. Quickly rebalancing product and service lines, hiring part-time help, and using overtime are three common approaches. Fast-food restaurants reassign tasks and develop a volume-flexible schedule to transition from the peak at lunch hour to the idle period in the afternoon. They may also use part-time help to handle such surges in demand. **Product mix flexibility** refers to the firm's ability to change its product mix at a given volume level. Two concepts useful in thinking about product mix flexibility are setup time and batch size.

Most processes produce more than one product type; **setup time** is the amount of time spent arranging tools, changing dies, setting machine speeds, cleaning equipment, and the like, in changing over from one product type to another. Setup time is typically independent of the number of units produced. However, setup time does not necessarily mean idle time for the task or process. It may be possible for a worker to do much of the setup for the production of a second product type "off-line" during the production of the first product type. This minimizes lost machine capacity due to setups.

The **batch size** is the number of units of a particular product type that will be produced before beginning production of another product type. Batch sizes may be constrained by physical limitations such as the capacity of materials handling equipment, or they may be based on the size of an order (for example, a customer orders 300 units of a special part). Often, the batch size is strictly a management decision. A firm making three colors of telephones, A, B, and C, for instance, may choose to mold 1,000 plastic casings of each color before changing over to another color. Alternatively, the process might produce one unit of A, then one unit of B, then one unit of C, and repeat this cycle until all units are produced. This approach provides high product mix flexibility. Long setup times, however, make it attractive to produce in large lot sizes, because the fixed cost of the setup can be spread over a larger production volume, thus reducing flexibility.

OM PRINCIPLE

High product mix flexibility results from small setup times and small batch sizes and can be a significant source of competitive advantage. Achieving high product mix flexibility requires creative design of production processes as well as a continual focus on improvement.

A lack of flexibility can impede competitiveness. For example, GM's Oshawa, Ontario plant shut down for three months to gear up for a new Chevrolet model and, after restarting, built only 288 cars in the first six weeks. Ford once took more than two months to switch its Kansas City, Missouri plant to produce the new year's models. In contrast, Honda's Maryville, Ohio plant produced its last Accord on a Friday, and began producing an all-new model the next Monday, reaching full speed of 48 cars per hour in six weeks. Many firms, such as Toshiba and Nissan, are focusing their strategies on flexibility and variety: more and better product features, factories that can change product lines quickly, expanded customer service, and continually improving new products (see the *OM Practice* box).

OM PRACTICE

Toshiba and Nissan
Toshiba and Nissan design factories for high flexibility.

Toshiba's computer factory assembles nine different word processors on the same production line and 20 varieties of laptop computers on another. The flexible lines guard against running short of a hot model or overproducing one whose sales have slowed. Nissan is another company with high flexibility. It describes its strategy as "five anys": to make *anything*, in *any volume*, *anywhere*, at *any time*, by *anybody*. Nissan's high-tech Intelligent Body Assembly System can weld and inspect body parts for any kind of car, all in 46 seconds. When U.S. automakers considered dropping entire car lines, Nissan was gearing up to fill market niches with more models. [28]

There are two key reasons for having accurate and relevant performance metrics. First, metrics that relate to customers' needs and expectations help the organization align and use its resources effectively. They help operations managers prioritize and focus on those objectives that are of critical importance to the organization's competitiveness. Second, metrics allow the organization to establish its operations strategy by providing a basis for assessing the synergies and tradeoffs across the various metrics. It may be impossible, for example, to design a factory that can deliver a customized product at the lowest cost and highest quality anytime, anyplace, in any volume. Rarely can a firm achieve superiority in every performance dimension, so it must make tradeoffs according to its specific "market-driven" strategies for achieving its desired goals.

For example, high-contact and low-contact service systems will emphasize different performance measures. Cost and productivity are of more concern to low-contact systems because of the importance of equipment and technology. In high-contact systems, quality assurance is more important, and cost reduction through economies of scale is more difficult to achieve. Low-contact systems are more amenable to statistical methods of process-quality control similar to those used in manufacturing. The presence of the customer makes quality control more difficult for high-contact systems. Training and motivation of employees are the principal means of quality assurance. Availability can be increased through careful scheduling and inventory control. Scheduling will emphasize personnel in high-contact systems, but will focus on tasks and jobs in low-contact systems. To some extent, "customer inventory" can be controlled in high-contact systems through appointments and reservation scheduling, which improve the dependability of service delivery. Flexibility is the source of competitive advantage in high-contact systems. The use of computer technology, for example, can greatly increase the flexibility of a service operation by allowing people to spend more time with customers and thus be able to respond faster and more flexibly to a wider range of customer demands.

Design and structural choices affect the way operations are managed. Turning tradeoffs into synergies is a critical management challenge. For instance, many managers believed (some still do) that high quality could be achieved only at a high cost because every input and output would have to undergo extensive inspection. However, by instituting better processes for managing suppliers and improving work methods and quality control policies, a firm can eliminate much unnecessary inspection and still achieve high quality. Many firms have found that improvements in quality often result in simultaneous reduction in costs. Similarly, reductions in lead-time result in inventory savings and more rapid cash recovery. Such opportunities are not always evident.

Summary of Key Points

- Strategic planning is the process of determining an organization's long-term goals, policies, and plans as a means for achieving competitive advantage. Two key elements of strategy are organizational resources (the functional strengths and assets of the organization) and posture (the key competitive priorities on which the organization chooses to focus).
- Operations strategy is an important component of overall business strategy. Operations strategy must focus on ensuring the production of high-quality goods and services, providing them in the proper quantities at the proper time, managing human resources, and adapting to organizational change.
- Operations strategy may be viewed from three major perspectives: rational, organizational, and political. The rational view considers strategy from a decision and choice framework; the organizational view centers on organizational processes by which strategy is defined and implemented; and the political view focuses on roles and behaviors in meeting strategic challenges and mitigating interfunctional conflicts. Understanding these perspectives provides guidance in addressing resource tradeoffs and characterizing an organization's posture.
- In manufacturing organizations, the five process types—projects, job shops, batch, line, and continuous operations—have varying capabilities and are suited for different markets. The product-process matrix captures the key tradeoffs implicit in making these operational choices.
- In service organizations, the degree of customer contact, service customization, and labor intensity provide a framework for identifying appropriate strategies and process choices.
- As an organizational process, strategic planning consists of strategy development and strategy deployment. Hoshin kanri, or policy deployment, is a process for implementing key strategic objectives based on a philosophy of continuous improvement. It involves active participation of employees at all levels and frequent evaluation and possible modification of plans and actions.
- The measurement of operations performance is vital to successfully managing operations and achieving strategic goals and objectives. Four key performance criteria define the scope of operations performance measurement: cost, quality, time, and availability. Cost and productivity have long been traditional operations performance measures, while the other categories have taken on increasing importance in recent years.
- Product and service quality focus on design quality and conformance quality. Measures of quality include fitness for use and measures of nonconformities during production or service delivery.
- Time is an important source of competitive advantage. In operations, key time-based metrics are product lead-time, including product development lead-time, manufacturing lead-time, and delivery lead time; and cycle time. Lead-times measure system performance, while cycle time measures system capacity.
- Availability and flexibility measures address the ability of firms to provide products and services to customers when they want them, where they want them, and in the form they want them. Specific measures include uptime, service levels, stockouts, fill rates, and setup times.
- Performance measures provide a means of assessing tradeoffs and synergies in making strategic operations decisions. Typically, the choices must reflect the match between a firm's operational capability and its competitive and market needs.

Questions for Review and Discussion

1. What is strategic planning? What are the two key elements in defining a strategy?
2. How does the traditional definition of strategy differ from the more contemporary "capability school" perspective? Outline the differences using examples.
3. Explain the difference between mission and vision. Find some corporate mission and vision statements. Do they meet our definitions?
4. Define operations strategy. How does it relate to the structural and infrastructural elements we introduced in Chapter 1?
5. Assess the operations strategy of a firm and outline the consistencies and inconsistencies in its operational choices. To complete this task, call an operations manager at a local firm and ask questions such as:
   a. How do operations contribute to overall business performance?
   b. How often is consistency between various operations decision areas discussed in the executive council or strategy sessions?
   c. Are the firm's people, processes, methods and technologies well aligned with customer expectations?
   d. What is the most frequent source of conflict in the organization?
6. Describe the three perspectives on operations strategy. How do they differ in content and focus?
7. Describe the basic features of the five major process types and give an example of each type in (a) food business, (b) health care, (c) manufacturing.
8. What is the product-process matrix? What conditions would make a firm choose off-diagonal strategies?
9. How does the product-process matrix differ from a service-process matrix? How does each matrix help in strategy formulation?
10. Discuss where each of the following industries would fit in the product-process matrix:
    a. Drugs
    b. Specialty chemicals
    c. Aerospace
    d. Machine tools
    e. Automobiles
    f. Paper
    g. Brewers
    h. Steel
    i. Electronics
11. What is the difference between high-contact and low-contact systems? Provide some examples. Would a hotel such as Holiday Inn be classified as a high-contact operation if a customer on a business trip spends 8 of the 16 hours on the trip sleeping in the hotel?
12. How does customer contact affect the operations strategy of a service organization?
13. What implications do high-contact and low-contact systems have for efficiency, quality, flexibility, and dependability? Use the example of HMOs pressuring hospitals to reduce the average length of stay in order to reduce the cost of operations.
14. Explain how the design elements of high-contact versus low-contact services in the restaurant business differ by discussing how typical processes (for instance, reservations, seating, providing menus, serving bread, taking orders, preparing orders, food options,

desserts, beverages, serving, and payment) would be implemented in a low- or high-contact environment. What general differences between the two systems can you identify?

15. Match each business strategy with the most appropriate manufacturing mission:

Business Strategy	**Manufacturing Mission**
a. Market dominance	___Introduce a variety of products
b. Specialty market niche	___Support new-product technology
c. Delivery response	___Lowest unit cost
d. Market coverage response	___Produce to changing schedules
e. Custom product response	___Manufacture to specification
f. Product innovation	___Manufacture all new products
g. Technical innovation	___Produce to small batch run

16. Why do some organizations fail to execute strategic planning effectively?
17. Explain the concept of policy deployment (hoshin kanri).
18. What are the four different kinds of strategic projects? Explain how projects fit into strategic planning activities.
19. Visit a local firm and find examples of the four different kinds of projects in this organization. You can also do this by calling a manager in a local firm. Explain the four categories and ask the manager to give you examples in each category.
20. The chapter lists propositions that result from the differing views of operations strategy and the guidance they suggest for its role. What factors might contribute to the violation of these propositions in many organizations?
21. Find and report on some current examples of how companies are using cost and productivity, quality, time, and availability and flexibility for competitive advantage.
22. Explain the differences among the various ways to measure productivity. How should operations managers make a choice?
23. Provide an example of the eight key dimensions of quality for both a product and a service.
24. Provide an example of a recent service encounter that you had where the five service quality dimensions were either addressed well or poorly.
25. How is conformance quality measured? State the common types of measures used.
26. Explain the differences among the following terms: product lead-time, product development lead-time, manufacturing lead-time, delivery lead-time, and cycle time.
27. What are the alternative ways of measuring availability and flexibility in operations?
28. Explain the importance of performance measurement, especially with respect to implementing operations strategy.

Internet Projects

To find Web links to carry out each of the following projects, go to the text's Web site at **http://raturi_evans.swlearning.com**.

1. Select one cover story of your choice that relates to operations strategy. Summarize the article, relating it to the material in this chapter.
2. Superfactory provides resources, communities, and tools supporting manufacturing excellence. Select a factory tour of your choice, and after going through the tour, summarize the operations strategy of the firm. Your summary should include the process positioning of the firm and its prioritization of cost, quality, time, and availability objectives as well as a brief discussion of its structural and infrastructural choices (see Chapter 1).

3. "A Guide to Performance Measurement and Nonfinancial Indicators" identifies quality, flexibility, and innovation as the nonfinancial measures that need to be factored into an assessment of the effectiveness of a process. Identify some ways of quantifying such metrics. For example, two common ways to assess the financial impacts of quality are to measure (1) the cost of poor quality and (2) the revenue and market share impacts of quality.

4. Strategic Horizons LLP provides several examples of mass customization from apparel to eyewear to industrial products. Write a brief summary of one example of mass customization.

EXPERIENCE OM

An Exercise on Strategy and Processes

1. In teams of three students, review the product-process matrix in Figure 2.2. Note that the upper left portion of the diagonal strategy focuses on processes, the lower right portion focuses on products, and the middle might be termed an "intermediate focus."

2. Discuss and draw conclusions about the characteristics of processes, using the templates provided in the Bonus Materials folder on the CD-ROM.

3. Summarize key management tasks and the dominant competitive mode for each category. Your answers should be based on sound reasoning of what you expect to find. A good approach is to think about firms in each column and make conjectures about their operations.

4. Based on your assessments, categorize the management tasks in the list below by placing 1 (process focus), 2 (intermediate focus), or 3 (product focus) before each task.

____Reacting quickly to changes

____Loading the facility and estimating capacity periodically

____Estimating costs and delivery times of products and services

____Breaking bottlenecks

____Tracing and expediting orders

____Systematizing diverse elements

____Developing standards and methods, improving guidelines

____Balancing resources across multiple process stages

____Managing large specialized and complex operations

____Assessing the cost of variety or using activity-based costing (ABC)

____Meeting the challenge of materials requirements complexity

____Meeting materials requirements reliably

____Running equipment at peak efficiency

____Timing expansion and technological change carefully

____Raising capital for expansion and growth

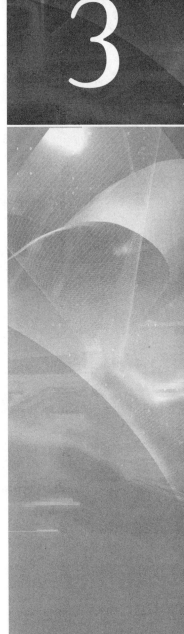

Product and Service Design and Development

3

Among the most important strategic decisions a firm makes are the selection and development of new products and services. The decisions it makes about what products and services to offer and how to position them in the marketplace determine its growth, profitability, and future direction. A firm can achieve a significant competitive advantage by paying attention to key operational issues associated with developing products and services. Operations management plays an important role in helping to reduce costs, improve speed-to-market, and ensure that product designs can be produced efficiently.

This chapter examines various aspects of product and service design and development. Specifically, we address:

- The strategic importance of product/service concept development and the impact of operations on product and service development (*Section 3.1*).
- The economic importance of design and development and tradeoffs in specifying the development budgets (*Section 3.2*).
- The role of design and development in time-based competition (*Section 3.3*).
- Structured approaches for enhancing the product development process to improve quality and performance (*Section 3.4*).
- The importance of taking an integrated, cross-functional approach to product development in coordinating successful product launch (*Section 3.5*).
- Emerging issues in product development (*Section 3.6*).

Material on the CD-ROM discusses some useful tools and techniques for product design decisions.
3. The Taguchi Loss Function
4. Reliability

3.1 THE ROLE OF OPERATIONS IN PRODUCT AND SERVICE DEVELOPMENT

The decision to develop new products and services is an important and difficult strategic decision that can make or break a firm in a highly competitive market. An effective product development approach offers three key benefits: *market position, resource utilization,* and *organizational renewal and enhancement.*[1] New products enhance market position by creating barriers to entry for competitors and establishing a leadership image that translates into market dominance, wider product lines, and increased market share. They improve resource utilization by leveraging the capacity of such resources as research and development, factories, the sales force, and field service personnel. The excitement associated with new product development efforts often renews a company by fostering creativity and demonstrating a commitment to innovation.

Many people think of design simply in terms of aesthetics—the features, shape, and color of a product, or the physical environment in which a service takes place. Yet having a well-designed, innovative product or service is not sufficient for success. For example, although Xerox has developed numerous new product ideas—its Palo Alto Research Center is famous for such innovations as the computer mouse, the graphical user interface, and the laser printer—many of them became commercial successes for other firms. Xerox's stock price declined from $92 a share in late 1999 to almost $5 a share in late 2000 and remained near $10 in 2003. Many of its problems have been related to a strategic realignment of the product development and delivery processes and an inability to follow through on successful development of innovative concepts at the same time that competitors were launching new products.

This is where the operations function enters the picture. New products and services must be produced and delivered efficiently, at low cost, on time, and within quality standards. Many designers do not understand these issues and, as a result, often propose products that cannot be produced or service designs that cannot be delivered because of inadequate technology or operational capabilities. Thomas Alva Edison, with as many as 1,300 inventions and 1,100 patents to his credit, said it best, "Genius is 1 percent inspiration and 99 percent perspiration." Many of Edison's contemporaries had the idea of creating a light bulb, but their bulbs would not stay lit.[2] Product development leaders today still use four key components of Edison's product development model:

1. **Lofty Goals:** For example, the ability of the bulb to stay lit for long periods of time.
2. **Right to Left Process:** Start with customers and move backward through operations to design.
3. **Structure:** Have "clear targets" instead of daydreaming and aimless experimentation.
4. **Fluidity:** Be driven by talent, not hierarchy.

The expertise of operations managers can help a firm remain focused on customers and follow a structured process that ensures that clear targets can be met.

Having a sound project management system in place can help a firm avoid problems such as the following during product development and launch:

OM PRINCIPLE

New product and service development activities must be coordinated closely with the operations function to ensure that designs are feasible, to minimize total costs, and to ensure that customers' requirements are satisfied.

○ Inferior project quality because the product was rushed or had inadequate funding.

○ Excessive unit costs because of delays and design changes, making the final product an unattractive value for the customer.

○ Poor tradeoffs between schedules, costs, and quality because the firm tried to beat its competitors to the market.

A **project** is simply a set of coordinated activities designed to achieve some result; managing these activities is called **project management**. (We will address the subject of project management thoroughly in Chapter 10.)

Four critical objectives must be considered in product development projects:

1. The project budget.
2. The time to launch.

3. The product/service performance characteristics.
4. The unit cost of the product/service.[3]

First, product development is an expensive activity, but early involvement of downstream functions such as operations and field service can reduce total product costs, especially those incurred after launch. Thus, allocating and managing the project budget is critical to success. Second, the need to improve speed-to-market creates unique requirements for operational flexibility. The typical problems associated with product/service development and launch processes often stem from inadequate assessment of the impact of operations. Third, the selection of product/service performance characteristics significantly affects the quality, flexibility, and cost of operations. Finally, the design process may account for 90 percent or more of the total manufacturing cost (which includes material, labor, logistic, and support costs) for a typical product with material costs accounting for 65 to 80 percent of the total manufacturing cost.[4] At Rolls Royce, for example, design determines 80 percent of the final production cost of some 2,000 of the company's components.[5] Managing these aspects of product development requires a disciplined approach that project management provides.

The best evidence of the value of good project management for product development is found in the automobile industry.[6] Japanese product development approaches are often recognized as the best. Teams typically spend more time early in the process identifying and resolving design problems. Early in a project's life, the *shusa* (a strong project leader in the Toyota system) has the team identify as many potential problems as possible. Japanese automakers also involve suppliers early in the design process, which helps to improve the product design and eliminates costly revisions later.

3.2 THE PRODUCT LIFE CYCLE AND THE ECONOMICS OF PRODUCT DEVELOPMENT

OM PRINCIPLE

The typical product life cycle consists of four stages: introduction, growth, maturity, and decline. Understanding the impact of operations on each of these stages is vital to an effective product development process.

Figure 3.1 shows a typical graph of a new product's sales volume over time—the **product life cycle.** In the first stage of the cycle, the product is developed and introduced, and sales grow slowly as the product gains acceptance in the market. Designs are often refined until a "dominant design" for the product or service is established. In the second stage, production accelerates to support a period of sales growth. This is followed by a period of maturity, when demand levels off and no new distribution channels are available. Market saturation occurs, and then sales begin to decline (Stage 4) unless the product or service is upgraded or replaced.

The development of a new product involves substantial investment. Significant expenses include initial development costs associated with design, prototyping, and testing; "ramp-up" costs associated with setting up the production system; actual production expenses; and costs for marketing and support. Figure 3.2 shows typical cumulative values of these cash flows through Stage 3 of the life cycle, when the market has matured and most of the development costs have been recouped. For this reason this stage is sometimes known as the "cash cow" period. As sales begin to decline, the cumulative profit may actually fall. Many firms make an early exit from the market for this reason.

OM PRINCIPLE

Higher levels of initial investment in the planning stages of product development generally lead to offsetting reductions in expenses or increased revenues in later stages of the life cycle by reducing unanticipated changes in designs and production processes.

FIGURE 3.1 | *The Product Life Cycle*

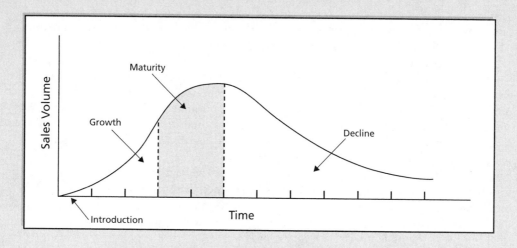

Of course, not all products are terminated when they reach the decline phase. Many consumer goods have long, almost unending mature phases or undergo major improvements (think software upgrades) to stimulate sales. In such cases, product development cycles overlap on a continuing basis.

Financial analysis of cash flows is typically used to rate product ideas on the basis of anticipated rate of return, payback, or other financial measures. Frequently, firms use a threshold rate of return—if anticipated earnings of a new product are below this hurdle, the idea will not be pursued. A new product may also be jeopardized by other concerns, however, such as incompatibility of the product or its manufacturing process with existing technology, ambiguity in the mind of the customer, lack of alignment with the organization's mission, cannibalization of other products, or failure to mesh with the current competitive priorities of the firm. Thus, assessments of the project should include qualitative evaluations as well as financial analysis.

OM PRINCIPLE

Three critical lessons for managing the product development process:
1. Early preparation and investment in the product development project have downstream payoffs.
2. The product development project should assess the impact of early design decisions through the entire life cycle of the product.
3. The cost-benefit analysis of product development projects should consider not just the cash flows associated with the project over the product life cycle, but also the qualitative competitive and organizational concerns.

3.3 SPEED-TO-MARKET

The importance of speed in product development cannot be overemphasized. To succeed in highly competitive markets, companies must churn out new products quickly. Whereas automakers once took four to six years to develop new models, most are now striving to do this in 24 months. In fact, Toyota's goal is just 18 months! General Motors plans to introduce a new or overhauled vehicle about every 28 days. Boeing would like to reduce the 54 months it took to design its 777 airplane to 10 months because the market changes so quickly. The ability to compete on speed is greatly influenced by the effectiveness of product development and operations management (see the *OM Practice* box on Moen).

FIGURE 3.2 | *Typical Cash Flows Associated with New Product Development*

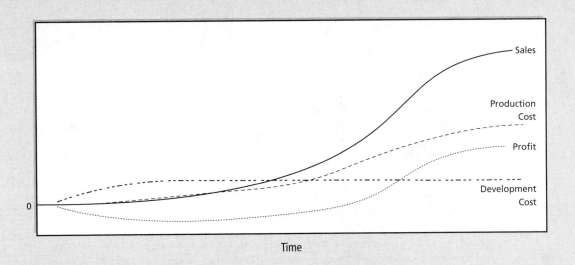

Time

OM PRACTICE

Moen, Inc.
Improved speed-to-market improves financial and market performance.

Moen, Inc. makes faucets for bathrooms and kitchens. In the mid-1990s, as plumbing fixtures became fashion statements, the company needed to expand its product line, which had been designed in the 1960s and 1970s, to include many more styles in silver, platinum, and copper. Moen revitalized its product design approach by using the Web and collaborating with its suppliers. Previously, engineers would spend six to eight weeks coming up with a new design, burning it onto CDs, and mailing it to suppliers in 14 countries. The suppliers would return a CD with changes

and suggestions, which had to be reconciled with other suppliers' responses. Redesign activities and tool design and production might extend this process to up to 24 weeks.

With the Web-based approach, a new faucet goes from drawing board to store shelf in 16 months, down from an average of 24 months. This time savings allowed Moen's engineers to work on three times as many projects, and introduce up to 15 new faucet lines each year. This helped boost sales by 17 percent from 1998 to 2001, well above the industry average of 9 percent over the same period, and moving Moen from number 3 in market share to a tie for number 1 with rival Delta Faucet Company.[7]

Japanese automakers continue to take an evolutionary approach to design, stressing continuous improvement in product development time.[8] In Japanese companies, if parts are working well, they are kept, not replaced; by using common components across a range of vehicles, Japanese designs cut down on variation. In contrast, U.S. automakers typically start with a clean slate whenever they redesign a vehicle, which leads to longer development times and often results in poor initial quality and reliability. Delays in the product development process can put a firm at a competitive disadvantage by reducing its ability to amortize the development costs before the product life cycle ends. By the time the product is introduced, the market may already be demanding the next generation. Firms have seen their equity value decline by as much as 5 percent when they announced a delay in the introduction of a new product.[9]

Delays may result from any of the following:

○ **Poor Project Management:** Failing to monitor a project's progress, not managing cross-functional meetings effectively, or poorly defining the roles of development team members are common problems. To successfully manage projects within time, cost, and desired performance/technology objectives, it is important to perform timely project status reviews, set milestones for the project to gauge progress, and properly define resources, roles, and the quantity and quality of the work being done. One firm changed the manufacturing location of a product four times before launch. Each change entailed months of delay and costly design modifications.

○ **Poor Definition of Product Requirements:** This can result from a failure to understand customers' needs, insufficient knowledge about a product's underlying technology, failure to properly consider environmental factors such as competition, and failure to assess downstream impacts when developing product requirements. Poorly defined requirements lead to frequent changes in the product's design and in product development and marketing plans. In addition, poor communication among the product development functions can contribute significantly to insufficient definition of product requirements and design specifications.

○ **Technological and Environmental Uncertainties:** Firms often think that incorporating the latest technology will make new products more marketable, but it can also result in reduced quality and reliability. Questions about compatibility with existing product components and the impact that the new technology will have on the firm's ability to make incremental product innovations need to be resolved early in the process.

○ **Lack of Senior Management Support:** Senior management's attitude toward product development can influence the mind-set of the entire organization. Products are delayed when senior management gives development projects a low priority, has unrealistic expectations or a short-term orientation, or takes a risk-averse approach. Senior management can support product development by taking a long-term strategic approach that views new product development as an opportunity and not as a risk.

Simply avoiding delays is not sufficient, however. A firm must proactively seek to accelerate its product introduction time to avoid the accumulation of substantial development expense. Such "accelerated" firms accrue several benefits:[10]

○ **Longer Sales Life:** Each day cut from a product's development cycle is a day added to its sales life.

○ **Larger Market Share:** For products that involve repeat purchases or high switching costs, the firm that introduces a new product first has a market share gain that is an annuity throughout the product life cycle.

○ **Increased Profit Margins:** Firms that are first to market enjoy greater freedom in pricing and thus achieve a higher profit margin. The price may decline when competitive products appear, but by then the first-entry firm will have moved down its manufacturing learning curve, ahead of its competition, thereby accruing a continuing profit margin advantage.

○ **Multiple Market Segments:** The firm that is able to develop products rapidly can serve multiple market segments more effectively. This is particularly important if consumers have diverse preferences. In many industries, product life cycles are being compressed and product variety is increasing. Consequently, the ability to introduce new products quickly to diverse market segments has become a source of competitive advantage.

With accelerated product life cycles, constant innovation prevents the product from becoming a commodity. This shifts the life cycle curve to the left, enabling the firm to stay ahead of the competition. At the same time, however, this acceleration poses serious challenges for the firm in the form of the following:

○ Quickly recovering its investment because the duration of the mature phase is reduced.

○ Maintaining constant and increasing rates of product innovation.

○ Achieving greater adaptability and flexibility in operations because they never reach a stage where methods and procedures can be systematized (some have referred to this situation as "constant change").

Furthermore, because the firm typically enters and leaves the market quicker than its competitors, it must develop alternative modes of competition. Another challenge is the "acceleration trap," which is the risk that volume will decline after an initial period of high sales.[11] To succeed in such "high-velocity" competitive environments requires dramatic changes in the managerial mind-set.[12] We will discuss approaches for accelerating product development later in this chapter.

One key decision a firm has to make is whether to develop products internally or outsource the design process. For instance, Volvo used an outside car design studio to create a less boxy, more exciting car. Cisco Systems admits that it cannot fully understand which new technologies will thrive in its Internet systems business, so it routinely buys business startups with promising new products. The need for state-of-the-art technology and speed-to-market clearly are driving Cisco's actions.

3.4 STRUCTURED PRODUCT DEVELOPMENT PROCESSES

> ### OM PRINCIPLE
>
> A structured product development process provides a framework for planning and managing development efforts and results in improved communication and coordination within the firm. It also leads to a final product that is focused on the customer's true needs.

BusinessWeek noted that the quality of U.S. automobiles in 2001 was at the level of Japanese vehicles in 1985 and that U.S. automakers and spend about $125 more per vehicle in warranty costs.[13] As one consultant noted, the real problem "has more to do with who designed it, how they designed it, and what processes and materials they used." Thus, a structured product development process is important.

The typical product development process, shown in Figure 3.3, consists of seven key phases:

1. Customer needs identification and idea generation.
2. Concept development and evaluation.
3. Product/service development.
4. Manufacturing process and service delivery development.

5. Ramp-up to full-scale production.
6. Market introduction.
7. Market evaluation.

Ames Rubber Corporation uses such a structured approach (see the *OM Practice* box).

OM PRACTICE

Ames Rubber Corporation
Product-development personnel at Ames maintain close communication with the customer.

Ames Rubber Corporation, a producer of rubber rollers for office machines and a Malcolm Baldrige National Quality Award winner, uses a four-step approach to product development. Typically, a new product is initiated through a series of meetings where Sales/Marketing or the Technical Services Group confers with the customer. From those meetings, a product brief is prepared listing all technical, material, and operational requirements. It is for-warded to internal departments, such as Engineering, Quality, and Manufacturing. The technical staff then selects materials, processes, and procedures and submits them to the customer. Upon the customer's approval, a prototype is made. The prototype is delivered to the customer, who evaluates and tests it and reports the results to Ames. Ames makes any requested modifications, and the prototype is returned to the customer for further testing. The process continues until the customer is completely satisfied. Next, a limited preproduction run is made, and data collected during the run are analyzed and shared with the customer. Upon approval, full-scale production is initiated.[14]

Customer Needs Identification and Idea Generation

New or redesigned product ideas should incorporate customer needs and expectations. In fact, W. Edwards Deming's introductory lecture to Japanese managers in 1950 contrasted the "old way" of product design—design it, make it, and try to sell it—with a "new way":

○ Design the product (with appropriate tests).

○ Make it and test it in the production line and in the laboratory.

○ Put it on the market.

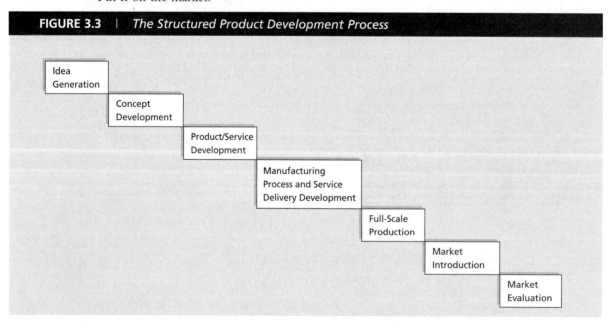

FIGURE 3.3 | *The Structured Product Development Process*

Idea Generation → Concept Development → Product/Service Development → Manufacturing Process and Service Delivery Development → Full-Scale Production → Market Introduction → Market Evaluation

- ○ Test it in service through market research; find out what the user thinks of it and why the nonuser has not bought it.

- ○ Redesign the product, in light of consumer reactions to quality and price.[15]

Ideas for new products can come from a variety of sources both internal and external. Many ideas come from customers or from employees. More often than not, however, new product ideas are developed through systematic research within the firm. Such research begins by listening to the "voice of the customer"—what customers say they want. Obviously, consumers want products that are affordable, easy to install and operate, perform to expectations, are reliable and durable, have clear instructions, and are easy to fix and maintain. But, in addition, they want products to have some very specific features. For example, they might want a pizza to be "tasty," or a portable stereo to have "good sound quality." A regional restaurant chain, listening to its customers, discovered that their most important requirement was "clean bathrooms," which they equated with a clean kitchen and healthful food. True innovations often transcend customers' expressed desires, however, simply because customers may not know what they like until they have it. A good example is Chrysler's decision to develop the minivan, despite research showing that people balked at such an odd-looking vehicle.[16]

In Chapter 2 we introduced the concept of order qualifiers and order winners from a strategic perspective. These also have important implications in the product design process. In the 1980s, for example, quality was considered an order winner, as many firms' quality was subpar; companies that were able to produce high-quality products easily captured the market. Today, however, quality is viewed as an order qualifier, as most consumers view it as a "given." Innovative design, customization, and exceptional service are typical order-winning characteristics today and must be integrated into products and services.

OM PRINCIPLE

A clear understanding of customer needs helps to identify both order qualifiers, which are characteristics that are needed for a product to even be considered, and order winners, which are characteristics that will win over the customer

Identifying customer needs early in the development process will ensure that proper technical tradeoffs are made during the later stages of the process. An effective process for identifying customer needs will ensure that

- ○ the product or service remains focused on customer needs;

- ○ no critical needs are missed and that both explicit needs and hidden needs are identified;

- ○ a common understanding of customer needs is developed among all members of the product development team; and

- ○ product specifications are developed from customer requirements.

Developing innovative ideas is laden with risk. For every 1,000 ideas, perhaps only 100 will have enough commercial promise to lead to a prototype; maybe only 10 of these will merit a substantial financial commitment, and only a few of these will be a commercial success. Hence, firms need effective R & D staffs and good tools for screening potential ideas.

Concept Development and Evaluation

The development of a concept for a new product or service begins with an idea in a customer's mind or in a laboratory. This is the essence of **innovation**—"something newly introduced, such as a new method or device." Marketing plays a key role in innovation by establishing customer needs and justifying proposals and expenditures to finance. Innovation often requires changes in basic operations and processes to ensure the appropriate operational capabilities. The importance of innovation for long-term success and the necessity of integrating it with the other management functions lead to the conclusion that every organization must develop an innovation-based product development strategy.

One decision that an organization will have to make is whether to *specialize* (narrow) or *diversify* (broaden) its product range. Specialist organizations focus on a limited range of skills and resources and thereby reduce process costs. But such a strategy can lead to disaster if technology or the market changes. For example, in 1930, Ford Motor Company suffered one of the largest corporate losses in history as its strategy of "you can have a Model-T in any color as long as it is black" backfired. Fixed resources and supplier capabilities had to be revamped over the next three years as the market and technology changes pushed Ford to consider newer products. Diversification spreads such risks but can lead to its own set of problems. For example, managing operations becomes much more complicated, and the accompanying loss of focus increases the cost of "variety."

Firms should evaluate two dimensions for any new product or service concept: the desired extent of technological change in the concept and the desired market positioning of the new product. These are illustrated in Figure 3.4. The *x*-axis plots the extent of technical and conceptual breakthrough; the *y*-axis plots the desired market positioning. For example, in an effort to maintain product leadership, the machine tool firm Hitachi Seiki chooses new product development projects based on the level of breakthrough.

A **technology push strategy** is characterized by innovation and product leadership. Such firms wish to be technology leaders and view technological innovation as an order-winning criterion. This strategy offers potential high rewards but entails high risks because the firm introduces breakthrough products for a market that does not yet exist, hoping to create demand by "pushing" these products to the market. If it is successful, it can make profits before its competitors catch up; by the time they do, the firm will have recovered much of the development costs and can cut prices to undercut the competitors. Microwave ovens, mobile telephones, video cameras and recorders, and nickel-cadmium batteries are all examples of products that were made possible by the development of new technology.

With a **market pull strategy,** firms uncover an unsatisfied need or demand through market research and customer feedback. They respond to it by adapting their existing products and services. Products are "pulled" by market demands. This strategy is reactive and therefore less risky; however the rewards are often less because competitors will also have detected the opportunity. An organization that chooses this approach must be able to respond rapidly before its competitors can enter the market and force down the price.

Concept evaluation focuses on determining how well a product/service concept will meet customer needs. It involves comparing the relative strengths and weaknesses of alternative concepts. The process may be as informal as selecting concepts that are intuitively appealing or have product champions. Many firms use formal decision or scoring models that filter out poor or infeasible concepts or rank them on their utility.

Scoring models provide a quantitative assessment of a concept by evaluating all key fac-

> **OM PRINCIPLE**
>
> The desired extent of technological change and the desired market positioning of the new product—that is the position on the graph of Figure 3.4—define different product development strategies. The two most common are the technology push and market pull strategies.

> **OM PRINCIPLE**
>
> The higher the economic consequences of product selection, the more rigorous should be the approach used to evaluate and select a concept.

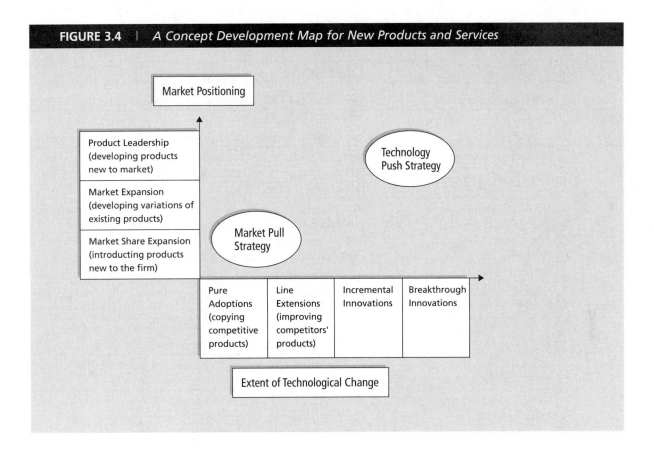

FIGURE 3.4 | *A Concept Development Map for New Products and Services*

tors and weighting them according to their relative priorities. For example, suppose that two key features for a car door are ease of handling (opening the door) and safety from side impact. If the weights are determined to be 60 percent for ease of handling and 40 percent for safety from side impact, then the scoring model for alternative designs is

Weighted score = 0.6 × (ease of handling score) + 0.4 × (safety score)

If two alternative designs are being considered, the assessment process might look like this:

Design Alternative	Ease of Handling Score (scale of 1 to 5)	Safety Score (scale of 1 to 5)	Total Score
A	3	5	(.6 × 3) + (.4 × 5) = 3.8
B	5	4	(.6 × 5) + (.4 × 4) = 4.6

In this case, design alternative B is preferred. Although this example is highly simplified, such approaches help managers to balance tradeoffs among complex sets of criteria. Scoring models essentially rationalize what might otherwise be a subjective, politically driven process. Table 3.1 describes the selection process in greater detail.

TABLE 3.1	Concept Evaluation and Selection Process	

Step	Task	Description
1	Select appropriate criteria.	Determine the most important customer and operational needs.
2	Determine the relative weights.	The relative weights reflect the importance of each criterion and are often derived from a pair-wise comparison of criteria.
3	Establish benchmarks.	Establish guidelines for evaluating each design proposal on each criterion. This involves specifying an operational definition for interpreting a score.
4	Rate each design concept on each criteria.	Assign a relative score to each concept based on the benchmarks established. Often, alternatives are compared to a reference design concept using a scale such as + (better than the reference concept), 0 (the same as the reference), − (worse than the reference).
5	Rank the concepts.	Rank alternative design concepts based on the calculation of the weighted score for each concept.
6	Evaluate the results.	Determine if any low rankings are due to some feature that could possibly be modified or improved.
7	Select the best concept(s).	Decide which concepts are to be selected for further refinement and analysis within resource limitations.
8	Conduct a postmortem review of the process.	It is important that all participants reach a consensus on the outcome. If they don't, then one or more important criteria might be missing, or the weighting process is flawed.

Product/Service Development

If an idea survives the concept stage—and many do not—the actual design process begins. This step consists of many different activities, including determining detailed specifications, deciding on product architecture, prototyping, and evaluating and reviewing the results.

Developing Specifications

The first question a designer must ask is: What is the product intended to do? As we noted earlier, a product's function must be driven by customer requirements. Other design considerations include the product's weight, size, appearance, safety, life, serviceability, and maintainability. When decisions about these factors are dominated by engineering considerations rather than by customer requirements, poor designs that fail in the market are often the result.

Developing a basic functional design involves translating customer requirements into measurable **product specifications** and, subsequently, into detailed design specifications. Product specifications, which spell out in precise detail what the product has to do, are intended to translate the voice of the customer into technical language. For example, consumers might want portable stereos with "good sound quality." Technical aspects of a stereo system that affect sound quality include the frequency response, flutter (the wavering in pitch), and the speed accuracy (inconsistency affects the pitch and tempo of the sound).

OM PRINCIPLE

Product specifications do not tell the development team *how* to address customer needs, but they should represent an unambiguous agreement as to *what* the team will attempt to achieve in order to satisfy those needs.

Every specification should include a metric and a value. For example, a specification for a commercial aircraft might be that *the aircraft will have a range of 8,400 nautical miles.* In this example, range is the metric and 8,400 nautical miles is the target value. Manufacturing specifications consist of **nominal dimensions** and **tolerances.** *Nominal* refers to the ideal dimension or the target value that a manufacturing or service process seeks to meet—for example, a drilled hole diameter of 0.60 mm. Recognizing the difficulty of meeting a target consistently, tolerance is the permissible variation—for instance, an allowance of $\pm$ 0.02 mm in a drilled hole. At Starbucks, the national chain of coffeehouses, milk must be steamed to at

OM PRINCIPLE

Tolerances are necessary because natural variation exists in every manufacturing and service process. Such variation cannot be reduced unless the technology—equipment, procedural steps, training, and so on—is changed.

least 150 degrees Fahrenheit but never more than 170 degrees, and every espresso shot must be pulled within 23 seconds of service or tossed.[17] Service specifications—particularly those that are behavioral in nature, such as a "friendly greeting"—generally are more difficult to define and measure. They require extensive research into customer needs and attitudes about timeliness, consistency, accuracy, and other service attributes.

Tolerances usually lead to conflicts between design and operations. Design would like narrow tolerances to improve product functionality; narrow tolerances increase the interchangeability of parts within the plant and in the field, and improve product performance, durability, and appearance. Operations would often prefer wide tolerances because they increase material utilization, machine throughput, and labor productivity and lower costs. Inappropriate tolerances can have a negative impact on product and quality characteristics. When Audi's TT coupe was first introduced, automobile columnist Alan Vonderhaar noted, "There was apparently some problem with the second-gear synchronizer, a device that is supposed to ease shifts. As a result, on full-power upshifts from first to second, I frequently got gear clashes." Observing that others had found the same problem, he concluded, "It appears to be an issue that surfaces just now and again, here and there throughout the production mix, suggesting it may be a tolerance issue—sometimes the associated parts are close enough to specifications to get along well, other times they're at the outer ranges of manufacturing tolerance and cause problems."[18]

Product Architecture Decisions

Designers face a variety of choices, known as *product architecture* decisions. Good product architecture can help designers to develop products quicker and at less cost. These choices also often have significant implications for operations. Consider, for instance the decision of whether to use standard or modular components. From an operations perspective, standard parts and components are more widely available and less expensive. Also, because they do not have to be designed in-house, the development time is lower. Modular design allows manufactured parts and services to be combined in a large number of ways, thus facilitating mass customization. For example, computing equipment is modular in the sense that different central processing units, video cards, CD/DVD peripherals, and other components can be combined. Thus, modular design offers the advantages of standardization in design without the accompanying disadvantage of "loss of uniqueness." Modular design also offers a major advantage when technology changes rapidly. For example, the central processing unit for personal computers obsolesces rapidly. A modular design allows the manufacturer to easily incorporate the latest technology, particularly if assembly is driven by customer orders.

Design approaches are often facilitated by technology such as **computer-aided design (CAD)** or simulation (see the *OM Practice* box on BMW). Up to 40 to 50 percent of the time involved in design can be saved through CAD. Many CAD systems electronically transfer information about the physical dimensions of the product and the manufacturing steps required to produce it to computer-aided manufacturing equipment. Some systems have simulation and animation capabilities that allow the operation of the product to be visualized. Thus, CAD technology not only increases the designers' productivity, but also improves the quality of the design and manufacturing process.

OM PRACTICE

BMW
Computer-aided design for the X5 sport utility reduces development time.

The BMW X5, built exclusively in Spartanburg, South Carolina, is the first BMW to be designed 100 percent digitally. BMW used three-dimensional CAD programs from development through testing to reduce development time (the X5 was the first BMW product developed within three years) and enable tighter manufacturing tolerances (reduced tolerances, together with a high level of quality during production, help ensure safety). CAD mod-

els efficiently defined possible problem points early in the design process and offered counter-measures. The models were also used for design tests and structural evaluations, including simulations, that provided highly reliable results and confirmed the accuracy and safety of virtual examinations for the future. BMW can conduct CAD-based tests to determine a vehicle's heating and air-conditioning efficiency, its body's behavior under varying wind pressure, the dynamics of vehicle movement and chassis load, the functionality of switches and displays, and even its performance in a crash.[19]

Prototyping

A **prototype** is a trial version of the actual product or part. Some prototypes are actual working models, while others are just rough, conceptual sketches. Prototypes serve four purposes.

First, prototyping helps the engineer or designer to evaluate a proposed design. Learning from the prototype will help the engineer create a better design. Second, a prototype enhances communication with people who are not familiar with the product. People find it is easier to understand a concept if they can look at a physical model or even a drawing. Third, the prototype can be tested to determine the product's physical properties or use under actual operating conditions and uncover any problems prior to ramp-up. For example, in developing the user interface for an automobile navigation system, BMW conducted extensive consumer tests with various prototypes, including a keyboard, a rotating push button, and a joystick (the push button was ultimately selected).[20] Finally, in large projects, a prototype could mean that a milestone has been met. The prototype could serve as a tangible goal for the product team.

> **OM PRINCIPLE**
>
> In product development, prototypes are used for four reasons: learning, communication, integration, and milestones.

The most time-consuming stage of product development is the making of a prototype. Today, using an approach known as **rapid prototyping,** ordinary CAD files can be converted rapidly into physical models. By allowing quick production of prototypes and fast verification of designs, this approach has significantly reduced product development times and improved quality.

Evaluation and Review

To ensure that all important design objectives are taken into account during the design process, many companies have instituted formal **design reviews.** Their purpose is to stimulate discussion and raise questions to generate new ideas and solutions to problems.

> **OM PRINCIPLE**
>
> Design reviews can facilitate standardization and reduce the costs associated with frequent design changes by helping designers anticipate problems before they occur.

Design reviews may focus on strategic issues of design that relate to customer requirements—and thus the ultimate quality of the product—such as completeness of specifications, value and appearance make-or-buy decisions, reliability requirements, and liability issues; or they may focus on detailed analyses for the purposes of cost reduction. In a **value analysis,** every component of a product, system, or service is analyzed to determine if its function can be accomplished more economically without degrading quality. Typical questions that might be asked include:

○ What are the functions of a particular component or process? Are they necessary? Can they be accomplished in a different way?

○ What materials are used? Can a less costly material be substituted? For example, can off-the-shelf items be used in place of custom-specified components?

○ How much material is wasted during operations? Can waste be reduced by changing the design?

OM PRINCIPLE

Value analysis typically leads to lower costs and higher profits, better products and services, improved product performance and reliability, higher quality, faster delivery through reduced lead-times, and increased standardization that leads to improved maintenance and lower repair costs.

One company originally made an exhaust manifold in an air compressor from cast iron, which required several machining steps. By switching to a powder metal process, it reduced four machine steps to one. The savings amounted to $50,000 per year. Another company formerly packed bottles of shampoo in plain chipboard cartons for distributors. By changing to a plastic six-pack holder similar to that used in the beverage industry, it saved more than $100,000 in the first year. Even simple ideas such as reusing packing material from incoming shipments to pack outgoing shipments have resulted in savings of more than $600,000 for many companies.[21]

Service Design

Similar considerations must be included when designing a service process. Some common examples of service processes are preparing an invoice, taking a telephone order, processing a credit card, and checking out of a hotel. Nonetheless, service design differs from product design in several ways. First, the outputs of service processes are not as well-defined as manufactured products. For example, even though all banks offer similar tangible goods such as checking, loans, and automated teller machines, the real differentiating factor among banks is the service they provide. Second, most service processes involve more interaction with the customer, often making it easier to identify needs and expectations. Often, though, customers cannot define their needs for service until they have some point of reference or comparison.

Designing a service essentially involves determining an effective balance among three basic components: (1) physical facilities, processes, and procedures; (2) employees' behavior; and (3) employees' professional judgment.[22] A restaurant, for instance, must consider the menu, the decor and atmosphere, the processes by which customers are seated and served, what employees say and how they say it, and how they react to problems and complaints. The goal is to provide a service whose elements are internally consistent and focused to meet the needs of a specific target-market segment. Fast-food restaurants have carefully designed their service delivery processes for a high degree of accuracy and fast response time.[23] Hands-free intercom systems, microphones that reduce ambient kitchen noise, and screens that display a customer's order are all focused on these requirements. Timers at Wendy's count every segment of the order completion process to help managers identify problem areas. Kitchen workers wear headsets to hear orders as they are placed. Even adding photos of certain items to drive-through order boards makes it more likely customers will select these items; less variety means faster order fulfillment.

Too much or too little emphasis on one component will lead to problems and poor customer perceptions. For example, too much emphasis on procedures might result in timely and efficient service, but might also suggest insensitivity and apathy toward the customer. Too much emphasis on behavior might ensure a friendly and personable environment, but service might be slow, inconsistent, or chaotic. Too much emphasis on professional judgment might lead to good solutions to customer problems but also to slow, inconsistent, or insensitive service.

Service designs are generally expressed as a standard operating procedure, or a template that service providers should follow when interacting with customers. For example, Figure 3.5 shows the Three Steps of Service of The Ritz-Carlton Hotel Company. Every employee is trained in this process, which defines the procedures for anticipating and complying with customer needs. When services are documented in this fashion, it is easy to conduct a "design review" to identify potential improvements and non-value-added steps or to use the template as a prototype in trying out a new service concept.

FIGURE 3.5 | *The Ritz-Carlton's Three Steps of Service Process*

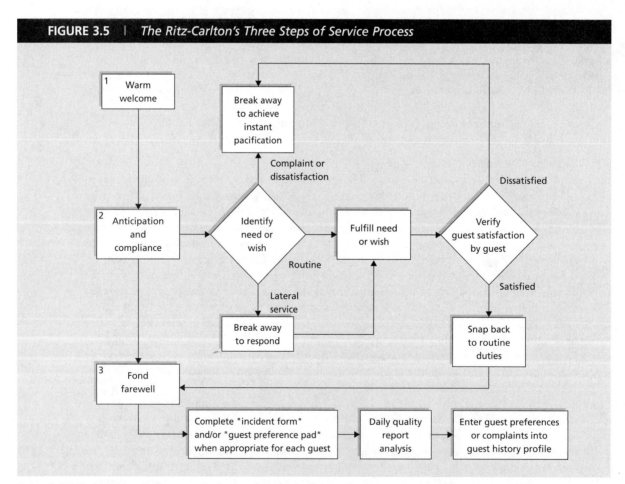

Source: © 1992, The Ritz-Carlton Hotel Company. All rights reserved. Reprinted with the permission of The Ritz-Carlton Hotel Company, L.L.C.

OM PRINCIPLE

The choices among customer contact, labor intensity, and customization significantly affect operations performance and its management.

Architecture decisions in services often involve customer contact and involvement in the service process, labor intensity versus technology, and levels of customization. Examples include an airline's choice to use automated e-ticketing check-in or human service representatives, or a bank's decision to have one long line feeding several tellers or an individual line for each teller.

Service organizations low in all three dimensions of this classification are more similar to manufacturing organizations. They should focus on the physical facilities and procedures; behavior and professional judgment are relatively unimportant. As contact and interaction between the customer and the service system increase, the latter factors become more important. In service organizations that are low in labor intensity, the customer's impression of the physical facilities, processes, and procedures is important. Such organizations must be careful to choose and maintain reliable, easy-to-use equipment.

As labor intensity increases, variations between individuals become more important, but behavior and professional judgment will remain relatively unimportant as long as customization, contact, and interaction remain low. As customization increases, professional judgment becomes more important in the customer's perception of service quality. In services that are high in all three dimensions, facilities, behavior, and professional judgment must be equally balanced.

Manufacturing Process and Service Delivery Development

OM PRINCIPLE

A simple design does not necessarily mean simple production. Product designs that use simple components sometimes result in complex or difficult assembly operations or in products that are difficult or expensive to service or support. Thus, operations involvement in the design stage is vital for reducing total life cycle costs

Product design decisions cannot be made without also considering the design of manufacturing processes and service delivery systems. Many aspects of product design can adversely affect operations performance.[24] Parts are sometimes designed with features that are difficult to produce consistently, or they are so fragile or so susceptible to corrosion or contamination that some are damaged during movement from one operation to the next. Thus, problems of poor design can show up as errors, poor yield, damage, or functional failure in fabrication, assembly, test, transport, and end use.

Design for manufacturability (DFM) is the process of designing a product for efficient production at the highest level of quality. DFM is intended to prevent product designs

OM PRINCIPLE

DFM guidelines must be interpreted with caution. For example, minimizing the number of parts during design might well result in a very complicated and costly production process.

that simplify assembly operations but require more complex and expensive components, designs that simplify component manufacture while complicating the assembly process, and designs that are simple and inexpensive to produce but difficult or expensive to service or support. DFM is a team-based approach that involves everyone associated with the development process, such as packaging, manufacturing, accounting, and supplier development. In an example of DFM in action, a team of designers at Thermos were designing an electric grill with tapered legs. The manufacturing team member noted that tapered legs would have to be custom-made and persuaded the designers to make them straight.[25]

DFM works on simplistic guidelines, such as the following:

○ Minimize the number of parts, including fasteners.

○ Minimize the number of fabrication or assembly operations.

○ Discover customers' functional requirements and match the design to them.

○ Determine process capabilities and design products to match them.

○ Specify standard components with proven quality levels whenever possible.

○ Design multifunctional modules and combine them.

○ Create designs that simplify fabrication, assembly, and servicing.

○ Design products to allow one-way assembly with no wasteful backtracking.

○ Avoid special-purpose fasteners or those that require special tools.

○ Make parts strong enough to withstand inevitable mishandling.

○ Anticipate potential misuse by customers and create a design that prevents it.

Design for assembly (DFA) is similar to DFM, but focuses on reducing assembly costs and increasing the quality of conformance by creating designs that fit well with assembly operations. This simple strategy begins by reducing as much as possible the number of parts needed to assemble the product. It then works to ensure that the remaining parts fit together as easily as possible. These goals are easier to state than to accomplish. One approach to assessing DFA is to use a quantitative scoring method for part features that identifies areas for potential savings and assigns penalty points for each feature of the design. The DFA team then seeks to redesign the product to improve this design score. Although no one can accurately measure the relative contribution of DFA, Ford has reportedly used it to achieve a cost advantage over General Motors in the range of $1,500 per vehicle.

Environmental concerns are placing unprecedented government and consumer pressures on product and process designs. Millions of home, personal care, and office appliances are disposed of each year.[26] The problem of what to do with obsolete computers is a growing design and technological problem today.[27] Pressures from environmental groups that are clamoring for "socially responsive" designs, states and municipalities that are running out of space for landfills, and consumers who want the most for their money have caused designers and managers to look carefully at the concept of **Design-for-Environment**, or **DfE**.[28]

DfE is the explicit consideration of environmental concerns during the design of products and processes; it includes such practices as designing for recyclability and disassembly. Recyclable products are designed to be taken apart and their components repaired, refurbished, melted down, or otherwise salvaged for reuse. Toner cartridges for laser printers, for example, are often remanu-

> **OM PRINCIPLE**
>
> DfE offers the potential to create more desirable products at lower costs by reducing disposal and regulatory costs, increasing the end-of-life value of products, reducing material use, and minimizing liabilities.

factured. Although recyclability appeals to environmentalists as well as city and state officials with overflowing landfills, it creates new issues for designers who must select materials that allow for reuse. Several U.S. firms including Whirlpool, 3M, and General Electric, are working on or marketing such products.[29] GE's plastics division, which serves the durable goods market, uses only thermoplastics in its products. Unlike many other varieties of plastics, thermoplastics can be melted down and recast into other shapes and products, thus making them recyclable. Designers must also refrain from using certain methods of fastening, such as glues and screws, in favor of quick connect-disconnect bolts or other such fasteners. These changes in design will have an impact on tolerances, durability, and quality of products. Such design changes also affect consumers who will be asked to recycle the products.

Both Xerox and IBM are examples of companies that have integrated DfE specialists directly into design teams. The use of snap-fits on IBM computer housings and reusable Xerox toner cartridges and bottles were introduced as a result of DfE.

Ramp-Up to Full-Scale Production

Ramp-up involves the building of production capability for full-scale production. Often this is done gradually over time to ensure proper coordination and quality and to identify and eliminate any problems that might arise in the actual production process. There are several approaches to ramp-up, and the decision is not always clear. For example, the automobile industry has a choice between a *mixed-model ramp-up process* (the old model is phased out at the same time that production of a new model begins) or a *clean-sheet ramp-up process* (production of the new model does not begin until production of the old model is finished). Figure 3.6 illustrates the two choices. In a mixed-model ramp-up, the firm uses the capacity of its operations better, but operators must work on two model types simultaneously, which may cause confusion. A clean-sheet ramp-up leads to lower capacity utilization of processes and disrupts supplier schedules during the transition.

No matter which approach is selected, problems will inevitably occur as the organization learns to manage production of the new product, and operations managers need to be prepared to address them until operations can operate smoothly and on a normal schedule. For example, in the pharmaceutical industry, new drugs are constantly being developed, and manufacturers must ramp up production during the clinical trial phase of the development process.[30] During the time between preclinical trials and final manufacturing, demand may increase as much as 16 times. The chances of a preclinical drug reaching the market are only about 1 in 9, however, so there is considerable risk in ramping up when the drug may not win regulatory approval and may never be sold.

FIGURE 3.6 | *Mixed-Model versus Clean-Sheet Ramp-up Process*

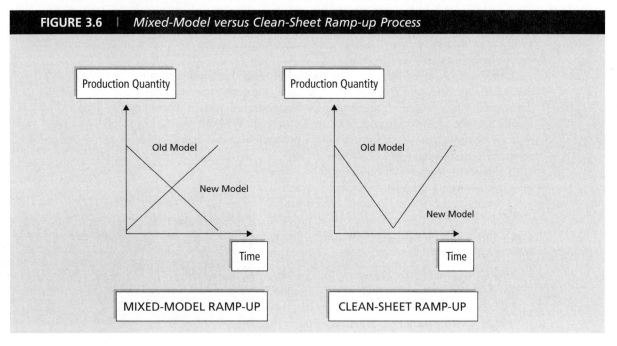

Market Introduction and Evaluation

How many times has a new startup venture introduced a great product, only to find that it lacked the proper infrastructure to produce the product in sufficient quantity to meet market demand, to deliver it on time, or to provide sufficient customer service? All these are operational activities that must be included in product development project plans. In addition, plans should include a process for obtaining customer feedback to initiate continuous improvements.

> **OM PRINCIPLE**
>
> Introducing a new product to the market requires considerable operational and logistical support as well as installation, customer support, and other service activities.

3.5 PRODUCT DEVELOPMENT AS A CROSS-FUNCTIONAL ACTIVITY

One of the most significant barriers to efficient product development is poor intra-organizational cooperation. All functions play crucial roles in the design process.[31] Whereas the designer's objective is to meet functional requirements, the manufacturing engineer's objective is to produce the designed product according to specifications and at the lowest cost. The salesperson wants the product to have features and a price that make it easy to sell, and finance executives want it to make a profit. Purchasing must ensure that purchased parts meet quality requirements. Packaging and distribution personnel must ensure that the product reaches the customer in good operating condition. All business functions

> **OM PRINCIPLE**
>
> Viewing product development as a cross-functional activity can improve the four key success factors associated with a product launch: development time, product performance, unit product cost, and development program expense.

have a stake in the product; therefore, all must work together. After Daimler-Benz merged with Chrysler, for example, CEO Dieter Zetsche began overhauling the vehicle development process to put more focus on the early stages. By pulling together teams from design, engineering, marketing, manufacturing, and purchasing—an approach that Chrysler developed in 1989 but could not sustain—he hoped to reduce waste and resolve quality problems without diminishing Chrysler's creative instincts.[32]

Unfortunately, many firms use a sequential product development approach. In this "over-the-wall" approach, as it is often called, design engineers dominate the early stages of the development process. Later, the prototype is transferred to manufacturing for production. Finally, marketing and sales personnel are brought in. Without good cooperation and communication from the beginning, the final product may not meet customer requirements, resulting in design changes and further delays.

Successful product development requires interactions among the many different functional groups within an organization to identify and solve design problems and to reduce product development and introduction times. These interactions include the following:

> **OM PRINCIPLE**
>
> The interactions among the core functions of marketing, design, manufacturing, and finance in the product development process are critical to successfully meeting product development objectives and should begin at the initial product concept phase and be carried on throughout the life of the project.

- ○ **From Marketing to Design:** The conflicts between the marketing (customer oriented) and design (innovation) perspectives are legendary.[33] The marketing function's role is to convey the "voice of the customer" to the design function in the initial phases of the product development process and ensure that new designs remain focused on customer needs. If communication between these groups breaks down, market failures often result.

○ **From Design to Operations:** Once the design is completed, the design team must present the operations function with a product or service that can be built or delivered to meet customer expectations at a targeted cost. If the product cannot be built to the quality and cost levels that customers demand, it will be hard to sell no matter how innovative the design may be. Design for manufacturability (DFM), discussed earlier in this chapter, helps the design and manufacturing teams coordinate their efforts and focus on these issues.

○ **From Operations to Marketing:** The interactions between marketing and operations are mainly concerned with the production capacity that will be required to meet demand for the product. If marketing forecasts sales and communicates these forecasts to manufacturing early in the product development process, manufacturing can better plan inventory and production; this can prevent lost sales due to insufficient inventory or high carrying costs due to overproduction. Product launches are often plagued by conflict over such issues.

○ **From Design, Operations, and Marketing to Finance:** Finance interacts with each of the other core product development functions to ensure that resources are available when they are needed. If enough money is not allocated to research and development, an organization can easily fall behind the competition in technical abilities. If not enough money is spent on developing new production process technologies, or if the investments are approved too late, then the firm's products may fail to meet the quality standards desired by its customers.

Integrated Product Development

Integrated product development (also called **concurrent engineering** or **simultaneous engineering**) is a term used to describe the cross-functional cooperation of all major functions in the product development process from conception through sales. Multifunctional teams, usually consisting of 4 to 20 members representing every specialty in the company, are responsible for all aspects of product development, including product design, production process design, design for manufacturability and assembly, and supplier issues (see the *OM Practice* box on Solar Turbines). Such an approach not only helps achieve trouble-free introduction of products and services, but also results in improved quality, lower costs, and shorter product development cycles. Typical benefits include 30 to 70 percent less development time, 65 to 90 percent fewer engineering changes, 20 to 90 percent less time to market, 200 to 600 percent improvement in quality, 20 to 110 percent improvement in white-collar productivity, and 20 to 120 percent higher return on assets.[34] Cooperative relationships may extend beyond the internal value chain. For example, strategic alliances with suppliers and other partners can help a company to gain access to key technologies necessary for effective product development.

If communication across an organization's functional groups is already a problem, adding an international dimension makes coordination much more challenging. Many product development projects in large firms with a global presence require both interfunctional and international cooperation; hence, efficient management of product development projects is essential. Such firms must find ways to encourage cross-functional cooperation within each subsidiary as well as cross-national cooperation across subsidiaries in different countries. Some have suggested that Japanese firms will find functional integration easier than international integration, whereas the situation will be the opposite for Western firms.[35]

OM PRACTICE

Solar Turbines

Solar Turbines employs a team-oriented New Product Introduction (NPI) process to meet customer needs and minimize development schedules and cost.

Solar Turbines, a division of Caterpillar that manufactures gas turbine products for the global market, is a recipient of the Malcolm Baldrige National Quality Award. The company introduced its team-oriented New Product Introduction (NPI) process to make product development more effective and efficient. The NPI process consists of four phases:

1. Market Requirements and Concept Development.
2. Product Planning.
3. Development.
4. Production.

NPI teams are formed at the start of the Market Requirements and Concept Development phase and are charged with bringing a new product from concept through field operation. They include representatives from manufacturing, customer service, finance, the firm's Products Committee, project engineering, marketing, package engineering, and turbine engineering, all coordinated by a team leader. Human resources representatives may observe the teams during startup to assess their effectiveness and recommend appropriate training.

In each phase of the NPI process, many activities are performed concurrently. For example, in the Product Planning phase, functional support team formation, market requirements determination, customer requirements determination, product requirement specification, competitive strategy evaluation, alternatives evaluation, risk assessment, business plan development, and Products Committee approval are all performed concurrently. Solar has found that conducting simultaneous product development activities with the early involvement of all key stakeholders contributes to higher product quality, shorter development schedules, and lower overall product development costs.[36]

Quality Function Deployment

When information is passed from marketing to design and from design to manufacturing, it is easy for customer needs to fall by the wayside as each function focuses on its own internal issues. Cross-functional coordination among marketing, design, and operations can be facilitated by **quality function deployment (QFD),** a methodology that links customer needs (the voice of the customer) to the technical (design) requirements throughout the product development and production process. The main tool used in QFD is the **House of Quality** (Figure 3.7). This is a matrix-style chart that correlates customer needs, called "the Whats," with technical requirements, called "the Hows." Ideally, the House of Quality should be developed by a cross-functional team with members from all core functions.

OM PRINCIPLE

QFD provides a means for improving communication and teamwork among all constituencies in the product development process—marketing and design, design and manufacturing, and purchasing and suppliers. It can help to ensure that products respond to customer needs, prevent misinterpretation of product objectives during the production process, and reduce the product development cycle time.

The process begins by identifying customer needs and the technical features of the design. These are related to one another in the center of the house, which is a relationship matrix that indicates how each technical requirement affects customer needs. The next step is to construct the "roof" of the house. This is a matrix indicating the relationships between the technical requirements with symbols denoting the strength of the relationships. For instance, a specification for an excessive takeoff weight for a commercial aircraft will strongly affect the required takeoff distance. The matrix helps in examining the product's features collectively rather than individually and in answering questions such as, "How does a change in one product characteristics affect others?" The roof of the House of Quality is a good indicator of design tradeoffs that may have to be made in the future and helps ensure that the impact of the tradeoffs on customer requirements will be considered.

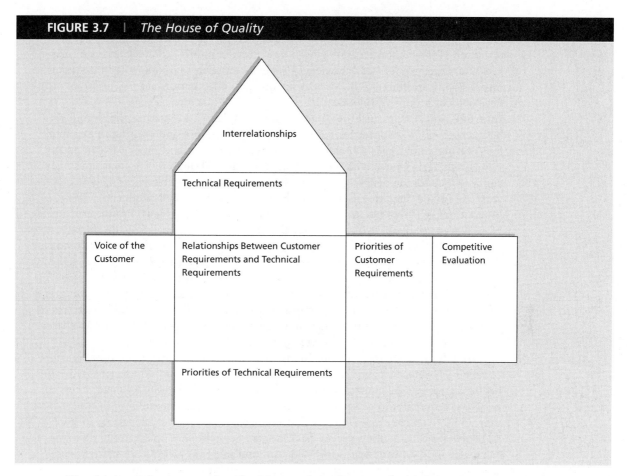

FIGURE 3.7 | *The House of Quality*

The third step in constructing the House of Quality is to build the "garage." This part describes customer perceptions of specific product attributes as well as evaluations of competing products. Competitive benchmarking information is often used to construct this portion of the house. The goal is to identify technical features that have a strong relationship to customer needs, have poor competitive performance, or are strong selling points.

The final step is to build the "basement," which provides the basis for setting target specifications and identifying the most important technical requirements that will need to be "deployed," or paid close attention to, in subsequent stages of the design and production process. These priorities result from a holistic assessment of the information contained in the House of Quality and are often expressed in quantifiable terms or against an appropriate rating system. For example, if a technical requirement receives a low evaluation on all competitors' products, but affects key customer needs, then focusing on that requirement can lead to a competitive advantage. *Supplementary Notes 3.1* in the Bonus Materials folder on the CD-ROM contains a detailed example of using QFD to develop a fitness center concept.

3.1

3.6 EMERGING ISSUES IN PRODUCT DEVELOPMENT

Three major trends appear to drive the need for continual improvement and redefinition of the product development function in organizations:

1. **Globalization:** With globalization of strategic partners such as suppliers and distributors, a firm's ability to innovate can provide a critical advantage in launching new

products, gaining market share, and securing important relationships worldwide. Thus, product development processes must be designed to encompass the needs of global operations. Information technology can now provide round-the-clock access to markets and other sources of knowledge (such as suppliers or competitors), so many organizations are looking at ways to encourage collaboration among research and development groups worldwide.

2. **Internet and E-Commerce:** Information networks are blurring the boundaries between economies, industries, organizations, and functions and creating more rapid, free-flowing communication among suppliers, distributors, and other partners in the value chain. This connectivity is catalyzing innovation. Though most applications of e-commerce are in the fledgling stage, it will surely become a viable sales channel in the years ahead and alter the relationships between customers and producers. With the Internet, information can be exchanged without heavy investments in infrastructure. Now five members of a cross-functional team can meet virtually on the Net for a minor product design decision, instead of having to fly 10,000 miles. Another trend is the growing shift of market power from producers to consumers. As consumers gather more information and knowledge, they are better able to bargain. Currently, 25 to 35 percent of car buyers access the Internet for information and pricing before going to a dealer showroom. At the same time, dealer employee turnover is approaching 70 percent per year. Defining new product and service "bundles" with altered market channels and altered power spectrums will continue to be a major challenge.

3. **Supply Chain Cost Reduction:** Innovations in the management and development of supply chains can make some companies highly valued partners. Supply webs are beginning to replace supply chains, resulting in quicker and more efficient access to suppliers. A significant portion of the product development activities can thus be outsourced more efficiently, leaving the firm to focus on the core elements. For example, many features in popular software packages are actually developed outside the firm. Microsoft and Netscape scan such "add-ons" and integrate them into their packages, allowing their developers to focus on the core content modifications.

Beating competitors with new products that anticipate customers' desires is critical for most organizations today. Leading firms are looking for ways to innovate the new product development process itself, since doing so leverages their ability to plan and introduce winning new products. Two issues are emerging as vital to product development and operations: managing information and the product portfolio.

First, the widespread use of information technology often creates a proliferation of incompatible computer systems ("islands of automation") that are developed and supported by different parts of the organization. Also, the quantity of product design data generated within a short period of time makes manual control of these data extremely difficult, if not impossible. As a result,

OM PRINCIPLE

A significant challenge for the future is the integration of information technology with the design, program management, final assembly, certification, and delivery of the product to the customer.

maintenance costs for legacy systems are soaring. Starting in the mid-1980s, a new class of applications called *Engineering Data Management (EDM)* emerged. EDM applications have a common purpose of providing **configuration management**—a disciplined approach to defining elements of product engineering data and controlling and tracking changes. Although the intent was to help bridge the gaps between islands of automation, EDM had limited use from a business perspective because it could manage only data generated by computer-aided design, manufacturing, and engineering tools.

In the 1990s, a new type of stand-alone application, called *Product Data Management (PDM)*, entered the market and allowed configuration management of almost any type of dataset. EDM/PDM has evolved into *Product Information Management (PIM)*. PIM solutions rely on well-defined benchmarks for product development and a centralized database that coordinates information flow for all product development activities.

OM PRINCIPLE

The strategic assessment of the product development portfolio—the set of product development projects in which a firm is engaged—will remain a vital source of competitive advantage for most firms.

The second key initiative for improving product development is to continually reassess the **product development portfolio**—the projects that an organization has undertaken. Wheelwright and Clark present a classification scheme of four primary types of development projects to help clarify resource needs for project planning as shown in Table 3.2.[37] Clearly, a sweeping project to develop a new core process or product or both requires more resources such as cross-functional product-innovation teams and more organizational flexibility. Small projects with limited scopes probably do not require as broad a resource base.

A balanced mix of product development projects allows the firm to hedge the risks of breakthrough projects with those that are guaranteed to produce incremental revenue. An interesting example comes from Toyota.[38] Toyota creates new products that share key components but utilizes separate development teams to ensure that each product will be different enough to be attractive to different product/market segments. Such multiproject thinking allows Toyota to leverage its product portfolio to produce a stream of new products rapidly and with the requisite amount of innovation. This requires both strong cross-functional coordination and strong interproject coordination. We believe that this will be the biggest challenge for many large firms in the coming decade.

Summary of Key Points

○ Effective product development processes lead to improved market position, efficient resource utilization, and organizational renewal and enhancement. Operations management plays a critical role in these efforts by providing the infrastructure to produce and deliver products and services efficiently and at low cost, on time, and within quality standards.

○ The typical product life cycle consists of four stages: introduction, growth, maturity, and decline. Higher investment in development early in the product development process often results in lower overall costs and better returns on investment.

○ The ability to compete on speed and agility is influenced greatly by the effectiveness of product development and operations management activities. Delays in development often arise from poor project management, poor definition of product requirements, technological uncertainties, and lack of senior management support. "Accelerating" product life cycles improves speed-to-market, as well as investment returns and flexibility, and promotes a mind-set of innovation.

○ A structured product development process enhances communication and helps keep the focus on the needs of the customer. A typical product development process consists of seven key phases: customer needs identification, concept development and evaluation, product or service development, manufacturing process and service delivery development, ramp-up to full-scale production or service delivery, market introduction, and market evaluation. Various tools and techniques support each phase and enhance the effectiveness of the product development management effort.

TABLE 3.2	*A Framework for Product Development Projects*		
Type of Project	**Description**	**Examples**	**Characteristics**
Advanced research and development	Pure research or advanced development to create fundamentally new products or process technologies	Electric or hybrid cars; Xenon microprocessor	• Requires high level of knowledge and skills. • May have no experience to draw from. • End results are unknown; success is uncertain.
Breakthrough	Product or process development using some entirely new technology	Mazda's development of the rotary engine; tablet PCs; BMW's i-drive system	• Can develop early market leadership. • Requires new integration across organizational functions.
Platform or new generation	Major overhaul of an existing product or development of a new class of product designs	Third generation Nintendo or X-box gaming systems; Pentium 4 processor	• Provides a basis for future product development without requiring extensive change. • May not be innovative enough to gain a competitive edge.
Derivative	Refinements or improvements to existing products or processes	Wireless PDAs; rewritable DVDs	• Requires only small modifications to existing processes and technology and few advanced skills. • Easy to copy; may not provide sustainable competitive advantage.

Source: Types of projects and descriptions based on Steven Wheelwright and Kim Clark, *Revolutionizing Product Development*, New York: Free Press, 1992, 28–29.

- ○ The core functions of product design include developing specifications, product architecture decisions, prototyping, and evaluation and review. The design of services must account for their unique characteristics and balance physical facilities, processes, and procedures; employee behavior; and employee professional judgment.
- ○ Anticipating the impacts of product and service designs on operations is facilitated by such techniques as design for manufacturability (DFM), design for assembly (DFA), and design for environment (DfE).
- ○ Product development is a cross-functional activity that involves interactions among marketing, design, manufacturing, and finance; these interactions are captured in the concept of integrated product development. Concurrent, or simultaneous, engineering is an approach to effectively managing product development through teamwork while reducing product development time and creating higher-quality designs.

- ○ Integrated product development is enhanced by such methodologies as quality function deployment (QFD), a process for ensuring that customer requirements are captured in the design of products and in production delivery processes. QFD relies on the House of Quality to evaluate the ability of a design to meet customer needs and respond to competitive threats and opportunities.

- ○ The key forces that will transform product development in organizations are globalization, the Internet and e-commerce, and changes in the supply chain. Emerging issues in product development include Product Information Management (PIM) for managing information as a corporate asset and strategic assessment of the product development portfolio.

Questions for Review and Discussion

1. Why is the selection and development of new products an important strategic decision?
2. Why is it important to study the operational consequences of the product development process?
3. How does the product life cycle influence cash flow in a typical firm? How does cash flow change as the product life cycle is compressed?
4. Explain the common reasons for product development delays. What effect do such delays have from a strategic viewpoint?
5. What benefits accrue from accelerating product introduction time?
6. Describe the general phases of a typical product development process. How do they differ for manufactured products versus services?
7. Explain the concept of the "voice of the customer." What are some ways to ensure that the voice of the customer is captured effectively?
8. Discuss the value of using scoring models for concept selection. What are some of the challenges associated with this methodology?
9. How do product specifications link the voice of the customer to engineering and manufacturing issues?
10. Explain the concepts of nominal specifications and tolerances. Provide at least two examples in both manufacturing and service activities.
11. What is product architecture? Describe the key product architecture decisions that are important to operations.
12. Discuss the product development issues associated with project management and information systems.
13. Explain the differences between the mixed-model and clean-sheet ramp-up approaches.
14. Why should product development be viewed as a cross-functional activity?
15. Explain the key interactions among marketing, design, manufacturing, and finance in product development.
16. Define concurrent engineering. Explain the differences between it and the traditional, "over-the-wall" approach to product development.
17. What is quality function deployment? How does the House of Quality help to address critical product development issues?
18. Suppose that you were developing a small pizza restaurant with a dining area and local delivery. Develop a list of customer requirements and technical requirements and try to complete a House of Quality.
19. Fill in the following relationship matrix of a House of Quality for a screwdriver. By sampling your classmates, develop priorities for the customer attributes and use these and the relationships to identify key technical requirements to deploy.

	Price	Interchangeable Bits	Steel Shaft	Rubber Grip	Ratchet Capability	Plastic Handle
Easy to Use						
Does not Rust						
Durable						
Comfortable						
Versatile						
Inexpensive						
Priority						

20. What is design for manufacturing? How does it differ from design for assembly? State some typical DFM rules that enhance the design and manufacturing processes.

21. Explain the benefits of computer-aided design and rapid prototyping.

22. How do analysis and design reviews support the objectives of product development?

23. Discuss emerging issues in product development. Why do many firms still struggle with their product development activities?

24. John Stark Associates provides a comprehensive resource for product development (see the text Web site at **http://raturi_evans.swlearning.com**). It suggests that the following 15 principles provide a sound basis for good engineering and product development:

   ○ A quality-focused approach
   ○ A bias for cycle time reduction
   ○ A bias for innovation
   ○ A coherent vision, strategy, plan and metrics
   ○ A product-family oriented business unit
   ○ Listening to the voice of the customer
   ○ A clearly defined and well-organized development process
   ○ Cross-functional product development teams
   ○ Supplier involvement early in the development process
   ○ A development methodology
   ○ Highly skilled, well-trained people

- Computer-aided design systems
- Digital product models controlled by EDM and PDM systems
- Simulation and rapid prototyping
- Best practice techniques

Do you strongly agree or disagree with any of these principles? Summarize the main logic of one of these principles (i.e., how does it enhance product development effectiveness?).

25. The Georgia Web group (see the text Web site at **http://raturi_evans. swlearning.com**) outlines the seven C's of Web-service design as follows:

- **Comprehensiveness:** Complete institutional coverage with respect to organization and functions as provided at the closest possible point of knowledge.
- **Currentness:** Accuracy of static information enhanced by the currentness of changing information.
- **Client Orientation:** Responsiveness to requests from the viewing audience.
- **Clarity over Coolness:** Simplicity of page design and directness of hyperlink pathways take precedence over visual techniques that clutter or compromise presentation.
- **Courtesy over Coolness:** The length of time required for a page to load useful information is reasonable.
- **Compatibility without Compromise:** Sensitivity to and support of different browser environments.
- **Cross-Linking and Validation:** Multiple access paths to the same information with a method in place to check the validity of site-wide links.

Do you think the cost (of creation and maintenance) and competence of the designers themselves are significant issues? What are some other dimensions that would affect the design of a Web service?

Internet Projects

To find Web links to carry out each of the following projects, go to the text's Web site at **http://raturi_evans.swlearning.com**.

1. Dr. William Boulton has summarized many of the contemporary issues of product development practice. In one paragraph, summarize the key issues of one of his articles.

2. Using examples from Clorox, Dupont, Invar, and Nortel, the University of California at Berkeley summarizes the main reasons why firms use design for manufacturability (DFM). Summarize the rationale for DFM and find examples of DFM in products and services that you use.

3. Marshall Brain's *How Stuff Works* gives a comprehensive summary of how things work. Choose one product that you've always wondered how it works. Review the design of this product and suggest at least three ways the product could be improved. Improvement in design can be interpreted as (1) enhancement of the product functionality, (2) enhancement of the design so that it is easier to make, or (3) enhancement of the design so that the product is environmentally more effective, e.g., easier to dispose of.

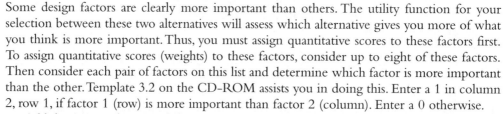

EXPERIENCE OM

Selecting a Service Concept

You have decided to open a Cajun-style restaurant in the downtown of a large Midwestern city. Two alternative opportunities (design concepts) are available. The first business plan positions the restaurant as a high-contact restaurant with all the frills including "hand-ground pepper" and a waiter describing entrées and specials. The second business plan takes the low-contact route with self-seating, a self-service salad bar, and the like. High-contact restaurant operations generally have lower efficiency, longer response time, greater customization, less automation, and greater flexibility. Your task is to discuss and evaluate the two extreme concepts (high versus low contact) and come to a conclusion about what kind of restaurant you will create.

Typical processes that need to be considered include taking reservations, seating customers, providing menus, serving water and bread, taking orders, preparing orders, making and delivering salads and entrées, providing desserts and beverages, and collecting the bill. Your first assignment is to characterize the features that might be present in a high-contact system versus a low-contact system for each of these processes. After completing this task, determine your restaurant configuration by performing the following steps, using the templates provided in the Bonus Materials folder on the CD-ROM.

Step 1 Selection of Design Variables
In selecting between the two alternatives, what kinds of factors do you want to evaluate? You may want to use the process elements from the table and add other factors to this list. For example, you may think that location is an important factor. Use Template 3.1 on the CD-ROM.

Step 2 Paired Comparison to Assign Weights to the Factors
Some design factors are clearly more important than others. The utility function for your selection between these two alternatives will assess which alternative gives you more of what you think is more important. Thus, you must assign quantitative scores to these factors first. To assign quantitative scores (weights) to these factors, consider up to eight of these factors. Then consider each pair of factors on this list and determine which factor is more important than the other. Template 3.2 on the CD-ROM assists you in doing this. Enter a 1 in column 2, row 1, if factor 1 (row) is more important than factor 2 (column). Enter a 0 otherwise.

Add the 1s in each row and the 0s in each column. Check that the total number of 1s and 0s is equal to SUM $= N(N - 1)/2$. Thus, for eight factors, this should be 28. Next, calculate the weight of each factor by taking the ratio of the sum of 0s and 1s for that factor to SUM. Thus, if factor 5 has three 1s across (total 1s $= 3$) and two 0s down (total 0s $= 2$), its weight is $(3 + 2)/28 = 0.18$. Finally, discuss your results and summarize them.

Step 3 Establish Benchmarks for Evaluating Alternatives
To evaluate the two alternatives across the eight factors, you will need to set up benchmarks that provide a scale for evaluation. Assume that each factor has three benchmarks. An example is given below. A higher number (3) is associated with a more preferred scenario (in this case, you much prefer "reservation over phone and Internet, with specific table selection")—you derive greater utility from it. Use Template 3.3 on the CD-ROM to record your information.

BENCHMARKING FACTORS

ENTER DESCRIPTION/BENCHMARK FOR EACH FACTOR

Factor	1	2	3
Reservation	No reservation	Reservation over phone	Reservation over phone/Internet
		No specific tables	Allow specific table selection

Step 4 *Evaluating Alternatives*

Now assess both service design alternatives by assigning the score for each alternative on Template 3.4 on the CD-ROM. For example, if you foresee Alternative 1 (high contact) as one where you will permit reservations over the phone only but will not allow assigned seating, then enter a score of 2 below system 1 in the row for the "reservation" factor on Template 3.4.

Now multiply the weight of that factor by the score for that factor to arrive at a weighted score for all factors for both systems. Then add the weighted scores across all factors to arrive at the total score for both alternatives (system 1 and system 2).

What alternative has the higher score?

Step 5 *Robustness and Sensitivity Analysis*

Check for robustness of the solution by changing the weights somewhat and seeing if your decision changes. First, change a weight (any two) by +2% and −2%. Do your results change? Second, change a weight (any two) by +5% and −5%. Do your results change? Third, change a weight (any two) by +10% and −10%. Do your results change? Finally, change a weight (any two) by +20% and −20%. Do your results change? Is your result a robust result?

Debrief

Write a report on your process and conclusions. Some suggest that in selecting the factors, less consideration should be given to what is an "important" factor and more to what is a more "discriminatory factor." Do you agree? Note that a factor that has a very high weight in your list (is very important) can easily change your selection with a simple benchmark misclassification. Also, if both alternatives have the same score on this high-weight factor, then the total score for both alternatives derives a high proportion of its value from this factor, making the total score somewhat insensitive to errors on other factors (it is easier to tell the difference between 3 and 4 then between 100,003 and 100,004). Your report should include a specific demonstration of your conclusion.

CHAPTER

4

Process Design and Improvement

Processes are the means by which goods and services are produced and delivered to customers. Designing and improving processes is one of the most important functions of operations management. For example, the layout of equipment and facilities and the level of automation used in processes can significantly influence cost, productivity, quality, time, availability, and flexibility. Tradeoffs exist in every process design; choosing the designs that best match a firm's competitive strategy is a key challenge. Another design decision—the choice of technology—also affects a firm's ability to meet customers' requirements and performance goals. In the face of ever-increasing competition, new information technology capabilities, and new work structures, operations managers must also focus on improvement and address two fundamental questions: Why are we doing it this way? How can we do it better? Because operations managers must be able to evaluate a process's ability to meet the organization's strategic objectives, they must understand both the technical and the managerial implications of process technology.

This chapter discusses important issues of process technology, design, and improvement. Specifically, we address:
- A taxonomy of processes and the strategic importance of process decisions (*Section 4.1*).
- Process thinking (*Section 4.2*).
- The role of technology in process design (*Section 4.3*).
- High-performance work systems and the role of people in processes (*Section 4.4*).
- Measuring process time performance (*Section 4.5*).
- Understanding process variability (*Section 4.6*).
- Facility design and flexibility (*Section 4.7*).
- Basic approaches to process improvement (*Section 4.8*).

Material on the CD-ROM discusses some useful tools and techniques for process design and improvement.

5. Queuing Models
6. Assembly-Line Balancing
4. Reliability
12. Poka-Yoke (Mistake-Proofing)

4.1 THE IMPORTANCE OF PROCESSES

In Chapter 1 we introduced the notion of a *process*—a set of linked activities that performs some manufacturing or service task. Organizations may take years to perfect a process that

delivers to the customer the results they desire. An example of a process that has been optimized to deliver highly reliable service in the shortest possible time is the pit stop process used in auto racing events such as NASCAR and the Indy 500. Its importance cannot be overstated, as cars may race for several hours only to win or lose the race in a matter of seconds during a pit stop. The typical pit stop looks something like this:[1]

0 seconds:　　Someone holds a sign (sometimes called the lollipop) over the pit wall, and the driver tries to stop with the nose of the car even with the sign. As many as six crew members begin service. One of them inserts an air hose to activate on-board hydraulic jacks that lift the car off the track.

1 second:　　Air wrenches are used to remove the nuts that secure the wheels, and the driver is handed a plastic squeeze bottle of water or an electrolyte replacement beverage.

2 seconds:　　Refueling begins. Two hoses are used. One allows fuel to flow from the storage tank into the car. The other catches any spill so that it can be pumped back into the tank.

3 seconds:　　All crew members wear fire-retardant suits. Those handling refueling also wear protective helmets. Methanol fuel burns with a virtually invisible flame, and the helmets can protect a refueler who might be on fire without knowing it.

4 seconds:　　All four wheels are loosened and removed.

5 seconds:　　Wheels are removed and placed on the ground. A bouncing or rolling tire is a safety hazard.

6 seconds:　　New wheels and fresh tires are put on the bare hubs.

7 seconds:　　If needed, aerodynamic changes are made to the car by adjusting front or rear wings or by making changes to shocks or other suspension components.

8 seconds:　　Wheels are tightened onto hubs with impact wrenches that run in reverse at the flick of a switch.

9 seconds:　　Refuelers have nearly refilled the 40-gallon fuel cell. Tire changers clear radiators of debris.

10 seconds:　　Refueling is completed. Hoses are disconnected, automatically resealing the cell.

11 seconds:　　Fuel hoses are handed to crew members behind the pit wall. Tire changers pick up the old tires and take them back to the wall.

12 seconds:　　Tire changers make sure hoses connected to their impact wrenches are cleared from around the car. The team is penalized if the car runs over a hose as it leave the pits.

13 seconds:　　The two refuelers move toward the rear of the car in anticipation of pushing it out of the pits.

14 seconds:　　Tire changers stand ready to help push should the car stall. The driver tosses the beverage bottle to one of the crewmembers behind the pit wall and waits for the signal to go.

15 seconds:　　The car has been refueled and now wears four fresh tires. The driver is told to "Go! Go! Go!" and roars out of the pits.

Fifteen seconds is all it takes. Imagine the level of efficiency and service that could be attained if business processes were addressed with the same level of attention!

Any organization has two basic kinds of processes:

1. *Value-creation processes,* which are the key design and production/delivery processes for goods and services.
2. *Support processes,* which support an organization's value-creation processes

Value-Creation Processes

Value-creation processes represent the value-added activities that directly contribute to the creation of a product or a service. In manufacturing, for example, they might include casting, stamping, machining, heat-treating, and assembly. In a service organization, these might be dispensing prescriptions and performing operations in a hospital, or providing loans or cashing checks in a bank. In either case, the ultimate goal is to meet customer needs. For example, AT&T Universal Card Services (UCS), which was subsequently acquired by Citigroup, identified key customer expectations for four important processes:

> **OM PRINCIPLE**
>
> The requirements of value-creation processes generally stem from external customer needs. This requires effective approaches for listening and learning from customers.

1. Applying for an account: *accessible, responsive, do it right, and professional.*
2. Using the card: *easy to use and hassle-free, features, credit limit.*
3. Billing: *accurate, timely, easy to understand.*
4. Customer service: *accessible, responsive, do it right, and professional.*

These expectations formed the basis for processes that UCS developed to serve its customers.

Support Processes

Support processes are necessary to enable the successful performance of value-creation processes and for conducting business. These include finance and accounting, facilities management, service recovery, legal, and human resource administration. Other support processes, such as product innovation and supply chain management, are more global in nature and focus on managing key activities in the enterprise. For example, Bose Corporation, maker of high-end audio components, recognized the need to look at its business as a strategy-driven, cross-functional effort, and identified four key support processes: time-to-market process (product concept to manufacture), integrated supply chain process (material and resource planning to production to order filling), market-to-collection process (market planning to collections), and the customer service process.[2]

> **OM PRINCIPLE**
>
> Support process requirements stem from internal customer needs. Failure to meet the support needs of customer-contact employees can have a detrimental effect on external customers.

Support processes are information-intensive and typically use information technology extensively. In a pizza delivery business, for example, a touch-sensitive computer screen can be linked to a computer in the kitchen to speed order entry and improve accuracy. When a customer places an order, the order-taker can easily enter the specific combination of toppings quickly on the screen to print the order for pizza preparation, eliminating errors due to misreading of handwritten orders.

4.2 PROCESS THINKING

Nearly every major activity within an organization involves a process that crosses traditional organizational boundaries. Figure 4.1 illustrates how processes typically cut across traditional functions in organizations. For example, an order fulfillment process might involve a salesperson placing the order; a marketing representative entering it on the company's computer system; a credit check by finance; picking, packaging, and shipping by operations personnel; invoicing by finance; and installation by field service engineers. A process perspective links all necessary activities together, rather than focusing on only a small part. Many of the greatest opportunities for improving organizational performance lie at the organizational interfaces—the spaces between the boxes on an organization chart. In a complete overhaul of its factory, Rolls-Royce created 16 zones of 60 to 100 workers each and then subdivided each of those zones into 10 smaller zones. Employees work in customer-supplier relationships with those in neighboring zones. As a result, cars spend only 32 days in the factory instead of 76, and the company lowered its break-even point from 2,700 cars annually to 1,300.

OM PRINCIPLE

Process thinking is vital to both service and manufacturing operations in that it does the following:

○ Provides a means to better understand how individual and group efforts affect other individuals and groups.

○ Allows the discovery of barriers that inhibit cooperation and performance between work groups.

○ Provides a means of analyzing and improving processes.

Process thinking is a structured approach that views a firm and its various activities and functions as a system of interrelated processes that managers must design, control, and continuously improve (see the *OM Practice* box on Gold Star Chili).

Interfaces that cross departmental boundaries—as most business operations do—create a challenge for process thinking. For example, forecasting customer demand, which is normally performed by marketing, is an important subprocess for operations planning and scheduling as well. Ineffective forecasts create ineffective schedules as

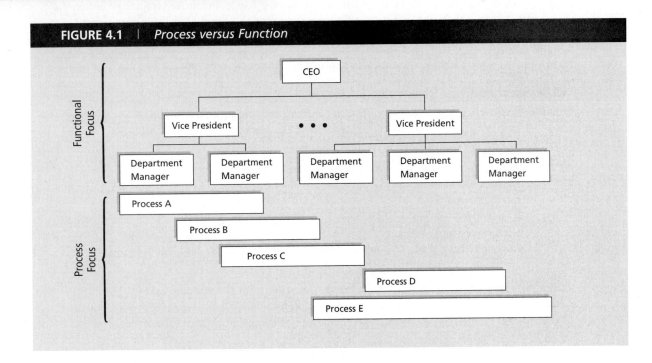

FIGURE 4.1 | *Process versus Function*

OM PRACTICE

Gold Star Chili

Gold Star Chili views processes as critical to its business success.

Figure 4.2 shows a process-based organization of Gold Star Chili, a chain of chili restaurants in the greater Cincinnati area. Three primary processes link the company's operations to its customers and other stakeholders: franchising, restaurant operations, and manufacturing/distribution. Sustaining these primary processes are various support processes, such as research and development, human resources, accounting, purchasing, operations, training, marketing, and customer satisfaction, as well as business processes for new products, menus, and facilities. The franchising process is designed to ensure a smooth and successful startup that meets company objectives. The process has been refined over time and includes extensive interaction with prospective and approved franchisees.

Restaurant processes include Cash Register, Steam Table, Drive-through, Tables, Bussers, and Management. These processes are designed to ensure that the principal requirements of all customers, such as being served in a timely manner and receiving their order accurately, are met. Chili production is performed at the Gold Star Commissary. A nine-member team, cross-trained to perform each process, is responsible for adding beef, spices, tomatoes, and water during production. The chili must pass a series of strict tests before being shipped to restaurants. Various pieces of equipment are used to maintain control during production. For example, a Bostwick Viscosity Meter measures the consistency of the chili, determining whether it is too thick or thin, and a flow meter adds the proper amount of water. Other equipment analyzes the fat content of the ground beef used in the chili. The final test, taste, is performed by members of the commissary to ensure that each batch meets established standards.

firms juggle operational priorities to meet ever-changing needs. Operations generally pays the penalty for ineffective forecasting in the form of excess inventories or poor capacity utilization; the originator of the forecast is seldom held accountable. Mazak Corporation, however, takes a unique approach. Once a product is made, it is transferred physically to the Sales and Service division, which also makes the forecasts that drive the production schedules. Since the responsibility for inventory lies with this division, it has an incentive to forecast better.

Effective information systems help to support process thinking. Thus, sales representatives who know what is currently being built in the factory or is in stock can make informed sales calls. Similarly, the sales reps can more easily check the feasibility of a customer requested-delivery date if they know the plant schedules.

Understanding Processes

Motorola has suggested a simple approach to understanding processes that requires six steps:

1. *Identify the Product or Service:* What work do I do?
2. *Identify the Customer:* Who is the work for?
3. *Identify the Supplier:* What do I need and from whom do I get it?
4. *Identify the Process:* What steps or tasks are performed? What are the inputs and outputs for each step?
5. *Mistake-Proof the Process:* How can I eliminate or simplify tasks and prevent mistakes from occurring?
6. *Develop Measurements, Controls, and Improvement Goals:* How do I evaluate the process? How can I improve it?

The first three steps focus on identifying the boundaries of the process. Steps 4 and 5 map the process flow and seek to refine it. The final step includes defining appropriate performance measures, such as cost, quality, service levels, or time, and provides the basis for evalua-

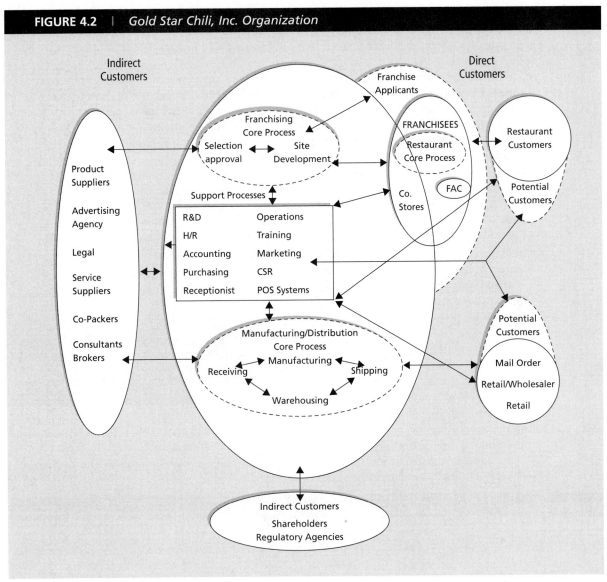

FIGURE 4.2 | *Gold Star Chili, Inc. Organization*

Source: Gold Star Chili, Inc.

tion and improvement. This approach can be applied to everything from an individual's job to broader processes that cut across the organization.

A process begins with a trigger that causes a specific action to be taken by an individual or work group and ends when the output or result is passed on to someone else. Both the trigger and the output can be physical, such as raw materials or semifinished parts, or intangible, such as an order. Every individual or work group has two roles:

1. The role of *customer* where they receive a trigger from a supplier (either external or internal).
2. The role of *supplier* where they pass the result on to a customer (either external or internal).

The actual process defines what happens between the start and end points; often this is referred to as the **process definition.** For example, a simple sales process might include the steps: introduce services, identify customer needs, suggest solutions, articulate benefits, negotiate a proposal, and close the sale.

Processes are often easier to understand when they are depicted with a flowchart. A **process flow diagram,** or **process map,** depicts the specific sequence of operations, transportations, inspections, storages, and delays that are the basic elements of any production process. Figure 4.3 shows the common symbols used in building a process map, and Figure 4.4 shows a process map for a pizza manufacturing and delivery operation. Many software packages are available for building such flowcharts and simulating process flows. Tasks (or operations) refer to the actual work being performed, transportations show flow or movement of products or customers, inspections are points where measurements are taken (usually for quality control purposes), storages show points where resources are held for future use, and delays are points where entities must wait (often unavoidably). At a minimum, a process flow diagram must show the tasks, flows, and storages or delays. **Parallel tasks** can be performed simultaneously, while **sequential tasks** must be performed in sequence. For example in Figure 4.4, preparation of the sauce, toppings, and dough are parallel tasks. The pizza is then assembled, baked in an oven, and packaged in a sequential flow. Arrows describe the sequence of tasks.

A process flow diagram may raise a number of questions. For example, Can some operations be eliminated or combined? Can transport operations be simplified or eliminated? Why do delays occur? In this way, the diagram may lead to changes in work methods, equipment, or even layout that can significantly reduce costs and

> **OM PRINCIPLE**
>
> Describing a process using a process flow diagram helps to determine if tasks occur in the proper sequence, if flows are routed properly, and if storage is necessary.

improve productivity. To ensure that tasks are done correctly and accurately, many companies use **standard operating procedures (SOPs).** An SOP documents how each step of a process should be carried out. Operator training and managerial intervention ensure that these documented procedures are followed.

FIGURE 4.3 | *Common Process Flowchart Symbols*

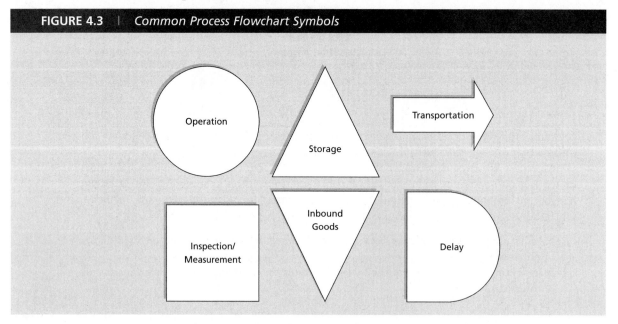

FIGURE 4.4 | *A Process Flow Diagram for Pizza Production*

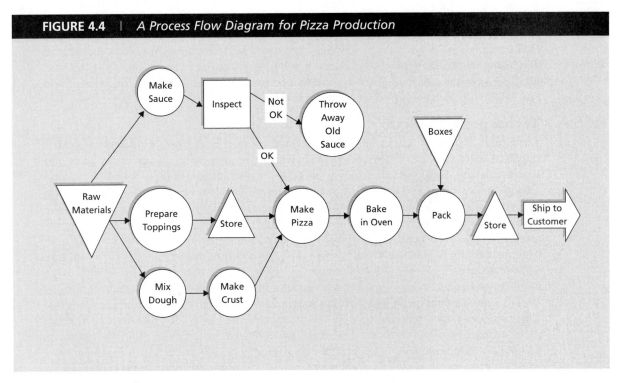

4.3 PROCESS TECHNOLOGY

Process technology consists of the methods and equipment used to manufacture a product or deliver a service. **Hard technology** involves the application of computers, sensors, robots, and other mechanical and electronic aids. Common applications of hard technology include robotic welding and painting, automated sorting and assembly, scanners and bar-code technology, and imaging. **Soft technology** refers to the computer software and other techniques that support manufacturing and service organizations. Examples include office-automation software, database management systems, electronic data interchange (EDI), computer-aided design/computer-aided engineering (CAD/CAE), manufacturing resource-management software, and, of course, the Internet.

> **OM PRINCIPLE**
>
> Process technology is an essential component of an organization's operations strategy. The ability of operations managers to use process technology effectively greatly influences a firm's ability to create and deliver customer value.

The effective combination of hard and soft technology leads to highly flexible production systems. For example, many companies have replaced paper instructions on the shop floor with computers that enable production workers to retrieve assembly instructions, current drawings, and other information whenever necessary. **Computer-assisted manufacturing (CAM)** was developed by combining information from databases with physical process control. A **flexible manufacturing system (FMS)** performs multiple functions under computer control. Such systems consist of numerical-control (N/C) machines linked by automated material-handing devices or robots. The union of CAD/CAE and CAM with FMS is known as **computer-integrated manufacturing (CIM).** Today, **enterprise resource planning (ERP) systems**, which are accounting-oriented information systems for identifying and planning the resources needed to take, make, ship, and account for customer orders, are widespread.

The Internet is clearly changing the way many organizations design their key business processes, as it improves communication between all links in the value chain. For example, Dell has linked its customers and suppliers through a digital network, and Cisco has shifted purchasing, sales, customer service, and other business processes online. Oracle found that handling a typical service call over the Internet cost under $20 (versus $350 for an in-person call) while improving accuracy, speed, and convenience.

Technology Choices

Technology choices are key strategic decisions, as they affect both internal efficiencies and the ability to meet customers' needs. With a strategy of limiting the number of products and processes, a firm might use technology to increase its productivity (through specialization and learning) and achieve a competitive advantage through low cost. For example, in the banking industry, having a teller take a deposit or cash a check costs $1.07 on average; performing the same transactions at an ATM costs only $0.27, while providing enhanced customer convenience. Nonetheless, a technology-driven strategy may not be sufficient in today's world; some banking customers prefer a friendly smile and conversation. Many manufacturers require "mass-customization" processes to be able to produce high volumes of increasingly large numbers of products. Sony, for instance, obtains information from actual sales of various Walkman models and then quickly adjusts its product mix to conform to those sales patterns. That approach requires the ability to quickly change product lines and processes, as consumer needs change. The Internet has provided increased flexibility in service industries—witness the growth of Amazon.com as a distributor of printed materials. An easy-to-navigate browser interface generates flexibility in selection; thereafter an automated warehousing and delivery system delivers exactly what you need efficiently.

Process technology can be thought of in terms of primary, secondary, and tertiary factors, defined broadly as follows:

> **OM PRINCIPLE**
>
> A simple way of understanding process technology is to think in terms of its primary (economic), secondary (technology requirements), and tertiary (non-economic) factors.

- ○ **Primary Factors:** What the technology costs. For example, economic factors in many technology decisions include rate of return on investment, budget limitations, purchase price, installation cost, operating expenses, training costs, labor savings, tax implications, and miscellaneous costs (such as computer software for programmable equipment).

- ○ **Secondary Factors:** What the technology requires. For example, appropriate cutting speeds depend on the type of material being cut and the cutting tool itself. Typical cutting speeds may be 600 meters per minute for aluminum and 50 meters per minute for titanium alloys; in some cases, speeds may even reach 9,000 meters per minute. One needs to know the effects of such speeds on the structural properties of the materials being cut, such as stress properties of aircraft wings, as well as the impact on tool life. Higher cutting speeds can cause cutting tools to wear out more frequently, and production must then be interrupted to replace them.

- ○ **Tertiary Factors:** Noneconomic factors such as installation time, availability of training, productivity improvements, vendor service, and adaptability and flexibility of the equipment.

A well-known example of these factors, attributed to Wickham Skinner of the Harvard Business School and summarized in Table 4.1, involves what one looks for in a lawnmower.

It has often been argued that managerial thinking about process technology is remiss in that most managers think only in terms of the primary effect of technology and not its sec-

TABLE 4.1	*Primary, Secondary, and Tertiary Factors in Purchasing a Lawnmower*

Factor	Type	Considerations
Cost to purchase	Primary	Initial investment
Cost to operate	Primary	Operating and maintenance requirements
Durability	Primary	Life of mower and life cycle costs
Engine type	Secondary	Two-cycle engine requires mixing oil with gasoline
Freewheeling device	Secondary	Easier to use if lawn has many turns and edges
Adjustable height	Secondary	Needed for different seasons of the year
Power	Secondary	Thickness of grass varies in sun and shade
Width of cut	Secondary	Wider cut needed for large yards
Brand	Tertiary	Easy starting and reliability
Adjustable width	Tertiary	Allows narrow cuts around landscaping and wide cuts for open lawns
Folding handles	Tertiary	Facilitates storage and transportation
Winter storage service with dealer	Tertiary	Provides more space in garage or shed

ondary or tertiary factors.[3] Viewing all factors makes process technology a source of competitive advantage.

OM PRINCIPLE

Defining the secondary and tertiary factors of new technology is much more difficult than establishing the primary factors because it requires the ability to project the operational consequences *after* the technology is acquired.

Technology decisions typically involve large sums of money, are difficult to reverse, and have a long-term effect on a firm's competitiveness. Thus, conventional thinking generally focuses only on acquisition, not on implementation. A process perspective requires one to think about both. An aversion to technology can hinder the performance of operations managers. Many managers feel inadequate and are reluctant to ask questions about technology or assume that understanding it takes a lot of time. As a result, they either make poor technology decisions or leave the decisions to scientists and engineers who lack the strategic, long-term vision to make wise choices. Skinner says managers don't have to master complex technologies, but they do need to visualize the process in which the technology will be embedded. Pictures, diagrams, and analogies can help a manager visualize a process. The manager should be able to understand why the process is necessary, what changes take place as a result of the process, what actions are performed by the equipment and what role an operator plays, what must be done *before* the process begins, what must be done *after* the process ends, what can go wrong, and what usually does go wrong.

4.4 WORK SYSTEM ISSUES IN PROCESS DESIGN

Though technology is certainly critical in work processes, much work is still done by people. Thus, a significant amount of attention must be paid to the design of work systems and jobs. **Work design** refers to how employees are organized in formal and informal units, such as departments and teams. **Job design** refers to responsibilities and tasks assigned to individuals. Both work and job design are vital to organizational effectiveness and personal job satisfaction.

The design of **high-performance work systems** should be addressed at three levels. At the individual level, work systems should enable effective accomplishment of work activities and promote flexibility and individual initiative in managing and improving work processes. This requires extensive employee involvement, empowerment, and training and education. At the process level, cooperation, teamwork, and communication are key ingredients. Finally, at the organizational level, the firm must address compensation, recognition, and factors of health, safety, and support services.

> **OM PRINCIPLE**
>
> High-performance work systems are characterized by flexibility, innovation, knowledge and skill sharing, alignment with organizational directions, customer focus, and rapid response to changing business needs and marketplace requirements.

Three approaches to work design—job enlargement, job rotation, and job enrichment—focus on motivation and job satisfaction. IBM was apparently the first to use **job enlargement,** in which jobs are expanded to include several tasks rather than a single, low-level task. This approach makes jobs less fragmented and generally results in greater worker satisfaction and higher quality. With **job rotation,** individual workers learn several tasks by rotating from one to another. The idea is to increase workers' interest and motivation and add to their complement of skills. Finally, **job enrichment** entails giving workers more authority, responsibility, and autonomy rather than simply more or different work to do. Job enrichment has been used successfully in a number of firms, including AT&T—which experienced better employee attitudes and performance—Texas Instruments, IBM, and General Foods.

Many work systems are designed around teams. A **team** is a small number of people with complementary skills who are committed to a common purpose, set of performance goals, and an approach for which they hold themselves mutually accountable.[4] Teams provide opportunities for individuals to solve problems that they may not be able to solve on their own. Teams may perform a variety of problem-solving activities, such as determining customer needs, developing a flowchart to study a process, brainstorming to discover opportunities for improvement, selecting projects, recommending corrective actions, and tracking the effectiveness of solutions. Teams may also assume many traditional managerial functions. For example, a self-managed assembly team at General Motors' Saturn plant interviews and hires its own workers, approves parts from suppliers, chooses its equipment, and handles its own budget.

Ergonomics and Safety

Ergonomics—the study of the human interface with products and the work environment—developed as a discipline during World War II, when analysts concluded that many pilots died because they had not mastered the complicated controls of their airplanes. Ergonomics is evident in a variety of consumer products today. Many computer keyboards are designed to reduce carpal tunnel injuries. The windshield-level brake light required in cars since 1986 resulted from ergonomic analysis that indicated such lights could reduce rear-end collisions by 50 percent.

> **OM PRINCIPLE**
>
> Process design must include attention to key human issues, particularly ergonomics and safety.

A primary occupational hazard in industry today is musculoskeletal injury involving constriction of nerves, tendons, and ligaments and inflammation of joints, particularly in the lower back, wrists, and elbows. It typically is caused by mismatching human physical abilities

OM PRACTICE

AT&T Credit Corporation
Teams streamline operations and improve productivity and service.

In most financial companies, the back-office jobs of processing applications, claims, and customer accounts are as dull and repetitive as assembly-line jobs. The division of labor into small tasks and the organization of work by function are characteristic of many service organizations. At AT&T Credit Corporation, which was established in 1985 to provide financing for customers who lease equipment, one department handled applications and checked the customer's credit standing, a second drew up contracts, and a third collected payments. No one person had responsibility for providing full service to a customer. Recognizing these drawbacks, the company president decided to hire his own employees and give them ownership of the process and accountability for it. Although his first concern was to increase efficiency, his approach had the additional benefit of providing more rewarding jobs.

In 1986 the company set up 11 teams of 10 to 15 newly hired workers in a high-volume division serving small businesses. The three major lease-processing functions were combined in each team. The company also divided its national staff of field agents into seven regions and assigned two or three teams to handle business from each region. The same teams always worked with the same sales staff and were able to establish personal relationships with the agents and their customers. Above all, team members took responsibility for solving customers' problems. Their slogan became, "Whoever gets the call owns the problem." Today, members make most decisions on how to deal with customers, schedule their own time off, reassign work when people are absent, and interview prospective new employees. The teams process up to 800 lease applications daily—twice as many as under the old system—have reduced the time for final credit approval from several days to 24 to 48 hours.[5]

and task-performance requirements. Jobs that require heavy lifting, repetition, or the use of improperly designed tools are common culprits. Workers' injuries can result in high health insurance costs and liability premiums for their employers.

Ergonomic studies and proper design of the workplace can reduce or eliminate on-the-job injuries. For example, if workpieces or operators have varying heights, an adjustable workbench or floor platform can be used. At Ford Motor Company, a worker who assembled a steering column from outside the vehicle had to bend over sideways, a position that resulted in a lot of pain and lost workdays. When an eight-inch pit was created, the worker could stand in it and do the job at a very slight angle without trauma.

To ensure safe and healthful working conditions and reduce hazards in the work environment, Congress passed the Occupational Safety and Health Act (OSHA) in 1970. It requires employers to maintain a workplace free from recognized hazards that are likely to cause death or serious physical harm. Firms that fail to do so face potential fines and penalties.

To ensure safe conditions, equipment should be designed so that moving parts are guarded or out of reach. At the same time, workers must be educated in the proper use of

OM PRINCIPLE

Safety is a function of the job, the human operator, and the surrounding environment. The job design should make it unlikely that workers will injure themselves.

equipment and the methods designed for performing the job. Finally, the surrounding environment must be conducive to safety. This might include nonslip surfaces, warning signs, or buzzers. Three key safety issues are lighting, temperature, and noise. For example, difficult inspection tasks and close assembly work require more light than operating a milling machine or loading crates in a warehouse. A temperature in the low 60s might be ideal for lifting boxes in overalls and gloves but may chill a typist's fingers. Intense noise over long periods of time can result in impaired hearing.

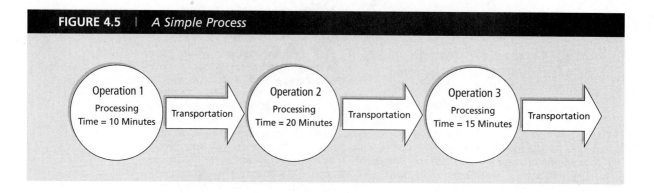

FIGURE 4.5 | *A Simple Process*

4.5 MEASURING PROCESS TIME PERFORMANCE

Two key metrics for evaluating process performance are *flow time* and *cycle time*. **Flow time** (also called **throughput time**) is the time it takes to complete a job—either a unit or batch of units—after release to production. This includes not only the actual processing time, but transportation from one machine to another, time spent waiting for parts or other units to be completed, and delays such as machine downtime. Thus, flow time depends on how the process is managed.

For example, consider the process depicted in Figure 4.5, which also shows the processing times for the individual operations. The total processing time for all three operations is 45 minutes; this represents the minimum possible flow time. Assume that jobs arrive every 10 minutes so that operation 1 may begin immediately upon their arrival and that no transportation time is required between operations. We would have the following production schedule:

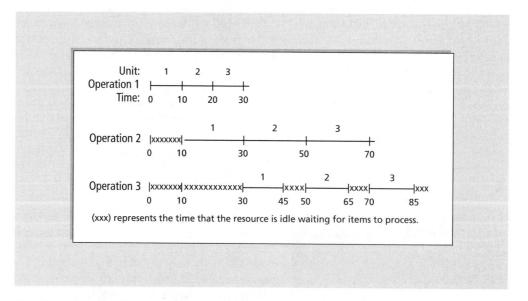

The flow time for the first unit is 45, because it proceeds through each operation without delay. The flow time for the second unit (which begins at time 10 and ends at time 65) is 65 − 10 = 55 minutes, however, and the flow time for the third unit is 85 − 20 = 65 minutes. Thus, if a new order arrives every 10 minutes, the flow time will grow without bound.

Cycle time is the average time between completions of successive units.[6] In this example, a unit is completed every 20 minutes (that is, at times 45, 65, 85, and so on); thus, the cycle time of the process is 20 minutes/unit. The **throughput** of the system—a measure of the system's actual capacity to deliver output expressed as a rate of units per time—is computed as 1/cycle time. Thus,

$$\text{Throughput} = 1/(20 \text{ minutes/unit}) \text{ or } 3 \text{ units/hour}$$

The relationship between throughput, work in process, and cycle time is reflected in a relationship known as **Little's law**, which states that

$$\text{Average throughput} = \text{work in process/cycle time}$$

For example, if 30 units await processing, and each unit takes 20 minutes, the average throughput is 30 units/(20 minutes) or 1.5 units/minute. This law explains why so many firms have attacked cycle time in recent years: a reduction in cycle time increases throughput. It is easy to count work in process every morning as well as process output each day to measure throughput. Little's law can then predict the impact that cycle time reductions will have.

Little's law can predict performance for a specific work operation, a production process, or even an entire factory. By writing it as

$$\text{Work in process} = (\text{Average throughput})(\text{Cycle time})$$

Little's law can be used to predict queue lengths at work stations.

Little's law is useful beyond the manufacturing floor. For example, a finance manager can use it to assess cash flow cycle times by using the analogy of sales = throughput, and accounts receivable = work in process.

In Figure 4.5, the three operations have the capacities of producing 6 units/hour, 3 units/hour, and 4 units/hour, respectively. The second operation, having the smallest capacity, is the **bottleneck** of the process—the operation that limits the capacity of the process and essentially defines the cycle time and throughput. In Figure 4.5, we see that one unit can be produced every 20 minutes (with the first unit completed at time 45); thus, the cycle time is 20 min/unit. Identifying the bottleneck in the simple process in Figure 4.5 is easy, but as the process configuration becomes more complex, identifying the bottleneck becomes more difficult.

Bottlenecks can be expensive when one considers the cost of idle equipment. In the construction industry, for example, having heavy earthmoving equipment sit idle for lack of a maintenance part not only incurs a high cost of capital but may also result in penalties for not meeting deadlines. Cycle times can be reduced by adding capacity to bottleneck processes. In Figure 4.5, for instance, reducing the time of the second operation from 20 minutes to 15 minutes will reduce the cycle time of the process to 15 minutes and increase the capacity of the system from 3 units/hour to 4 units/hour. In a practical sense, this would entail moving 5 minutes of work from operation 2 to operation 1. For example, some order-taking tasks at a drive-through, such as telling the customer the total amount of the bill, may be done either at the order window or at the payment/pickup window. In many cases, however, shifting tasks may not be practical or possible because of constraints in technology or work requirements.

If every step in a process has the same cycle time, then the process is said to be perfectly balanced. If a system is not perfectly balanced, then idle time will exist at the nonbottleneck operations. **Balancing** is the process of allocating work in sequential operations equally (or at least as close as possible). Henry Ford's assembly lines

OM PRINCIPLE

By removing bottlenecks and balancing production lines, lower manufacturing lead-times and cycle times can be achieved, thereby improving efficiency, productivity, and cost.

were efficient because they were balanced. We address the topic of balancing assembly lines in the supplementary material on the CD-ROM.

Now let us consider a more complex process configuration. Figure 4.6 shows a pizza-making operation with two pizza-making assembly lines and one packaging line. We might start a new pizza on both pizza-making lines every 30 minutes. Both would be completed in 20 minutes; one pizza would move immediately to packaging, for a flow time of 35 minutes; the other would have to wait 15 minutes while the first pizza is packaged and then would take 15 minutes for packaging, for a total flow time of 50 minutes. This cycle would be repeated continually (draw a timeline to convince yourself). Thus, the average flow time would be 42.5 minutes. Alternatively, if we start a new pizza every 20 minutes, *alternating* between the two pizza-making lines, each pizza will be able to proceed directly to packaging, resulting in a shorter average flow time of 35 minutes, but with less throughput (3 versus 4 per hour).

To reduce flow time, firms such as Dell, Inc. often maintain inventories of semifinished components. Many firms create modular product designs so that, in a Lego-like fashion, the end product can be customized to customer specifications in a very short time. Other firms store finished units and reconfigure them at a marginal cost, which is often lower than the cost of modifying production schedules to match customer demand. In the machine tool industry, firms often find that the marginal cost of selling the product with more than the customer wants is less than the cost of reconfiguring the system or of modifying production schedules to meet the variations in customer requirements.

FIGURE 4.6 | *A Pizza Production Process*

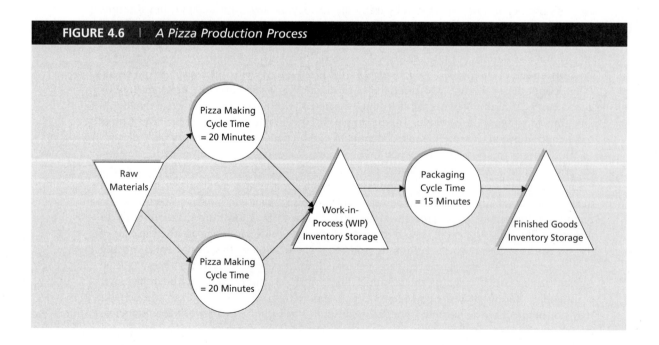

In a manufacturing firm, flow time is directly related to the amount of working capital, and decreasing it often releases unproductive capital for other investment opportunities. In a service organization, the analogy to flow time is often called **contact time;** it is divided into two parts:

1. *Active contact time,* which is the time a customer is involved in value-adding activities.
2. *Passive contact time,* which is the time the customer is waiting for services to be performed.

Service quality often is perceived as directly proportional to active contact time. Thus, minimizing passive contact time improves the perception of quality. For example, self-serve facilities provide higher active contact time as tasks associated with organizing peripherals into customer bundles are eliminated; customers do the bundling themselves (see the *OM Practice* box for an example in the airline industry).

OM PRACTICE

Improving Airline Service
Technology improves flow time at airports.

At airports nationwide, fliers are spending more time in lines than ever before. Overall, average time spent at U.S. airports has increased to almost 70 minutes. Some travel analysts blame the airlines for not adding enough staff at the counters and gates. Passenger loads at Southwest Airlines, for example, have risen 26 percent since 1997, but the passenger-handling staff has increased by only 17 percent. Security screening measures added since the terrorist attacks of September 11, 2001, have made the problem even worse.

Most airlines acknowledge the longer lines, and some have taken steps to reduce them. Northwest has begun rolling out "portable agent worksta-

tions," which are wireless devices that allow agents to roam the terminal and check in passengers (and their bags) at points other than the ticket counter or gate. Delta Air Lines is spending $500 million on technology upgrades and now offers curbside check-in services at nearly 90 percent of its U.S. destinations. Several carriers, including Northwest, Continental, Southwest, and Alaska Airlines, are installing self-service kiosks that offer the entire range of ticketing and check-in services. But even with such technological advances, most analysts think the lines could get even longer—if only because passenger numbers are expected to increase 3 to 4 percent a year during the next decade. Dean Headley, a Wichita State University professor who publishes an annual airline-quality rating, says that in the future, "every day is going to look a little bit more like the Wednesday before Thanksgiving."[7]

4.6 PROCESS VARIABILITY

Typically, processes are designed based on average processing rates, but this ignores the effects of variability. Consider the process shown in Figure 4.7. Assume that the processing time for operation X is constant while that of operation Y is variable, but has the same average as operation X, 10 minutes.

FIGURE 4.7 | *A Two-Step Process*

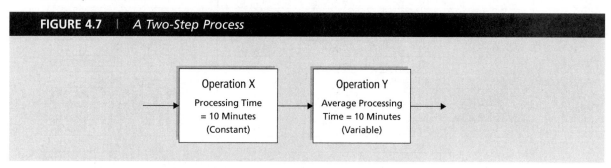

It is easy to see that if operation Y has no variability, each unit will be completed exactly 20 minutes after the previous one, resulting in an average flow time[8] of 20 minutes and an average cycle time of 10 minutes, as shown below:

Start Time at X	Processing Time for X	Completion Time at X	Processing Time for Y	Completion Time at Y	Flow Time	Cycle Time
0	10	10	10	20	20	
10	10	20	10	30	20	10
20	10	30	10	40	20	10
30	10	40	10	50	20	10
40	10	50	10	60	20	10
50	10	60	10	70	20	10
60	10	70	10	80	20	10
70	10	80	10	90	20	10
80	10	90	10	100	20	10
90	10	100	10	110	20	10
100	10	110	10	120	20	10
				Average:	20.00	10.00

Now, suppose that the processing time for operation Y is either 9, 10, or 11 minutes, each with a probability of 1/3. The simulation results below show that both the flow time and the cycle time increase (partially due to a positive bias in processing time):

Start Time at X	Processing Time for X	Completion Time at X	Processing Time for Y	Completion Time at Y	Flow Time	Cycle Time
0	10	10	10	20	20	
10	10	20	11	31	21	11
20	10	30	9	40	20	9
30	10	40	10	50	20	10
40	10	50	11	61	21	11
50	10	60	10	71	21	10
60	10	70	10	81	21	10
70	10	80	10	91	21	10
80	10	90	11	102	22	11
90	10	100	9	111	21	9
100	10	110	11	122	22	11
110	10	120	11	133	23	11
120	10	130	10	143	23	10
130	10	140	11	154	24	11
140	10	150	10	164	24	10
150	10	160	11	175	25	11
160	10	170	11	186	26	11
170	10	180	9	195	25	9
180	10	190	9	204	24	9
190	10	200	9	213	23	9
200	10	210	10	223	23	10
210	10	220	10	233	23	10
220	10	230	10	243	23	10
				Average:	22.43	10.14

Further, if the processing time for operation Y exhibits more variability, say, 8, 10, or 12 minutes, again equally distributed, the average flow time and cycle time increase more, as the following simulation shows:

Start Time at X	Processing Time for X	Completion Time at X	Processing Time for Y	Completion Time at Y	Flow Time	Cycle Time
0	10	10	12	22	22	
10	10	20	8	30	20	8
20	10	30	10	40	20	10
30	10	40	12	52	22	12
40	10	50	10	62	22	10
50	10	60	10	72	22	10
60	10	70	8	80	20	8
70	10	80	10	90	20	10
80	10	90	10	100	20	10
90	10	100	8	108	18	8
100	10	110	10	120	20	12
110	10	120	12	132	22	12
120	10	130	12	144	24	12
130	10	140	12	156	26	12
140	10	150	12	168	28	12
150	10	160	8	176	26	8
160	10	170	12	188	28	12
170	10	180	10	198	28	10
180	10	190	12	210	30	12
190	10	200	8	218	28	8
200	10	210	10	228	28	10
210	10	220	12	240	30	12
220	10	230	12	252	32	12
				Average:	24.17	10.45

OM PRINCIPLE

Increased variability decreases the effective capacity of a system. In designing processes and configuring production systems, operations managers need to account for variability and should not base decisions only on average processing rates.

Now, suppose that operation X has variable processing times while the times for operation Y are constant. In general, we will find that both the average flow time and the average cycle time for the system increase, as the following simulation shows:

Start Time at X	Processing Time for X	Completion Time at X	Processing Time for Y	Completion Time at Y	Flow Time	Cycle Time
0	8	8	10	18	18	
10	8	18	10	28	18	10
20	12	32	10	42	22	14
30	10	42	10	52	22	10
40	12	54	10	64	24	12
50	12	66	10	76	26	12
60	12	78	10	88	28	12

(continues)

Start Time at X	Processing Time for X	Completion Time at X	Processing Time for Y	Completion Time at Y	Flow Time	Cycle Time
70	10	88	10	98	28	10
80	12	100	10	110	30	12
90	8	108	10	120	30	10
100	8	116	10	130	30	10
110	8	124	10	140	30	10
120	10	134	10	150	30	10
130	10	144	10	160	30	10
140	10	154	10	170	30	10
150	12	166	10	180	30	10
160	10	176	10	190	30	10
170	10	186	10	200	30	10
180	12	198	10	210	30	10
190	12	210	10	220	30	10
200	10	220	10	230	30	10
210	8	228	10	240	30	10
220	8	236	10	250	30	10
				Average:	27.65217	10.54545

High variability early in a process is more likely to lead to poor performance than high variability later in the process. This suggests that operations managers should focus on reducing variability in the early stages of a process rather than downstream. Further, if we are to add capacity to a system (and decrease processing time) in a two-stage process when processing times of both stages are variable, we are better off adding capacity to the second stage. Variability in multistage systems tends to build up as we move down the process chain—thus, the last process faces the most variability. To cope with this higher variability, that process needs relatively more capacity than early processes. These process insights are useful in designing larger, more complicated systems and in understanding system behavior as well. Operations managers need to address the performance of process combinations when there is process variation; in addition, they need to consider process bottlenecks, which we discuss next.

OM PRINCIPLE

In connected processes with variability, increased capacity toward the end of the process results in better performance than increased capacity at the start. Unbalanced processes—processes with greater capacity toward the end of the process than at the beginning—lead to enhanced performance.

Process Design and the Theory of Constraints

As we observed earlier, bottlenecks restrict any system from performing better than what can be accomplished at the bottleneck. Although we tend to think of bottlenecks as constraining capacity, they can also constrain the quality, time, or availability objectives desired from a process. Typically, they lead to consistently late orders or constant expediting of jobs that have not met their schedules.

Using bottlenecks to identify targets for process improvement is also known as the **Theory of Constraints (TOC),** popularized by Eliyahu Goldratt in his book *The Goal.* The TOC consists of three parts:

1. A set of problem-solving tools—called the TOC Thinking Processes—which logically and systematically answer three questions essential to any process of ongoing improvement: "What to change?" "What to change to?" and "How to cause the change?"
2. A set of daily management tools that can be used to significantly improve vital management skills, such as communication, effecting change, team building, and empowerment.
3. Innovative, proven solutions created by applying the TOC Thinking Processes to specific application areas, such as production, distribution, marketing and sales, and project management.

The principal objective of the TOC is to establish a process of continuous improvement, based on the premise that constraints determine the performance of any system. A **constraint** is any resource lack that prevents the system from achieving continuously higher levels of performance. Limited capacity at work centers, inflexible work rules, inadequate labor skills, and an ineffective management philosophy are all forms of constraints.

OM PRINCIPLE

Constraints determine the throughput of the facility because they limit a plant's throughput level to their own capacity; the excess capacity of nonconstraint resources cannot be used.

The TOC assumes that material flows in small batches, called **transfer batches,** consisting of the required number of units that need to be processed before the next operation is done. Since the number of such constraints is typically small, the TOC focuses on identifying them, managing them carefully, and linking them to the market to ensure an appropriate product mix. Thereafter, the firm can schedule the nonconstraint resources to enhance the competitiveness of the production process. In addition to improving throughput, constraint management can help to reduce inventories, lower operating costs, and improve responsiveness.

The general steps in synchronizing a manufacturing process using constraint management are as follows:[9]

1. Identify the constraints—that is, the work centers where inventory accumulates.
2. Place buffers at key points in the process to protect throughput. This should be done in front of the constraint resources to keep them running, at assembly points where parts that have been processed on the constraint resource converge, and at the finished goods shipping area.
3. Determine the production schedule for the constraint resource. The schedule for a constraint resource is based on that resource's limited capacity, the market demand, and the lead-times from the constraint resource to the shipping buffer. The idea is to trade off the limited capacity between process and setup times at the constraint resource.
4. Release materials to feed the constraint resources. Backward schedule from the constraint buffer to the gateway operation.
5. Forward schedule workstations that follow a constraint resource by allowing transfer batches and process batches to vary to ensure a smooth materials flow.

Scheduling Technology Group in the United Kingdom provides TOC-based software solutions based upon an approach called Optimized Production Technology (OPT). *Supplementary Notes 4.1* on the CD-ROM summarizes nine key principles on which OPT is based.

Constraint management goes beyond the scheduling function, however. Once the constraint resources are identified, the nature of key management decisions—product costing, performance measurement, product and process design, and so on—changes. Through these changes, constraint management helps a firm to achieve the desired global or plantwide coordination of its manufacturing resources.

Binney & Smith, maker of Crayola crayons, and Procter & Gamble both use the TOC in their distribution efforts. Binney & Smith had high inventory levels yet poor customer service. By using the TOC to better position its distribution inventories, it was able to reduce inventories and improve service. Procter & Gamble reported $600 million in savings through inventory reduction and elimination of capital improvement through the TOC. The TOC applies to administrative functions, as well as manufacturing, as Stanley Furniture has shown (see the *OM Practice* box).

OM PRACTICE

Stanley Furniture
Stanley Furniture applied TOC concepts to its order-entry process.

Stanley Furniture in Stanleytown, Virginia, had implemented efficient manufacturing concepts in its assembly line, but soon discovered that order entry was a key constraint in the administrative process, which accounted for nearly half of the customer lead-time. Order entry was a batch manufacturing process using a first-come, first-served scheduling rule. Key process steps were to receive orders, enter orders into a sales-order system, obtain credit approval, notify master production scheduling (MPS), modify the MPS, modify the final assembly schedule, and consolidate orders for shipping. Waiting before each of those steps lengthened lead-times. A team analyzed this process and found that credit approval was the constraining activity. After streamlining the credit-approval process, the company was able to establish new procedures that better integrated order entry and inventory management. Having eliminated credit approval as a system constraint, the team tackled problems in the shipping function. Once this constraint was broken through several improvements, they identified the assembly line as the constraining resource. As a result, over 60 percent of orders are now shipped within 7 days of receipt, and 95 percent are shipped within 15 days of receipt, a substantial improvement from the original 45-day lead-time.[10]

4.7 PROCESS DESIGN AND FLEXIBILITY

Process design and flexibility are closely connected; in Chapter 2 we saw that dedicated, linear processes such as those found on an assembly line inhibit the flexibility of the process, while job shops, which have disconnected flows and are not very efficient, offer high levels of process flexibility. The importance of design and flexibility can be seen at Ford Motor Company. Many years ago, every major piece of equipment in Ford's most automated factory was designed to accommodate a narrow range of processing operations. The machines were so tightly wedded to the production of eight-cylinder engines that a shift to six-cylinder engines would have necessitated changes throughout the plant. When market conditions forced Ford to opt for the smaller engines, the company had to close the plant because it could not convert its specialized equipment to a different set of tasks.[11]

Another important driver of the process design decision is the customer; higher levels of customization require a make-to-order environment (high flexibility) as opposed to a make-to-stock system (low flexibility). A compromise is to

OM PRINCIPLE

The requisite level of flexibility in any process depends on the process positioning strategy as well as the product concept that the firm sees best meeting the needs of the customer.

use an assemble-to-order approach, in which a firm maintains an inventory of modular components and mixes and matches the modules to meet customer needs.

Two issues are critical in assessing process flexibility:(1) the kind of flexibility the process needs and (2) whether time or range is more critical for a flexible response.[12] When an organization faces uncertain demand for its products or services, it needs greater flexibility in its product mix. Range and time refer to the two dimensions of flexible response: a process may have to respond with a wider range of products, or it might have to respond with a mix of products very quickly. For example, Wal-Mart may require that all of its suppliers be capable of producing three different types of fishing rods sold at its stores. This challenge is quite different from the challenge that occurs when Wal-Mart makes significant changes in the volume purchased from a supplier across the three models every week. Thus, even though the supplier may have the design capability to produce all three models, it may not have the operational capability to respond to changing volumes within the lead-time of one week. Table 4.2 summarizes these dimensions for six different types of flexibility.

To better understand this, consider a firm with a high level of uncertainty in aggregate product demand. This is common for firms in the fashion goods industry—a new line of clothes may turn out to be a hot seller, or it may not attract any customers. Forecasting is difficult; forecasts are typically off by 50 to 100 percent for such products. Such a firm has two choices to create volume flexibility. First, it can acquire more than the necessary capacity (say, the capacity to make 1,000 dresses when it forecasts that only 500 might be sold). Alternatively, it can add a second shift or hire people on overtime to manufacture additional clothing. All three of these options increase the range of volume-flexible responses for the firm but also have consequences in terms of increased cost of production, quality, and the like. The ability to respond to a surge in demand quickly, however, is best achieved by acquiring increased capacity, even though this might be a very expensive option (see Table 4.3). The single most important decision that limits or enhances an organization's flexibility in responding to market and environmental uncertainties is the physical arrangement of its processes.

Facility Layout

The physical design of facilities can have a significant impact on process performance. **Facility layout** refers to the specific arrangement of physical facilities. Good facility layout

TABLE 4.2	*Characteristics of Process Flexibility*		
Flexibility Type	**Range**	**Time**	**Nature of Uncertainty**
Mix	Variety of parts	Lead-time	Demand for products offered
Changeover	Variety of major design changes	Startup time	Product life cycles
Modification	Variety of minor design changes	Time to make a minor design change	Appropriate product characteristics
Volume	Amount of change in the production level	Time to change production level	Amount of aggregate product demand
Rerouting	Degree that operations sequence can be changed	Time to reroute and process	Machine downtime
Material	Range of composition and dimensional variation	Time to make the adjustments	Meeting raw material standards

TABLE 4.3	*Characteristics of Volume Flexibility*	
Volume Flexibility Responses	**Cost**	**Time**
Acquire and operate with more than needed capacity	Very expensive since the plant has very low utilization and much idle capacity is reserved for a demand surge	Almost instantaneous response to a surge in demand
Produce more on overtime	Moderately expensive since overtime labor is paid at 150% of the normal rate; quality problems due to overwork	Can respond to a demand surge fairly quickly
Produce more by going from one shift to two shifts	Not very expensive since scale of operations fits level of demand and factory operates at high utilization levels	Very slow as additional workers have to be hired and trained, additional equipment and resources have to be bought, etc.

helps to minimize delays in materials handling, maintain flexibility, use labor and space effectively, promote high employee morale, and provide for good housekeeping and maintenance (see the *OM Practice* box on Sun Microsystems).

OM PRACTICE

Sun Microsystems
Sun Microsystems improved productivity and quality through facility design

Sun Microsystems illustrates the benefits that can be achieved through effective facility layout. Founded in 1982, Sun Microsystems produces computer workstation products. Sun's manufacturing facility evolved in stages as the company grew and more capacity was needed. As a result, there was no coordinated process design. Materials, paper, and people were everywhere, often in conflicting flow patterns. Things got done because of the effectiveness of the workers, not because there was

an effective process flow. Moreover, the product mix was constantly changing. Consequently, managers decided that a new facility was needed. They had several goals in designing the new facility:

- Provide flexibility to meet product changes.
- Improve materials handling and process flow to ensure high quality.
- Provide the ability to track and control materials through computerized systems.
- Improve employee morale by providing a pleasant work environment.

The new plant increased on-time delivery by 50 percent and dramatically improved quality, even with a higher volume of production.[13]

Three major layout patterns are commonly used in designing production processes: product layout, process layout, and group layout. **Product layouts** are used when a single product or a closely related set of products is manufactured in high volumes and the product flows in a fixed sequence from one operation or department to another. Continuous flow, mass-production, and batch-processing production processes are

OM PRINCIPLE

Because all products move in the same direction, product layouts provide a smooth and logical flow of products and/or customers and enable the use of specialized handling equipment.

usually organized by product layout. A common type of product layout is the **assembly line**—a sequence of workstations, connected together by a materials-handling system, which is used to assemble components into a final product. For example, at Harley Davidson's York, Pennsylvania plant, three-person teams build and assemble motorcycles on the Sportster line from start to finish.[14] The process is a straight-line assembly line, consisting of 15 primary stations, and a Sportster rolls off the line about every 45 to 48 minutes. As the bikes are built, they move from station to station via a moving floor conveyor. What is unique about this process is that the assemblers—three per bike—move, station by station, with each motorcycle.

A **process layout** consists of a functional grouping of machines or activities that do similar work. For example, all drill presses may be grouped together in one department and all milling machines in another. Depending on the processing they require, parts may be moved in different sequences among departments. Such layouts are common in older plants and in job shops, which use process layouts to provide flexibility in the products that can be made and the utilization of equipment and labor. Many services, such as hospitals, are designed as process layouts: different patients may visit different functions such as radiology and the pharmacy in different orders. Another example is a self-service cafeteria with different food stations (in contrast to a traditional cafeteria line that would exhibit a product layout design).

> **OM PRINCIPLE**
>
> Materials-handling cost is usually the principal design criterion for process layouts. In general, departments with a large number of moves between them should be located close to one another.

A **group,** or **cellular, layout** is designed around groups of different machines (called **cells**) needed for producing families of parts. Each cell has its own materials-handling system, typically a robot or a conveyor system. If possible, a component part is completely processed in a single machine cell. Components are then routed to assembly areas.

Table 4.4 summarizes the features of product, process, and group layouts. The basic trade-off among these layout types is flexibility versus productivity. Process layouts offer high flexibility but low productivity, while product layouts have limited flexibility but high productivity. Because a product layout clearly defines the flow of product and customers, it is easier to use dedicated equipment as well as to automate. Group layouts balance the advantages of both types.

TABLE 4.4   *Comparison of Basic Layout Patterns*

Factor	Product Layout	Group Layout	Process Layout
Volume of flow	High	Moderate	Low
Setup costs and requirements	High	Moderate	Low
Equipment utilization	High	Moderate	Low
Automation potential	High	Moderate	Low
Type of equipment	Dedicated/specialized	Some specialization	Flexible/general purpose
Amount of flexibility	Low	Moderate	High
Focus	Cost/efficiency	Time/quality	Flexibility/customization

4.8 PROCESS IMPROVEMENT

Well-designed processes have improvement routines built into them.[15] Improvement in processes is often approached from one of two perspectives:

1. Frequent improvements in all processes, no matter how small (*continuous process improvement*).
2. Large, radical changes in major business processes (*breakthrough improvement*).

Operations managers need both approaches, which are depicted in Figure 4.8. In successful companies, continuous improvement and break-through improvement feed off each other. Jack Welch, former CEO of General Electric, said it best: "The big breakthrough opens the way for countless small improvements, and the accumulation of small gains builds the organization's confidence to attempt yet another quantum leap."

OM PRINCIPLE

Continuous improvement provides the performance measurements and problem-solving data to signal when it is time to make more radical changes.

Continuous process improvement is a never-ending effort to discover and eliminate causes of problems; it is a fundamental part of a total quality philosophy and lean thinking, which we address in more detail in Chapters 6 and 9. Many opportunities for process improvement exist, including the obvious reductions in manufacturing defects, productivity, and cycle times. A good illustration is Dell, Inc. Although it had some of the highest quality ratings in the PC industry, Michael Dell became obsessed with finding ways to reduce machine failure rates. He concluded that failures were related to the number of times a hard drive was handled during assembly and insisted that the number of "touches" be reduced from the existing level of more than 30 per drive. Production lines were revamped, and the number was reduced to fewer than 15. Soon after, the reject rate of hard drives fell by 40 percent and the overall failure rate dropped by 20 percent.[16] See the *OM Practice* box on Diamond Packaging for another example.

Benchmarking and Reengineering

Breakthrough improvement refers to *discontinuous* change, as opposed to gradual, continuous improvement. Breakthrough improvements result from innovative and creative thinking and are often achieved through benchmarking and reengineering.

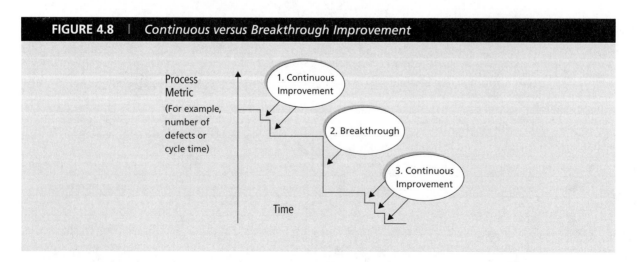

FIGURE 4.8 | *Continuous versus Breakthrough Improvement*

OM PRACTICE

Diamond Packaging
Diamond Packaging uses kaizen to reduce changeover time.

At the Diamond Packaging Plant in Rochester, New York, the semiautomatic carton line packages various types of products (film) into cartons and also shrink-wraps and collates different types of displays. This requires short production runs and frequent changeovers. A plant team had reduced changeover time from 3.0 to 1.5 hours, and a kaizen team was convened to reduce this by an additional 50 percent to help improve customer service.

The team reviewed a videotape of the changeover and identified four areas of opportunity: labor allocation and movement, material movement, equipment upgrades, and employee expectations and training. An analysis of the machine setup showed operators walking more than 500 feet back and forth during the changeover, and similar opportunities were identified on the rest of the line. The team recommended increasing the setup team from two to six to eight persons, which would theoretically result in a 13.5-minute changeover. Other recommendations included moving the line to allow better access to the back of the carton machine to reduce material movement, making inexpensive equipment upgrades to make the carton machine more "changeover friendly," and developing specific training plans for the new changeover specialist positions. By implementing these changes, the team was able to reduce changeover time to 22 minutes.[17]

Benchmarking is defined as "measuring your performance against that of best-in-class companies, determining how the best-in-class achieve those performance levels, and using the information as a basis for your own company's targets, strategies, and implementation"[18] or, more simply, "the search of industry best practices that lead to superior performance."[19] **Best practices** are approaches that produce exceptional results, are usually innovative in their use of technology or human resources, and are recognized by customers or industry experts.

The concept of benchmarking is not new.[20] In the early 1800s, Francis Lowell, a New England industrialist, traveled to England to study manufacturing techniques at the best British mills. Henry Ford created the assembly line after touring a Chicago slaughterhouse and watching carcasses, hung on hooks mounted on a monorail, move from one workstation to another. Toyota's just-in-time production system was influenced by the replenishment practices of U.S. supermarkets. Modern benchmarking was initiated by Xerox—an eventual winner of the Malcolm Baldrige National Quality Award—and has since become a common practice among leading firms. Xerox studied the warehousing and distribution practices of L. L. Bean for its spare parts distribution system. As another example, a General Mills plant in Lodi, California had an average machine changeover time of three hours. Then somebody said, "From three hours to 10 minutes!" Employees went to a NASCAR track, videotaped the pit crews, and studied the process to identify how the principles could be applied to the production changeover processes. Several months later, the average time fell to 17 minutes.[21]

OM PRINCIPLE

Benchmarking should not be restricted to one's industry, but should seek improvements and best practices from any source.

Reengineering has been defined as "the fundamental rethinking and radical redesign of business processes to achieve dramatic improvements in critical, contemporary measures of performance, such as cost, quality, service, and speed."[22] Reengineering is based on the following premises:

1. Business processes make mistakes, take time, and cost money.
2. Business processes waste time on non-value-added activities.
3. Business processes do 1 and 2 because of the way they are "engineered," or designed.

Reengineering involves asking basic questions about processes: Why do we do it? Why is it done this way? Such questioning often uncovers obsolete, erroneous, or inappropriate assumptions.

Radical redesign involves tossing out existing procedures and reinventing the process, not just incrementally improving it. The goal is to achieve quantum leaps in performance. For example, IBM Credit Corporation cut the process of financing IBM computers, software, and services from seven days to four hours by rethinking the process. Originally, the process was designed to handle difficult applications and required four highly trained specialists and a series of handoffs. The actual work took only about 1.5 hours; the rest of the time was spent in transit or delay. By questioning the assumption that every application was unique and difficult to process, the company was able to replace the specialists with a single individual supported by a user-friendly computer system that provided access to all the data and tools that the specialists used. Black & Decker Accessories—Europe (B&D) reengineered its development process, reducing its new package introduction cycle time by 60 percent. A B&D improvement team mapped major steps in its development process, compared how long each work step took to its work content, moved workers and combined tasks to eliminate unnecessary paperwork, focused resources by assigning teams to product lines, developed tighter links with internal customers and suppliers, and updated its desktop publishing equipment and other technology. Another example is given in the *OM Practice* box on American Express.

> ## OM PRINCIPLE
>
> Successful reengineering requires fundamental understanding of processes, creative thinking to break away from old traditions and assumptions, and effective use of information technology.

Reengineering can be facilitated in various ways including the following:

1. **Simplifying:** Eliminating approvals, unnecessary steps, and the like.
2. **Focusing:** Better aligning people and resources to support process thinking.
3. **Energizing and Motivating:** Eliminating artificial job classifications and work rules to develop worker pride, giving individuals and teams more authority.
4. **Refining:** Striving to eliminate sources of variability, balancing capacities and smoothing work flows.

Benchmarking can greatly assist reengineering efforts. Reengineering without benchmarking probably will produce 5 to 10 percent improvements; benchmarking can increase this percentage to 50 or 75 percent. When GTE reengineered eight core processes of its telephone operations, it examined the best practices of some 84 companies from diverse industries. By studying outside best practices, a company can identify and import new technology, skills, structures, training, and capabilities.[23]

Summary of Key Points

○ Processes—value creation and support—are vital to creating customer value. A firm's process technology affects its ability to manufacture products or deliver services that meet customer requirements and strategic objectives.

○ Process thinking involves viewing work activities across traditional organizational boundaries as a system of interrelated processes. It promotes understanding of how work actually gets done, allows improvement opportunities to be discovered, and provides a basis for analyzing and improving performance.

○ Process thinking involves customers and suppliers, inputs and outputs, process activities, and approaches for mistake-proofing and measuring performance. Process maps are useful in accomplishing this.

OM PRACTICE

American Express
Reengineering leads to service improvements at AMEX

The Travel Services' Group at American Express (AMEX) needed a change. Business had more than tripled over the past three years, the group had acquired a number of entrepreneurial companies (each with its own way of doing things), customers were demanding more global services, and the threat of terrorism and airfare wars had changed the economics of the business. Major gaps in cost, quality, and speed could no longer be bridged with continuous improvement efforts. These issues led AMEX to consider reengineering.

The group embarked on a series of improvement efforts to bring their short-term economics into line (analogous to getting a patient well enough to operate) and brought in top-level field executives to coordinate the quality and reengineering activities of their improvement teams. The oversight team (executive committee) began with a high-level process map of travel services consisting of five processes; two of these were identified for possible redesign—*service delivery* and *reinforcing customer relations*. Two reengineering teams were chartered. Both teams began by validating recent customer research findings with focus groups and individual open-ended questions. Next, they constructed their own high-level process map to prioritize the subprocesses for reengineering. Once they had formulated a high-level redesign and gained approval from the executive committee, they began to implement several short-term improvements, standardize best practices, and assess the technical systems infrastructure for a more thorough redesign.

The preliminary results showed a 7 percent improvement in customer satisfaction, dramatic improvement in on-call resolution of customer service issues, a 6 percent gain in productivity, and a 6 percent reduction in cost.[24]

- Process technology consists of both hard technology (equipment and mechanical devices) and soft technology (computers and information systems). The choice of technology depends on a variety of economic and noneconomic factors and its impact on operations performance.

- High-performance work systems are characterized by flexibility, innovation, knowledge and skill sharing, alignment with organizational directions, customer focus, and rapid response to changing business needs and marketplace requirements; these systems should be addressed at the individual, process, and organizational levels. Job satisfaction, teamwork, and ergonomics and safety issues are key components in work and job design.

- Process variability results in increased flow time and cycle time and decreases the effective capacity, or throughput, of a system; thus, it should be taken into account in designing processes. Bottlenecks and constraints also limit capacity and system performance. The Theory of Constraints provides an approach for addressing constraints and achieving better coordination of resources.

- Process flexibility depends on the physical arrangement of facilities and whether the firm uses a make-to-stock or make-to-order system. Three major layout patterns are product, process, and group. Product layouts are based on the sequence of operations performed, and products move in a continuous path. Process layouts consist of functional groupings of machines or activities that do similar work. Group layouts place machines in cells to produce families of parts. Group layouts can provide significant improvements in productivity and flexibility. These layouts differ in production volume, variety, use of automation, labor skills needed, machine setup requirements, and unit costs.

- Continuous process improvement allows firms to incrementally change the process to deliver better value to customers, while breakthrough improvement focuses on radical change. Both are needed in the long term. Reengineering and benchmarking are common breakthrough improvement approaches that have proven track records of success.

Questions for Review and Discussion

1. Define value-creation and support processes, and provide several examples of each.

2. What are the primary value-creation processes at your college or university? How do they support the products offered?

3. What is process thinking? How does it facilitate designing the "right" processes in an organization?

4. Use the Motorola approach described in this chapter to design a process for each of the following:

   a. Preparing for an exam

   b. Writing a term paper

   c. Planning a vacation

   Draw a flowchart (process map) for each process and discuss ways in which the process might be improved.

5. Legal Sea Foods operates several restaurants and fish markets in the Boston area. The company's standards of excellence mandate that it serve only the freshest, highest-quality seafood. It guarantees the quality by buying only the "top of the catch" fish daily. Although Legal Sea Foods tries to make available the widest variety every day, certain species of fish are subject to migratory patterns and are not always present in New England waters. Weather conditions may also prevent local fishermen from fishing in certain areas.

   Freshly caught fish are rushed to the company's quality control center where they are cut and filleted in an environmentally controlled state-of-the-art facility. All shellfish come from government-certified beds and are tested in an in-house microbiology laboratory for wholesomeness and purity. All lobsters are held under optimum conditions, in clean, pollution-free water in special storage tanks. Every seafood item is inspected for quality eight separate times before it reaches the table.

   At Legal Sea Foods' restaurants, each meal is cooked to order. Though servers try to deliver all meals in an order within minutes of each other, they will not jeopardize the quality of an item by holding it beneath a heat lamp until the entire order is ready. The service staff are trained to work as a team for better service. More than one service person frequently delivers food to a table. When any item is ready, the closest available person serves it. Customer questions can be directed to any employee, not just the person who took the initial order.

   a. What are the major processes performed by Legal Sea Foods?

   b. How does the process design support the company's goal of serving only the freshest, highest-quality seafood?

6. Explain the difference between hard and soft technology.

7. Consider the choice of a desktop computer, notebook computer, or personal digital assistant (e.g., Palm Pilot). List the primary, secondary, and tertiary factors that would influence this technology choice.

8. What do we mean by high-performance work systems, work design, and job design?

9. Why are teams an important element of many process designs? Provide some examples of how teams support a high-performance environment.

10. Why are ergonomics and safety important issues in designing work processes?

11. What impact does variability have on process performance? How can a manager reduce variability in processes?

12. Briefly explain the Theory of Constraints and its impact on process design.

13. How do different facility layouts affect production flexibility? Discuss the advantages and disadvantages of product, process, and group layouts.

14. Discuss the type of facility layout that would be most appropriate for each of the following:

    a. Printing books

    b. Performing hospital laboratory tests

    c. Manufacturing home furniture

    d. A photography studio

    e. A library

15. Describe the layout of a typical fast-food franchise such as McDonald's. What type of layout is it? How does it support performance objectives? Do different franchises (e.g., Burger King or Wendy's) have different types of layouts? Why?

16. What are the differences between continuous and breakthrough improvement?

17. What are best practices? How can an organization identify them?

18. Explain the difference between benchmarking and reengineering.

19. The president of Circle H has assigned you to determine the causes of certain problems and to recommend appropriate corrective action. You have authority to talk to any person in the company.

    The early stages of your investigation establish that the three most common customer complaints are symptomatic of some major quality problems in the company's operations. You decide to review all available data, which may indicate the root causes of these problems.

    Further investigation reveals that, over a recent four-month period, a procedural change was made in the order-approval process. You decide to find out whether this change caused a significant difference in the time required to process an order from field sales through shipping.

    Your investigation reveals that the change in the order-approval process has increased the amount of time required to restock goods in customers' stores. You want to recommend corrective action, but you first investigate why the change was made. You learn that because of large losses on delinquent accounts receivable, the credit manager was required to approve all restock orders. This change added an average of three hours to the amount of internal processing time needed for a restock order.

    On review of your report, the president of Circle H takes note of administrative problems whose existence he had never suspected. To assure that corrective action will be effective and sustained, the president assigns you to take charge of the corrective action program.[25]

    a. What types of data would be most useful to review for clues as to the reasons for the three major customer complaints?

    b. How would you investigate whether the change in the order-approval process had a significant effect on order processing time?

    c. Given your knowledge of problems in both order processing and accounts receivable, what should you do?

20. Construct a spreadsheet model for the process in Figure 4.7 similar to those in the chapter to simulate the impact of variability in upstream and downstream processes. Assume that processing times are random with values of either 5, 10, or 15. To do this, use the Excel formula =IF(RAND()<0.33333333,5,(IF(RAND()<0.6666666,10,15))). Run each system (X constant, Y variable; X variable, Y constant) for 1,000 time units and

compute the average flow time and cycle time for each process. By pressing the F9 key, you can replicate the simulation with different random inputs. Repeat this for 10 replications and summarize the average differences in performance.

21. A study of the admission process in a local hospital gathered the following data for the nine activities in which a typical patient engaged. Some activities need to be repeated, as indicated in the last column of the table.

   a. Assuming that each activity is staffed by a person working 8 hours/day, what activity is the bottleneck? How many patients can be processed in a day?

   b. What is the throughput time of a patient? What assumptions did you need to make to answer this question?

   c. If three of the workers can perform any activity at 125 percent efficiency (thereby reducing the time taken by 1.25), how would you assign them to the activities? How would this change alter the capacity of the process?

   d. If you could group some activities to be performed by a single worker, how would you group them? How many workers could be moved to other departments without altering the overall capacity of this department?

Activity	Standard Time (minutes)	Average Number of Times Activity is Repeated per Patient
A	7	1
B	3	1
C	4	1
D	8	1.25
E	3	1.25
F	9	1.50
G	12	1
H	4	1.20
I	6	1

22. The shipping department receives packages in batches with a variable number of units. They are then processed and shipped. The number of packages waiting processing during random inspections was 73, 65, 84, 103, 58, and 79. The department ships an average of 50 packages per day. How much of the delay in the packages reaching their final customers is due to the shipping department?

23. Part X is first processed by operator A for 1 minute, then processed by operator B for 3 minutes, and then tested by operator C for 4 minutes. Of the tested units, 10 percent are defective and must be rejected. Part Y is first processed by operator A for 2 minutes and then assembled with one unit of X (from the process described above) by operator B, taking 4 minutes. The assembly is then tested by operator C in 2 minutes. Of these final products, 5 percent are found defective and are rejected. Draw a process flow diagram, showing the flows of materials, and find the process capacity in number of completed units per hour.

24. Consider the department that reviews mortgage applications in a financial institution. A printer prints the applications that were inputted by the different branches the previous day. One employee reviews the documentation to ensure that it is complete and adds any missing fields. Once the application is reviewed, it is placed on a tray. This tray is taken once a day (at 7 a.m.) to the Risk Evaluation Committee that will analyze each application and decide to accept or reject it. The printer outputs five applications per hour con-

tinuously from 7 a.m. until 5 p.m. The employee who reviews the applications works the following periods: 8–10 a.m., 11a.m.–2 p.m., and 3–6 p.m. It is estimated that it takes 10 minutes on average to review (and complete) an application. The Risk Evaluation Committee usually handles 10 applications per hour. Every morning at 8 a.m. the committee starts evaluating the applications received and does not stop until the whole tray is cleared.

   a. Draw charts for the cumulative number of applications arriving at and departing from the reviewing employee station.

   b. How much employee time is wasted waiting for the applications?

   c. What is the maximum number of applications that wait to be inspected? When does this situation occur?

   d. How long does it take for an application to go from printer to decision (focus on the best case and the worst case)?

Internet Projects

To find Web links to carry out each of the following projects, go to the text's Web site at **http://raturi_evans.swlearning.com**.

   1. Korry Electronics of Seattle, Washington, has absorbed a number of "lean manufacturing principles." Visit their Web site and then select *Lean Manufacturing* from their menu. From its presentation, outline the key concepts of "lean manufacturing" with a brief example of how the concept is used at Korry.

   2. At the Interactive Warehouse Web site, you can learn about methods of determining order-picking routes. For example, a store orders a few products from a warehouse. The products are stored throughout the warehouse. How should the order picker walk (or drive) to get these products as fast as possible? Follow the five-step process of setting up a layout, creating an order and a route, and then testing the results using different routing methods.

   3. Go to the Web link for case studies of various companies in different industrial environments. Each study contains a wealth of information about the company, details of its structure, production process, and related topics. Contrast the product-oriented layouts at United Distillers and BC Cement with the group layouts at Safeway distribution center and the process layouts at Wyman Gordon.

EXPERIENCE OM

Understanding Variability and Bottlenecks

This game was first developed by Dr. Eliyahu Goldratt and then refined by Professor Robert Jacobs. It demonstrates (1) the impact of variability on a process; (2) the effect of automation (reduced variance of processes) on capacity, buffers, and throughput time; and (3) bottlenecks in a variable process. Experienced operations managers have a sense of these results based on their intuition. This game gives you the chance to delve beyond the obvious and get a fresh perspective on how typical operations really work; specifically, it allows you to see the impact of the combination of statistical fluctuations and dependent events.

All those playing are operating a production plant whose product is chips (you may use poker chips, pennies, or Pringles—it doesn't matter!). The chips arrive at your plant (handed out at the game's start) as raw material. There are two production lines: one is a "dice" line and the second a "coin" line. A die and coin will be used to determine each day's production. Each line has six workstations. It is your job to process these chips through the six workstations in the plant so that they become finished product and can be shipped out as sold goods. Chips between workstations are work-in-process (WIP) inventory.

At a real manufacturing facility, the goal of this game is to maximize the goods shipped out the door and to minimize inventory. The game is played over a 20-"day" period, or roughly a month's work. At the end of 20 rolls, each team of six players (one player for each workstation) calculates the total number of shipped chips and the total of all WIP inventories. The team with the best score (highest number shipped, lowest inventory) wins.

Two important phenomena existing in a real manufacturing plant also exist here:

1. **Dependent Events:** Chips cannot move on to Workstation 2 without first passing through Workstation 1. Likewise all chips must move from 1 to 2 to 3 and so on and can be shipped only after passing through Workstation 6.

2. **Statistical Fluctuations:** These are simulated by rolling a die and tossing a coin. The number of chips that can be processed by Workstation 1 and moved to Workstation 2 is controlled by Workstation 1's die toss. In a real plant, average output is made up of good days and bad days. On good days with perfect attendance and no breakdowns or distractions, output is high. On bad days, with breakdowns, process and quality problems, accidents, excessive absenteeism, material shortages, and the like, output is low. In any case, output will vary around an average according to the latter factors. All workstation forepersons toss their dice at the same time. One round of tosses constitutes a day of production in the plant. After the toss, each foreperson moves the number of chips forward indicated by the die. If the die toss exceeds the total number of chips available in WIP, only the existing number of chips is moved forward. On the coin line, each station produces four units on the throw of a head and three units on the throw of a tail. Thus, their average output is the same as the dice line ($1/2 \times 3 + 1/2 \times 4 = 3.5$ units for the coin line and $1/6 \times 1 + 1/6 \times 2 + \ldots + 1/6 \times 6 = 3.5$ units for the dice line). Suppliers ship to both lines just in time—four units on day 1 and three units on day 2, then four on day 3 and three on day 4, and so on.

Questions to Consider Prior to Start of Game

1. How many chips do you expect to complete during the 20-day period for the coin line? For the dice line?

2. How much work-in-process (WIP) should you have at the end of the 20-day period for the coin line? For the dice line?

3. How much time should it take to process a chip from raw materials to completion at Workstation 6 for the coin line? For the dice line?

Questions to Consider after Playing the Game

1. How many chips did you actually complete during the 20-day period in each line?

2. How did WIP inventory vary during the game? How much did you have at the beginning of the game? How much at the end? How did these answers differ across the two lines? Why?

3. How much time did it take to process a chip from beginning to end? Did this time vary as the game was played for each line? How did it vary across the two lines? Why?

4. Is the dice line operationally better than the coin line? Why?

5. If you were to add capacity to the line, would you add it to the first station or the last station? Does this answer differ across the two lines?

6. If you were to add inventory buffers to the line, would you add them to the first station or the last station? Does this answer differ across the two lines?

7. If you wanted to use standard operating procedures or automation (both of which would reduce the variability in the number of units processed on a given day), would you use it at the first station or the last station? Why?

You may use the template in the Bonus Materials folder on the CD-ROM to keep track of work in process (WIP or the number of chips in your incoming pile), production (die toss), and lost production (units you could not ship in any period since you did not have enough chips).

One Absolute Rule

Give before you receive. In other words, the output of the previous station is available to you tomorrow, NOT TODAY. So throw a die (or toss a coin), pass the number of units to the next work center (you may not have enough so you lose some production that day), and then receive from the previous workstation.

5

Facilities and Capacity Planning

Facilities and capacity planning is the process of determining the type, amounts, and timing of resource and capacity decisions. The objective is to specify the proper mix of facilities, equipment, and labor required to meet both current and future product demand in the appropriate locations. Because these decisions are strategic in nature, capacity and facilities planning involves a joint effort among the organization's operations, marketing, and finance functions. Important questions to be answered include the following:

1. What kind of facilities and capacity do we need? Can existing facilities accommodate new products and adapt to changing demand for existing products? How is the market for existing products changing, and how will current and future technological innovations affect operations?
2. How much capacity do we need? How large should facilities be? Should new facilities be built? Should existing ones be modified, expanded, or closed? What are the financial implications of such decisions? How do we generate forecasts that provide crucial information for capacity planning?
3. When do we add more capacity? When should we think of downsizing?

This chapter focuses on understanding the role of facilities and capacity decisions in operations. Specifically, we address:
○ The strategic role of facilities (*Section 5.1*).
○ Facility charters (*Section 5.2*).
○ Capacity planning decisions (*Section 5.3*).
○ Timing of additions (or downsizing) of capacity and facilities (*Section 5.4*).

Material on the CD-ROM discusses some useful tools and techniques for facilities and capacity planning.
7. Decision Analysis
10. Forecasting

5.1 STRATEGIC IMPORTANCE OF FACILITIES AND CAPACITY

Property and facilities represent a significant portion of the book value of a firm's assets; they also represent key investments that can sustain or impede a firm's long-run competitiveness (see the *OM Practice* box on Ford). Wal-Mart and Disney create competitive positions through their facilities strategies.

Wal-Mart, which receives $1 out of every $5 spent in U.S. retail stores, operates an ever-expanding chain of over 3,600 stores. Capacity and location decisions for every new store go through a rigorous assessment of the viability of the proposal, competitive and social reactions, and forecasts of store sales and profitability. When Walt Disney built Disneyland in Anaheim, California, in 1954, he was short of cash and could afford only 160 acres of land. Hotels, restaurants, and other organizations in the immediate vicinity of Disneyland cashed in on its popularity. When planning for Disney World in Orlando, The Walt Disney Company developed a different strategy: it purchased 29,500 acres of land around the theme park location for only $200 per acre. Today, less than half of that land is in use—the rest is valued at more than $1 million per acre—but the Disney-owned properties play a large role in its profitability as well as attracting more guests to its theme parks.[1]

OM PRACTICE

Henry Ford's Rouge Complex
"The 100-acre Rouge complex is Henry Ford's shrine to mass production."

Henry Ford was obsessed with building cars as quickly and efficiently as possible. Buying from outside suppliers was inherently wasteful, so he decided to assemble a car at one site along the Rouge River. Once a swamp, the Rouge complex has contained ship berths for ore boats; coke ovens; two iron foundries; a steel mill; a rolling mill; 110 miles of railroad tracks; a final assembly plant; other plants making engines, glass, tires, batteries, transmissions, radiators, and electrical parts; and its own power plant, powerful enough to illuminate Boston. It once had the distinction of being the only place in the world a car could go from raw materials to finished product in 48 hours.

The Rouge complex was an outgrowth of the success of the Model T. In 1909–1910, its first year,

18,000 were built. In the next two years, when the price was reduced from $845 to $600, output doubled to 78,000. Nonetheless, capacity was a serious problem and output was restricted.

Ford's ingenuity resulted in a moving assembly line at Highland Park in 1913. Borrowing ideas from arms makers and meat packers, Ford started to build flywheel magnetos on a crude assembly line, bringing assembly time down from 20 minutes to 13 minutes to 5 minutes. Applying the idea to other components, Model T production increased to 585,388 in 1916, as Ford cut the price to $360. The company that was founded in 1903 with a dozen shareholders and less than $100,000 in capital had accumulated $58 million in profits. Nevertheless, Henry Ford was obsessed with growth and decided that all profits would be reinvested in new plants along the Rouge River instead of dividends for shareholders.[2]

One might wonder whether the Internet reduces the value of developing a sound facilities and capacity strategy, since delivery of products and services is made "virtual," lessening the impact of facilities on a firm's competitiveness. On the contrary, says one of Charles Schwab's executives. "When you have a problem affecting customers, that's when you know the true meaning of the word mortar." Schwab, with over $10 billion a week in online transactions continues to pay close attention to its 337 branch offices and four service centers. Recognizing the importance of tangible facilities in tandem with e-commerce, it pursues a strategy that has become known as "clicks and mortar."[3]

Market Drivers of Facilities and Capacity Decisions

OM PRINCIPLE

Facilities are constructed or modified for two key reasons: changes in existing products, markets, or processes; or the emergence of new products, markets, or processes.

Organizations confront facilities decisions because of changes in their products, processes, or markets. For example, the firm may have outgrown its current facilities because of market growth or the addition of new product lines; the current facilities may have become obsolete; or the firm might consider a new "greenfield" site for entering new markets, launching newly developed product lines, or adopting radically different technology and processes. Table 5.1 summarizes these issues.

Decisions become even more complex with competitive "gaming"—for example, firms have been known to announce nonexistent capacity expansion plans just to induce panic in smaller competitors. Restaurant chains often clone competitors' concepts or locate right next door (however, this can result in a win-win situation by increasing traffic, as competitive store co-locations in malls have demonstrated). Firms also face the question of whether to plan expansions during economic downturns (when resources such as land and buildings can be acquired cheaply) or when the economy is booming (when resources are more expensive, but are needed to grow a business). Such complexities make the development of a rigorous facilities and capacity strategy very important.

> ## OM PRINCIPLE
>
> Facilities and capacity decisions generally are very expensive and irreversible. Thus, when making such decisions in a dynamic environment, the organization must make a thorough assessment of the future scenarios that might evolve.

In developing this strategy, the firm must consider the product life cycle (see Figure 3.1), which we introduced in Chapter 3. During the growth state, capacity is often limited, operations managers must maintain a high degree of flexibility to be responsive to design changes, and the workforce must be highly skilled to adapt quickly to changing product and process requirements. At some point, however, the simultaneous demands for flexibility and efficiency may require a decision to produce at a different location, in a different facility, or on a different production line. This "breakaway" point is critical, as it becomes a pretext for rationalizing the product or the service at a new facility. Thus, the growth phase is the best time to increase capacity in anticipation of future sales volume increases. The

> ## OM PRINCIPLE
>
> Both the size and timing of facility and capacity decisions depend on the growth (or decline) of demand for products and services as characterized by the product life cycle.

TABLE 5.1   Factors Influencing Facility and Capacity Changes

	Markets	Products	Processes
Changes	Responsiveness pressures (access time for customers or delivery time for goods) require the creation of a new facility. An example is a bank opening nearly full service automated branches in malls.	Product life cycle changes (sales growth) trigger facility changes. An example is Amazon.com building many large warehouses across the country.	Antiquated processes or equipment requires shutting down an old facility and launching a new one. For example, Coca-Cola closed old bottling plants and built new ones.
Emergence	New markets in specific geographic regions require that new facilities be developed. For example, BMW built its facility in South Carolina in response to growing U.S. demand.	A new product line requires being close to a specific asset base. For instance, many Japanese auto firms built plants in the United States to produce only U.S. models.	A new process or technology is implemented in a "greenfield" site. For example, hospitals locate MRI technologies in separate testing facilities.

decision of how much capacity to add depends on accurate forecasting of future sales growth. One must also recognize, however, that the rapid growth experienced during the initial stages of the product life cycle will not continue indefinitely, and adding too much capacity can saddle the firm with obsolete resources.

As the product moves into the maturity stage of the product life cycle, capacity utilization becomes critical for the product or service to compete on cost as opposed to innovation. If capacity decisions are delayed until this stage, however, the lead-time required until capacity becomes available may result in lost market share opportunities. Also, insufficient capacity can easily result in poor quality if pressures for output increase.

Finally, as demand declines and the product is phased out of the marketplace, the firm must maintain control over cost. Capacity needs are reduced, and overcapacity typifies the decline phase. Downsizing capacity is not easy, though—reallocation of resources to other product lines or other divisions requires careful planning. Today, many firms are evaluating their product and service portfolio, often to focus on pockets of excellence. This also can reduce capacity needs.

The product life cycle clearly demonstrates that resource and facility needs change over time. With multiple products, life cycles may overlap, reducing some of the demands for facility expansion and contraction. Forecasts of aggregate demand for facilities can be obtained by combining demand estimates over product life cycles. Thus, facility planning must account for the forecast product mix and the aggregate effect of different life cycles on resource requirements.

Key Components of Facilities and Capacity Planning

Facilities and capacity planning involves three basic questions:

○ *What will be done at the facility?* This question is often referred to as the **facility charter.** Charters can be defined around core competencies (for example, research and development), markets (North America), or processes (assembly).

○ *How much capacity is needed?* Aggregate capacity is usually defined in terms of quantity of products or volume of customers. Economies of scale suggest having a few large facilities; however, factors such as proximity to customers or suppliers may require smaller, responsive branch facilities. Further, a firm facing uncertain demand must consider the incremental cost of adding capacity and having resources lie idle some of the time versus the cost not having enough capacity and turning customers away at other times.

> ## OM PRINCIPLE
>
> The answers to three basic questions:
> 1. What is to be accomplished at the facility?
> 2. How much capacity is needed?
> 3. When should capacity changes take place?
>
> are vital for successful facilities and capacity planning.

○ *When should capacity be changed?* When demand changes over time with the product life cycle, timing of decisions is crucial. Preemptive investments in facilities can make it more difficult for competitors to enter the market or attract customers. Alternatively, a firm can wait and build facilities after it has some assurance that there will be enough customers to warrant the expansion.

The following sections outline the critical issues affecting these decisions and provide examples of the methods used by organizations.

5.2 FACILITY CHARTERS

Determining the range of products or services that the facility will have the capability to produce or deliver can be a very complicated decision. Facility charters define the focus of a facility, that is, the area of expertise in which the facility specializes. Specifying a facility charter entails defining:

○ *The Core Competency of the Facility:* For example, is it focused on cost reduction, customer access, or innovation?

○ *The Breadth of Products and Services Provided by the Facility:* An important decision is whether to outsource any products or services.

○ *The Span of Process of the Facility:* Many manufacturing firms, for example, do final assembly and testing at distribution centers, leaving component manufacturing to a central plant.

Matching facilities with products, processes, and markets is not an easy task, particularly for organizations offering multiple products and services through multiple facilities. As David Garvin observes:

> Multiple plants . . . create a new set of problems: how to match products with plants, what relationships to establish among facilities, and the proper basis for comparing the performance of dissimilar organizations. Operating decisions become more complex. . . . Deciding how a factory should be focused—the range of products to include, and the variety of production processes—has important links to competitive positioning.[4]

For example, banks must often decide whether a new branch should offer the full range of services or a limited subset. Large consumer products companies must decide whether to dedicate facilities to a single product or consolidate several products (usually with similar technologies) within the same facility. Retail stores like K-Mart are considering smaller and more conveniently located facilities. Toyota decided to manufacture the Camry-based coupe in its Cambridge, Ontario plant rather than its primary Camry plant in northern Kentucky. The Cambridge plant was set up to produce the Corolla (also manufactured in California) and four-cylinder Corolla engines, which are also manufactured in West Virginia.[5]

Sometimes firms decide to focus a facility on a few products. For example, American Power Conversion Corporation has created "focused factories" designed to produce a limited number of uninterruptible power supply (UPS) products. It opened a new facility in Rhode Island in 1996 to produce its Matrix-UPS line and larger KVA Smart-UPS units. The Matrix-UPS line, geared

OM PRINCIPLE

The logic of establishing a facility focus is that a facility cannot be all things to all customers—it must carefully choose its priorities and excel in a few of them, lest it perform poorly on all of them.[6]

toward data centers driven by PC LANs, minicomputers, or mainframes, and the Smart-UPS products, designed for server applications, formerly were manufactured at the company's headquarters in West Kingston, Rhode Island. "In the past, we were small enough in that our West Kingston facility had every unit there, and it meant that if one [unit] was down, or one needed more people, you swapped people over," said Elise Hamann, director at APC. "The advantage of that is that you have people there, but [the disadvantage is] they may not be up to speed on that particular product."[7] Focused facilities overcome this disadvantage.

Facility charters for multifacility configurations can be classified according to whether they are based on products, market areas, processes, or general configurations.[8] For example, with a product configuration, the firm produces entire products (product lines) under one roof. Thus, every new facility in an organization with a product facility charter has a product or a product line associated with it. Typically, the facility is identified by saying "We make paper products there" or "We make detergents there." Table 5.2 summarizes some advantages and disadvantages of these types of facilities charters.

Facilities charters can also be classified according to six strategies:[9]

○ *Product focus strategy,* which establishes plants based on products or product lines.

○ *Process focus strategy,* which establishes plants based on specific processes in the product value chain.

○ *Regionalization strategy,* which is similar to a market-oriented facilities strategy and focuses plant activity on the needs of a geographic region.

○ *Consolidation strategy,* which is similar to a general-purpose facilities strategy and allows plants to manufacture for disparate markets with disparate processes under one roof.

○ *Vertical integration strategy,* which assimilates vertically integrated processes under one roof.

The *OM Practice* box explores the choices confronting Seagate, Inc., a multibillion dollar hard disk drive (HDD) manufacturer.

TABLE 5.2	*Advantages and Disadvantages of Various Types of Facilities Charters*		
Facility Charter	**Advantages**	**Disadvantages**	**Examples**
Product	The facility can focus on product excellence by limiting its scope and exploiting economies of scale.	Supply chain costs may be high if customers demand a bundle of products from different facilities. Facilities may be susceptible to risks associated with a dedicated product line.	Consumer products (soap, paper, food), income tax preparation
Market	The facility can focus on customer response and service by providing a wide variety of products or services in one facility.	Process and product expertise is disbursed across many facilities, inhibiting learning. Diseconomies of scale result in increased costs.	Retail stores, banks, automotive services
Process	For complex products or services, a process-based facility charter can focus on efficiency and customization.	Coordinating schedules and product flow is difficult. Changes in products and services can severely disrupt operations.	Automobiles, health care, consulting
General	Facilities can focus on meeting multiple requirements of the market, product, and process simultaneously.	Establishing a viable facilities charter is complicated. Lack of a unified charter can create confusion and inefficiency.	Defense contractors, universities

OM PRACTICE

Facility Charters at Seagate

Seagate's regional network of vertically integrated plants in Southeast Asia reduces supply disruptions in the procurement of critical components.

The two critical components of a hard disk are the head and the recording media (DISC). Previously, "thin film inductive heads" (TFIH) were capable of sustaining increasing customer demands for more disk capacity. Now, however, "magneto resistive heads" (MRH) manufactured using a new technology are utilized in high capacity hard drives.

Figure 5.1 shows the facilities strategy at Seagate. Plant 1 is dedicated to manufacturing

recording media—common components for any type of hard disk. This reduces the capacity required for disc production as the demand variance for both products is pooled. Plant 2 manufactures MRH and TFIH. These components are then assembled into two different types of hard disks at Plant 3, an assembly plant. In reality, Seagate is using a pure process focus strategy with some consolidation—by consolidating head production (MRH and TFIH) as well as assembly, it can operate with three plants, rather than five. Its main reason for specifying facility charters is to eliminate confusion about the stated goals and purposes of a facility.[10]

FIGURE 5.1 | *Seagate Plant Configuration*

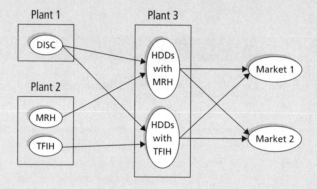

Three key issues affect a firm's choice of a facilities charter. First, the level of vertical integration within a facility is often a consequence of a sequence of incremental "make-buy" decisions over time. A strategic perspective on facility charters would entail reassessing them with every make-buy decision that significantly alters the span of process within a facility. Second, broad

> ### OM PRINCIPLE
> An effective facilities charter is characterized by a portfolio of products and services that absorb demand variations within product lines and at the same time do not impose an unnecessarily high demand for mix flexibility.

facility charters create unfocused operations and unbundled priorities, which make designing appropriate facilities more difficult. Finally, achieving mix and volume flexibility requires that the firm balance "choking facilities with variety" on the one hand with creating dedicated facilities that are susceptible to volume variations on the other.

Vertical Integration and Outsourcing

The choices of what processes are performed within a facility and which ones are outsourced, which characterize the degree of **vertical integration,** critically affect a firm's facility and capacity strategy. On the one hand, an organization might consolidate all processes for a specific product or product line—Ford's Rouge complex so impressed Japanese automotive executives that even today Japanese auto assembly plants are much larger on average than their American counterparts.[11] However, such a strategy is risky when markets and demand change radically. When customers wanted a car other than a black model T, the lack of flexibility in Ford's vertical integration strategy resulted in financial losses.[12] More recently, such firms as Amazon.com, Barnes and Noble, and Borders incurred massive investments for regional warehouses. After borrowing more than $1 billion to build its distribution network, Amazon.com is testing a new outsourcing strategy—letting someone else manage its inventory. **Outsourcing** is the process of letting an external agency manage a firm's operations, such as inventory management, call centers, or human resources.

Why is Amazon.com outsourcing inventory management when the economics typically favor in-house production? In reality, the cost of in-house production is almost always understated. Consider a firm that assembles a product from two components. In assessing the make-buy decision for one of the components, it evaluates the cost of buying the product from a supplier against the cost of in-house production, which includes the direct cost of buying raw materials for the components and the processing costs. What the firm cannot predict (and often does not) is the increased overhead associated with materials planners, purchasing agents, and coordinators. Adding to this are managers' inclinations to grow their empires, making in-house production a self-fulfilling prophecy.

Too much vertical integration, however, can result in problems. Consider the two simple scenarios in Figure 5.2. Suppose that the firm decides to add making component A to the charter at facility X. It gains control of both the delivery of A and the direct cost of making A, thereby adding to its bottom line the profit margin it would have paid to the supplier. Now, however, the facility has two things to do and requires process experts who know something about fabrication. Furthermore, facility X has become a competitor to all suppliers of component A—and the firm is locked out of the free market for product and process innovation on this component. If component manufacturing is run as a cost center, it has little incentive to improve because it has a captive, internal market. If it sells the component externally, it now has two customers, a situation that usually results in internal customers being

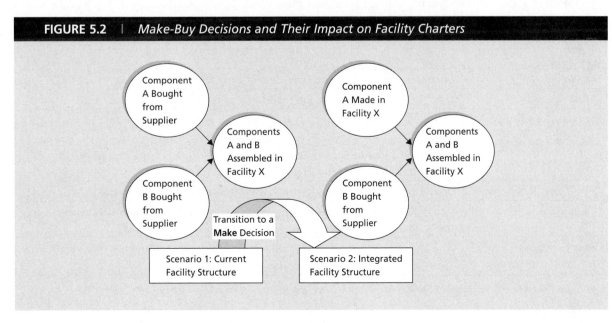

FIGURE 5.2 | *Make-Buy Decisions and Their Impact on Facility Charters*

assigned lower priority. If the firm continues to make such decisions, it will eventually become very unfocused and unmanageable. By choosing to outsource inventory control, Amazon.com can better focus on its core competency—its Web presence. Table 5.3 summarizes some other arguments for in-house production.

Outsourcing of noncore processes in the manufacturing sector gained momentum in the early 1980s and has continued to expand through almost every industry.[13] Criteria for an objective decision on whether to outsource are not very easy to find and apply, however, as each case is different.[14] Consequently, such decisions often lead to altercations between managers holding opposing beliefs. Questions that should be considered when making outsourcing decisions include:

> ## OM PRINCIPLE
>
> Firms decide to outsource when they believe that the supplier or contractor can deliver better value for products/services than in-house production.

1. What costs are associated with outsourcing versus in-house production? Can economies of scale be exploited?
2. Do outside suppliers have the capability of providing the required quality and reliability levels?
3. Does the firm have the technological capability for in-house production?
4. What impact will outsourcing have on the firm's human resources?

Focused Facilities

The growth of outsourcing has been attributed to a loss of focus in facility charters. As facilities become more complex, conflict over priorities arises, and the facility tries to become all

| TABLE 5.3 | Some Arguments for In-house Production |

Reason	Argument
Economies of scale	Quantity required is so small that external suppliers cannot produce at a reasonable cost.
Quality	Suppliers do not have the capability of achieving required quality.
Reliability of supply	Limited suppliers may not provide reliable delivery.
Technology	Suppliers may not have the right equipment and process technology.
Costs	With in-house production, internal overhead is allocated more effectively.
Economic conditions	During economic downturns, surplus capacity may be used to manufacture in-house.
Collusion	Supplier coalitions might engage in collusion, obtain legislative protection, and/or engage in unfair pricing practices.
Long-term employment	Producing in-house can protect jobs and maintain the organization.
Patent protection	Outsourcing may lead to loss of patents and/or may disburse internal innovations to the open market too quickly.
Emotive response	Size and integration are often "emotionally held beliefs" among executives who favor in-house production.

Source: Summarized from discussions in Wilbur B. England, *Modern Procurement Management: Principles and Cases,* Homewood, IL: Richard D. Irwin, 1970.

OM PRINCIPLE

Facilities often lose focus for a variety of reasons: product and process proliferation, market and technological changes, product life cycle changes, economies of scale leading to uncontrolled incremental expansion, executive ambition, and the firm's inability to quantify real and opportunity costs.

things to all people—for instance, attempting to be efficient yet flexible, low cost yet innovative—and eventually it satisfies no one. Also, as organizations decide to build or modify facilities incrementally, the network of facilities that may emerge often loses a systems perspective, resulting in inefficiencies and unnecessary costs.

A typical firm may have several product lines and process technologies serving different market segments all under one roof and cannot afford to create separate, focused facilities. An alternative is to segment the facility into a set of subfacilities, each with a unique charter—a "plant-within-a-plant" concept. The firm must choose an appropriate basis for focusing—one that gives it maximum competitive and market leverage. Table 5.4 summarizes different strategies for focusing facilities. For example, separating the physical (and managerial) structures needed to support two products provides a high level of product specialization, eases the product engineering support required, and results in better allocation of overhead by product line.

Reconsidering facility charters from a strategic perspective also allows the organization to identify redundancies and inconsistencies. It also enables the organization to assess the long-term competitive implications of the entire global network and rationalize the contributions of individual facilities within the network. As the *OM Practice* box on Procter & Gamble, shows, companies that can view location and facility charter decisions from a systems perspective can enhance their critical capabilities and create lasting competitive advantage.

OM PRACTICE

Procter & Gamble
Strategic product sourcing improves Procter & Gamble's bottom line.

A few years ago, Procter & Gamble was facing product life cycles that had declined from three to five years a few decades earlier to approximately 18–24 months, requiring plants to change equipment more frequently. Several corporate acquisitions had resulted in excess capacity, and the company thought consolidation would lower product costs. Accordingly, P&G began an effort called Strengthening Global Effectiveness (SGE) to streamline work processes, drive out non-value-added costs, and eliminate duplication. A principal component of SGE was the North American Product Supply Study, designed to reexamine and reengineer P&G's product-sourcing and distribution system for its North American operations, with an

emphasis on reconfiguring plant charters by choosing the best location and scale of operation for making each product. The need to consolidate plants was driven by the move to global brands and common packaging and the need to reduce manufacturing expense, improve speed-to-market, avoid major capital investments, and deliver better consumer value.

Some 30 product strategy teams consisting of individuals from major business categories, finance, manufacturing, distribution, purchasing, R&D, and plant operations developed options for plant locations and capacities that were evaluated using simple optimization models. Top options were subjected to more thorough financial and risk analysis. Within three years, based on the study's recommendations, P&G had closed 12 plants and reconfigured the charters of many others, resulting in over $250 million in pre-tax savings.[15]

Product Mix and Volume Flexibility

Facility charters should consist of a portfolio of products and services that balance the need to keep resources utilized fully with the desire to maintain high levels of product and service availability. This tradeoff is best captured by contrasting the **mix flexibility** (the ability to

TABLE 5.4	Facility Focus Strategies		
Strategy	**Description**	**Advantages**	**Disadvantages**
Product based	Product lines or clusters are segregated within a facility. For example, hospitals segregate emergency rooms, outpatient clinics, and intensive care units.	High level of product focus, specialization, and responsiveness. Smoother new product introduction. Cleaner product costing. Better development of employee expertise.	Imbalances can occur as product volumes grow at different rates. Coordination of customer "product bundles" may be difficult.
Market/customer based	Product/process clusters within a facility respond to the needs of specific market segments. For example, a law office that has divisions for estate planning, tax, and real estate.	Permits specialization by market segments. Promotes customer relationship building.	Resources across several facilities are duplicated. Reduced emphasis on process and technical skills.
Process based	Parts of the value-adding process are segregated within the facility. For example, an automobile plant with fabrication, assembly, painting, and other departments.	Concentrates technology and process expertise. Encourages standardization. Utilization can be kept high as demands from downstream process segments are pooled, resulting in reduced variation.	Reduces the ability of the organization to respond to major shifts in products or markets and limits its ability to introduce radical changes in products or processes. Makes coordination across processes more difficult.
Volume/product life cycle based	A facility is segmented by the volume of product/service or the stage of the product life cycle.	High-volume segments exploit economies of scale. Low-volume segments can focus on flexibility and responsiveness. Separate process segments for newly developed products (pilot production lines) can focus on product and process innovation.	Duplicates resources, resulting in high overhead costs. If segments vie for resources based on profitability, low-volume segments may not receive appropriate attention.
Priority based	Plants-within-a-plant are created based on the competitive priorities—cost, quality, time, and availability.	Allows focus on most critical priorities within segments.	Multiple market segments, products, and processes may be difficult to coordinate.

Source: Based on T. J. Hill, *Manufacturing Strategy: Text and Cases,* 2nd ed., Homewood, IL: Richard D. Irwin, 1994.

change products quickly) and **volume flexibility** (the ability to "ramp up" and "ramp down" quickly and efficiently with changes in demand) of a facility with a wide range of products with that of a facility with a narrow range of products.

The ability to change capacity quickly can be a source of competitive advantage or simply a competitive necessity, particularly for firms that compete with multiple short-cycle products and services. For example, forest products, consumer goods, and glass manufacturing firms seldom need the flexibility to make rapid capacity changes; however, makers of personal computers, toys, automobiles, and other products with short product life cycles require mix and volume flexibility. As we have noted, however, facilities that have a charter of multiple products or services can become unfocused and incur high costs of variety (the costs incurred solely for managing the complexity that accompanies variety). Organizations must carefully consider these issues in developing appropriate facility charters.

5.3 CAPACITY MEASUREMENT AND PLANNING

Capacity planning is a crucial element of a firm's operations strategy because it has significant implications for cost and customer satisfaction. **Capacity planning** involves carefully balancing the needs of the market with resource efficiency and utilization. In many cases, capacity changes involve large capital expenditures. For example, adding rooms to a hotel or building a new factory requires costly and lengthy construction. Such capacity decisions must be made in the face of considerable uncertainty about future product demand. Furthermore, capacity needs change over time. By the time capacity changes are implemented, the environment may have changed significantly. In the 1960s and early 1970s, for example, U.S. firms could sell all they could produce, so they increased manufacturing capacity as fast as possible; in the late 1970s and through the 1980s, however, foreign competition and higher interest rates resulted in a substantial decrease in demand.

As a result, overcapacity led to many layoffs and plant closures. In other situations, capacity may be adjusted to meet short-term fluctuations in demand. For instance, airlines can move larger planes to high-demand routes during peak holiday and vacation periods, and multiplex movie theaters can show a popular movie on multiple screens.

Measuring Capacity

To plan capacity effectively, one must understand how to measure it. **Capacity** can be measured in a variety of ways, but the most common is the *rate of output per unit of time.* This concept of capacity can best be understood using the analogy in Figure 5.3. The input rate (for example, customer orders or output from upstream work centers) creates demand. The *load* is the volume of work that remains to be completed at any time; it is the difference between the cumulative flows into the system and the cumulative flows out of it, adjusted for any increases due to lags in transformation-process activities. If the input rate exceeds capacity, the load increases; if it is less than capacity, the load decreases.

The load of a process can be measured by its *backlog* or *work in process*. The relationships among lead-time, demand, capacity, and load are

Load at time t = cumulative demand (input rate until time t) −
cumulative capacity (output rate) until time t

Lead-time = load/capacity

For example, consider a fast-food drive-through facility that can process a customer in a cycle time of 3 minutes. The capacity is 20 customers per hour. If a total of 50 cars have arrived at the facility by 12:00 noon (the cumulative demand), and 40 have been processed, then the load is 10 cars waiting to be served. The lead-time until the last customer will be processed is

10 cars/20 cars per hour = 0.5 hours, or 30 minutes

This example shows the importance of assessing flow by establishing what the right amount of capacity for a system is.

As we discussed in Chapter 4, for processes with multiple operations, the slowest operation defines the bottleneck and limits the capacity of the system. Thus, capacity improvements and investment decisions should be focused on bottleneck operations.

When operations managers state process capacities, they must clearly indicate which of three types of capacity they are specifying: *maximum, effective,* or *actual* capacity. **Maximum, or theoretical, capacity** defines the highest rate of output that a process or activity can achieve. Operations managers calculate the maximum capacity of a process based on the number and duration of available shifts, the number of available machines and employees per shift, and the number of workdays in the period of calculation. For example, suppose a small machine shop that is designed to operate one shift per day for five days per week can produce 500 units per shift with its current equipment, product mix, and workforce. The maximum capacity of the shop is

(500 units/shift)(1 shift/day)(5 days/week) = 2,500 units/week

This calculation requires some very important simplifying assumptions: equally skilled workers, no loss of time to product changeovers or differences in products, and no loss of capac-

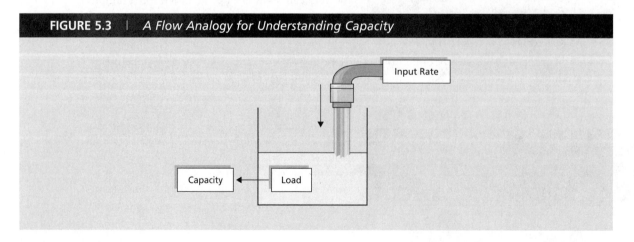

FIGURE 5.3 | *A Flow Analogy for Understanding Capacity*

ity due to machine breakdowns, preventive maintenance, worker problems, scrap, and salvage. In practice, other capacity measures are more useful for operations decisions.

Effective, or **planned, capacity** is the output rate that managers expect for a given activity or process. Effective capacity is generally less than maximum capacity. In the example above, if 10 percent of the productive time is used for preventive maintenance and product changeover setups, the output would be $0.90(2,500) = 2,250$ units/week, which would be the effective capacity. Operations managers often base production plans and schedules on this measure of output for several reasons. First, because effective capacity is less than the maximum available, any excess capacity can accommodate unexpected demand. No practical shop-floor scheduler expects to receive all orders with normal lead-times. Important customers often submit rush orders that require rapid response. Second, excess capacity allows time for preventive maintenance, which reduces the chances of unplanned breakdowns and can reduce system variance. Third, unplanned maintenance and repair will generally be necessary and reduce available capacity. Finally, running at maximum capacity can severely strain equipment and people; thus, planning for a more reasonable capacity level reduces anxiety. Effective capacity is a function of utilization and efficiency:

$$\text{Effective capacity} = \text{maximum capacity} \times \text{utilization} \times \text{efficiency}$$

Utilization is a measure of how intensively a resource is being used. Mathematically, utilization is expressed as

$$\text{Utilization} = \text{actual hours used/scheduled hours available}$$

For example, suppose that a machine is scheduled for 40 hours for production during a week. If it is actually used for only 30 hours, the utilization is $30/40 = 0.75$ or 75 percent. Note that utilization can never exceed 100 percent. Historically, for U.S. manufacturing firms, utilization has hovered around 80 percent with a variation of plus or minus 3 percent across the years. In service-oriented firms, 60% utilization is considered optimistic.

Efficiency measures how well something is performing relative to expectations; it is expressed as the ratio of the actual units produced to the standard rate of production expected in a time period or the standard time to actual time:

$$\text{Efficiency} = \text{actual units produced/standard production rate}$$
$$\text{or}$$
$$\text{standard time/actual time}$$

Unlike the utilization rate, efficiency can exceed 100 percent when an experienced employee performs planned tasks; it can fall below 100 percent if, say, the employee is inexperienced. For example, if the standard time to complete a task is 2.0 hours, and it is completed in 2.4 hours, efficiency is $2.0/2.4 = 0.83$ or 83 percent. If it is completed in 1.9 hours, efficiency is $2.0/1.9 = 1.053$ or 105.3 percent.

Operations managers often need to estimate both efficiency and utilization rates to develop feasible production plans. They base estimates of actual times on workers' experience and familiarity with planned jobs, the condition of plant equipment, and the quality of raw materials. For example, if the maximum capacity is 2,500 units/week, utilization is estimated at 75 percent, and efficiency at 95 percent, then the effective capacity is $(2,500)(0.75)(0.95) = 1,781.25$. Such calculations provide realistic information on which to base delivery promises or job completion dates.

The third type of capacity measure is **actual capacity**—the actual level of output for a process or activity over a period of time. In our example, because of unanticipated machine breakdowns, defective output, material shortages, and other unplanned delays, the actual output might only be 1,500 units/week.

Actual capacity can be reduced by many factors including workers' lack of training or experience, uncertain demand, unplanned requests by customers, poor-quality incoming materials that require preprocessing or rework, setup times and changeovers across products, condition of the equipment and yield problems, power failures, and seasonal drops in efficiency.

Note that aggregate capacity measures can also be affected by product mix. If a plant produces only one type of product, capacity is usually easy to define. In a sugar refinery, for example, a logical measure of capacity is tons of sugar per month (or per day, per week, and so on). However, consider a small winery. A measure of capacity might be the number of gallons or barrels of wine produced per month. Red wine takes longer to age than white wine. If the winery is producing half red wine and half white wine and then changes to a 30 and 70 percent mix, the capacity will clearly increase, even though the physical facilities and labor do not change.

Some organizations measure capacity in terms of *units of input*, such as hours of available time. Thus, one shift/day for 5 days/week provides a theoretical capacity of 40 hours/week. If managers wish to keep a 20 percent cushion for planned or unplanned contingencies, the effective capacity would be only 32 hours/week. Such measures can be misleading, however, as the *OM Practice* box on hospitals suggests.

OM PRINCIPLE

Managers calculate theoretical values for maximum and effective capacity to guide their production plans. Actual capacity provides feedback to assess performance because it deals with actual rather than planned production.

OM PRINCIPLE

Maximum capacity cannot be increased unless the facility or the labor force is expanded (possibly through the use of overtime) or modified. Actual capacity can often be increased by operational improvements such as reducing setup times or purchasing machines with lower maintenance requirements.

OM PRACTICE

How Hospitals Measure Capacity
It's the output, not the input, that really counts.

There are 1,960 excess beds in 25 hospitals in the Greater Cincinnati area. Studies suggest that this amounts to about $60 million in wasted resources. Over the years as inpatient services have declined because of reductions in the average length of stay, more effective medical treatments, and migration of inpatient procedures to outpatient services, hospitals have reconfigured their facilities with more offices, clinics, and conference rooms. Nonetheless, they have maintained these "paper" beds on their books because size conveys market power, and the size of hospitals is usually measured by the number of beds.

Number of beds is a wonderful measure of capacity when all a hospital does is perform inpatient services and all beds are occupied. Obviously, though, a 500-bed hospital with one doctor has much less capacity than a 50-bed hospital with four doctors. Also, as the hospital's product mix shifts from inpatient to outpatient services, bed capacity becomes a less useful indicator of the size of the hospital. "Shouldn't we judge our hospitals by the number of patients they take care of and how they stack up on the basis of quality, efficiency, and costs? Rather than saying the Christ Hospital is a 550-bed hospital, I'd like to say that we took care of 148,644 people last year," concludes Jack Cook, president of Christ Hospital.[16]

Capacity Tradeoffs

Capacity costs include both the initial investment in facilities and the annual cost of operating and maintaining the facilities. Excess capacity can be extremely expensive, especially for capital-intensive firms such as paper mills and steel mills, although in industries such as aircraft production, which operate with a continual backlog of orders, higher capacity will allow faster delivery times. Not having sufficient capacity also entails a cost, however—the opportunity cost incurred from lost sales and reduced market share, as well as any necessary overtime

> ## OM PRINCIPLE
>
> In developing a long-range capacity plan, a firm must make a basic economic tradeoff between the cost of capacity and the opportunity cost of not having adequate capacity.

or outsourcing premiums. Too little capacity can result in the inability to meet customer demand, particularly in service industries. However, tight capacity allows for higher equipment utilization and a better return on investment. Complicating the decision is the fact that the capacity plan must be based on long-term forecasts, which are usually uncertain. Other factors to consider include interest rates, technology improvements, construction costs, competition, and government regulations.

The tradeoffs between the cost of capacity and shortages because of lack of capacity can be conceptualized in economic terms by computing a **capacity cushion**—the amount of capacity in excess of expected demand.[17] Let C_s represent the opportunity loss per unit of not having enough capacity along with any penalties (such as overtime premiums) associated with not being able to meet demand during a given time period, and C_x represent the annualized cost of having an unneeded unit of capacity.

Suppose that the demand for a product has a simple probability distribution:

Demand	Probability	Cumulative Probability
5	0.2	0.2
10	0.3	0.5
15	0.4	0.9
20	0.1	1.0

The expected demand is 12 units. However, if the firm builds capacity for this amount, then it faces an expected shortage of $[0.4(15 - 12) + 0.1(20 - 12)] = 2.0$ units. If it builds 15 units of capacity, the expected shortage will be only 0.5 units. The decision of how much capacity to build can be determined as a function of the costs, C_s and C_x. The optimal level of capacity will be the minimum amount satisfying the equation

$$\text{Cumulative probability} > C_s/(C_s + C_x)$$

Suppose that $C_s = 3$ and $C_x = 1$. Thus, $C_s/(C_s + C_x) = 0.75$, and the capacity should be set at 15 units, or a capacity cushion of 25 percent over expected demand. In capital intensive industries such as steel or paper, the cost of capacity is fairly large and the resulting cushion is generally small, while in other industries such as fashion goods, the margins (and hence the value of C_s) are high and cushions are also therefore rather large.

Though this model illustrates the fundamental tradeoffs, it does not capture all the realities that managers face in making capacity decisions. For example, opportunity costs of shortages are very difficult to quantify, and the model assumes a single period, as opposed to incremental capacity changes. The firm may not be able to acquire the financial resources required for a major capacity expansion and may face substantial risks if its forecasts are incorrect. If the time period is long and aggregate demand exhibits steady growth, the facility will be under-utilized for a long period of time, since the level of capacity is planned for the end of the time horizon. Other disadvantages include new and unforeseen products and technology, government regulations, and other factors that may alter capacity requirements. Practical approaches to capacity planning focus on the amount, timing, and form of capacity changes.

Economies and Diseconomies of Scale

For a fixed facility size, the average unit production cost is

$$C = V + F/O$$

where V = variable production cost (constant for all levels of output, O)
        F = fixed costs of the system
        O = planned output rate

The model suggests that as output, O, increases, F/O decreases, because the fixed costs are spread over more units, resulting in lower total cost per unit. Increased utilization levels strain a facility, however, with undesirable consequences including the following:

○ Premium for overtime or temporary help.

○ Cost of expediting orders and express freight services.

○ Reduced customer service and quality, for example, incomplete and backlogged orders.

○ Tired workers and increased machine breakdowns.

This suggests that beyond some optimal point, costs will begin to increase. Larger facilities do provide some economies of scale: up to a point, larger facilities typically result in a lower cost per unit for products and services as illustrated in Figure 5.4. The figure shows the typical profile of average unit costs as a function of production volume for three potential plant sizes. For each, average total cost declines as utilization increases until the process reaches its actual capacity. Beyond the

OM PRINCIPLE

The optimal, or best, operating level of capacity is the lowest point on the cost curve, as a function of the anticipated volume. If demand is expected to grow or decline dynamically, however, a more thorough analysis that evaluates discounted costs over time should be done.

OM PRACTICE

OM at the Movies
Bigger is better in the cinema business.

The megaplex is here to stay. The average multiplex movie theater offers 5 screens, and some have as many as 30 screens. At a cost of over $30 million per complex, the screening business is restricted to the large firms that can afford such capital-intensive investments. With the number of screens growing at a faster rate than box-office grosses, the average take per screen is declining, making it vital to cut costs and generate revenues from other sources such as concession stands and games. AMC Theaters converted all of its theaters to 14- and 30-screen megaplexes at a cost of $509 million. New and upgraded facilities with babysitting services and cappuccino bars are intended to attract customers and induce them to stay longer (and spend more). As "economies of scale from size and regional concentration make consolidation all but inevitable," mergers are becoming common. Some 3 percent of the chains now control 60 percent of the screens.[18]

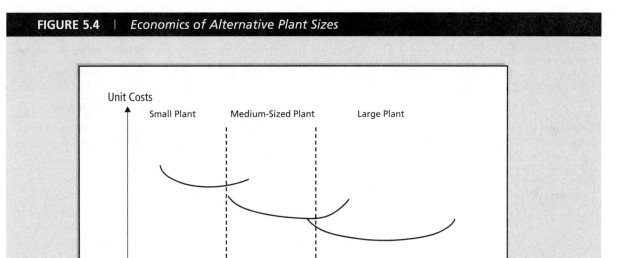

FIGURE 5.4 | *Economics of Alternative Plant Sizes*

optimal point, diseconomies of scale due to overextended resources drive up costs, offsetting the incremental benefits of additional production.

In addition, large facilities can have disadvantages resulting from diseconomies of scale. A larger workforce requires more supervisors and managers, leading to a larger bureaucracy. Large facilities can reduce the focus of the plant and lead to inefficiencies and loss of strategic position. If larger facilities must be located very far from some customers, the firm may incur increased logistics costs because of the larger lead-times required for transportation and the greater probability of delays. In addition, one large plant is more vulnerable to natural disasters, strikes, and future reductions in demand. With smaller facilities, a firm can sell off or realign the facilities much more easily.

Economies of scale are created by **static efficiency.** At any given point in time, the scale of operation affects the unit cost of production through three economies:

> **OM PRINCIPLE**
>
> Understanding the source of efficiency often helps operations managers more precisely estimate the impact of the amount of capacity acquired on costs.

1. Economies of volume, achieved through better allocation of the fixed cost.
2. Economies of capacity, achieved because of the indivisibility of resources.
3. Economies of technology, achieved because the organization can procure and implement more efficient (advanced) process technology.

An example of each is provided in Table 5.5.

Efficiencies are also derived over time as a firm builds more and more of a product; these **dynamic efficiencies** are best captured by a learning curve, as we discuss later in this chapter.

	Scale	Volume Produced	Cost per Unit	Explanation
TABLE 5.5		*Examples of Economies of Scale: Volume, Capacity, and Technology*		
	100 units	90 units	$1.11	Current scale, level of production, and cost
Economies of volume	100 units	100 units	$1.00	This cost reduction is due to the increased level of volume produced with the same capacity, thus spreading the fixed cost over a larger volume.
Economies of capacity	200 units	200 units	$0.90	This cost reduction is due to the ability of the organization to reduce overall fixed costs. For example, the firm may have to hire a purchasing manager who has only 20 hours of work with a scale of 100 units. With a scale of 200 units, the purchasing manager has 40 hours of work, and his or her salary is allocated over this larger volume. It is the indivisibility of resources (not being able to hire a part-time purchasing manager) that creates economies of capacity.
Economies of technology	400 units	400 units	$0.70	At a scale of 400 units, the organization can afford to procure more efficient technology, for example, a more automated machine, resulting in further reductions in the cost per unit.

The Capacity Planning Process

Figure 5.5 provides an overview of the strategic capacity planning process. The business plan sets the direction of the organization by specifying the types of goods or services that will be offered, and the forecast develops the needs for the whole organization. Typically, the forecast is best represented by the firm's quarterly projections. The forecast should take into account such factors as industry trends, the rate and direction of technological innovation, the likely behavior of competitors, and the impact of international markets and sources of supply. Note that capacity planning is not always for growth; sometimes downsizing is necessary. This can be an emotional decision, so the capacity planning process should include processes that can deal effectively with the human and organizational consequences of downsizing.

Forecasts of demand for goods and services must then be translated into a measure of capacity needed. For instance, from the forecast of product demand, a manufacturing firm might conclude that 2,400 machine hours will be needed in the milling department next year and that the number of machine hours needed will grow by 5 percent a year over the next five years. An airline might translate a forecast of demand for flight services into an estimate of the number of flight attendants needed to meet that level of demand.

Aggregate capacity plans must be translated into facility, equipment, and labor plans. Facility needs can be met by expanding or contracting existing facilities, constructing new facilities, or closing old ones. The firm needs to ask whether it should have one large facility or several smaller ones; where plants, warehouses, and so on should be located; and what the focus of each facility should be. Equipment needs might be met by purchasing additional machines or by replacing old machines with newer and faster technology. Hiring new workers or retraining present employees might meet labor needs. Automation issues have an impact on both equipment and labor needs.

Both equipment and labor plans must be consistent with the capacity and facility plans. Also, although they are not discussed here, the financial issues associated with meeting capacity requirements naturally influence the capacity plan. For example, at the Easton, Pennsylvania plant of Pfizer, Inc., a producer of industrial materials used in paints, plastics, foods, cosmetics, and other products, the long-term planning for plant facilities is done on a divisional basis. A computer model converts forecast product demand over a 10-year horizon into capacity needs by type of production process. Those needs are matched against current plant capacities so that capacity additions and cash requirements can be planned. The end result is a pro forma cash flow and profit/loss statement. Changes in the timing of capital additions are tested iteratively, as are different assumptions about the marketplace. The analysis is performed annually, and the result is the long-range capacity plan. Detailed capacity planning involves determining specific facility, equipment, and labor requirements for supporting the aggregate capacity needs identified through long-range forecasts.

FIGURE 5.5 | *The Strategic Capacity Planning Process*

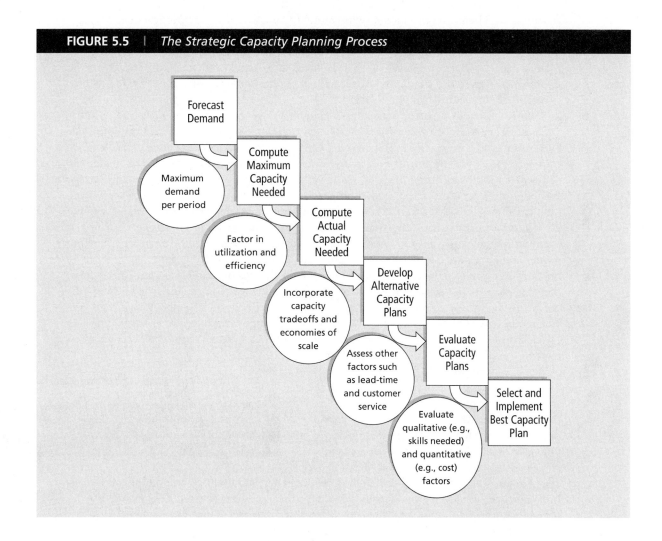

In balancing supply and demand for resources in the short term, it is useful to separate demand management from supply management. Demand management incorporates decisions that modify demand to bring it in line with available resources; examples of demand management include off-peak pricing to encourage demand in the slow period, complementary services that compensate for unavailable resources, and schedule-driven demand as created by appointment and reservation systems. Supply management involves changing the capacity available to accommodate variations in demand; examples include creating flexible capacity, using part-time help or temporary services, and outsourcing some services.

> **OM PRINCIPLE**
>
> Capacity is rarely in perfect balance with demand. Demand management attempts to change the demand while supply management tries to change the resource structure necessary to support variations in demand.

Capacity Planning in Services

Having adequate capacity is as vital for service organizations as for manufacturers, but capacity planning poses different problems for service organizations. In manufacturing, if demand is cyclical, shortages can usually be avoided by building up inventory during slow periods or arranging to subcontract production with another firm. A service organization does not have these options, although it can adjust capacity to some extent by scheduling additional staff during periods when demand is high. As in manufacturing organizations, it is important to balance capacity at various stages of a service process to avoid bottlenecks. In fact, balancing is probably even more important for service organizations—manufactured goods do not complain about waiting, but people do!

Before changing capacity, service and manufacturing organizations must make similar decisions. They must be concerned with the amount, timing, and form of capacity additions. It is easy to add the wrong kind of capacity for producing services. For instance, to increase passenger capacity, some airlines purchased jumbo jets. That turned out to be a poor strategic decision when competitors increased capacity by flying more frequently with smaller jets. Although their total capacity was the same in terms of seats per day, the airlines with more frequent flights provided better customer service and gained market share. Another strategic error a service organization can make is to increase only a portion of its service capacity. For example, if a hotel adds more rooms, it must also increase capacity in its restaurants, meeting rooms, and recreational facilities to accommodate a larger number of guests.

Service capacity decisions must be aligned with the customer service goals specified in the strategic plan. In a service organization, these generally relate to the location and the timing of demand since customers often expect immediate, convenient responses to their service requests. When you are hungry, your craving for a Big Mac can often be satisfied by one of McDonald's competitors if its service is closer to you. A bank's service reputation often depends on how quickly customers' transactions can be processed.

Service organizations can manage capacity in two ways: directly, by fixing resources or setting a schedule, or indirectly, by controlling the timing or rate of demand. As examples of the first approach, doctor's offices set appointment schedules based on physician availability, airlines publish a calendar of plane arrivals and departures, and pizza delivery chains adjust cooks and drivers during peak weekend demand times. As an example of the second approach, airlines manage demand through pricing policies (see the *OM Practice* box on revenue management). If a firm does not or cannot influence its customers' demand, then it must maintain sufficient capacity to accommodate anticipated demand.

> **OM PRINCIPLE**
>
> Service capacity depends not only on the scheduling of resources available to the firm, but also on how the firm manages and influences demand.

OM PRACTICE

Revenue Management as a Capacity Strategy

Revenue management has enabled the airlines to maximize revenue and profits by stratifying and segmenting the market.

For service industries, revenue management (originally known as yield management) is the process of allocating the right type of capacity, to the right kind of customer, at the right price, in order to maximize revenue or yield. The objective is to balance capacity in relation to demand, while maximizing the sales price for each unit. In other words, revenue management is a way for companies to maximize capacity and profitability by balancing supply and demand through price management. Pioneered by the airlines 20 years ago, revenue management has been successfully used in numerous other industries, including utilities, cruise lines, trucking companies, amusement parks, hotels, and rental car companies. A revenue management system is not appropriate for all industries, however. For such a system to be effective, the industry must have six characteristics:

1. *The product or service is perishable.* At some point, the product becomes worthless because it can no longer be sold, and it cannot be held in inventory for future demand, generally because the time of its availability has passed. For example, once an airplane has taken off, its empty seat cannot be sold.

2. *Capacity of the product is limited.* A fixed amount of product is available, and additional inventory cannot be added without a long lead-time, a significant amount of capital, or both. For example, a hotel has a certain number of rooms and cannot add more without costly, lengthy construction. However, airlines can move planes to differ-

ent routes temporarily when demand is high or low.

3. *The industry faces segmented markets.* The nature of the product is such that it can be priced to appeal to and target different market segments. The time of purchase is often used to segment markets. The airlines are a prime example of market segmentation. All airline seats on a given flight within the same class are the same, but the airlines have implemented a segmentation strategy that differentiates customers who are willing and able to pay higher prices from those who are willing to change their behavior in exchange for a lower price. In other words, if you are price sensitive, you book your ticket well in advance of the flight; if you are not price sensitive, you wait until it is convenient for you to book your ticket.

4. *The product or service can be sold in advance.* Often this is done through reservation systems that, when combined with other technologies, enable the firm to forecast and manipulate demand and pricing.

5. *The variable costs of the product are low.* An incremental sale does not cost the vendor much, but enables the product to be sold at a wide range of prices rather than letting it spoil and go unsold. For example, a hotel operation has high fixed costs and relatively low variable costs. Therefore once it has reached the break-even point with respect to the fixed costs, any revenue generated in excess of the variable costs will go toward profits.

6. *Demand for the product varies over time.* Revenue management can help to smooth the demand curve by stimulating demand during low demand times and increasing revenue during high demand times.[19]

Table 5.6 outlines some parameters and illustrates how they are different in three industries that use revenue management extensively. It points out the differences in demand management (for example, extent of discounting and number of different prices per unit) and supply management (number of capacity types, mobility and duration of resources) across the three industries.

The Role of Forecasting in Capacity Planning

Forecasting is used in many OM applications. Consider a consumer products company, such as Procter & Gamble or Colgate-Palmolive, that makes many different products in various sizes. Long-range forecasts might be expressed in total sales dollars for use in financial planning by top managers. At lower organizational levels, however, managers of the various product groups need aggregate forecasts of sales volume for their products in units that are more meaningful to them—for example, pounds of a certain type of soap—to establish production

TABLE 5.6	*Examples of Revenue Management in Service Businesses*

Parameter	Airline	Hotel	Car Rental
Unit of capacity	Seat	Room	Car
Number of capacity types	2–3 (coach, first class, business class)	2–10 or more (single, double, suite, etc.)	5–20 or more (subcompact, compact, midsize, SUV, etc.)
Amount of capacity per location	Fixed	Fixed	Variable
Mobility	Small	None	Considerable
Pricing structure	3–7 or more (30-day advance, 7-day advance fares, etc.)	2–3 or more ("rack" room, weekend, corporate price, etc.)	4–20 or more; numerous discounts from corporations, travel partners, professional organizations, etc.
Duration of use	Fixed	Variable	Variable
Corporate discounts	Occasional	Yes	Yes
How capacity is managed	Centrally	Centrally or locally	Centrally, regionally, or locally

Source: Adapted from W. J. Carol and R. C. Grimes, "Evolutionary Change in Product Management: Experiences in the Car Rental Industry," *Interfaces* 25, no. 5 (1995): 84–104.

plans. Finally, managers of individual manufacturing facilities need forecasts by brand and size—for instance, the number of 64-ounce boxes of Tide—to plan material purchase and production schedules. Service organizations have some unique characteristics that affect forecasting. For instance, demand in many service industries, such as the airline and hotel industries, is highly seasonal. Demand for services may also vary with the day of the week or the time of day. Grocery stores, banks, and similar organizations need very short-term forecasts to schedule work shifts and route vehicles and make other operating decisions to accommodate variations in demand. Forecasting demand is especially critical for good capacity planning in both the long and the short term (see the *OM Practice* box on American Hoist and Derrick).

Various statistical and judgmental techniques are available to assist in forecasting (see the Tools and Techniques supplement on the CD-ROM). Surveys of practicing managers reveal that they rely more on judgmental methods of forecasting than on quantitative methods, although they are very familiar with many quantitative approaches. Quantitative forecasts often are adjusted judgmentally as managers incorporate environmental knowledge that is not captured in quantitative models. When no historical data are available, only judgmental forecasting is possible. But even when historical data are available and appropriate, they cannot be the sole basis for prediction.

The demand for products and services is affected by a variety of factors such as interest rates, inflation, and other economic conditions. Competitors' actions and government regulations also have an impact. Thus, some element of judgmental forecasting is always necessary. An interesting example of the role of judgmental forecasting occurred during the recession of the mid-1970s. All economic indicators pointed toward low demand for machine tools in the future. Nonetheless, the forecasters at one machine tool company recognized that new government regulations on automobile pollution control would require the auto industry to purchase new tools. As a result, this company was prepared for the new business.

OM PRACTICE

American Hoist and Derrick
Accurate forecasting is a crucial element of American Hoist and Derrick's capacity planning process.

American Hoist and Derrick is a manufacturer of construction equipment. Its sales forecast is an actual planning figure and is used to develop the master production schedule, cash flow projections, and workforce plans. As part of the forecasting process, the company uses the Delphi method of judgmental forecasting.

This method was adopted initially because top managers wanted an accurate five-year forecast of sales to plan for expansion of production capacity. They used the Delphi method in conjunction with regression models and exponential smoothing to generate the forecast. A panel of 23 key personnel was established, consisting of persons who had been making subjective forecasts, those who had been using or were affected by the forecasts, and those who had a strong knowledge of the market and corporate sales. Three rounds of the Delphi method were performed;

each requested estimates of gross national product, shipments of the construction equipment industry, shipments of American Hoist and Derrick's construction equipment group, and the value of American Hoist and Derrick's shipments. As the Delphi technique progressed, responses for each round were collected, analyzed, summarized, and reported back to the panel. The third-round questionnaire included not only the responses of the first two rounds, but also additional related facts, figures, and views of external experts.

As a result of the Delphi experiment, the sales forecast error was less than 0.33 percent; in the following year, the error was under 4 percent. Those levels represented considerable improvement over previous forecast errors of plus or minus 20 percent. In fact, the Delphi forecasts were more accurate than regression models or exponential smoothing, which had forecast errors of 10 to 15 percent. As another benefit of the exercise, managers developed a uniform outlook on business conditions and corporate sales volume and thus had a common base for decision making.[20]

5.4 TIMING OF CAPACITY DECISIONS

The timing of capacity decisions is complicated by the fact that capacity cannot be acquired instantaneously: it takes time to build facilities, hire people, train them, and make the facility fully functional for delivery of products and services. Two factors critically affect the time needed to acquire capacity:

OM PRINCIPLE

Changing capacity at the right time is critical. Delays in capacity expansion may result in losses of market share, but adding too much capacity too quickly or failing to decrease excess capacity can saddle the firm with underutilized resources and poor financial results.

○ **The Lead-Time Required to Make and Implement the Decision:** Capacity acquisition requires money, and such capital expenditures typically go though some formal approval process that has been set up to prevent excessive risk taking by overzealous managers. In addition, external regulations, such as environmental concerns and zoning requirements, increase the length of time it takes to get facilities operational.

○ **The Lead-Time for Facility Construction and Ramp-Up:** Designing, constructing, and setting up the infrastructure to bring a facility up to speed can take from one month to 10 years. This includes hiring and training workers, developing a network of suppliers, and setting up delivery, distribution, and quality assurance systems.

Lead, Lag, and Saddle Strategies

Figure 5.6 shows three basic capacity expansion strategies: straddle, lead, and lag. A firm chooses a strategy based on the needs of its customers and its strategy for meeting those needs.

The three strategies are driven by two simplifying assumptions: (1) capacity is added in "chunks," or discrete increments, and (2) demand is steadily increasing. Though demand for mature products and commodities may exhibit a linear growth trend, newer products often grow in rising and falling patterns driven by their product life cycles.

OM PRINCIPLE

In an expanding market, firms either implicitly or explicitly adopt one of three basic capacity expansion strategies—straddle, lead, and lag—as shown in Figure 5.6.

The first strategy (Figure 5.6a), called a **capacity straddle strategy,** matches capacity additions with demand as closely as possible. It calls for capacity expansions only when managers expect that they can sell at least some of the additional output, but before they know that they can sell it all. When the capacity curve is above the demand curve, the firm has excess capacity; when the capacity curve is below the demand curve, it has insufficient capacity to meet demand. During periods of capacity shortage, there are several alternatives. The firm can lose sales opportunities and possibly lose market share, or it can make short-term capacity expansions through subcontracting, overtime, additional shifts, and so forth. It seems clear that a firm that follows this strategy must maintain some volume flexibility in the short term to provide for excess (or a shortfall in) capacity within each capacity expansion. Riding the "saddle" strategy is difficult for firms that must add capacity in large increments. For example, automobile assembly plants are not economically feasible below a volume of 300 cars per day (75,000 cars per year), limiting the use of the saddle strategy. If demand for a model grows by 25,000 cars per year, three years will have to pass before an assembly plant expands capacity.

A firm employs a **capacity lead** or "expansionist" **strategy** (Figure 5.6b) when it invests in capacity in advance of demand to eliminate the chance of losing sales to competitors. It believes that the risks due to losses in market share far outweigh the financial risk of having excess (and unneeded) capacity. The economic tradeoff requires that incremental profits from making those sales exceed the incremental costs of operating the facility below full capacity. As an alternative, the firm may value its current customers so highly that it invests in the extra capacity despite the cost in order to protect its customer service reputation. Since the firm always has excess capacity, it has a cushion, as described earlier, against unexpected large orders or new customers. This cushion also enables the firm to provide good customer service, and backorders will rarely occur.

FIGURE 5.6 | *Three Capacity Expansion Strategies: (a) Matching Capacity with Demand, (b) Excess Capacity Policy, (c) Capacity Shortage Policy*

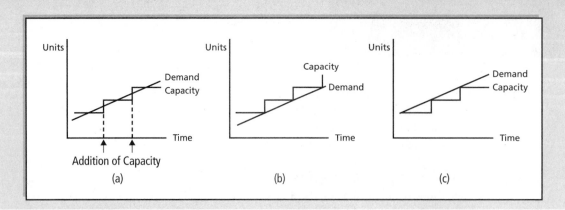

A **capacity lag** or "wait and see" **strategy** (Figure 5.6c) calls for capacity changes only after confirming changes in demand in order to maintain a high utilization rate. The firm believes that the risks associated with *ex ante* expansion of capacity are greater than the risks associated with market share losses should it not have enough capacity. In the long run, such a policy can lead to a permanent loss of market position. This strategy requires less investment and provides for high capacity utilization and thus a higher rate of return on investment; it is often used by firms that produce either a homogeneous commodity or a standard product that appeals to customers based primarily on cost. This choice makes the important assumption that customers will return after buying from competitors when the firm cannot fill their needs. However, this strategy can also reduce long-term profitability through overtime and productivity losses that occur as the firm scrambles to satisfy demand.

> **OM PRINCIPLE**
>
> For any capacity strategy, the firm has the option of making either frequent, small capacity increments or infrequent, large increments. This decision should be based on careful economic analysis of the cost and risks associated with excess capacity and capacity shortages.

In choosing a strategy, the ability and desire of the firm to make short-term capacity adjustments must also be taken into account. Finally, one must consider learning effects. For instance, larger volumes of operation in a capacity lead strategy result in a faster accumulation of learning, which drives down cost. The product or service is thus made affordable to a larger market, driving up volumes further. Firms that intend to dominate markets for products and services through volume and market share obviously find this approach very attractive. However, a major change in technology or market downturn will cause this strategy to backfire.

One problem in justifying incremental additions to existing capacity is projecting the revenue for additional capacity acquired. Lacking concrete demand data, many firms use historical utilization (utilization of existing capacity) to project revenues. This can result in serious problems, especially if the firm operates with seasonal demand.

Consider the capacity expansion problem for a firm that has an average demand of 100 customers per month but high seasonality in two months—June and July (see Figure 5.7). The firm has a capacity of handling 150 customers per month and is investigating a capacity addition to increase this figure to 200. With a total demand of 1,210 customers for the entire year and a total capacity of 1,800, the firm has an average utilization level of 67.22 percent

> **OM PRINCIPLE**
>
> Capacity expansions can be justified on the basis of incremental revenue, but the incremental revenue should be calculated based on forecast utilization of capacity as opposed to historical utilization of capacity.

(1,210/1,800). One assumption the firm could make at this stage is that additional capacity would operate at this utilization level, resulting in additional net revenues from an additional $50 \times 0.6722 = 33.61$ customers every month. This translates to $12 \times 33.61 = 403$ additional customers every year. This is erroneous, however: by looking at the graph, we can see that unless demand increases substantially, the additional resources will be utilized in only two months—July and August—or a paltry 16.7 percent of the year. The additional capacity will serve *only* the 100 customers who are now turned away in the months of July and August—not 404 as calculated above.

For firms operating with seasonal, monthly, weekly, or daily variations in demand, expanding capacity to meet all demand becomes increasingly difficult; much of the capacity will remain unused except during periods of peak demand.

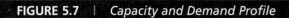

FIGURE 5.7 | *Capacity and Demand Profile*

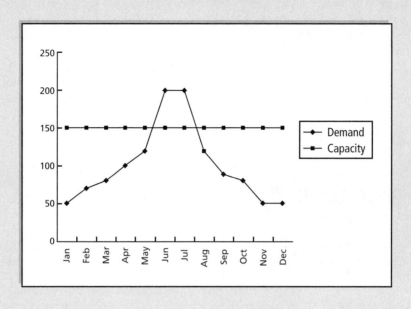

Learning and Capacity Requirements

If you have ever learned to type or play a musical instrument, you know that the longer and more often you work at it, the better you become. The same is true in production and assembly operations, as was recognized in the 1920s at Wright-Patterson Air Force Base in the assembly of aircraft. Studies showed that about 80 percent as many labor hours were required to produce the fourth plane as were required for the second; the eighth plane took only 80 percent as much time as the fourth; the sixteenth plane 80 percent as much time as the eighth, and so on. As production doubles from x units to $2x$ units, the time per unit of the $2x$th unit is 80 percent of the time of the xth unit. This is called an 80 percent **learning curve.** Such a curve exhibits a steep initial decline and then levels off as workers become more proficient in their tasks.

Learning curves can apply to individual operators or, in an aggregate sense, to the entire process for a new product. The terms *improvement curve* and *experience curve* are often used to describe the learning phenomenon in the aggregate context. Those curves can be used for cost estimating and pricing, short-term work scheduling, and setting

OM PRINCIPLE

When a learning curve is present, capacity is implicitly increased without changing the physical facilities. Failure to understand the effects of learning can result in unanticipated overcapacity.

manufacturing performance goals in addition to capacity planning. Learning-curve theory is most applicable to new products or processes that have a high potential for improvement and whose benefits will be realized only when appropriate incentives and effective motivational tools are used. See *Supplementary Notes 5.1* on the CD-ROM for a discussion of the mathematics of learning curves.

5.1

Summary of Key Points

- Facilities and capacity planning represent important strategic decisions that affect the ability of operations to support an organization's objectives. Facility and capacity changes typically result from changes in products, markets, or processes or the emergence of new ones; they often follow the evolution of the product life cycle.

- Facility charters set the focus for what is to be accomplished in a facility, its capacity requirements, and when capacity changes should take place. This entails defining the core competency, breadth of products and services, and span of process associated with the facility.

- Facilities are often "focused" by establishing priorities on which to excel. The focus might be on products, processes, markets, volumes, or priorities. Facilities may also be segmented into smaller components, each with a unique charter to focus it appropriately for competitive advantage.

- Vertical integration—which processes are performed within a facility and which are outsourced—is a key facilities decision. Too much or too little vertical integration can result in competitive disadvantages, so this decision should be addressed from a strategic perspective. The growth of outsourcing has been attributed to a loss of focus in facility charters.

- Mix flexibility (the ability to change products quickly) and volume flexibility (the ability to "ramp up" and "ramp down" quickly and efficiently with changes in demand) can provide important sources of competitive advantage.

- Capacity planning involves carefully balancing the needs of the market with resource efficiency and utilization to ensure the right quantity of goods or services at the right time and with the best use of available resources. Capacity can be measured in a variety of ways; the most common is the rate of output per unit of time. Theoretical, planned, and actual capacity measures allow operations managers to better manage resources to meet customer demand. Utilization and efficiency are related measures for evaluating resource usage.

- Capacity is often adjusted as market conditions change. A capacity cushion is often maintained to guard against sudden increases in demand. The best operating level of capacity is the lowest point on the production cost curve, as a function of the anticipated volume. Facility size decisions should account for economies of volume, capacity, and technology.

- Capacity planning includes using demand forecasts to compute maximum and actual capacity needed, developing and evaluating alternative capacity plans, and selecting the best capacity plan. Capacity planning is different for services than for manufacturing because service firms do not have inventories of goods that can be stored and must account for peak demand and customer service goals. This is usually accomplished either by adjusting resources or schedules or by trying to influence customer demand.

- Forecasting is an important input for capacity planning at all levels of an organization. Various statistical and judgmental tools are available to establish useful forecasts.

- Three key timing strategies for adjusting capacity are straddle (matching capacity to demand), lead (investing in capacity in advance of demand), and lag (expanding or decreasing capacity after demand changes). Each has different advantages and disadvantages. A strategy should be selected by analyzing the economics and risks associated with excess capacity and shortages.

- Learning can affect capacity requirements and calculations and should be considered when appropriate.

Questions for Review and Discussion

1. Explain the strategic importance of facilities and capacity in manufacturing and service firms.
2. Why are facilities constructed or modified? Explain how the product life cycle influences these decisions.
3. What are the three basic questions that facilities and capacity decisions involve?
4. What is a facility charter? Why is it important? What issues must be considered in specifying a facility charter?
5. Why is facility focus important to an organization? Discuss some approaches for focusing facilities and their advantages and disadvantages.
6. What are vertical integration and outsourcing? What issues must a firm consider in making vertical integration and outsourcing decisions? What tradeoffs must be evaluated?
7. What are mix and volume flexibility? How can they create competitive advantage?
8. What is the purpose of capacity planning?
9. Explain how to measure capacity. What is the difference between load and capacity?
10. Define theoretical, planned, and actual capacity and explain how they differ.
11. What is utilization? How does it differ from efficiency?
12. What tradeoffs must a firm make in developing a long-range capacity plan?
13. Explain the concept of a capacity cushion. What practical implications does it have for capacity planning?
14. How do economies and diseconomies of scale affect capacity planning?
15. How do economies of volume, economies of capacity, and economies of technology affect costs and operations?
16. Describe the generic capacity planning process. What specific activities must be performed?
17. How does capacity planning differ for manufacturing and service firms?
18. What issues affect the timing of capacity decisions?
19. Explain lead, lag, and straddle strategies for capacity expansion. What advantages and disadvantages does each have?
20. How do learning curves affect capacity decisions?
21. An automobile transmission assembly plant normally operates one shift per day five days per week. During each shift, 400 transmissions can be completed. Over the next four weeks, the plant has planned shipments according to the following schedule:

Week	1	2	3	4
Shipments	1,800	1,700	2,000	2,100

   a. What is the plant's theoretical capacity?

   b. At what percentage of capacity is the plant actually operating?

22. The roller coaster at an amusement park consists of 15 cars, each of which can carry up to three passengers. If each run takes 1.5 minutes and the time to unload and load riders is 3.5 minutes, what is the maximum capacity of the system in number of passengers per hour? Would the actual capacity equal that value? Explain.
23. A pizza-making process consists of (1) preparing the pizza, (2) baking it, and (3) cutting and boxing (or transferring to a platter for dine-in service). It takes five minutes to prepare a pizza, eight minutes to bake it, and one minute to cut and box or transfer. If the restaurant has only one preparer, what is the theoretical capacity of the pizza-making operation? What if two preparers are available? Will this change the bottleneck?

24. A grocery store has five regular checkout lines and one express line (12 items or less). Based on a sampling study, it takes 11 minutes on average for a customer to go through the regular line and 4 minutes to go through the express line. The store is open from 9 a.m. to 9 p.m. daily.

    a. What is the store's maximum capacity?
    b. What is the capacity if the regular checkout lines operate according to the schedule in the table below? (The express line is always open.)

Hours/Day	Mon	Tue	Wed	Thur	Fri	Sat	Sun
9–12	1	1	1	1	3	5	2
12–4	2	2	2	2	3	5	4
4–6	3	3	3	3	5	3	2
6–9	4	4	4	4	5	3	1

25. A company manufactures four products on three machines. The table below shows the production schedule for the next six months.

Production Schedule

Product	Jan	Feb	Mar	Apr	May	Jun
1	200	0	200	0	200	0
2	100	100	100	100	100	100
3	50	50	50	50	50	50
4	100	0	100	0	100	0

The next table gives the number of hours each product requires on each machine.

Hours/Product/Machine

	PRODUCT			
Machine	1	2	3	4
1	0.25	0.15	0.15	0.25
2	0.33	0.20	0.30	0.50
3	0.20	0.30	0.25	0.10

Setup times are roughly 20 percent of the operation times. The next table gives the machine hours available during the six months.

Machine Hours Available

Machine	Jan	Feb	Mar	Apr	May	Jun
1	120	60	60	60	60	60
2	180	60	180	60	180	60
3	120	60	120	60	120	60

Determine whether there is enough capacity to meet the product demand.

26. Ships arrive at an unloading dock at the rate of four every hour from 7 a.m. to 12 noon. They are unloaded in 30 minutes starting at 9 a.m. and stopping at 7 p.m. Ships waiting to be unloaded use up valuable port space, so the port authority has increased demurrage charges from $500 per hour to $1,000 per hour that the ship is docked. The shipping firm is considering two proposals: (a) a capacity increase that would allow a ship to be unloaded in 20 minutes at a cost of $1 million, and (b) beginning the unloading process

at 7 a.m., which would involve intense renegotiations of the labor contract (and a possible strike). However, workers are willing to start at 7 a.m. if they are paid overtime wages (cost = $60,000 per day) from 7 a.m. to 9 a.m. Plot graphs of the number of ships that have arrived, number waiting, and number unloaded as a function of time for the current scenario and both proposals. Compute and compare the total demurrage charges. What impacts do the proposals have?

Internet Projects

To find Web links to carry out each of the following projects, go to the text's Web site at **http://raturi_evans.swlearning.com.**

1. Visit the Web site for *Building Operations Management* magazine. Read the article "Taking the long view of facilities" in the March 2001 issue. Comment on the importance of an effective facilities strategy for a university.

2. The personal computer industry typifies economies of scale. Most PC components are produced in such large quantities that the final price to the user drops far below the off-the-shelf price of the individual chips, connectors, and other hardware. Visit the Web site for Airborn Electronics and summarize the main arguments for economies of scale. Contrast this with the diseconomies of scale in the U.S. public transport bus operations. What are the main sources of economies and diseconomies of scale from an operations perspective?

3. Airlines may use either a hub and spoke network or a point-to-point network, as shown in Figure 5.8. Visit the links to the Web sites to find different perspectives on the capacity implications of these systems.

   Summarize the main capacity implications of both networks. In your summary include the implications of both models for the following:

   a. Number and size of aircraft.

   b. Number and capacity of airports.

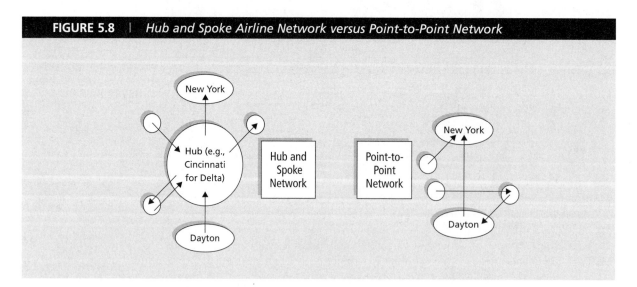

FIGURE 5.8 | *Hub and Spoke Airline Network versus Point-to-Point Network*

  c. Number and size of gates at airports.

  d. Capacity of baggage-handling systems.

  e. Capacity of ancillary services (e.g., short-term and long-term parking lots, restaurant and shopping services at airports, and airport shuttles).

4. At the Web site that summarizes the Toyota facilities in Japan, examine the table entitled "Production Sites and Sales Network in Japan," which shows where different Toyota models are produced. What logic is used in establishing facility charters in Toyota plants? You will need some familiarity with Toyota car models to understand the names of cars, particularly those marketed outside the United States. (Note that like other auto manufacturing firms, Toyota makes a number of key components in affiliated company plants.)

EXPERIENCE OM

Volume Flexibility in a Facilities Network

This exercise demonstrates the concept of volume flexibility in a multiple product, multiple plant network.[21] It allows the participants to do the following:

1. Understand the relationship between capacity utilization and service levels as measured by the probability of a stockout and fill rate.
2. Understand how multiple plant networks create flexibility.
3. Develop a working definition of flexibility (specifically, volume flexibility).
4. Understand the concept of chaining and how limited flexibility gives almost the same results as complete flexibility.

Work in groups of four to five students and answer the questions following the problem description.

Scenario 1 Two Products and Two Plants
Your firm makes two products, A and B, in two plants, 1 and 2. The demand for products A and B is independent and identically distributed and could be 5, 10, or 15 with probability 1/3 each. Each plant has 10 units of capacity.

○ **Case 1:** The plants have no product flexibility (that is, plant 1 makes product A and plant 2 makes product B only). What is the probability of meeting the demand for products A and B? What is the fill rate of products A and B? (The fill rate is the amount of demand met divided by the expected demand.)

○ **Case 2:** The plants have complete flexibility (that is, plant 1 and plant 2 can make both products A and B). Thus, when demand for product A is 15 and demand for product B is 5, plant 1 makes 10 A and plant 2 makes 5 B and 5 A. What is the probability of meeting demand for products A and B? What is the fill rate of products A and B?

Scenario 2 Four Products and Four Plants
Now consider a four-product, four-plant network. Use the same demand data as before (each product has a demand of 5, 10, or 15 with probability 1/3 each). The capacity of each plant is 10. Analyze the configurations below.

○ **Case 1:** No flexibility: each plant produces a single product.

○ **Case 2:** Full flexibility: each plant has the capability to produce all four products.

The following table should help you analyze the data.

Total Demand	Realizations by Product	Frequency	Total
20	(5,5,5,5)	1	1
25	(5,5,5,10)	4	4
30	(5,5,5,15) or (5,5,10,10)	4 + 6	10
35	(5,5,10,15) or (5,10,10,10)	12 + 4	16
40	(10,10,10,10) or (5,5,15,15) or (5,10,10,15)	1 + 6 + 12	19
45	(10,10,10,15) or (5,10,15,15)	4 + 12	16
50	(10,10,15,15) or (5,15,15,15)	6 + 4	10
55	(10,15,15,15)	4	4
60	(15,15,15,15)	1	1

○ **Case 3:** Partial flexibility: in this case, the products and plants are "chained." Plant 1 can make products A and B, plant 2 can make B and C, plant 3 can make C and D, and plant 4 can make D and A. *Hint:* In this case the only situations to analyze are (5,5,10,15), (5,5,15,15), and (5,10,10,15). Find out which combinations result in a stockout. There are 3 such cases out of 12 in (5,5,10,15), 4 out of 6 in (5,5,15,15), and 8 out of 12 in (5,10,10,15).

Quality Management

In 1887, William Cooper Procter, grandson of the founder of Procter & Gamble, told his employees, "The first job we have is to turn out quality merchandise that consumers will buy and keep on buying. If we produce it efficiently and economically, we will earn a profit, in which you will share." Procter's statement addresses three issues that are critical to operations managers: productivity, cost, and quality. Of these, the most significant in determining the long-run success or failure of any organization is quality. High-quality goods and services can provide an organization with a competitive edge; reduce costs due to returns, rework, and scrap; increase productivity, profits, and other measures of success; and, most importantly, generate satisfied customers, who will reward the organization with continued patronage and favorable word-of-mouth advertising. **Quality management** refers to the policies and procedures used to ensure that goods and services are produced with appropriate levels of quality to meet the needs of customers. The concept of quality is fundamental to all business operations.

This chapter focuses on the philosophy of modern quality management. Specifically, we address:

- Different perspectives on defining quality (*Section 6.1*).
- A brief history of the quality movement and its impact on operations (*Section 6.2*).
- The fundamental principles of total quality (*Section 6.3*).
- The philosophies of Deming, Juran, and Crosby (*Section 6.4*).
- Quality management frameworks, in particular the Baldrige Award, ISO 9000, and Six Sigma (*Section 6.5*).
- Systems for quality control (*Section 6.6*).
- Quality improvement (*Section 6.7*).

Material on the CD-ROM discusses some useful tools and techniques for quality management.

11. The Seven QC Tools
12. Poka-Yoke
13. Process Capability Analysis
14. Statistical Process Control (necessary for the Experience OM exercise).

6.1 DEFINING QUALITY

Quality can be a confusing concept, partly because people view quality in relation to differing criteria based on their individual roles in the organization. In addition, the meaning of quality has evolved as the quality profession has grown and matured. Neither consultants nor business professionals agree on a universal definition. A study that asked managers of 86 firms in the eastern United States to define quality produced several dozen different responses, including perfection, consistency, eliminating waste, speed of delivery, compliance with policies and procedures, providing a good, usable product, doing it right the first time, delighting or pleasing customers, and total customer service and satisfaction.[1] For an operations manager, however, design quality and conformance quality are of particular importance.

A product's **design quality** is an output of the firm's product innovation process. This process involves first understanding the needs and wants of customers and, then, developing products and delivery processes that are capable of meeting and exceeding those expectations. A Cadillac and a Jeep Cherokee serve different needs of different groups of customers. If you want a highway-touring vehicle with luxury amenities, then a Cadillac might be your choice. If you want a vehicle for camping, fishing, or skiing trips, a Jeep might be better.

Conformance quality measures the extent to which a process is able to deliver a product that conforms to the product's design specifications. **Specifications** are targets and tolerances determined by designers of products and services. Targets are the ideal values for which production is to strive; **tolerances** are the permissible variation. As Chapter 3 explained, tolerances are specified because designers recognize that it is impossible to meet targets all of the time in manufacturing. For example, if a part dimension is specified as "0.236 ± 0.003 cm," then any dimension in the range 0.233 to 0.239 centimeters is deemed acceptable and is said to conform to specifications. Specifications also apply to services. For example, "on-time arrival" for an airplane might be specified as within 15 minutes of the scheduled arrival time. The target is the scheduled time, and the tolerance is specified to be 15 minutes. FedEx's guarantee that every package is delivered by 10:30 a.m. each business day clearly establishes a target with a zero tolerance of being late.

It is vital to focus quality improvement efforts on *both* design and conformance, as shown in Figure 6.1. A product's value in the marketplace is influenced by the quality of its design. Improvements in design will differentiate the product from its competitors, improve a firm's reputation for quality, and improve the perceived value of the product. This allows the company to command higher prices as well as to increase its market share. This in turn leads to increased revenues, which offset the costs of improving the design.

> **OM PRINCIPLE**
>
> In today's global marketplace, the absence of defects is regarded as the price of entry, rather than a source of competitive advantage. Competitive success now depends on such attributes as the speed of new product development, flexibility in production and delivery, and extraordinary customer service.

The integration of design and conformance quality is summarized by a powerful, customer-driven definition of quality. *Quality is meeting or exceeding customer expectations.* Customers may be consumers, external customers, or internal customers. For instance, Wal-Mart is an external customer of Procter & Gamble, and an assembly department is an internal customer of the machining department. By viewing linkages among consumers and external and internal customers, one can easily characterize a firm's value chain and identify the key value-added processes on which the firm should focus.

Customer expectations can be understood by considering the different dimensions of quality as suggested by David A. Garvin:[2]

1. **Performance:** A product's primary operating characteristics. For an automobile, these would include such things as acceleration, braking distance, steering, and handling.
2. **Features:** A product's "bells and whistles." A car may have engine options, a tape or CD deck, antilock brakes, and power seats.

FIGURE 6.1 | *Quality and Profitability*

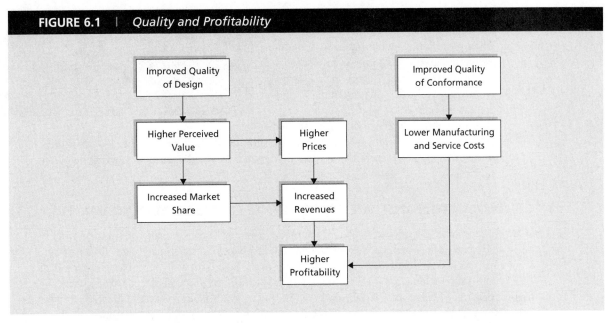

3. **Reliability:** The probability of a product's surviving over a specified period of time under stated conditions of use. A car's ability to start on cold days and frequency of failures are reliability factors.

4. **Conformance:** The degree to which a product's physical and performance characteristics match preestablished standards. A car's fit and finish and freedom from noises and squeaks can reflect this.

5. **Durability:** The amount of use one gets from a product before it physically deteriorates or until replacement is preferable. For a car, this might include corrosion resistance and the long wear of upholstery fabric.

6. **Serviceability:** The speed, courtesy, and competence of repair work. For an automobile, this might include access to spare parts, the number of miles between major maintenance services, and the expense of service.

7. **Aesthetics:** How a product looks, feels, sounds, tastes, or smells. A car's color, instrument panel design, control placement, and "feel of the road," for example, may make it aesthetically pleasing.

For services, research has shown that five key dimensions of quality contribute to customer perceptions:

1. **Reliability:** The ability to provide what was promised, dependably and accurately. Examples include customer service representatives responding in the promised time, following customer instructions, providing error-free invoices and statements, and making repairs correctly the first time.

2. **Assurance:** The knowledge and courtesy of employees and their ability to convey trust and confidence. Examples include answering questions accurately, being able to do the necessary work, monitoring credit card transactions to avoid possible fraud, and being polite and pleasant during customer transactions.

3. **Tangibles:** The physical facilities and equipment and the appearance of personnel. Tangibles include attractive facilities, appropriately dressed employees, and well-designed forms that are easy to read and interpret.

4. **Empathy:** The degree of caring and individual attention provided to customers. Examples include willingness to schedule deliveries at the customer's convenience, explaining technical jargon in layperson's language, and recognizing regular customers by name.

> **OM PRINCIPLE**
>
> Understanding the product and service dimensions of quality helps organizations to focus on the most important customer requirements and better manage the processes that create customer value.

5. **Responsiveness:** The willingness to help customers and provide prompt service. Examples include acting quickly to resolve problems, promptly crediting returned merchandise, and rapidly replacing defective products.

6.2 EVOLUTION AND IMPORTANCE OF QUALITY MANAGEMENT

Why the emphasis on quality? It helps to review a bit of history. Quality assurance, usually associated with some form of measurement and inspection activity, has been an important aspect of production operations throughout history.[3] Egyptian wall paintings from around 1450 B.C. show evidence of measurement and inspection. Stones for the pyramids were cut so precisely that even today it is impossible to put a knife blade between the blocks. The Egyptians' success was due to their consistent use of well-developed methods and procedures and precise measuring devices.

During the industrial revolution, the use of interchangeable parts and the separation of work into small tasks necessitated careful control of quality, leading to the need for inspection to identify and remove defects. Eventually, companies created separate quality departments. This artificial separation of production workers from responsibility for quality assurance led to indifference to quality among both workers and their managers. During World War II, many quality specialists were trained to use statistical tools, and the manufacturing industries gradually adopted statistical quality control. Nonetheless, because upper managers had delegated so much responsibility for quality to others, they knew little about quality, and when the quality crisis hit years later, they were ill prepared to deal with it. Concluding that quality was the responsibility of the quality department, many managers turned their attention to output quantity and efficiency because of the shortage of civilian goods.

During this time, two U.S. consultants, Dr. Joseph Juran and Dr. W. Edwards Deming, introduced statistical quality control techniques to the Japanese to aid them in their rebuilding efforts. A significant part of their educational activity was focused on upper management, rather than quality specialists alone. With the support of top managers, the Japanese integrated quality throughout their organizations and developed a culture of continuous improvement. Improvements in Japanese quality were slow and steady; some 20 years passed before the quality of Japanese products exceeded that of Western manufacturers. By the 1970s, primarily due to the higher quality of their products, Japanese companies had significantly penetrated Western markets. Most major U.S. companies answered the wake-up call by instituting extensive quality improvement campaigns, focused both on conformance and on improving design quality. One vice president of corporate productivity and quality summed up the situation by quoting Dr. Samuel Johnson: "Nothing concentrates a man's mind so wonderfully as the prospect of being hanged in the morning."

As organizations began to integrate quality principles into their management systems, the notion of **total quality management,** or **TQM,** became popular. Quality took on a new meaning of organization-wide performance excellence, rather than an engineering-based technical discipline, and permeated services, health care, education, and government.

OM PRINCIPLE

Failures of quality initiatives usually are rooted in poor organizational approaches and management systems, such as shortsighted leadership, inadequate resource allocation, poor training, or bad execution, and *not* in the underlying principles of quality.

Unfortunately, with all the hype and rhetoric, many companies scrambled to institute quality programs, which subsequently failed becaue they were hastily thrown together. Those organizations that have succeeded in building and sustaining quality have reaped the rewards associated with higher customer loyalty, employee satisfaction, and business performance.

Quality, Competitive Advantage, and Organizational Performance

The importance of quality in achieving competitive advantage was demonstrated by several research studies during the 1980s. PIMS Associates, Inc., a subsidiary of the Strategic Planning Institute, maintains a database of 1,200 companies and studies the impact of product quality on corporate performance.[4] PIMS researchers found that:

1. Product quality is an important determinant of business profitability.
2. Businesses that offer premium-quality products and services usually have large market shares and were early entrants into their markets.
3. Quality is positively and significantly related to a higher return on investment for almost all kinds of products and market situations.
4. Instituting a strategy of quality improvement usually leads to increased market share, but at the cost of reduced short-run profitability.
5. High-quality producers can usually charge premium prices.

The beneficiaries of quality are many. Obviously, the customer benefits, but all players within the supply chain benefit as well. When raw materials and component parts are delivered in conformance with the buyer's specifications, the buyer does not have to engage in wasteful activities, such as inspection and the maintenance of "just-in-case" inventory. Manufacturing processes benefit because their activities can be performed more efficiently if everything fits better. Indeed, Henry Ford could not operate his assembly lines effectively until he was able to buy parts made sufficiently precise to permit easy assembly operations. Workers benefit if they experience a sense of accomplishment whenever they do things well that delight customers. Finally, downstream distribution and retailing activities have an easier task stocking and marketing goods when they can rely on a firm's product to be made according to specifications. Nobody in the distribution channel wants products to be returned. A returned product is a symptom of poor quality, and it costs more money than most people realize.

OM PRINCIPLE

Organizations that invest in quality management efforts experience outstanding business results and improvements in operational performance.

In 1997, Kevin Hendricks and Vinod Singhal published one of the most celebrated studies of quality and performance.[5] Based on objective data and rigorous statistical analysis, the study showed that when implemented effectively, TQM approaches improve financial performance dramatically. Using a sample of about 600 publicly traded companies that have won quality awards either from their customers (such as automotive manufacturers) or through Baldrige and state and local quality award programs, Hendricks and Singhal examined performance results from six years before to four years after winning their first quality award. The primary performance measures tracked were the percent change in operating income and a variety of measures that might affect operating income: percent change in sales, total assets, number of employees, return on sales, and return on assets. These results were compared to a set of control firms that were similar in size to the award winners and in the same industry. The analysis revealed significant differences between the sample and the control group. Specifically, the winners' growth in operating income averaged 91 percent versus 43 percent for the control group. The winners also experienced a 69 percent jump in sales (compared to 32 percent for the control group), a 79 percent increase in total assets (compared to 37 percent), a 23 percent increase in the number of employees (compared to 7 percent), an 8 percent improvement in return on sales (compared to 0 percent), and a 9 percent improvement in return on assets (compared to 6 percent). Small companies actually outperformed large companies, and over a five-year period, the portfolio of winners beat the S&P 500 index by 34 percent. The *OM Practice* box provides some examples of specific organizational results from quality initiatives.

OM PRACTICE

Impacts of Quality Initiatives
Organizations taking a total quality path have achieved substantial improvements in performance.

- Among associates at Clarke American Checks, Inc., overall satisfaction improved from 72 percent in 1996 to 84 percent in 2000. Rising associate satisfaction correlates with the 84 percent increase in revenue earned per associate since 1995. Annual growth in company revenues increased from a rate of 4.2 percent in 1996 to 16 percent in 2000, compared to the industry's average annual growth rate of less than 1 percent over the five-year period.
- Dana Corporation's Spicer Driveshaft Division lowered internal defect rates by more than 75

percent. Employee turnover is below 1 percent, and economic value added increased from $15 million to $35 million in two years.

- Pal's Sudden Service, a privately owned quick-service restaurant chain in eastern Tennessee, had customer quality scores averaging 95.8 percent in 2001, compared with 84.1 percent for its best competition, and improved order delivery speed by over 30 percent since 1995.
- Parent satisfaction at Pearl River School District increased from 62 percent in 1996 to 96 percent in 2001.
- SSM Health Care's share of the St. Louis market has increased substantially while three of its five competitors have lost market share. It has received an AA credit rating from Standard and Poor's for four consecutive years, a rating attained by less than 1 percent of U.S. hospitals.

6.3 PRINCIPLES OF TOTAL QUALITY

The customer is the principal judge of quality. A quality-focused company's efforts need to extend well beyond merely meeting specifications, reducing defects and errors, or resolving complaints. The firm must also know what the customer wants and how the customer uses its products; anticipate needs that the customer may not even be able to express; design new products and services that truly delight the customer; respond rapidly to changing consumer and market demands;

OM PRINCIPLE

Total quality is based on three fundamental principles:
1. A focus on customers and stakeholders.
2. A process focus supported by continuous improvement and learning.
3. Participation and teamwork by everyone in the organization.

and continually develop new ways of enhancing customer relationships. This focus on the customer is one of the principles of total quality.

As we described in Chapter 4, many processes cross traditional organizational boundaries. A second principle of total quality is a process perspective that links all necessary activities together and focuses on the entire system, rather than on only a small part. This perspective is supported by **continuous improvement,** which, as Chapter 4 explained, refers to both incremental (small and gradual) and breakthrough (large and rapid) improvements in processes. Real improvement depends on *learning*, which requires feedback and analysis of results to understand why changes are successful and enable better approaches to be adopted.

In any organization, the person who best understands his or her job and how to improve both the product and the process is the one performing it. When managers give employees the tools to make good decisions and the freedom and encouragement to make contributions, they virtually guarantee that better quality products and production processes will result. Employees who are allowed to participate—both individually and in teams—in decisions that affect their jobs and the customer can make substantial contributions to quality. Empowering employees to make decisions that satisfy customers without constraining them with bureaucratic rules shows the highest level of trust. Another important element of total quality is teamwork, which focuses attention on both internal and external customer-supplier relationships and encourages the involvement of everyone in attacking systemic problems, particularly those that cross functional boundaries.

6.4 FOUNDATIONS OF MODERN QUALITY: PHILOSOPHIES OF DEMING, JURAN, AND CROSBY

No individual has had more influence on quality management than Dr. W. Edwards Deming. Deming received a Ph.D. in physics and was trained as a statistician. He worked for Western Electric during its pioneering era of statistical quality control in the 1920s and 1930s. Deming recognized the importance of viewing management processes statistically. During World War II he taught quality control courses as part of the U.S. national defense effort, but he realized that teaching statistics only to engineers and factory workers would never solve the fundamental quality problems that manufacturing needed to address. Despite numerous efforts, his attempts to convey the message of quality to upper-level managers in the United States were ignored.

Unlike other management gurus and consultants, Deming never defined or described quality precisely. In his last book, he stated, "A product or a service possesses quality if it helps somebody and enjoys a good and sustainable market."[6] The Deming philosophy focuses on improving product and service quality by reducing uncertainty and variability in the design and manufacturing process. In Deming's view, variation is the chief culprit of poor quality. In mechanical assemblies, for example, variations from specifications for part dimensions lead to inconsistent performance and premature wear and failure. Likewise, inconsistencies in human behavior in service frustrate customers and hurt companies' reputations. To reduce variation, Deming advocated a never-ending cycle of product/service design, manufacture/service delivery, test, and sales, followed by market surveys and then redesign and improvement. Deming argued that higher quality would set off a "chain reaction," in which quality would lead to higher productivity and lower costs, which in turn would lead to increased market share.

> **OM PRINCIPLE**
>
> Higher quality leads to higher productivity and lower costs, which in turn lead to improved market share and long-term competitive strength and stronger national economies.

In his early work in the United States, Deming preached his "14 Points." Although management practices are vastly different today, the 14 Points still convey important insights for managers.

○ **Point 1:** *Create a vision and demonstrate commitment.* An organization must define its mission, vision, and values to provide long-term direction for its management and employees in order to serve its customers. This should provide the basis for the implementation of operations strategy, as we discussed in Chapter 2.

○ **Point 2:** *Learn the new philosophy.* Today, quality principles are ingrained in most organizations. Still, people change jobs, and organizations generally have a short memory—both need to continually renew themselves to learn new approaches and relearn many older ones. This is reflected in the concept of "organizational learning."

○ **Point 3:** *Understand inspection.* Routine inspection acknowledges that defects are present, but does not add value to the product. While most companies today do not rely on inspection as the primary means of assuring quality, few managers truly understand the concept of variation and how it affects their processes and inspection practices. By understanding and seeking to reduce variation, managers can eliminate many sources of unnecessary inspection, thereby reducing non-value-added costs associated with operations.

○ **Point 4:** *Stop making decisions purely on the basis of cost.* Purchasing departments have long been driven by cost minimization without regard for quality. Deming urged businesses to establish long-term relationships with fewer suppliers, leading to loyalty and opportunities for mutual improvement. Today's emphasis on supply chain management (SCM) reflects the achievement of Point 4. SCM takes a system's view of the supply chain with the objective of minimizing total supply chain costs and developing stronger partnerships with suppliers. This will be addressed further in Chapter 7.

○ **Point 5:** *Improve constantly and forever.* Traditionally, continuous improvement was not a common business practice; today, it is recognized as necessary for survival in a highly competitive global environment. The tools for improvement are constantly evolving, and organizations need to ensure that their employees understand and apply them effectively. This requires training, the focus of the next point.

○ **Point 6:** *Institute training.* For continuous improvement, employees—both management and workers—require the proper tools and knowledge. Training must transcend basic job skills like running a machine or following the script when talking to customers. Training should include tools for diagnosing, analyzing, and solving quality problems and identifying improvement opportunities. Today, many companies have excellent training programs for technology related to direct production, but still fail to enrich the ancillary skills of their workforce. Consequently, some of the most lucrative opportunities to improve key business results are in this area.

○ **Point 7:** *Institute leadership.* Deming recognized that one of the biggest impediments to improvement was a lack of leadership. Leadership was, is, and will continue to be a challenging issue in every organization, particularly as new generations of managers replace those who have learned to lead. Thus, this point will always be relevant to organizations.

○ **Point 8:** *Drive out fear.* Driving out fear underlies many of Deming's 14 Points. Fear is manifested in many ways: fear of reprisal, fear of failure, fear of the unknown, fear of relinquishing control, and fear of change. Fear encourages short-term thinking. Fear is a cultural issue for all organizations. Creating a culture without fear is a slow process that can be destroyed in an instant with a change in leadership and corporate policies. Therefore, today's managers need to be sensitive to the impact that fear can have on their organizations.

○ **Point 9:** *Optimize the efforts of teams.* Teamwork helps to break down barriers between departments and individuals. Barriers between functional areas arise when managers fear they might lose power. Internal competition for raises and performance ratings and conflicts between unions and management contribute to barriers. The lack of cooperation leads to poor quality because other departments cannot understand what their "customers" want and do not get what they need from their "suppliers."

○ **Point 10:** *Eliminate exhortations.* Posters, slogans, and motivational programs calling for Zero Defects, Do It Right the First Time, Improve Productivity and Quality, and the like are directed at the wrong people. These motivational programs assume that all quality problems are due to human behavior and that workers can improve simply through motivation. Workers become frustrated when they cannot improve or are penalized for defects. Motivational approaches overlook the source of many problems—the system, which is the responsibility of management.

○ **Point 11:** *Eliminate numerical quotas and management by objective (MBO).* Many organizations manage by the numbers. This does not encourage improvement, particularly if rewards or performance appraisals are tied to meeting quotas. Workers may take shortcuts on quality to reach the goal. Once a standard is reached, workers have little incentive to continue production or to improve quality; they will do no more than they are asked to do. Management must understand the system and continually try to improve it, rather than focus on short-term goals.

○ **Point 12:** *Remove barriers to pride in workmanship.* Factory workers have little incentive to excel when they are given monotonous tasks; are provided with inferior machines, tools, or materials; are told to run defective items to meet sales pressures; and report to supervisors who know nothing about the job.

○ **Point 13:** *Encourage education and self-improvement.* The difference between this point and Point 6 is subtle. Point 6 refers to training in specific job skills; Point 13 refers to continuing, broad education for self-development. Today, many companies understand that elevating the general knowledge base of their workforce—outside of specific job skills—offers many benefits. Others, however, still view this as a cost that can be easily cut when financial tradeoffs must be made.

○ **Point 14:** *Take action.* The transformation begins with top management and includes everyone. Applying the Deming philosophy launches a major cultural change that many firms find difficult, particularly when many of the traditional management practices Deming felt must be eliminated are deeply ingrained in the organization's culture.

The 14 Points have become the basis for many organization's quality approaches (see the *OM Practice* box on Hillerich & Bradsby).

Joseph Juran was born in Romania in 1904 and came to the United States in 1912. He joined Western Electric in the 1920s as it pioneered the development of statistical methods for quality. He spent much of his time as a corporate industrial engineer and, in 1951, was responsible for the *Quality Control Handbook.* This book, one of the most comprehensive quality manuals ever written, has been revised several times and continues to be a popular reference.

Juran proposed a simple definition of quality: "*fitness for use.*" This definition suggests that quality should be viewed from both external and internal perspectives; that is, quality is related to "(1) product performance that results in customer satisfaction; (2) freedom from product deficiencies, which avoids customer dissatisfaction." How products and services are designed, manufactured and delivered, and serviced in the field all contribute to fitness for use.

Unlike Deming, Juran did not propose a major cultural change in organizations, but rather sought to improve quality by working within the system familiar to managers. He argued that employees at different levels of an organization speak in their own "languages." (Deming, on

OM PRACTICE

Hillerich & Bradsby

The Deming philosophy formed the basis for improving labor-management relations.

Hillerich & Bradsby Company (H&B) has been making the Louisville Slugger baseball bat for more than 115 years. In the mid-1980s, the company faced significant challenges from market changes and competition. After CEO Jack Hillerich attended a four-day Deming seminar, he decided to see what changes that Deming advocated were possible in an old company with an old union and a history of labor-management problems. Hillerich persuaded union officials to attend another Deming seminar with five senior managers. Following the seminar, a core group of union and management people developed a strategy to change the company. They talked about building trust and changing the system "to make it something you want to work in."

Employees were interested, but skeptical. To demonstrate their commitment, managers examined Deming's 14 Points and picked several they believed they could make progress on through actions that would demonstrate a serious intention to change. One of the first changes was the elimination of work quotas that were tied to hourly salaries and a schedule of warnings and penalties for failures to meet quotas. Instead, a team-based approach was initiated. Though a few workers took advantage of the change, overall productivity improved as rework decreased because workers were taking pride in producing things the right way first. H&B also eliminated performance appraisals and commission-based pay in sales. The company has also focused its efforts on training and education, resulting in more openness for change and capacity for teamwork. Today, the Deming philosophy is still the core of H&B's guiding principles.[7]

the other hand, believed statistics should be the common language.) Thus, to get top management's attention, quality issues must be cast in the language they understand—dollars. Hence, Juran advocated the use of quality cost accounting and analysis to focus attention on quality problems. The **costs of quality (COQ)**—or more specifically, the costs of *poor* quality—are those associated with avoiding poor quality or incurred as a result

OM PRINCIPLE

Top management speaks in the language of dollars; workers speak in the language of things; and middle management must be able to speak both languages and translate between dollars and things.

of poor quality. These include **prevention costs,** which are investments made to keep nonconforming products from occurring and reaching the customer; **appraisal costs,** which are associated with efforts to ensure conformance to requirements, generally through measurement and analysis of data to detect nonconformances; **internal failure costs,** which are incurred as a result of unsatisfactory quality found before the delivery of a product to the customer; and **external failure costs**, which occur after poor-quality products reach the customer. By measuring these costs, organizations can readily identify improvement projects.

At the operational level, Juran focused on increasing conformance to specifications through elimination of defects, supported extensively by statistical tools for analysis. Juran's prescriptions focus on three major quality processes, called the **Quality Trilogy:** (1) quality planning, the process of preparing to meet quality goals; (2) quality control, the process of meeting quality goals during operations; and (3) quality improvement, the process of breaking through to unprecedented levels of performance. At the time he proposed this structure, few companies were engaging in any significant planning or improvement activities. Thus, Juran was promoting a major cultural shift in management thinking.

Philip B. Crosby was corporate vice president for quality at International Telephone and Telegraph (ITT) for 14 years after working his way up from line inspector. After leaving ITT, he established Philip Crosby Associates in 1979 to develop and offer training programs. He also authored several popular books. His first book, *Quality Is Free*, sold about one million copies and was largely responsible for bringing quality to the attention of top corporate managers in the United States. The essence of Crosby's quality philosophy is embodied in what he calls the "Absolutes of Quality Management":

◦ Quality means conformance to requirements, not elegance.

◦ There is no such thing as a quality problem.

◦ There is no such thing as the economics of quality; doing the job right the first time is always cheaper.

◦ The only performance measurement is the cost of quality, which is the expense of non-conformance.

◦ The only performance standard is "Zero Defects (ZD)."

Unlike Juran and Deming, Crosby took a primarily behavioral approach. He emphasized using management and organizational processes, rather than statistical techniques, to change corporate cultures and attitudes.

6.5 QUALITY MANAGEMENT FRAMEWORKS

The philosophies of Deming, Juran, Crosby, and others have provided much guidance and wisdom in the form of "best practices" to managers around the world and have led to numerous awards and certifications that recognize the effective application of quality principles. Although awards justifiably recognize only a select few, the award or certification criteria provide frameworks for managing organizations effectively. The two frameworks that have had the most impact on quality management practices worldwide are the U.S. Malcolm Baldrige National Quality Award and the international ISO 9000 certification process. Recently, the concept of "Six Sigma" has evolved into a unique framework for managing quality.

The Malcolm Baldrige National Quality Award

Created in 1987, the Malcolm Baldrige National Quality Award (MBNQA) has been one of the most powerful catalysts of total quality in the United States and, indeed, throughout the world. Although the award receives the most attention, its primary purpose is to provide a framework for business improvement through self-assessment and encourage information sharing of best practices among organizations. Up to three companies can receive an award in each of the original categories of manufacturing, service, and small business. Congress approved award categories in nonprofit education and health care in 1999.

The award has evolved into a comprehensive National Quality Program, administered through the National Institute of Standards and Technology in Gaithersburg, Maryland, of which the Baldrige Award is only one part. The National Quality Program is a public-private partnership, funded primarily through a private foundation. A link to the program's Web site, which provides current information about the award, the performance criteria, award winners, and a variety of other information can be found on the text's Web site at **http://raturi_evans.swlearning.com.**

The Criteria for Performance Excellence

The award examination is based upon a rigorous set of criteria, called the *Criteria for Performance Excellence*, designed to encourage companies to enhance their competitiveness through an aligned approach to organizational performance management that results in the following:

1. Delivery of ever-improving value to customers, resulting in improved marketplace success.

2. Improvement of overall company performance and capabilities.
3. Organizational and personal learning.

The criteria consist of seven key categories that essentially define a set of high-performance management practices:

1. **Leadership:** This category is concerned with how an organization's senior leaders address values, directions, and performance expectations, as well as a focus on customers and other stakeholders, empowerment, innovation, and learning. Also considered are an organization's governance and how the organization addresses its public and community responsibilities.

2. **Strategic Planning:** This category is concerned with how an organization develops strategic objectives and action plans. Also addressed is how the chosen objectives and plans are deployed and how progress is measured.

3. **Customer and Market Focus:** This category looks at how an organization determines requirements, expectations, and preferences of customers and markets. Also included is how the organization builds relationships with customers and determines the key factors that lead to customer acquisition, satisfaction, loyalty, and retention, and to business expansion.

4. **Measurement, Analysis, and Knowledge Management:** This category addresses how an organization selects, gathers, analyzes, manages, and improves its data, information, and knowledge assets.

5. **Human Resource Focus:** This category looks at how an organization's work systems and employee learning and motivation enable employees to develop and utilize its full potential in alignment with the organization's overall objectives and action plans. Also addressed are the organization's efforts to build and maintain a work environment and employee support climate conducive to performance excellence and to personal and organizational growth.

6. **Process Management:** This category addresses the key aspects of an organization's process management, including key product, service, and business processes for creating customer and organizational value, and key support processes involving all work units.

7. **Business Results:** This category looks at an organization's performance and improvement in key business areas: customer satisfaction, product and service performance, financial and marketplace performance, human resource results, operational performance, and governance and social responsibility, as well as performance levels relative to competitors.

The seven categories form an integrated management system, as illustrated in Figure 6.2.

Although the criteria provide an overall business management framework, many aspects of the criteria are particularly relevant to operations managers, notably, categories 5 and 6. For example, in category 5, the criteria include the following questions:

OM PRINCIPLE

The Criteria for Performance Excellence are designed to apply to all types of organizations: manufacturing, service, small business, health care, education, government, and not-for-profit. Though each sector has its own unique language, the principles of managing for high performance are universal.

○ How do you organize and manage work and jobs to promote cooperation, initiative, empowerment, innovation, and your organizational culture? How do you organize and manage work and jobs to achieve the agility to keep current with business needs?

FIGURE 6.2 | *Baldrige Criteria Framework*

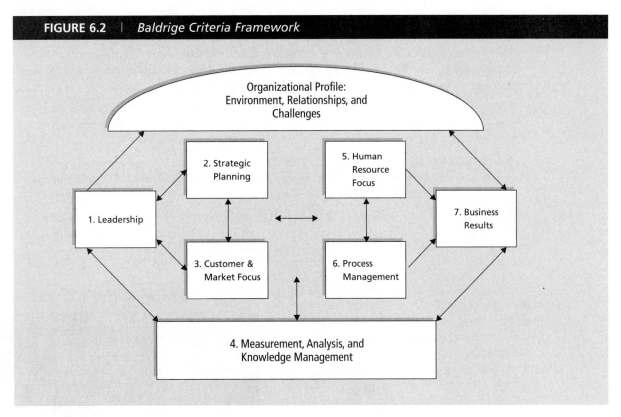

- How do you achieve effective communication and skill sharing across work units, jobs, and locations?

- How do you motivate employees to develop and utilize their full potential? How does your organization use formal and/or informal mechanisms to help employees attain job- and career-related development and learning objectives? How do managers and supervisors help employees attain job- and career-related development and learning objectives?

- How do you improve workplace health, safety, and ergonomics? How do employees take part in improving them? What are your performance measures or targets for each of these key workplace factors?

- How do you relate assessment findings [of employee well-being, satisfaction, and motivation] to key business results to identify priorities for improving the work environment and employee support climate?

These certainly are vital issues that operations managers must consider as they work to build and sustain a productive work environment.

In the Process Management category (category 6), the criteria focus on approaches for designing and managing value-creation and support processes—also critical issues for operations managers. Key assessment questions include the following:

- How does your organization determine its key value-creation processes? How do you determine key value-creation process requirements, incorporating input from customers, suppliers, and partners, as appropriate?

- How do you design these processes to meet all the key requirements? How do you incorporate new technology and organizational knowledge into the design of these processes? How do you incorporate cycle time, productivity, cost control, and other efficiency and effectiveness factors into the design of these processes? How do you implement these processes to ensure that they meet design requirements?

- What are the key performance measures or indicators that you use for the control and improvement of your value-creation processes? How does your day-to-day operation of these processes ensure that you meet key process requirements?

- How do you minimize overall costs associated with inspections, tests, and process or performance audits, as appropriate? How do you prevent defects and rework, and minimize warranty costs, as appropriate?

- How do you improve your value-creation processes to achieve better performance, reduce variability, improve products and services, and keep the processes current with business needs and directions? How are improvements shared with other organizational units and processes?

Even if they have no intention of applying for the award, organizations use the Baldrige criteria for self-assessment or internal recognition programs. The benefits of using the criteria for self-assessment include accelerating improvement efforts, energizing employees, and learning from feedback—particularly if external examiners are involved. For instance, Honeywell, Inc. uses the criteria as a company-wide framework for understanding, evaluating, and improving its business. Honeywell's mandate is to use the model for managing the business and engage senior management in an annual assessment process. General managers use this framework to exchange information, ask for help, and learn from each other.[8]

> **OM PRINCIPLE**
>
> Attempting to answer the questions in the Baldrige criteria can provide considerable insight into gaps in design and delivery processes that can lead to significant improvements. In this fashion, the Baldrige criteria become a useful tool for self-assessment and improvement of operational capabilities.

ISO 9000:2000

As quality became a major focus of businesses throughout the world, various organizations developed standards and guidelines. As the European Community (the predecessor of the European Union) moved toward the European free trade agreement, which went into effect at the end of 1992, quality management became a key strategic objective. To standardize quality requirements for European countries within the Community and those wishing to do business with those countries, the International Organization for Standardization (IOS), founded in 1946 and composed of representatives from the national standards bodies of 91 nations, adopted a series of written quality standards in 1987. They were revised in 1994 and again (significantly) in 2000. The most recent version is called the **ISO 9000:2000** family of standards. The standards have been adopted in the United States by the American National Standards Institute (ANSI), with the endorsement and cooperation of the American Society for Quality (ASQ), and are recognized by about 100 countries.

ISO 9000 defines *quality system standards*, based on the premise that certain generic characteristics of management practices can be standardized and that a well-designed, well-implemented, and carefully managed quality system provides confidence that the outputs will meet customer expectations and requirements. The standards were created to meet five objectives:

1. Achieve, maintain, and seek to continuously improve product quality (including services) in relationship to requirements.

2. Improve the quality of operations to continually meet customers' and stakeholders' stated and implied needs.
3. Provide confidence to internal management and other employees that quality requirements are being fulfilled and that improvement is taking place.
4. Provide confidence to customers and other stakeholders that quality requirements are being achieved in the delivered product.
5. Provide confidence that quality system requirements are fulfilled.

The ISO 9000 standards were originally intended to be advisory in nature and to be used for two-party contractual situations (between a customer and a supplier) and for internal auditing. However, they quickly evolved into criteria for companies that wished to "certify" their quality management or achieve "registration" through a third-party auditor, usually a laboratory or other accreditation agency (called a registrar). This process began in the United Kingdom. Rather than a supplier being audited for compliance to the standards by each customer, the registrar certifies the company, and this certification is accepted by all of the supplier's customers. The standards are intended to apply to all types of businesses, including electronics and chemicals, and to services such as health care, banking, and transportation. In some foreign markets, companies will not buy from suppliers that are not certified to the standards.

The ISO 9000:2000 standards consist of three documents:

1. ISO 9000 provides fundamentals, including definitions of key terms.
2. ISO 9001 sets out the basic requirements for quality management system.
3. ISO 9004 provides guidance for performance improvement beyond the minimum requirements of ISO 9001.

The ISO 9000:2000 standards are structured into four major sections—Management Responsibility; Resource Management; Product Realization; and Measurement, Analysis, and Improvement—and are supported by eight quality principles:

- **Principle 1:** *Customer-Focused Organization.* Organizations depend on their customers and therefore should understand current and future customer needs, meet customer requirements, and strive to exceed customer expectations.

- **Principle 2:** *Leadership.* Leaders establish unity of purpose and the direction of the organization. They should create and maintain an internal environment in which people can become fully involved in achieving the organization's objectives.

- **Principle 3:** *Involvement of People.* People at all levels are the essence of an organization, and their full involvement enables their abilities to be used for the organization's benefit.

- **Principle 4:** *Process Approach.* A desired result is achieved more efficiently when related resources and activities are managed as a process.

- **Principle 5:** *System Approach to Management.* Identifying, understanding, and managing a system of interrelated processes for a given objective improves the organization's effectiveness and efficiency.

- **Principle 6:** *Continual Improvement.* Continual improvement should be a permanent objective of the organization.

- **Principle 7:** *Factual Approach to Decision Making.* Effective decisions are based on the analysis of data and information.

○ **Principle 8:** *Mutually Beneficial Supplier Relationships.* An organization and its suppliers are interdependent, and a mutually beneficial relationship enhances the ability of both to create value.

Many organizations have realized significant benefits from ISO 9000. At DuPont, for example, ISO 9000 has been credited with increasing on-time delivery from 70 to 90 percent, decreasing cycle time from 15 to 1.5 days, increasing first-pass yields from 72 to 92 percent, and reducing the number of test procedures by one-third. Sun Microsystems' Milpitas, California plant was certified in 1992, and managers believe that meeting the requirements has helped the plant deliver improved quality and service to customers.[9] In Canada, Toronto Plastics, Ltd. reduced defects from 150,000 per million to 15,000 per million after one year of ISO implementation.[10] The first homebuilder to achieve registration, Michigan-based Delcor Homes, reduced its rate of correctable defects from 27.4 to 1.7 in two years and improved its building experience approval rating from the mid 60s to the mid 90s on a 100-point scale.[11]

Six Sigma

Motorola pioneered the concept of **Six Sigma.** Six Sigma can be described as a business improvement approach that seeks to find and eliminate causes of defects and errors in manufacturing and service processes by focusing on outputs that are critical to customers and a clear financial return for the organization. This is facilitated through the use of basic and advanced quality improvement and control tools by teams whose members are trained to provide fact-based decision-making information. The term *six sigma* represents a quality level of at most 3.4 defects per million opportunities (dpmo). An ultimate "stretch" goal of all organizations that adopt a Six Sigma philosophy is to have all critical processes, regardless of functional area, at a six-sigma level of capability. The theoretical basis for six-sigma quality is explained by Figure 6.3 in the context of manufacturing specifications.

Motorola chose the figure of 1.5 standard deviations because field failure data suggested that its processes drifted by this amount on average. Allowing some shift in the distribution is necessary because no process can be maintained in perfect control. The area under the shifted curves *beyond* the six-sigma ranges (the tolerance limits) is only 0.0000034, or 3.4 parts per million. If the process mean is held exactly on target (the shaded distribution in Figure 6.3), only 2.0 defects per billion would be expected.

OM PRINCIPLE

A six-sigma quality level corresponds to a process variation that is equal to half of the design tolerance while allowing the mean to shift as much as 1.5 standard deviations from the target, resulting in a quality level of at most 3.4 dpmo.

In a similar fashion we could define three-sigma quality, five-sigma quality, and so on. A five-sigma level corresponds to 233 dpmo, four sigma to 6,200 dpmo, and three sigma to 66,803 dpmo. Note that a change from three to four sigma represents a 10-fold improvement; from four to five sigma, a 30-fold improvement; and from five to six sigma, a 70-fold improvement—difficult challenges for any organization. Many companies have adopted Six Sigma to challenge their own improvement efforts. The efforts by General Electric in particular, driven by former CEO Jack Welch, attracted significant media attention to the concept and have made Six Sigma a very popular approach to quality improvement.

Although originally developed for manufacturing in the context of tolerance-based specifications, the Six Sigma concept has been operationalized to any process and has come to signify a generic quality level of at most 3.4 dpmo. It has been applied in product development, new business acquisition, customer service, accounting, and many other business functions. For example, suppose that a bank tracks the number of errors reported in customers' checking account statements and finds 12 errors in 1,000 statements. That is equivalent to an error rate of 12,000 dpmo (somewhere between the 3.5- and 4-sigma levels).

FIGURE 6.3 | *Six-Sigma Quality*

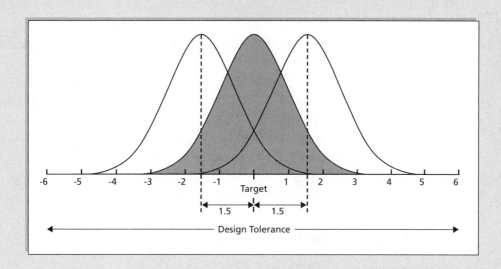

Six Sigma has developed from simply a way of measuring quality to an overall strategy to accelerate improvements and achieve unprecedented performance levels within an organization by finding and eliminating causes of errors or defects in processes by focusing on characteristics that are critical to customers.[12] The core philosophy of Six Sigma is based on some key concepts:[13]

1. Thinking in terms of key business processes and customer requirements with a clear focus on overall strategic objectives.
2. Focusing on corporate sponsors responsible for championing projects, supporting team activities, helping to overcome resistance to change, and obtaining resources.
3. Emphasizing such quantifiable measures as defects per million opportunities (dpmo) that can be applied to all parts of an organization: manufacturing, engineering, administrative, software, and so on.
4. Ensuring that appropriate metrics are identified early in the process and that they focus on business results, thereby providing incentives and accountability.
5. Providing extensive training followed by project team deployment to improve profitability, reduce non–value-added activities, and reduce cycle time.
6. Creating highly qualified process improvement experts ("green belts," "black belts," and "master black belts") who can apply improvement tools and lead teams.
7. Setting stretch objectives for improvement.

OM PRINCIPLE

In many ways, Six Sigma is the realization of many fundamental concepts of TQM, notably, the integration of human and process elements of improvement.[14]

Six Sigma includes both human issues such as management leadership, a sense of urgency, focus on results and customers, team processes, and culture change; and process issues such as the use of process management techniques, analysis of variation and statistical methods, a disciplined problem-solving approach, and management of fact. Nonetheless, Six Sigma it is more than simply a repackaging of older quality approaches, such as the traditional notion of TQM. Some of the differences include the following:

○ TQM is based largely on worker empowerment and teams; Six Sigma is owned by business leader champions.

○ TQM activities generally occur within a function, process, or individual workplace; Six Sigma projects are truly cross-functional.

○ TQM training is generally limited to simple improvement tools and concepts; Six Sigma focuses on a more rigorous and advanced set of statistical tools and a structured problem-solving methodology.

○ TQM focuses on improvement with little financial accountability; Six Sigma requires a verifiable return on investment and focuses on the bottom line.

The recognized benchmark for Six Sigma implementation is General Electric. GE's Six Sigma problem-solving approach (**DMAIC**) employs five phases:

1. Define (D):
   ○ Identify customers and their priorities.
   ○ Identify a project suitable for Six Sigma efforts based on business objectives as well as customer needs and feedback.
   ○ Identify CTQs (**critical to quality characteristics**) that the customer considers to have the most impact on quality.
2. Measure (M):
   ○ Determine how to measure the process and how is it performing.
   ○ Identify the key internal processes that influence CTQs and measure the defects currently generated relative to those processes
3. Analyze (A):
   ○ Determine the most likely causes of defects.
   ○ Understand why defects are generated by identifying the key variables that are most likely to create process variation.
4. Improve (I):
   ○ Identify means to remove the causes of the defects.
   ○ Confirm the key variables and quantify their effects on the CTQs.
   ○ Identify the maximum acceptable ranges of the key variables and establish a system for measuring deviations of the variables.
   ○ Modify the process to stay within the acceptable range.
5. Control (C):
   ○ Determine how to maintain the improvements.
   ○ Put tools in place to ensure that the key variables remain within the maximum acceptable ranges under the modified process.

The tools used in Six Sigma efforts have been around for a long time and may be categorized into seven general groups:

○ *Elementary statistical tools* (basic statistics, statistical thinking, hypothesis testing, correlation, simple regression).

○ *Advanced statistical tools* (design of experiments, analysis of variance, multiple regression).

○ *Product design and reliability* (quality function deployment, failure mode and effects analysis).

○ *Measurement* (process capability, measurement systems analysis).

- ○ *Process control* (control plans, statistical process control).

- ○ *Process improvement* (process improvement planning, process mapping, mistake-proofing).

- ○ *Implementation and teamwork* (organizational effectiveness, team assessment, facilitation tools, team development).

Some of these topics are addressed in other chapters of this book, in the Tools and Techniques materials on the accompanying CD-ROM, or in other courses that you may have taken.

Many companies have used Six Sigma very successfully. From 1996 to 1998, General Electric increased the number of its Six Sigma projects from 200 to 6,000. From all these efforts, GE expected to save $7 billion to $10 billion over a decade. For example, GE credits Six Sigma with a 10-fold increase in the life of CT scanner X-ray tubes, a 400 percent improvement in return on investment in its industrial diamond business, a 62 percent reduction in turnaround time at railcar repair shops, and $400 million in savings in its plastics business.[15] Other companies have also reported significant results. Between 1995 and the first quarter of 1997, Allied Signal (now part of Honeywell) reported cost savings exceeding $800 million from its Six Sigma initiative. Citigroup reduced internal callbacks by 80 percent, credit process time by 50 percent, and cycle times of processing statements from 28 days to 15 days.[16] Samsung Electronics integrated Six Sigma into its entire business process as a way to perfect its fundamental approach to product, process, and personnel development. In 2000 and 2001, the company completed 3,290 Six Sigma projects, which have contributed to an average reduction in defects of 50 percent.[17]

Design for Six Sigma (DFSS) is a relatively new approach that is rapidly becoming recognized and incorporated into traditional product development processes. It is being applied not only to engineered products, but also to business transactions and production processes. DFSS represents a set of tools and methodologies used in the product development process for ensuring that goods and services will meet customer needs and achieve performance objectives, and that the processes used to make and deliver them achieve six-sigma capability. DFSS consists of four principal activities:[18]

1. *Concept development*, in which product functionality is determined based upon customer requirements, technological capabilities, and economic realities.
2. *Design development*, which focuses on product and process performance issues necessary to fulfill the product and service requirements in manufacturing or delivery.
3. *Design optimization*, which seeks to minimize the impact of variation in production and use, creating a "robust" design.
4. *Design verification*, which ensures that the capability of the production system meets the appropriate sigma level.

DFSS can be viewed as a key process within the overall product development process that we discussed in Chapter 3.

Comparing Baldrige, ISO 9000, and Six Sigma

We have described three major frameworks for quality management systems: the Baldrige Criteria for Performance Excellence, ISO 9000, and Six Sigma. Although they are all process-focused, data-based, and management-led frameworks, each offers a different emphasis in helping organizations improve performance and increase customer satisfaction. For example, Baldrige focuses on performance excellence for the entire organization in an overall management framework, identifying and tracking important organizational results; ISO focuses on product and service conformity for guaranteeing equity in the marketplace and concentrates on fixing quality system problems and product and service nonconformities; and Six Sigma concentrates on measuring product quality and driving process improvement and cost savings throughout the organization.

Although the 2000 revision of ISO 9000 has incorporated many of the principles of the Baldrige criteria, it still is not a comprehensive business performance framework. Nevertheless, it is an excellent way to begin a quality journey. In fact, ISO 9000 offers more detailed guidance on process and product control than Baldrige and

> **OM PRINCIPLE**
>
> ISO 9000 provides a good set of basic practices for initiating a quality system and is an excellent starting point for companies with no formal quality assurance program.

provides systematic approaches to many of the Baldrige criteria requirements in the Process Management category. Thus, for companies in the early stages of developing a quality program, the standards enforce the discipline of control that is necessary before they can seriously pursue continuous improvement. The requirements of periodic audits reinforce the newly installed quality system until it becomes ingrained in the company.

Implementing Six Sigma fulfills many of the elements of ISO 9000:2000.[19] For instance, Six Sigma helps to demonstrate management commitment through the periodic review of six-sigma plans and projects, the provision of champions to sponsor projects, the addition of training resources, and the communication of progress and achievements.

A critical question is whether an organization using Baldrige will be more successful if it also uses Six Sigma and vice versa. If Six Sigma is viewed as only a small part of the Process Management category, the impact would seem to be marginal. In reality, however, Six Sigma plays a role in each of the seven Baldrige categories. Six Sigma enhances the ability of leadership to focus on the critical factors that make a business successful and select appropriate strategies and action plans. Therefore, Six Sigma can strengthen management practices in Leadership and Strategic Planning. Understanding customer requirements and linking them to processes and delivery systems is a principal focus of Baldrige. By focusing on "critical to quality" (CTQ) customer requirements—one of the important concepts in Six Sigma—organizations gain better knowledge about customer requirements, a key component of the Customer Focus category. Six Sigma methodology is driven by a management-by-fact methodology. This can improve an organization's ability to meet the requirements in the Measurement, Analysis, and Knowledge Management category. People play a vital role in championing projects and providing technical and application-specific knowledge. Six Sigma can improve work systems, training, and the work environment—all critical components of the Human Resource Focus category. With Six Sigma, process management is not a by-product, but one of the primary organizational goals. The DMAIC methodology provides a structured approach to the Process Management category. Finally, Six Sigma's focus on business results leads organizations to track and monitor appropriate metrics. Many

organizations, including Texas Instruments, Motorola, Hewlett-Packard, Solectron, and Boeing, have successfully married the two approaches.

So how should an organization choose? The answer is that this should not be an "either/or" decision. Instead, the organization should choose any combination that fits its needs.

> **OM PRINCIPLE**
>
> Though different, Baldrige and Six Sigma are highly compatible and can both have a place in the management system of a successful organization (see the *OM Practice* box on Baxter).

6.6 QUALITY CONTROL SYSTEMS

Control is the activity of ensuring conformance to requirements and taking action when necessary to correct problems and maintain stable performance. Goals and standards, which

OM PRACTICE

Baxter Health Care International
Synergies result from merging Baldrige with Six Sigma.

The Business Excellence organization within Baxter Healthcare International is a small group of people focused on helping internal clients improve their operations. Specific areas of responsibility in Business Excellence include:

- The Baxter Award for Operational Excellence (an internal Baldrige Award).
- Deployment of the Baxter Integrated Management System (the Baldrige model).
- The Corporate Quality Manual.
- The Baxter Quality Institute (an internal quality training group).
- The Quality Leadership Process (a method of deploying performance excellence in manufacturing).
- The Lean Manufacturing Initiative.
- Six Sigma initiatives.

Business Excellence has rolled all of these together into a unified service offering. For example, consider the following fictitious scenario. The Supply Chain organization has determined that its operating cost and cash flow contributions are not meeting its targets and consults Business Excellence. First, Business Excellence will work with members of the leadership team to develop an organizational profile of the Supply Chain organization. This helps the team members focus on who they are and what their specific challenges are. Next, Business Excellence will perform a simple Baldrige assessment online and use the output to generate a feedback report of strengths and opportunities for improvement with strong emphasis on the integration of the model. Then Business Excellence will distill the feedback report down to 10 to 12 cross-cutting themes for the leadership team to focus on. These are built into an Excel spreadsheet for a "prioritization matrix" exercise, designed to identify the top two or three critical opportunities or issues that the group will focus on. Next, Business Excellence will bring in the Six Sigma approach and drill down into these opportunities to determine potential projects. When these have been identified and scoped sufficiently to make a decision to move forward, project charters are developed and assigned to Six Sigma specialists to implement them.[20]

OM PRINCIPLE

Any control system has three components: (1) a standard or goal, (2) a means of measuring accomplishment, and (3) the comparison of actual results with the standard, along with feedback to form the basis for corrective action.

are one of the components of any control system, are defined during the planning and design processes. They establish what is supposed to be accomplished. The goals and standards have measurable quality characteristics, such as dimensions of machined parts, numbers of defectives, customer complaints, or waiting times (see the *OM Practice* box on golf balls).

OM PRACTICE

A Quality Spin on Golf Balls
To be conforming under the Rules of Golf, golf balls must meet five standards: minimum size, maximum weight, spherical symmetry, maximum initial velocity, and overall distance.[21] Methods for measuring such quality characteristics may be automated or performed manually by workers. For instance, a golf ball is measured for size by trying to drop it through a metal ring—a conforming ball sticks to the ring while a nonconforming ball falls through. Digital scales measure weight to one-thousandth of a gram, and initial velocity is measured in a special machine by finding the time it takes a ball struck at 98 mph to break a ballistic screen at the end of a tube exactly 6.28 feet away. Thus, although you might not be able to control your swing, controlling golf ball quality is easy.

The need for control arises because of the inherent variation in any system or process. Walter Shewhart is credited with recognizing the distinction between common and special causes of variation at Bell Laboratories in the 1920s. **Common causes of variation** are the result of complex interactions of variations in materials, tools, machines, operators, and the environment. Variation due to any of these individual sources appears at random; individual sources cannot be identified or explained. Their combined effect is stable, however, and can usually be predicted statistically. Common causes of variation generally account for about 80 to 95 percent of the observed variation in a production process. Common cause variation can be reduced only by providing better technology and training.

The remaining variation in a production process is the result of **special causes of variation**, often called *assignable causes*. Special causes arise from external sources that are not inherent in the process. They appear sporadically and disrupt the random pattern of common causes. Hence, they tend to be easily detectable using statistical methods and are usually economical to correct. Factors that lead to special causes are a bad batch of material from a supplier, a poorly trained substitute machine operator, a broken or worn tool, and miscalibration of measuring instruments. Unusual variation that results from such isolated incidents can be explained or corrected.

A system governed only by common causes is called a **stable system.** Understanding when a system is stable is crucial for making proper business decisions. Managers often make one of two fundamental mistakes in attempting to improve a process:

OM PRINCIPLE

Understanding a stable system and the differences between special and common causes of variation is essential for managing any system. If managers don't understand the variation in a system, they cannot predict its future performance.

1. They treat any fault, complaint, mistake, breakdown, accident, or shortage as a special cause when it actually is due to common causes.
2. They attribute any fault, complaint, mistake, breakdown, accident, or shortage to common causes when it actually is due to a special cause.

In the first case, tampering with a stable system can increase the variation in the system. In the second case, the opportunity to reduce variation is missed because the amount of variation is mistakenly assumed to be uncontrollable.

Short-term corrective action generally should be taken by those who own the process and are responsible for doing the work, such as machine operators or order-fulfillment workers. For example, DaimlerChrysler manufactures the PT Cruiser at the company's Toluca Assembly Plant in Mexico. To ensure quality, the Toluca plant verifies parts, processes, fit, and finish every step of the way—from stamping and body to paint and final assembly. The quality control practices include visual management through quality alert systems, which are designed to call immediate attention to abnormal conditions. The system provides visual and audible signals for each station for tooling, production, maintenance, and material flow.[22] Long-term corrective action is the responsibility of management.

Quality control systems should include documented procedures for all key processes; a clear understanding of the appropriate equipment and working environment; methods for monitoring and controlling critical quality characteristics; approval processes for equipment; criteria for workmanship, such as written standards, samples, or illustrations; and maintenance activities. For example, Cincinnati Fiberglass, a small manufacturer of fiberglass parts for trucks, has a control plan for each production process that includes the process name, tool used, standard operating procedure, tolerance, inspection frequency, sample size, person responsible, reporting document, and reaction plan. Of particular importance is the ability to trace all components of a product back to key process equipment and operators and to the original material from which they were made. Process control also includes monitoring the accuracy and variability of equipment, operator knowledge and skills, the accuracy of measurement results and data used, and environmental factors such as time and temperature.

Designing the Quality Control System

A basic quality control system includes a number of key elements, some of which are discussed here.

Contract Management, Design Control, and Purchasing

Because the ultimate objective of quality assurance is to provide goods and services that meet customer requirements, the quality control system should provide for contract review to ensure that customer requirements are adequately defined and documented and that the company and its suppliers have the capability to meet these requirements. The purchasing function is critical because designs often require components or materials supplied by other firms. The purchasing function should include processes for evaluating and selecting suppliers on the basis of their ability to meet requirements, appropriate methods for controlling supplier quality, and means of verifying that purchased products conform to requirements.

Inspection and Testing

Data for process control generally come from some type of measurement or inspection activity. Inspection and/or testing for quality control generally is performed at three major points in the production process: at the receipt of incoming materials, during the manufacturing process, and upon completion of production. The purpose of receiving inspection is to ensure conformance to requirements before value-adding operations begin. Historically, the receiving function evaluated the quality of incoming materials

> **OM PRINCIPLE**
>
> The true purpose of inspection is to provide information to control and improve processes, not to separate the good from the bad.

by using **acceptance sampling,** in which the decision to accept or reject a group of items (formally called a **lot**) is based on specified quality characteristics. However, acceptance sampling yields no beneficial results if the supplier's process is stable. The labor cost and tied-up inventory add no value to the product. Also, acceptance sampling can only detect poor quality, not prevent it. Today, most companies rely on certifying the supplier's control systems to ensure the receipt of conforming product.

In-process quality control inspection is needed because of unwanted variation that may arise during production, for example, from machines going out of adjustment, worker inattention, or environmental conditions. In-process inspection allows process operators to quickly recognize special causes of variation and make immediate adjustments to stabilize the process. The quality control indicators used for in-process inspection should be closely related to cost or performance, be economical to measure, and provide information for improvement.

Quality control measurements and indicators fall into one of two categories. An **attribute** is a performance characteristic that is either present or absent in the product or service under consideration. For example, a dimension is either within tolerance or out of tolerance, an order is complete or incomplete, or an invoice can have one, two, three, or any number of errors. Thus, attributes data are discrete and tell whether the characteristic conforms to specifications. Attributes can be measured by visual inspection, such as assessing whether the correct zip code was used in shipping an order; or by comparing a dimension to specifications, such as whether the diameter of a shaft falls within specification limits of 1.60 ± 0.01 inch. Attribute measurements are typically expressed as proportions or rates, for example, the fraction of nonconformances in a group of items, number of defects per unit, or rate of errors per opportunity. The second type of performance characteristic is called a **variable.** Variables data are continuous—for instance, length, weight, or time. Variables measurements are concerned with the *degree* of conformance to specifications. Thus, rather than determining whether an airline flight is on time, a measure of the actual deviation from the scheduled arrival time is recorded. Variable measurements are generally expressed with such statistics as averages and standard deviations.

The decision of where to perform in-process inspection is fundamentally an economic one. An organization must consider tradeoffs between the explicit costs of detection, repair, or replacement and the implicit costs of allowing a nonconformity to continue through the production process. These costs are sometimes difficult or even impossible to quantify. As a result, several rules of thumb influence this decision. For example, one might inspect before relatively high-cost operations, or where significant value is added to the product, or before processing operations such as painting, that may make detection of defectives difficult or costly by masking or obscuring faulty attributes.

The final question is how much to inspect: that is, should all outputs be inspected or just a sample? One must first ask: What would be the result of allowing a nonconforming item to continue through production or on to the consumer? If the result might be a safety hazard, costly repairs or correction, or some other intolerable condition, the conclusion would probably be to use 100 percent inspection rather than sampling.

Final inspection is the last point in the manufacturing process at which the producer can verify that the product meets customer requirements and avoid external failure costs. For many consumer products, final inspection consists of functional testing. For instance, a manufacturer of televisions might do a simple test on every unit to make sure it operates properly. However, the company might not test every aspect

> ## OM PRINCIPLE
>
> Final inspection should not be the primary means of quality control; however, it is still an important part of the overall quality assurance system.

of the television, such as picture sharpness or other characteristics. These aspects might already have been evaluated through in-process controls. Computerized test equipment is quite widespread, allowing for 100 percent inspection to be conducted rapidly and cost-effectively.

Preventing Defects and Errors

Human beings tend to make mistakes inadvertently.[23] Typical mistakes in operations are omitted processing, processing errors, setup errors, missing parts, wrong parts, and adjustment errors. **Poka-yoke** (POH-kah YOH-kay) is an approach for mistake-proofing processes using automatic devices or methods to avoid simple human error. The poka-yoke concept was developed and refined in the early 1960s by the late Shigeo Shingo, a Japanese manufacturing engineer who developed the Toyota production system.[24] Poka-yoke focuses on two aspects: prediction, or recognizing that a defect is about to occur and providing a warning, and detection, or recognizing that a defect has occurred and stopping the process. Detailed examples in both manufacturing and services are provided in the Tools and Techniques supplement on the CD-ROM.

Metrology

Measuring quality characteristics generally requires the use of both the human senses—seeing, hearing, feeling, tasting, and smelling—and some type of instrument or gauge to measure the magnitude of the characteristic. Gauges and instruments used to measure quality characteristics must provide correct information, which is assured through **metrology**, which is defined broadly as the collection of people, equipment, facilities, methods, and procedures used to assure the correctness or adequacy of measurements.

Metrology is vital to quality control because of the emphasis on quality by government agencies, the implications of measurement error for safety and product liability, and the reliance on improved quality control methods such as statistical process control. The need for metrology stems from the fact that every measurement is subject to error.

> ## OM PRINCIPLE
>
> Whenever variation is observed in measurements, some portion is due to measurement system error, which can be systematic (called bias) or random. The size of the errors relative to the measurement value can significantly affect the quality of the data and resulting decisions.

The evaluation of data obtained from inspection and measurement is not meaningful unless the measurement instruments are accurate and precise. **Accuracy** is defined as the closeness of agreement between an observed value and an accepted reference value or standard; it is measured as the amount of error in a measurement in proportion to the total size of the measurement. The lack of accuracy reflects a systematic bias in the measurement such as a gauge out of calibration, worn, or used improperly by the operator. **Precision** is defined as the closeness of agreement between randomly selected individual measurements or results as measured by the variance of repeated measurements. A measuring instrument with a low variance is more precise than one having a higher variance.

When an individual inspector or technician measures the same unit multiple times, the results will usually show some variability. **Repeatability**, or **equipment variation**, is the variation in multiple measurements by an individual using the same instrument. This is a measure of how precise and accurate the equipment is. **Reproducibility**, or **operator variation**, is the variation in the same measuring instrument when it is used by different individuals to measure the same parts; reproducibility indicates how robust the measuring process is to the operator and environmental conditions. Causes of poor reproducibility might be poor training of the operator in the use of the instrument or unclear calibrations on the gauge dial. Statistical approaches can be used to quantify and evaluate equipment and operator variation.

> ## OM PRINCIPLE
>
> The total observed variation in production output is the sum of the true process variation (which is what we actually want to measure) plus variation due to measurement:
>
> $$\sigma^2_{total} = \sigma^2_{process} + \sigma^2_{measurement}$$
>
> If the measurement variation is high, the observed results will be biased, leading to inaccurate assessment of process capabilities.

Process Capability

Process capability is the range over which the natural variation of a process occurs as determined by the system of common causes; that is, it is what the process can achieve under stable conditions. For example, suppose that customer intelligence finds that a firm's online customers expect delivery within three business days of placing an order. Assuming a two-day Priority Mail delivery, this allows only one day to process, pick, pack, and ship the order. If it turns out that the average time to perform these tasks is two days, then the process is not capable of meeting customer requirements. Management then faces two possible decisions: (1) develop a better process by investing in more people and perhaps better technology, or (2) try to change customer expectations and work within the existing capability.

> ## OM PRINCIPLE
>
> Process capability is important to both product designers and operations managers and is critical to achieving Six Sigma performance. Knowing process capability allows one to predict, quantitatively, how well a process will meet specifications and to specify technology requirements and the level of control necessary.

Unfortunately, product design often takes place in isolation, with inexperienced designers applying tolerances to parts or products while having little awareness of the capabilities of operations to meet these design requirements. Similarly, salespeople make delivery commitments without knowing the firm's capability to meet those commitments. Process capability should be carefully evaluated in determining product and service specifications and operations technology. The Tools and Techniques supplement on the CD-ROM describes quantitative methods for analyzing process capability.

Statistical Process Control

Statistical process control (SPC) is a methodology for monitoring a process to identify special causes of variation and signal the need to take corrective action when appropriate. When special causes are present, the process is deemed to be *out of control*. If the variation in the process is due to common causes alone, the process is said to be *in statistical control*. SPC relies on *control charts*, which are relatively simple to use and have three basic applications: (1) to establish a state of statistical control, (2) to monitor a process and signal when the process goes out of control, and (3) to determine the capability of a process to conform to specifications. Control charts provide diagnostic tools to tell managers whether or not process variation is normal, thus helping them to know when to take action and, more importantly, when to leave a process alone. Making adjustments to a stable process only increases variation and results in lower quality. The Tools and Techniques supplement on the CD-ROM describes how to use control charts in detail.

Quality Control in Services

The most common quality characteristics in services are time (waiting time, service time, delivery time) and number of nonconformances, both of which can be measured rather easily. Insurance companies, for example, measure the time to complete different transactions such as new issues, claim payments, and cash surrenders. Hospitals measure the percentage of nosocomial infections and the percentage of unplanned readmissions to the emergency room, intensive care, or operating room within, say, 48 hours. Other quality characteristics are observable. These include the types of errors (wrong kind, wrong quantity, wrong delivery date, etc.) and behavior (courtesy, promptness, competency, etc.). Hospitals might monitor the completeness of medical charts and the quality of radiology readings, measured by a double-reading process.

Internal measurements of service quality are commonly performed with some type of data sheet or checklist. Time is easily measured by taking two observations: starting time and finishing time. Many observed data assume only "yes" or "no" values. For example, a survey of pharmaceutical operations in a hospital might include the following questions:

- Are drug storage and preparation areas within the pharmacy under the supervision of a pharmacist?

- Are drugs requiring special storage conditions properly stored?

- Are drug emergency boxes inspected on a monthly basis?

- Is the drug emergency box record book filled out completely?

Simple check sheets can be designed to record the types of errors that occur.

Even though human behavior is easily observable, describing and classifying the observations is far more difficult. The major obstacle is developing operational definitions of behavioral characteristics. For example, how does one define courteous versus discourteous, or understanding versus indifferent? Defining such distinctions is best done by comparing behavior against understandable standards. For instance, a standard for "courtesy" might be to address the customer as "Mr." or "Ms." Failure to do so is an instance of an error. "Promptness" might be defined as greeting a customer within five seconds of entering the store or answering letters within two days of receipt. These behaviors can easily be recorded and counted.

Like measuring equipment, service surveys are also prone to both systematic and random error; thus, the reliability of any survey should be understood and evaluated. An example of quality control at The Ritz-Carlton Hotel Company is given in the *OM Practice* box.

OM PRACTICE

The Ritz-Carlton Hotel Company

Quality control is vital to The Ritz-Carlton's focus on personalized attention.

The Ritz-Carlton Hotel Company uses a proactive approach to control quality because of its intensive personalized service environment. Systems for collecting and using quality-related measures are widely deployed and used extensively throughout the organization. For example, each hotel tracks a set of Service Quality Indicators on a daily basis. The Ritz-Carlton recognizes that many customer requirements are sensory and, thus, difficult to measure. However, by selecting, training, and certifying employees in their knowledge of The Ritz-Carlton Gold Standards of service, the company is able to assess their work through appropriate sensory measurements—taste, sight, smell, sound, and touch—and take appropriate actions.

The company uses three types of control processes to deliver quality:

1. Self-control of individual employees based on their spontaneous and learned behavior.
2. A basic control mechanism carried out by every member of the workforce. The first person to detect a problem is empowered to break away from routine duties, investigate and correct the problem immediately, document the incident, and then return to his or her routine.
3. A critical success factor control for critical processes. Process teams use customer and organizational requirement measurements to determine quality, speed, and cost performance. These measurements are compared against benchmarks and customer-satisfaction data to determine the need for corrective action and resource allocation.

In addition, Ritz-Carlton conducts both self and outside audits. Self-audits are carried out internally at all levels, from one individual or function to an entire hotel. Process walk-throughs occur daily in hotels, and senior leaders assess field operations during formal reviews at various intervals. Outside audits are performed by independent travel and hospitality rating organizations. All audits must be documented, and any findings must be submitted to the senior leader of the unit being audited. The senior leaders are responsible for action and for assessing the implementation and effectiveness of recommended corrective actions.[25]

6.7 QUALITY IMPROVEMENT

Operations managers should never be content with simply maintaining control, but should seek to improve all processes and operations, such as reducing cost, better meeting delivery schedules, enhancing employee safety and skill development, developing better products, or improving productivity.

Kaizen

Kaizen, a philosophy that originated in Japan and has been adopted by many organizations around the world, means gradual and orderly continuous improvement. At Nissan Motor Company, Ltd., for instance, management seriously considers any suggestion that saves at least 0.6 seconds in a production process. The concept of kaizen is so deeply ingrained in the minds of both managers and workers that they often do not even realize they are thinking in terms of improvement. The Kaizen Institute (see the text Web site at **http://raturi_evans.swlearning.com**) suggests some basic tips for implementing kaizen: discard conventional fixed ideas; think of how to do something, not why it cannot be done; do not seek perfection; do not make excuses, but question current practices; and seek the wisdom of 10 people rather than the knowledge of one.

> ## OM PRINCIPLE
>
> Kaizen seeks improvements that minimize financial investment and capitalize on the participation, knowledge, creativity, and experience of all employees.

Some companies use **kaizen blitz**—an intense and rapid improvement activity in which a team or a department throws all its resources into an improvement project over a short time period, as opposed to traditional kaizen applications, which are performed on a part–time basis. Blitz teams generally include employees from all areas involved in the process who understand it and can implement changes on the spot. Improvement is immediate, exciting, and satisfying for all those involved in the process.

The Deming Cycle

A key aspect of the kaizen philosophy is the use of the **Deming cycle**—a simple methodology for improvement (originally called the *Shewhart cycle* after its original founder, Walter Shewhart). The Deming cycle is composed of four stages: *plan, do, study*, and *act* (PDSA). The plan stage consists of studying the current situation and describing the process including its inputs, outputs, customers, and suppliers; understanding customer expectations; gathering data; identifying problems; testing theories of causes; and developing solutions and action plans. In the do stage, the plan is implemented on a trial basis, for example, in a laboratory, in a pilot production process, or with a small group of customers, to evaluate a proposed solution and provide objective data. Data from the experiment are collected and documented. The study stage determines whether the trial plan is working correctly by evaluating the results, determining what can be learned from them, and determining if any further issues or opportunities need be addressed. Often, the first solution must be modified or scrapped. New solutions are proposed and evaluated by returning to the do stage. In the last stage, act, the improvements become standardized, and the final plan is implemented as a "current best practice" and communicated throughout the organization.

Seven simple tools—flowcharts, check sheets, histograms, Pareto diagrams, cause-and-effect diagrams, scatter diagrams, and control charts—termed the **Seven QC** (quality control) **Tools** by the Japanese, support the Deming cycle and kaizen activities.[26] These tools are described in detail in the Tools and Techniques supplement on the CD-ROM. The following *OM Practice* box demonstrates the use of some of these tools to improve customer service in a department store.

OM PRACTICE

Quality Improvement in a Department Store

The Mitsukoshi Department Store in Japan provides services to customers ranging from advice on gifts to gift wrapping and other product-specific services. Concerned about improving customer service, the members of the Quality Control team decided to focus on how long customers had to wait while their watch batteries were being replaced. In Japan, customers can have watch batteries replaced at almost any watch shop, and clerks working in watch sections handle these requests frequently. The solution to the problem would affect a sales clerk's work routine.

The QC team assessed the current situation using various quality tools and techniques, such as check sheets, histograms, and cause-and-effect diagrams. When data were collected on wait times, the team found that wait time exceeded 5 minutes 32 percent of the time. The team also recorded the reasons for waiting. The most frequent causes of long waits were the inability to open the back of the watch easily and the search for the appropriate

battery. Using a cause-and-effect diagram, the team realized that lack of materials and equipment was the primary cause of delayed installations. Their action plan consisted of the following recommendations:

1. Purchase tools applicable to all brands.
2. Request a tool cabinet and organize the tools.
3. Assign a person to be in charge of battery stock.
4. Train employees in how to change batteries from each watchmaker.
5. Organize the worktable and counter, removing batteries and tools from this area.

After this plan was implemented, the frequency of wait time exceeding 5 minutes was reduced from 32 percent to 8.4 percent. In addition, no one waited more than 10 minutes. The team created a culture of "don't make them wait" that improved customer service, and this spirit has led to enhanced teamwork and sharing of ideas among the sales clerks. As this example shows, quality improvement can be applied to any process, no matter how simple.[27]

Summary of Key Points

- Quality has a variety of meanings; in operations, the most important views of quality are quality of design (how well goods and services meet customers' needs) and quality of conformance (the extent to which a process is able to deliver a product that conforms to design specifications). Both influence a firm's profitability.

- Although the emphasis on quality has changed dramatically throughout history, the concepts of total quality—a focus on customers and processes, continuous improvement and learning, and participation and teamwork by everyone—have emerged as the foundation for high-performance operations.

- The impact of quality is evident in both the financial and the operational results that companies have achieved as a result of good quality management.

- The philosophies of Deming, Juran, and Crosby had a powerful influence on management thinking in the late twentieth century and continue to be influential today. They provide a rational basis for focusing on quality in operations and throughout an organization, as well as key principles for managers to follow.

- The two most prominent frameworks for quality management are the Malcolm Baldrige National Quality Award and the ISO 9000 standards. The Baldrige criteria provide an approach for a comprehensive assessment of an organization's management system, and for seeking opportunities for improvement relative to best management practices. Operations managers can obtain specific guidance from the Process Management category. ISO 9000 is a set of quality system standards that seek to establish consistency of performance in operations to meet customer requirements.

- Six Sigma has emerged as a leading approach to improving quality and linking results to the bottom line. Through quality measurement, use of advanced statistical and other tools, problem-solving methodology, and a focus on results, Six Sigma has allowed many firms to achieve unprecedented levels of performance.

- Common causes of variation are the result of complex interactions of variations in materials, tools, machines, operators, and the environment. Special causes arise from external sources that are not inherent in the process; they appear sporadically and disrupt the random pattern of common causes. Special causes can be identified and removed through quality control approaches, whereas common causes must be attacked by improving technology and systems.

- Key elements of an effective quality control system are contract management, design control, purchasing, inspection and testing, and metrology. Quality control methods are crucial in both manufacturing and service operations.

- Kaizen is a philosophy that seeks to improve all processes and operations, such as reducing cost, better meeting delivery schedules, enhancing employee safety and skill development, developing better products, and improving productivity. Kaizen is supported by the Deming cycle (PDSA), the Seven QC Tools, and other approaches such as kaizen blitz.

Questions for Review and Discussion

1. Consider the nine "definitions" of quality that arose from the survey of managers described in Section 6.1. Which relate to design quality, and which relate to conformance quality?

2. Cite an example in which you experienced poor quality in a product or service. Did you complain to the company? Did you tell others about the problem? Has that experience changed your purchasing practices?

3. Explain the difference between targets and tolerances. Why are tolerances necessary?

4. Explain the implications of the quality definition of "meeting or exceeding customer expectations" for operations managers.

5. Why do improvements in design and conformance quality lead to higher profitability?

6. As the historical review suggested, the quality movement in the United States arose because of crises that manufacturers faced from foreign competitors. Through the 1980s and into the 1990s, Ford Motor Company moved to the top in quality of U.S. automobiles as a result of its quality efforts only to fall behind General Motors and DaimlerChrysler by the turn of the century. In early 2002, Ford closed five plants and cut 35,000 jobs. Chairman William Clay Ford, Jr., stated "We strayed from what got us to the top of the mountain and it cost us greatly." What lessons does this provide to other companies?

7. Summarize the three key principles of total quality. What implications do they have for operations managers?

8. Describe Deming's philosophy and explain how and why it differs from traditional management practices.

9. What implications do Deming's 14 Points have for the daily management of operations? How do they relate to the other structural and infrastructural decisions discussed in Chapter 1?

10. How do Juran's and Crosby's philosophies differ from Deming's?

11. Why was the Malcolm Baldrige National Quality Award instituted? Explain the impact the award has had on U.S. business.

12. List and explain the seven categories of the Baldrige criteria.

13. "Operations managers need only pay attention to the Process Management category of the Baldrige criteria." Do you agree with this statement? Why or why not?

14. Obtain a copy of the current year's Malcolm Baldrige National Quality Award criteria. Develop a short questionnaire that a company might use to assess its management practices based on the criteria.

15. Select a past winner of the Baldrige award, and find some articles describing that company's quality system (many articles are published about the winners). Write a case about the company.

16. What is ISO 9000? How does it differ from the Baldrige criteria? How do the eight principles of ISO 9000:2000 correspond to Baldrige concepts?

17. Explain the concept of Six Sigma. How is it measured? How has it evolved into a comprehensive improvement philosophy?

18. Explain the DMAIC process. What are the advantages of using such a structured process?

19. Explain the difference between common causes and special causes of variation.

20. Provide some examples of control systems that illustrate the three components (standards, measurement, and feedback) discussed in the chapter.

21. Gather information about a local company's quality control system. Evaluate its design and suggest some steps the company might take to improve.

22. Explain the difference between accuracy and precision. Why is it important to measure and evaluate repeatability and reproducibility in a manufacturing process?

23. How does quality control differ between manufacturing and services? In what ways is it similar?

24. What is kaizen? How does it differ from kaizen blitz?

25. Explain the Deming cycle. Describe how it might be used to address a problem that you face in your business or personal life.

Internet Projects

To find Web links to carry out each of the following projects, go to the text's Web site at **http://raturi_evans.swlearning.com**.

1. The Deming Institute is dedicated to keeping the philosophy of W. Edwards Deming alive. Visit the Web site and write a brief report on how Deming's philosophy continues to be promoted.

2. The Kaizen Institute is a global management consulting company, recognized as the international leader in helping companies implement continuous improvement tools and strategies. Visit the Web site, click on the menu item *Reading,* and select *Kaizen* case from the list. Read the NUMMI case and summarize the lessons learned about continuous improvement.

3. Six Sigma Qualtec is a provider of training and implementation services. Their Web site documents the results of several case studies. Click on "case studies" and select "Transactional services case studies" at the bottom of the page. Summarize how service firms can benefit from quality improvement programs.

EXPERIENCE OM

Applying Statistical Process Control

The Dean Door Company (DDC) manufactures steel and aluminum exterior doors for commercial and residential applications. DDC landed a major contract as a supplier to Walker Homes, a builder of residential communities in several major cities throughout the upper Midwest. Because of the large volume of demand, DDC had to expand its manufacturing operations to three shifts and hire additional workers.

Not long after DDC began shipping doors to Walker Homes, it began receiving complaints about excessive gaps between the door and the frame. The problem was somewhat alarming to DDC because its reputation as a high-quality manufacturer was the principal reason that it was selected as a supplier to Walker Homes. In reviewing the complaints, the company president suspected that the expansion to a three-shift operation and pressures to produce higher volumes and meet just-in-time delivery requirements was causing a breakdown in quality.

On the recommendation of the plant manager, DDC hired a quality consultant to train the shift supervisors and selected line workers in SPC methods. As a trial project the plant manager wants to evaluate a critical cutting operation that he suspects might be the source of the gap problem. The nominal specification for this cutting operation is 30.000 inch with a tolerance of 0.125 inch; therefore the acceptable specification limits are 29.875 and 30.125. Anything outside these limits is considered a defect. The following table shows the results of inspecting five consecutive door panels in the middle of each shift over a 10-day period and recording the dimensions of the cut.

			OBSERVATION				
Shift	**Operator**	**Sample**	**1**	**2**	**3**	**4**	**5**
1	Terry	1	30.046	29.978	30.026	29.986	29.961
2	Jordan	2	29.972	29.966	29.964	29.942	30.025
3	Dana	3	30.046	30.004	30.028	29.986	30.027
1	Terry	4	29.997	29.997	29.980	30.000	30.034
2	Jordan	5	30.018	29.922	29.992	30.008	30.053
3	Dana	6	29.973	29.990	29.985	29.991	30.004

			OBSERVATION				
Shift	**Operator**	**Sample**	**1**	**2**	**3**	**4**	**5**
1	Terry	7	29.989	29.952	29.941	30.012	29.984
2	Jordan	8	29.969	30.000	29.968	29.976	29.973
3	Cameron	9	29.852	29.978	29.964	29.896	29.876
1	Terry	10	30.042	29.976	30.021	29.996	30.042
2	Jordan	11	30.028	29.999	30.022	29.942	29.998
3	Dana	12	29.955	29.984	29.977	30.008	30.033
1	Terry	13	30.040	29.965	30.001	29.975	29.970
2	Jordan	14	30.007	30.024	29.987	29.951	29.994
3	Dana	15	29.979	30.007	30.000	30.042	30.000
1	Terry	16	30.073	29.998	30.027	29.986	30.011
2	Jordan	17	29.995	29.966	29.996	30.039	29.976
3	Dana	18	29.994	29.982	29.998	30.040	30.017
1	Terry	19	29.977	30.013	30.042	30.001	29.962
2	Jordan	20	30.021	30.048	30.037	29.985	30.005
3	Cameron	21	29.879	29.882	29.990	29.971	29.953
1	Terry	22	30.043	30.021	29.963	29.993	30.006
2	Jordan	23	30.065	30.012	30.021	30.024	30.037
3	Cameron	24	29.899	29.875	29.980	29.878	29.877
1	Terry	25	30.029	30.011	30.017	30.000	30.000
2	Jordan	26	30.046	30.006	30.039	29.991	29.970
3	Dana	27	29.993	29.991	29.984	30.022	30.010
1	Terry	28	30.057	30.032	29.979	30.027	30.033
2	Jordan	29	30.004	30.049	29.980	30.000	29.986
3	Dana	30	29.995	30.000	29.922	29.984	29.968

a. Using control charts, interpret the data shown in the table. Is the overall process in statistical control? If not, what might be the likely cause? Compute revised control limits after eliminating any out-of-control points.

b. Examine the data in relation to the acceptable specification limits. What do you conclude?

c. After establishing control, additional samples were taken over the next 20 shifts, as shown in the table below. What conclusion can you reach about the process now? Is there any evidence that the process has changed relative to the control limits established in part (a)?

OBSERVATION

Shift	Operator	Sample	1	2	3	4	5
1	Terry	31	29.970	30.017	29.898	29.937	29.992
2	Jordan	32	29.947	30.013	29.993	29.997	30.079
3	Dana	33	30.050	30.031	29.999	29.963	30.045
1	Terry	34	30.064	30.061	30.016	30.041	30.006
2	Jordan	35	29.948	30.009	29.962	29.990	29.979
3	Dana	36	30.016	29.989	29.939	29.981	30.017
1	Terry	37	29.946	30.057	29.992	29.973	29.955
2	Jordan	38	29.981	30.023	29.992	29.992	29.941
3	Dana	39	30.043	29.985	30.014	29.986	30.000
1	Terry	40	30.013	30.046	30.096	29.975	30.019
2	Jordan	41	30.043	30.003	30.062	30.025	30.023
3	Dana	42	29.994	30.056	30.033	30.011	29.948
1	Terry	43	29.995	30.014	30.018	29.966	30.000
2	Jordan	44	30.018	29.982	30.028	30.029	30.044
3	Dana	45	30.018	29.994	29.995	30.029	30.034
1	Terry	46	30.025	29.951	30.038	30.009	30.003
2	Jordan	47	30.048	30.046	29.995	30.053	30.043
3	Dana	48	30.030	30.054	29.997	29.993	30.010
1	Terry	49	29.991	30.001	30.041	30.036	29.992
2	Jordan	50	30.022	30.021	30.022	30.008	30.019

7

Supply Chain Management

A **supply chain** is a network that describes the flow of materials from suppliers through facilities that transform them into useful products and, finally, to distribution centers that deliver those products to customers. **Supply chain management (SCM)** is an integrated approach to procuring, producing, and delivering products and services to customers; it includes the management of materials, as well as associated information and the flow of funds. Supply chains exist in both manufacturing and service industries. Their principal purpose is to create value for customers, and they are therefore an important component of the value chain we described in Chapter 1.

This chapter focuses on the role of supply chains. Specifically, we address:
- The concept of integrated supply chain management (*Section 7.1*).
- The role of inventory in supply chains (*Section 7.2*).
- Guidelines for measuring and evaluating supply chain performance (*Section 7.3*).
- A strategic view of supply chains (*Section 7.4*).
- Variability and the "bullwhip" effect in supply chains (*Section 7.5*).
- Managing supply chains (*Section 7.6*).
- Some emerging trends in supply chain management (*Section 7.7*).

Material on the CD-ROM discusses some useful tools and techniques for supply chain management.
2. Linear Optimization Modeling
8. Scoring Models for Facility Location
9. Center of Gravity Method

7.1 SUPPLY CHAINS

Supply chains play a very critical role in organizations. The Commerce Department estimates that in the United States, $1.1 trillion in inventory results in $3.2 trillion in annual retail sales. Of this, $400 billion in inventory is at retail locations, $290 billion at wholesalers or distributors, and $450 billion with manufacturers. One would imagine that with almost four months of sales in stock—calculated as $(1.1/3.2) \times 12$—stockouts would be very rare. Yet studies show that 8.2 percent of shoppers, on average, fail to find their product in stock. These stockout events represent 6.5 percent of all retail sales. Even after recouping some of the loss with sales of alternative products and rainchecks, retailers suffer net lost sales of 3.1 percent. This takes an enormous toll on retailers, whose margins are generally very thin, not to mention the loss of customer goodwill. The problem is that many organizations do not have the right product, at the right place, at the right time to service customers.[1] "For a company with annual sales of $500 million and a 60 percent cost of sales, the difference between being at median in terms of supply chain performance and in the top 20 percent is $44 million of additional working capital."[2] Thus, the economic potential of effective supply chain management, or SCM, is significant.

SCM is an outgrowth and synthesis of traditional inventory management and logistics. **Inventory management** focuses on managing physical stock to ensure availability of materials for work-in-process operations as well as for external customers. Inventory management began over a century ago when Ford Harris first used mathematics to answer the question "How many units should I make in one batch?" He established the classic economic order quantity formula, which, along with other quantitative inventory models, is discussed in the Tools and Techniques supplement on the CD-ROM. **Logistics** is the discipline of managing the flow of materials and transportation activities to ensure adequate customer service at reasonable cost. The unique characteristic of SCM is that whereas inventory and logistics managers typically focused on activities within the span of their manufacturing and distribution processes, SCM encompasses the entire value chain, from suppliers to customers, with a clear focus on and understanding of the interactions among all parts of the system. For example, managers of consumer products supply chains recognized that their unwanted inventory and/or unmet demand often stemmed from independent decisions among the players within the supply chain. "Special carload" price promotions would cause buyers to buy in an intermittent pattern, creating operational disruptions throughout the supply chain that affected both costs and customer service. A supply chain focus and partnerships among customers and suppliers such as the relationship between Wal-Mart and Proctor & Gamble help to support a true systems perspective.

Figure 7.1 illustrates a supply chain network for a typical manufacturing or service organization. It includes the material management functions of receiving and storing raw materials and components; key processing functions of manufacturing, distribution, and delivery; information-processing and decision-making functions; and functions related to managing transfers of funds. Working capital in the form of payables and receivables is just as important as working capital in the form of inventory and equipment and thus is a critical part of a supply chain.

SCM comprises a wide variety of activities, including forecasting and scheduling product and material flows, inventory management, identifying sources of supply and procuring materials, supplier management, production and assembly, order capture and scheduling, billing, accounts receivable, order consolidation, picking and packing, transportation, dealing with returns and allowances, financial planning, information systems, performance measurement, customer relationship management, and many others. Dealing with all these activities can be quite complex, and coordinating them can be a significant challenge (see the *OM Practice* box

OM PRINCIPLE

Integrated supply chain networks are critical to the successful performance of all firms in the value chain used to deliver goods and services to the customer. A business that does not view supply chains as an integrated system runs the risk of suboptimizing resources, failing to meet critical customer needs, and failing to support key business strategies.

on Nabisco). For example, to reconcile material, information, and fund flows with suppliers, every organization needs to constantly monitor all aspects of the ordering process. Doing so not only enables a firm to identify tardy or ineffective suppliers or those with unacceptable credit policies but also can be helpful in identifying opportunities. For example, one firm chose a supplier with a longer delivery lead-time and higher cost because it had an easier credit policy (60 days) than the more effective supplier (30 days).

Projecting a cash flow crisis, the firm decided that the extra 30 days in accounts payable was worth the incremental cost it would pay to the less effective supplier. The need for such com-

FIGURE 7.1 | *Material, Information, and Fund Flows in a Supply Chain*

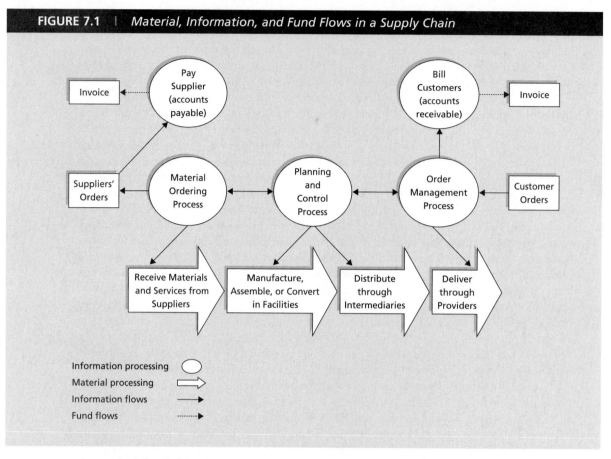

plex analysis has led businesses to recognize the importance and potential of taking an integrated view of SCM.

The **Supply Chain Operations Reference (SCOR) model,** which is based on the following four basic functions involved in managing a supply chain, provides an excellent framework for understanding the complexity in a supply chain as well as the right metrics for improving performance:[3]

1. **Plan:** Developing a strategy that balances aggregate supply and demand.
2. **Source:** Procuring goods and services to meet planned or actual demand.
3. **Make:** Transforming goods and services to a finished state to meet demand.
4. **Deliver:** Managing orders, transportation, and distribution to provide the goods and services.

Since other chapters focus on the plan (Chapter 8) and make (Chapter 4) functions, we will restrict our attention to source and deliver issues in this chapter.

Sourcing decisions involve developing and managing a set of suppliers that can provide the appropriate inputs to the organization at the right time, quality, and cost. Today, many organizations are outsourcing peripheral functions so that they can focus on their core competence. With this growth in outsourcing, the sourcing function is becoming even more important. Consider a firm that sources only 40 percent of its final product value (cost of goods sold) versus one that sources 80 percent. A 1 percent reduction in sourcing cost delivers only

OM PRACTICE

Nabisco's Supply Chain
Nabisco struggles and succeeds with supply chain management.

Nabisco began to reassess its supply chain in the mid-1980s so that it would be able to compete successfully in today's business environment. The company learned "that supply chain management is about moving from being internally-focused and functionally driven to externally-focused and process driven." One principle was that *any customer could order and expect delivery of Nabisco products on a single purchase order.* Accomplishing this was not easy because Nabisco has multiple manufacturing plants run by independent Nabisco operating companies. Thus, the company spent a great deal of time making sure everyone understood his or her part in the process. It needed to "convey the benefits of [SCM], the trade-offs with other business functions and—perhaps most impor-

tantly—the risks associated with not pursuing enlightened supply chain management." Employees needed to understand that this was not an inventory reduction plan and that the concept was centered on delighting the customer.

To facilitate this effort, Nabisco initiated an internal communications and outreach program. Through this program, for example, operations personnel were given access to the same systems and information that the logistics department had. Now SCM is assuming a position as a core competency at Nabisco. Senior executives now recognize that an "extremely agile supply chain is vital to generate and sustain profitable growth." Nabisco's emphasis is on "producing the right product and positioning it at the right place at the right time to drive down dwell time and increase turns with reduced inventory investment." To be truly successful, everyone involved with the supply chain must share this focus.[4]

0.4 percent to the first firm's profit margin but contributes 0.8 percent incrementally to the second firm's profit margin.

With the advent of the Internet and Web-based distribution channels, firms face many new challenges in ensuring that they have an effective infrastructure to deliver the products and services to the final customer. Many industries have achieved benefits for the end customer through **disintermediation,** in which the role of intermediaries such as wholesalers and distributors in a supply chain is reduced or even eliminated altogether. The primary driving forces here are simplification of the delivery process and creation of new methods to respond to customer demands effectively and with greater agility. Both Amazon.com and Dell, for example, have reinvented their delivery systems through disintermediation to enhance the value to the end customer.

Supply Chains and Competitive Advantage

Supply chains have been a source of competitive advantage throughout history (see the interesting story of Alexander the Great in the *OM Practice* box). Today, companies no longer compete on products—they compete through supply chains.[5] A study by Pittiglio, Rabin, Todd & McGrath found that companies in the "top quintile for supply chain performance achieve savings equal to 3 percent to 7 percent of revenues." Consequently, companies such as the following are focusing significant efforts on streamlining their supply chains to reduce costs and provide better customer service and value:

○ Eastman Kodak has developed what it calls "stream inventory management." The company looks at its supply chain as one continuous pipeline. A computer system called Globiis (Global Business Integrated Information System) is used to run its inventory management system.

○ General Electric Transportation Systems has seen great benefits by developing close relationships with its suppliers. GE even allows its suppliers to tap into its design drawings and quality information online. As the suppliers have taken on more of the production process, they work with the company in what GE calls "flawless execution."

○   A.W. Chesterton has trimmed its supply chain by reducing the number of vendors from 1,300 in 1993 to 125 today. Chesterton has also reduced inventory by 35 percent and increased profits threefold. The firm now focuses on quality and service instead of price.

Without any specific effort to coordinate the overall supply chain system, each organization in the network (suppliers, providers of goods and services, and distributors) has its own

---

OM PRACTICE

Alexander the Great and Supply Chain Management

Modern business can learn many lessons from Alexander the Great.

Alexander the Great was born in 356 B.C. and became one of history's greatest military leaders, inspiring Julius Caesar and Napoleon among others. Alexander's ability to consistently defeat enemy armies and expand his kingdom was a result of his proactive preparation and logical approach to warfare. His 35,000-man army could carry no more than a 10-day supply of food when away from sea transport, yet because he had included logistics and SCM in his strategic plans, his troops were able to march over thousands of miles at a rate of 19.5 miles a day without major problems.

If Alexander were a CEO today, he would:

○   Include logistics and SCM in strategic planning.
○   Consistently make changes that were demonstrated to provide specific benefits to his organization.

○   Develop a working knowledge and detailed understanding of his customers and their products, competition, industry, logistics requirements, and technologies, and utilize this knowledge, along with other assets, to develop competitive advantages, market share, and profit.
○   Appoint a single person to lead all logistics (SCM) functions and participate in strategic planning sessions.
○   Develop alliances with key suppliers and service providers and access their infrastructure by allowing them to entrench themselves in his own company.
○   Utilize technology and other business tools only to the extent that they further the goals of profitability and competitive advantage.

In fact, if Alexander the Great were a CEO today, he would strike fear into the hearts of the competition![6]

---

agenda and operates independently from the others. Such an unmanaged network results in inefficiencies, however. For example, a plant may have the goal of maximizing throughput in order to lower unit costs. But if the distributors don't or can't use this output, inventory will accumulate in the distribution network. Clearly, much can be gained in performance and efficiency by managing the supply chain network in an integrated fashion. Volkswagen, for example, is working with its dealers to get advance order information and actual orders electronically and feed the data directly into the daily automobile production planning. VW is also working with its in-house supply plants and contract suppliers to issue electronic orders for parts and subassemblies to be delivered in a just-in-time mode according to the daily production schedule. VW plans to use this integrated supply chain operation to reduce its present order-to-delivery cycle time from many weeks to two weeks and eventually to a matter of days.

The VF Corporation makes popular lines of clothing such as Jantzen, Vanity Fair, and Wrangler. After installing computer-aided design (CAD) in its design centers, computer-aided manufacturing (CAM) at its world-dispersed plants, and a telecommunications network to interconnect them in near-real time, VF realized three benefits:

OM PRINCIPLE

Integrated supply chain management can lead to lower costs, improved customer service, and enhanced revenues *simultaneously*.

lower costs, improved customer service, and a 17 percent increase in revenue. Developing new products quickly using CAD, VF can update designs and forecasts and electronically feed the information to the agile CAM manufacturing plants (and suppliers) for prompt rescheduling. Fast air transportation brings the right quantities of the right product to the retail shelves. These supply chain innovations improved sales in the peak season and reduced leftover product to be sold at a discount. So revenues rose, *and* the customers got better service, *and* inventory and resale costs went down.

Demand Chains

Converting from a supply-based company to a responsive, customer-centric organization is a major challenge. When a supply chain is viewed from the customer's perspective, the result is a concept known as the **demand chain.** Although the concepts of supply chain and demand chain are often used interchangeably, a demand chain focuses on a demand-driven "pull" model of operation. This model seeks to identify and react to market demand, giving price and margin stability a high weight, while accepting the risk of underutilized capacity in the short term. In contrast, a supply-driven "push" model gives unit cost reduction a high weight, while accepting the periodic need for discounting to clear stocks. The two have completely different implications for operations, logistics, and sales. The supply chain is focused on making products in a highly predictable, highly efficient way; the demand chain is the counterpoint, focused on customers.[7]

Because demand chain management focuses on demand, information technology (IT) applications such as data mining can provide useful information for merchandising decisions, promotion plans, and new product development decisions. In the supply chain, data are predictable and easily categorized and can be tuned to flow down the chain. But the opposite is true of demand chains. Interpretation of demand data, elasticity to price changes, and cross-elasticity with other options or competitors' prices and features can make responding to customer needs very difficult. The *OM Practice* box on Benetton provides a good example of a firm that has learned to exploit demand chain management.

Increasing the flexibility of the supplier or the manufacturing facility is a key focus in demand chain management. Flexible operations can better respond to market needs. As at

OM PRACTICE

Benetton as McFashion: A Quick-Response Demand Chain

Benetton has invested heavily in demand chain management over the last two decades.

Benetton's extensive EDI network linking its design center with the network of outsourced manufacturers, sales agents, retail outlets, transportation carriers, and logistics centers makes the demand chain transparent. Its investments in flexible manufacturing lines with its famous postponement concepts in manufacturing, cycle time reduction, and its state-of-the art distribution center also enable it to respond to demand signals promptly. The ability to change production schedules enables Benetton to distribute the right products to the right markets to meet the highly seasonal demands for apparel. The firm has also invested in CAD tools linked to CAM tools, concurrent design processes, and cross-trained design teams so as to reduce new product development time. This enables the company to introduce new products in the middle of a season in response to fashion trends. It is no wonder that Benetton is known as the "smart operator" of the apparel industry and has earned the nickname "McFashion," in recognition of its success as a "quick-response" provider.[8]

Benetton, this means providing the technology for flexible operations and developing systems and procedures that are geared to responsiveness. Aligning the product portfolio (such as the variety of products offered) with customer needs, operational capabilities, and profitability is a challenging task since each of these goals typically pulls an organization in a different direction.

7.2 THE ROLE OF INVENTORIES IN SUPPLY CHAINS

Inventory is any asset held for future use. Inventories support the supply chain by providing materials and goods where and when they are needed—for production and delivery to customers. Therefore, inventory management is one of the most important functions in SCM.

> **OM PRINCIPLE**
>
> Inventory is generally the largest short-term asset on any corporate balance sheet. High inventories are not always bad, but they often are a symptom of ineffective business practices.

Firms carry inventory primarily for four reasons:

1. **Economies of Scale:** Quantity discounts offered by suppliers often lead to reduced total costs of procurement, and manufacturing costs are lower if they are spread across more units.
2. **Production and Capacity Smoothing:** Rather than change processing rates to match varying demand, it may be more economical to process at a constant rate and use inventory as a buffer.
3. **Protection against Supply Disruptions and Demand Surges:** Supply disruptions may result in process starvation, downtime, and throughput reduction. Demand surges can result in delayed deliveries, lost sales, and customer dissatisfaction.
4. **Profit from Price Changes:** Speculative inventories can be used to protect and profit from sudden price changes, especially in the commodities market.

Inventory takes many forms. Purchased raw materials and components are called **lot-size inventory. Work-in-process (WIP) inventory** acts as a buffer between work centers or departments to enable the production system to continue operating when machines break down, supplier shipments are late, or a large proportion of parts is defective. **Finished goods inventory** minimizes the effects of varying demand for finished goods and provides better customer service. It is rarely possible to predict sales accurately, and a firm runs the risk of losing many customers if it runs out of stock. **Fluctuation inventory** or **safety stock** is maintained in case of such an event. Another reason for having inventory is that many items have high seasonal demand. Limited production capacity may make it impossible to produce enough during a short selling season. **Anticipation inventory** is therefore built up during the off-season to meet future increase in demand.

Three primary decisions must be made in relation to inventory: (1) how to monitor inventory, (2) how much should be ordered, and (3) when orders should be placed. Each of these decisions has an important impact on cost. The greater the control placed on monitoring inventory levels, the higher the cost of administrative work and information processing. On the other hand, better control may result in fewer stockouts and improved customer service. The quantity and frequency of ordering also affect inventory costs. If large lots are ordered, more inventory is carried on the average. Consequently, fewer orders are placed and ordering costs are low, but holding costs are high. On

> **OM PRINCIPLE**
>
> Excessive inventory can have disadvantages, including increased response time to changes in market demand; increased time to change to new products; delay in detecting quality problems; and decoupling stages of the process flow, discouraging teamwork.

7.1

the other hand, if frequent small orders are placed, ordering costs are high, but holding costs are low. These costs must be balanced to achieve a minimum-cost inventory policy. Quantitative models in the Tools and Techniques supplement on the CD-ROM address these issues.

Inventory decisions relate to both the design and the management of the supply chain. A key strategic system design issue is the placement of inventory within a supply chain. For example, in an assemble-to-order environment, there is little or no finished goods inventory, but high levels of component inventories must be maintained in order to respond quickly to customers' requests. Examples of operational decisions include the routine replenishment of inventories. *Supplementary Notes 7.1* in the Bonus Materials folder on the CD-ROM provides a discussion of analytical approaches for some basic inventory calculations.

7.3 MEASURING SUPPLY CHAIN PERFORMANCE

OM PRINCIPLE

Supply chain metrics provide vital information for both managing daily operations and evaluating key strategic tradeoffs such as customer response and cost-effectiveness in designing supply chains.

We discussed the importance of measuring operations performance in Chapter 2. Unless the right metrics are established to support the organization's strategy, the supply chain may be poorly designed and managed.

Longs Drug Stores captures and uses various metrics to monitor its supply chain and operate it at peak efficiency.[9] These include product availability (99 percent), inventory reduction at its distribution centers (65 percent reduction in four years), store inventory (38 percent reduction), and inventory turns (62 percent better than the industry average). The OM Practice box on Koppers provides a good example of the use of metrics in supply chains.

OM PRACTICE

Supply Chain Measurement at Koppers Industries
The supply chain is the key to growth at Koppers.

In late 1994, Koppers Industries, Inc. launched an initiative to improve the way the 82-year-old company managed its supply chain. Now a $600 million company, it has already saved between $6 million and $7 million through its supply chain strategy. A total SCM program entails getting control of the flow of materials from the supplier's supplier to the customer's customer. To pull it all off, the company first had to revamp its logistics process. To measure its logistics performance, it developed a set of eight metrics including the dollar value of inventory, the number of inventory turns, the percentage of shipments made using each mode of transportation, the load factor for each shipment, on-time shipment record, equipment utilization, backhaul, and

demurrage. It also designed an overall metric to calculate its total logistics costs as a percentage of the cost of sales.

To better position itself for the long haul, Koppers reorganized to focus on total supply chain costs. With help from Mercer Management Consulting and the Center for Logistics Research, Koppers learned that logistics costs, which include transportation and inventory costs, comprised between 15 and 20 percent of sales costs in some business units.

Koppers has seen dramatic savings from backhauls, mode shifts, and load optimization. All these results sprouted from cross-functional cooperation and accurate shipping data. With the proper software in place, Koppers' functional departments can examine costs on a total supply chain basis. The performance of the supply chain is measured in terms of profit, average product fill rate, response time, and capacity utilization.[10]

Inventory System Metrics

A practical approach for measuring inventory management performance is to classify inventory into five categories:[11]

1. **Operating Inventory:** Any inventory less than or equal to the maximum allowable level to sustain normal operations.
2. **Surplus Inventory:** Any inventory exceeding the operating inventory maximum, but less than "excess" inventory. Most companies have a policy defining excess inventories based on financial policies.
3. **Excess Inventory:** Inventory beyond surplus as defined by financial policy.
4. **Obsolete Inventory:** Inventory classified as obsolete because of discontinuation of a product, expiration of shelf life, and so forth.
5. **New Product Inventory:** A classification suggested because demand for new products is slow in the early stages of the product life cycle.

This classification system can be applied to finished goods, raw materials, work in process, or any other categories that a company may define. The existence of surplus inventory should be viewed as an indication of a control problem requiring attention. A manager might compare the total excess and obsolete inventory to the reserve provided in the balance sheet and bring any discrepancies to financial management. The classification also helps in determining whether there are any overall problems in the inventory management process and provides the basis for any needed corrective action and process modifications.

Inventory costs provide objective measures on which to base many supply chain decisions. The cost of maintaining inventory is the principal criterion for determining inventory policy—how much inventory to carry and the frequency of ordering. Inventory costs fit into four major categories: cost of the items themselves, order-preparation costs, inventory-holding costs, and shortage costs. The cost of items is an important consideration when quantity discounts are offered; it may be more economical to purchase large quantities at a lower unit cost. **Ordering costs** are incurred because of the work involved in placing purchase orders with suppliers and organizing the ordered items for production within a plant. For purchased items, they can include the costs of order processing, filling out forms, selecting suppliers, fixed handling costs, processing receiving documents, and inspecting goods when they arrive. Within a plant, the ordering costs (generally called **setup costs**) include paperwork, machine setup, and startup scrap. Ordering costs depend on the number of orders placed, not on the number of items purchased or manufactured.

Inventory-holding (inventory-carrying) costs include all direct and opportunity costs incurred to store the product. They include such items as rent, electricity, heat, insurance, taxes, spoilage, obsolescence, and the cost of capital. Rent, utilities, and the like are fixed costs associated with maintaining the storage facilities and are relatively easy to measure from accounting data. Spoilage and obsolescence costs apply to food and drug items, which may have only a limited shelf life, or to novelty and seasonal items such as large toy stocks or Christmas trees. The cost of capital invested in inventory normally accounts for the largest component of inventory-holding costs. Cost of capital is the product of the value of a unit of inventory, the length of time held, and an interest rate associated with a dollar tied up in inventory. The interest rate can be highly volatile and depends on the prime interest rate, the risk environment of the firm, and management goals for rates of return on investment. Since many of these factors are difficult to determine, holding charges are often based on managers' judgment, rather than on strict accounting principles.

Shortages are classified as backorders or lost sales. A **backorder** occurs when a customer waits for an item that is not available in stock; a **lost sale** occurs when the customer refuses to wait but goes to another supplier or buys a substitute product. Backorders may incur additional costs for shipping, invoicing, and labor involved in handling the paperwork, receiving the goods, and notifying customers. Lost sales result in lost profit opportunities and in possible future loss of revenues, which are referred to as **goodwill costs.**

Supply Chain System Metrics

Supply chain managers use numerous other metrics that provide a more aggregate view of performance. These include the following:

- **Perfect Order Fulfillment:** A "perfect order" is defined as an order that is delivered complete on the customer's request date, in perfect condition, and with all supporting documentation such as packing slips, bills of lading, and invoices.

  Perfect order fulfillment = number of perfect orders/total number of orders

- **Customer Satisfaction:** Customer satisfaction includes *customer perception* of whether customers receive what they need when they need it, as well as such intangibles as convenient time of delivery, product and service quality, helpful manuals, and after-sales support. Customer satisfaction is often measured on a perception scale that might range from Extremely Dissatisfied to Extremely Satisfied.

- **Order Fulfillment Lead-Time:** This is the time to fill a customer's order. In 1996, it took 50 days to order a Ford Mustang and have it delivered to a dealer. Within two years, e-technology had reduced this time to 15 days; a customer could specify options via a computer, view the car on the monitor, order it, and get a confirmed delivery date.[12] Today, companies are even visualizing next-day delivery for a custom car! An alternative to lead-time is to calculate the proportion of deliveries that were on time as well as complete, called **perfect delivery fulfillment:**

  Perfect delivery fulfillment =
  number of orders delivered on time/total number of orders

- **Total Supply Chain Costs:** Total supply chain costs include total overhead cost for order fulfillment, material acquisition, inventory holding, logistics, and information systems support. These are often broken down into order fulfillment costs, which include costs for order entry and maintenance, installation, distribution, and accounting; total inventory-carrying costs, which include the opportunity costs of holding inventory calculated as a percentage of the inventory value, costs associated with breakage, pilferage, and obsolescence, and insurance and taxes; finance costs associated with paying invoices, coordinating supply/demand processes, auditing physical counts, and performing inventory accounting; and costs associated with the development and maintenance of information systems.

- **Cash-to-Cash Cycle Time:** Some firms go beyond such direct metrics and measure the supply chain performance in terms of the **cash-to-cash cycle time,** which is the average time to convert a dollar spent to acquire raw materials into a dollar collected for finished product.

$$\text{Cash-to-cash cycle time} =$$
$$\text{total inventory days of supply} + \text{days sales outstanding} - \text{days payables outstanding}$$

Inventory days of supply is the total dollar value of production (raw material and work in process), plant-finished goods, and field-finished goods inventories divided by the average daily cost of sales. *Days sales outstanding* is measured by the average accounts receivable divided by average daily sales. *Days payables outstanding* is measured by dividing the year-ending accounts payable (A/P) by the average daily material receipts for the year.

For example, suppose that a firm has an average daily cost of sales of $800: $16,000 in total inventories and $32,000 in average accounts receivable. Last year, at year-end closing, the firm had accounts payable of $14,000 and average daily receipts of material of $700 per day. Then the cash-to-cash cycle time is

$$\text{Cash-to-cash cycle time} = \$16{,}000/\$800 + \$32{,}000/\$800 + \$14{,}000/\$700$$
$$= 20 \text{ days} + 40 \text{ days} + 20 \text{ days} = 80 \text{ days}$$

○ **Inventory Turnover Ratio:** This is the inverse of average days of supply scaled to an annual basis:

$$\text{Inventory turnover ratio} = (\text{operating days/year}) \times$$
$$(\text{average daily cost of sales/total inventory})$$

Continuing the previous example, if the firm operates 250 days per year, the inventory turnover ratio would be $(250 \times \$800)/\$16{,}000 = 12.5$ per year. This means that the firm turns over its inventory an average of 12.5 times per year.

○ **Supply Chain Response Time:** This is the time, in cumulative calendar days, to recognize a major shift in marketplace demand, internalize that finding, replan demand, and increase production by 20 percent. This value is a standard that has been established by the Supply-Chain-Council and will be different in different industries.

$$\text{Supply chain response time} = \text{forecast cycle} + \text{replan cycle} +$$
$$\text{time to increase production by 20\%}$$

The *forecast cycle* is the time between forecast regeneration that reflects true changes in marketplace demand for shippable end products. The *replan cycle* measures the time between the initial creation of the regenerated forecast and its release to the end-product production facilities, expressed in calendar days. The time to achieve a 20 percent production increase is the typical time, in calendar days, to achieve a sustainable unplanned 20 percent volume increase in production output.

Such aggregate measures require that supply chain managers also pay attention to other metrics such as forecast accuracy, warranty costs, time for resolution of customer complaints, expenses incurred due to inventory writedowns, and supplier and shipper lead-times.

Impacts of Lead-Time Reduction

Shortening the leadtime for delivery in a supply chain does more than just reduce the wait time for a customer. Figure 7.2 shows the cause-and-effect relationships that a typical firm

FIGURE 7.2 | *Impact of Lead-Time Reduction on Supply Chain Metrics*

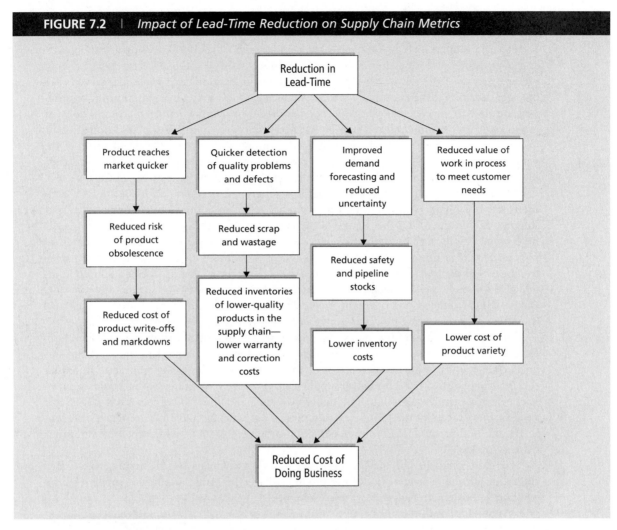

experiences as delivery lead-time for products and services is reduced. By reducing the time window for uncertainty, during which a firm must guess what the demand for its products is going to be, the risk associated with obsolescence is reduced as is the need for safety (buffer) stock. This simultaneous reduction in cycle, anticipation, pipeline, and buffer inventories results in great improvements to the bottom line. A good rule of thumb is that for every x percent reduction in lead-time, a firm experiences a $(x + \sqrt{x})$ percent reduction in inventory level.[13] For example, reducing the delivery lead-time from 10 to 8 weeks (a 20 percent reduction) would reduce inventory levels from \$1.8 million to \$1.36 million (a 24.47 percent reduction).

OM PRINCIPLE

Developing a supply chain strategy is similar to the concept of aligning products and processes as we discussed with the product-process matrix in Chapter 4: that is, the structure of a supply chain should support the basic product and business strategy chosen by the firm.

7.4 SUPPLY CHAIN STRATEGY AND STRUCTURE

The first step in devising an effective supply chain strategy is to consider the nature of the demand for the firm's products.[14] In doing so, the firm must consider the product life cycle, demand predictability, product variety, and market standards for lead-times and customer service. Based upon their demand patterns, products can be classified as either *functional* or *innovative*. Functional products include the staples that people buy in a wide range of retail outlets, such as grocery stores and gas stations. Since such products satisfy basic needs that do not change much over time, they have stable, predictable demand and long life cycles. However, such products also face stiff competition, which often leads to low profit margins. Innovative products are new or modified products companies create to achieve higher margins. These are common in the fashion and technology industries and give customers an additional reason to buy. Although these products can enable companies to achieve higher profit margins, the very newness of innovative products makes demand for them unpredictable. In addition, their life cycle is short because imitators eventually erode any initial competitive advantage.

There are two basic modes of structuring a supply chain: *efficient* and *responsive*. An **efficient supply chain** focuses on high productivity in material flow and minimizing costs of shipping the product from the factory to the customer. A **responsive supply chain** focuses on customer availability and responsive service. Design decisions that support an efficient supply chain strategy might include using a few large warehouses centrally located (as opposed to many small ones located closer to customers in a responsive design), slower and more cost-effective shipment modes (such as water- and rail-based transportation as opposed to trucks and air), more efficient management of pipeline inventories, and optimization models that minimize costs of routing products from factory to warehouses to retail stores.

The design of a responsive supply chain often trades off cost and efficiency considerations for better customer response. The firm might use multiple and redundant products and services, or it might pay the additional cost of abundant inventories at the retail level to reduce the chances of a stockout. Further, all supply chain processes are geared toward quick responsiveness—for example, air freight and higher-cost general delivery providers (such as UPS and FedEx) are commonly used modes of transport. Most catalog and Internet retailers, recognizing the immediacy of customer needs, often provide customers with expensive but quick delivery options.

Reminiscent of the product-process matrix concept in Chapter 4, the supply chain design should match the characteristics of the products that it supports: an efficient supply chain is better suited to functional products, and a responsive supply chain to innovative products. Attempting to use an efficient supply chain structure for an innovative product strategy, or a responsive supply chain structure for a functional product line, will create problems for both the customer and for the firm.

> **OM PRINCIPLE**
>
> Functional products and services require an efficient supply chain process, whereas innovative products and services require a responsive supply chain processes.

Designing Supply Chains

In designing a supply chain, companies must ask: How do we choose suppliers? How many total manufacturing sites are needed? Where should they be located? What products should be produced at each site? What is the best distribution network to support the delivery of the product to customers? Two key decisions that must be addressed are (1) the amount of centralization/decentralization in the location of facilities and

> **OM PRINCIPLE**
>
> Attention to the design of a supply chain is essential to determine the best structure for providing customers with the right quantity of goods, at the right places, at the right time, while minimizing the total delivered cost—manufacturing, warehousing, and transportation—of the product at its final destination.

(2) The type of planning system used. The *OM Practice* box on FreshDirect provides a good example of an effective supply chain design.

OM PRACTICE

Designing the Supply Chain at FreshDirect

FreshDirect has an effective supply chain design for rapid home delivery of food products.

FreshDirect's strategy is to offer higher-quality fresh products at a lower cost by eliminating waste throughout the grocery supply chain in each individual processing step, while exploiting e-commerce. The typical grocery store carries about 25,000 different packaged items and roughly 2,200 perishable products. In contrast, FreshDirect offers 5,000 perishable products but only 3,000 choices in packaged goods. The location of its processing facility is the most critical factor in FreshDirect's cost-efficient delivery model. FreshDirect built a 300,000-square-foot facility in Long Island City, called a processing center rather than a distribution center to underscore its emphasis on high-quality fresh foods rather than the delivery process. This gives FreshDirect easy access to the greatest population density in the United States.

FreshDirect uses a make-to-order approach, similar to that of Dell, Inc., and scaled, vertical integration to shorten the supply chain. For example, FreshDirect applies the Dell model to coffee beans: it offers 55 standard varieties of coffee from 22 different coffee beans, which are roasted and ground to order. But if those options don't fit the consumer's needs, FreshDirect will prepare a customized blend by combining the 22 beans in any proportion desired. Although roasting and blending add further costs, the raw beans can be procured for as little as 70 cents per pound, leaving room for both low consumer prices and attractive margins. In its seafood operation, representatives place initial orders at the docks in lower Manhattan as the catch arrives during the day and into the evening. At midnight, FreshDirect stops taking consumer orders for the following day and provides an exact order quantity to the seafood buyers. The prescribed quantities arrive at the Long Island City processing facility around 3 a.m. and are cut to customers' orders by early to mid-morning. Deliveries begin at 4 p.m. the same day, resulting in a "dock-to-door" time that is often less than 24 hours.

FreshDirect relies on direct sourcing and leverages vertical integration in its operations to provide value to its commodity suppliers. For example, the company buys "Raised Right" branded chicken from College Hill Poultry in Fredericksburg, Pennsylvania. Because FreshDirect cuts and packs the chicken to order, bypassing the traditional grocery supply chain, it is able to sell Raised Right chicken at a price comparable to that of unbranded poultry. To control the cost of the "necessary evil" of home delivery, FreshDirect doesn't offer same-day delivery—only next-day delivery. In addition, it delivers only between 4 p.m. and midnight and promises delivery within a two-hour window.[15]

Location decisions have significant influence on the cost and service characteristics of the value chain and also influence market size and market share. This is particularly important for some services whose competitive advantage depends on having a facility located near customers. A firm might choose to locate a plant in a new geographic region not only to reduce distribution costs, but also to create cultural ties between the firm and the local community. The relationships established may attract new business and improve the firm's market position in relation to distant competitors. But location decisions can also be a source of problems, as Honda discovered when locating its automobile plant near Marysville, Ohio. An important factor in that decision was the state's agreement to build a four-lane highway linking the site to the interstate highway system. Subsequently, the state announced a delay of at least six years in completing the highway.[16]

Broadly speaking, a firm may choose to locate all its products closer to the factory (centralized system) or closer to the retail outlets (decentralized system) in a supply chain (see Figure 7.3). With centralized systems, inventories are aggregated or "pooled," thereby reducing overall inventory levels. Generally, the response time to the customer increases as the firm takes longer to route the product through its supply chain upon the initiation of an order. This is reminiscent of the efficient (as opposed to the responsive) supply chain design that we discussed earlier. With a centralized distribution system, both the cycle inventory and the safety stock levels are reduced. *Supplementary Notes 7.2* in the Bonus Materials folder on the CD-ROM discusses the key principles and factors used in making location decisions for manufacturing and service organizations.

The second strategic choice for the firm is its planning system. Two basic alternatives— pull versus push—are illustrated in Figure 7.4. In a **pull distribution system,** upstream entities respond to the demand signals from downstream entities in the supply chain. For example, as customer demand spikes, retailers send orders upstream to distribution centers, which respond by increasing orders from the factories. Most order-point systems at the retail level are pull systems and easy to implement. The retailer or the distribution center reviews its inventory position and, based on its assessment of demand and its inventory policy, places orders as needed. Although such systems are widely used, they can amplify the variability of demand (the bullwhip effect), creating problems in the supply chain. In addition, orders are placed without consideration of the needs of other distribution centers.

FIGURE 7.3 | *Centralized and Decentralized Distribution System*

Supplier

Warehouse

Retailer

Centralized Distribution System

Supplier

Warehouses

Retailer

Decentralized Distribution System

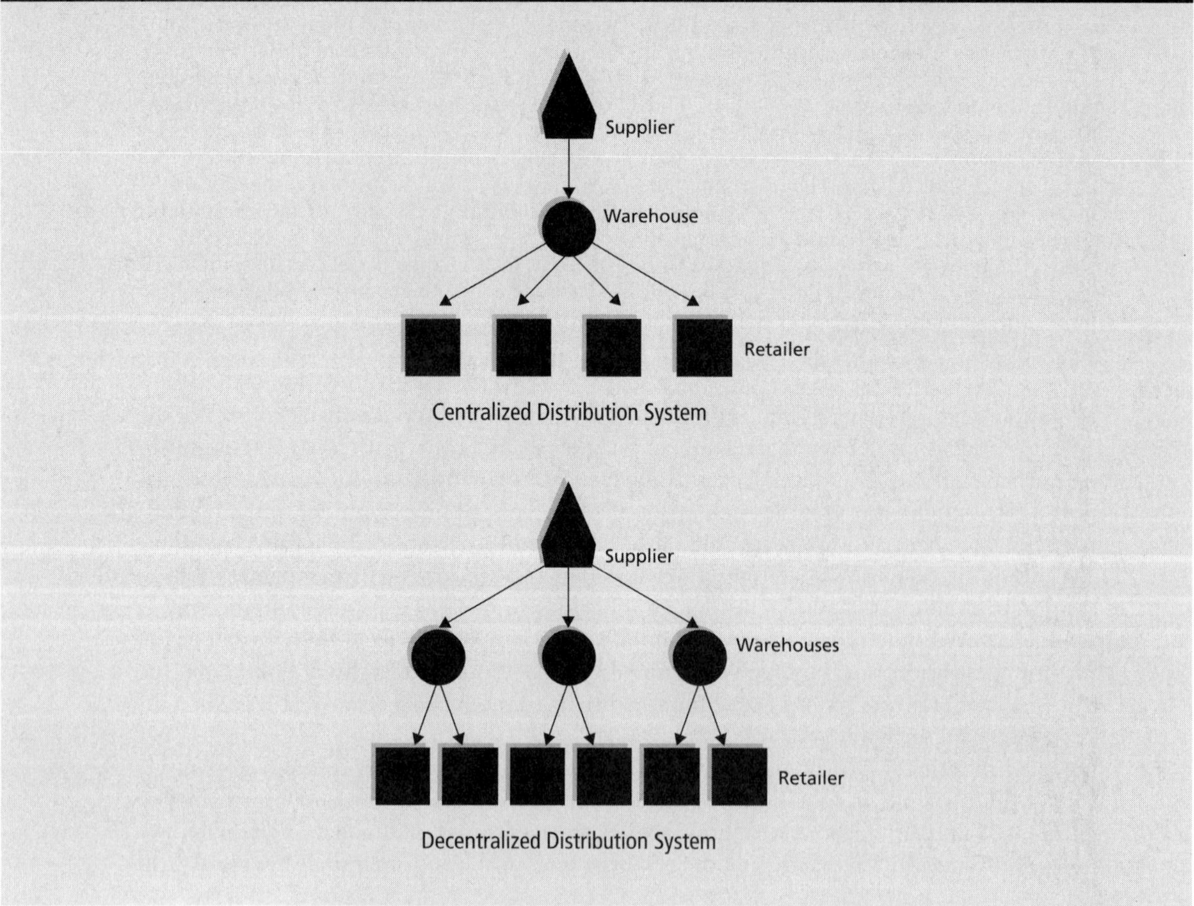

Supplementary Notes
7.3

In a **push distribution system,** factory production levels are based on a forecast (as opposed to real demand), and product is *pushed* downstream to distributors and retailers. Push systems allow consolidation and result in cost savings; they also better allocate items that are in short supply. However, information management is more complex than for a pull system. In a push system the factory makes replenishment decisions using some mechanism such as **fair shares allocation.** *Supplementary Notes 7.3* provides an explanation and example of this process.

Base stock systems are a combination of push and pull. The demand and inventory information is sent to the factory, which calculates a "base stock" for each downstream entity that is equal to the expected demand (over the order cycle and lead-time) plus any safety stock. Shipping quantities are determined based on the base stock **echelon inventory**—all inventory of the product at that location and all downstream locations—and orders. Thus, the factory sees changes in the distribution pipeline, not just those in end consumption. A base stock system allows the firm to gain the benefits of both inventory reduction (as in push systems) and customer service (as in pull systems).

Global Facilities Networks

Traditional supply chain models seek to balance facility costs, transportation costs, taxes, and other such costs to determine the locations that will minimize a firm's total cost. This approach is limited in many ways, however. First, cost considerations, proximity to customers or suppliers, and other such factors may not remain sustainable advantages. Thus, if a firm starts manufacturing overseas, it may gain a temporary advantage based on differences in costs of labor, transportation costs, and the like, but there is nothing to stop another firm from following the same path and enjoying the same "factor" advantages, thereby neutralizing any difference that might have existed. Second, in many cases, currency appreciation over time will result in

FIGURE 7.4 | *Pull versus Push Distribution Systems*

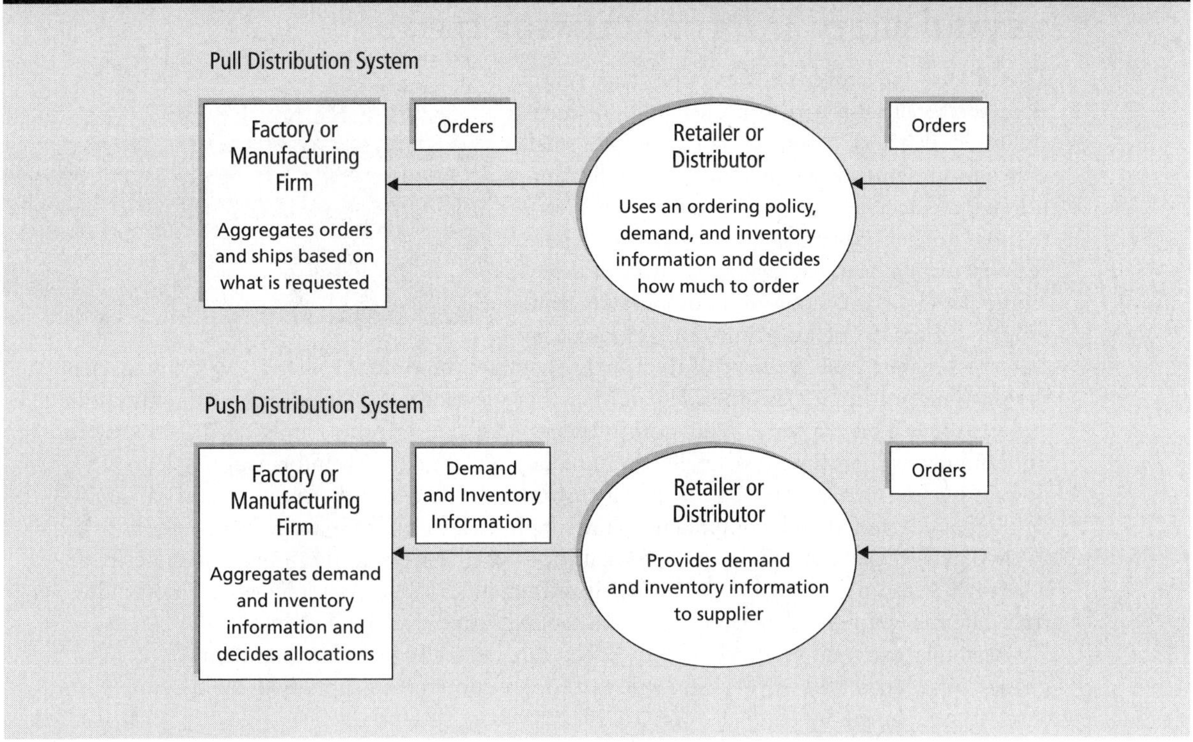

Pull Distribution System

Factory or Manufacturing Firm

Aggregates orders and ships based on what is requested

Orders

Retailer or Distributor

Uses an ordering policy, demand, and inventory information and decides how much to order

Orders

Push Distribution System

Factory or Manufacturing Firm

Aggregates demand and inventory information and decides allocations

Demand and Inventory Information

Retailer or Distributor

Provides demand and inventory information to supplier

Orders

increases in labor and material costs. Even in countries with no such appreciation, costs will be affected by what Ken Ohmae calls the "expense of cheap labor." He notes that "the chip-makers have learned first-hand what CTV and textile industries discovered earlier: inexperienced labor must be trained and, once trained and experienced, labor does not stay cheap very long."[17]

Today, many firms are building global networks of facilities. The evolution of multiplant networks has been driven by economic, marketing, and operational factors. For example, firms such as Toyota and BMW create a multiplant network to leverage the exchange rate differentials across national boundaries. Others are motivated by production factors such as labor costs, logistics ease and efficiency, and market presence.

> ## OM PRINCIPLE
> Multiple plants in different global locations generally offer benefits of increased responsiveness, ease in local customization, and logistical gains afforded by simplification of the distribution network, and allow organizations to hedge against socio-political and currency risks. Accompanying these benefits, however, is the increased managerial complexity associated with planning and operating multiple units.

Whether the strategic advantage of a global facilities network will be sustainable depends on the logic used to configure the capabilities of the network.[18] Strategic thinking about facilities leads firms to analyze carefully the core capabilities and strategic roles of individual facilities within their network. Three key dimensions of such a capability-focused approach are related to process advantages, employee advantages, and market advantages. While the traditional approach takes a static view of conditions and benefits, the capability-focused approach tries to capture benefits that are dynamic and self-renewing. The traditional approach tends to view facilities location decisions from the perspective of the operations function alone, while the capability-focused approach takes the cross-functional business process view. Finally, the objective of the traditional approach is often tactical competitive improvement, whereas the capability-focused approach targets long-term strategic advantage.

7.5 VARIABILITY AND THE BULLWHIP EFFECT

The farther one moves up the supply chain away from the retail customer, the greater is the variability in demand observed. For example, small increases in demand by customers cause distribution centers to increase their inventory. This leads to more frequent or larger orders to be placed with manufacturing. Manufacturing, in turn, increases its purchasing of materials and components from suppliers. Because of lead-times in ordering and

> ## OM PRINCIPLE
> A supply chain is a dynamic system because of time lags in the flow of materials and information from the beginning of the supply chain to the end. Demand variability increases as one moves back up the supply chain away from the retail customer.

delivery between each element of the supply chain, by the time the increased supply reaches the distribution center, customer demand may have leveled off or even dropped, resulting in an oversupply. This triggers a reduction in orders back through the supply chain, resulting in undersupply later in time. Essentially, the time lags associated with information and material flow cause a mismatch between the actual customer demand and the supply chain's ability to satisfy that demand as each component of the supply chain seeks to manage its operations from its own perspective. This results in large oscillations of inventory in the supply chain network. This phenomenon is known as the **bullwhip effect** and has been observed across most industries. The bullwhip effect increases costs and reduces service to the customer.

A simple example of the bullwhip effect can be constructed by simulating a demand change for a retailer whose decision rule is to order enough to keep a two-month supply on hand. As Table 7.1 shows, the retailer starts with a beginning inventory of 400 units. Observing sales of 200 in period 1 and the resulting ending inventory of 200, the retailer places an order for

$$Q = (2 \times \text{current sales}) - \text{ending inventory} = (2 \times 200) - 200 = 200 \text{ units}$$

The order placed in period 0 is received instantaneously (in period 1) and so on. As can be seen from the table, when sales increase by 5 percent in period 4 (to 210), the order size becomes

$$Q = (2 \times 210) - 190 = 230 \text{ units}$$

Thus, a 5 percent increase in sales results in a 15 percent increase in the order size. Figure 7.5 illustrates the change of demand and orders placed by the retailer over time. As can be seen, the variance of demand is amplified by the retailer's simple ordering rule.

When the lead-time to deliver the product to the retailer is increased, the impact is more dramatic. For example, when orders are received one period after they are placed, the results are as shown in Table 7.2 and Figure 7.6.

OM PRINCIPLE

The bullwhip effect increases as the supply chain becomes more complex and lead-time increases.

Figure 7.7 illustrates the typical amplification in the variance of the orders as one moves upstream in the supply chain. We may make the following observations:

1. The factory that produces the product sees greater demand variance than distributors, and distributors see greater variance than retailers. Most factories incur a cost of

| TABLE 7.1 | *Order Sizes in a Two-Stage Supply Chain* |

Time	Beginning Inventory	Sales	Distribution Center Inventory	Ending Inventory	Order Size
0					200
1	400	200	400	200	200
2	400	200	400	200	200
3	400	200	400	200.	200
4	400	210	420	190	230
5	420	220	440	200	240
6	440	230	460	210	250
7	460	230	460	230	230
8	460	230	460	230	230
9	460	230	460	230	230
10	460	220	440	240	200
11	440	210	420	230	190
12	420	200	400	220	180

FIGURE 7.5 | *Variance Amplification with Zero Lead-Time*

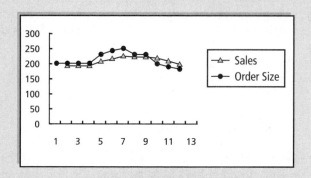

TABLE 7.2   *Order Sizes in a Two-Stage Supply Chain with Positive Lead-Time*

Time	Beginning Inventory	Sales	Distribution Center Inventory	Ending Inventory	Order Size
0					200
1	400	200	400	200	200
2	400	200	400	200	200
3	400	200	400	200	200
4	400	210	420	190	230
5	390	220	440	170	270
6	400	230	460	170	290
7	440	230	460	210	250
8	500	230	460	270	190
9	500	230	460	270	190
10	520	220	440	300	140
11	490	210	420	280	140
12	420	200	400	220	180

       varying this production (see Chapter 8); either they are underutilized in some periods, or they cannot meet demand at other times.

2. The longer the supply chain, the greater the amplification of variance at the factory.
3. Longer lead-time (in information or material transfer) exaggerates the variance amplification.
4. Though point-of-sale (POS) data inform the factory what the real demand looks like, the factory would provide ineffective service to its immediate downstream customer (the wholesaler) if it followed a production schedule based on POS data.

FIGURE 7.6 | *Variance Amplification with Increased Lead-Time*

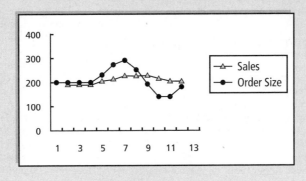

The *OM Practice* box on Procter & Gamble describes how that company uses value pric-ing as one strategy to reduce the bullwhip effect.

Managing the Bullwhip Effect

According to some authors,[19] the bullwhip effect is caused by four factors, which can be dealt with as follows:

1. **Demand Forecast Updating:** Ordinarily, every firm in a supply chain forecasts its demand myopically—that is, by looking at historical demands from its own direct cus-tomers. The orders of those customers, however, are based on the demand they see as well as their own ordering policies. In addition, managers in the chain often add a "fudge factor" to demand estimates, further obscuring true customer demand. One strategy to counteract this problem is for all components of a supply chain to use the same demand data obtained from the furthest point downstream. Technologies such as POS data collection, electronic data interchange (EDI), and vendor-managed inven-tories (VMI), as well as lead-time reduction, which are described later, can all help to support this.

FIGURE 7.7 | *Variance Amplification in a Multistage Supply Chain*

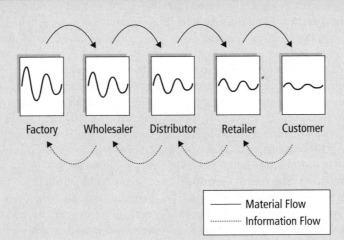

OM PRACTICE

Value Pricing at Procter & Gamble
Value pricing strategies seek to reduce the bullwhip effect.

Saying that "consumers won't pay for a company's inefficiency," former Procter & Gamble CEO Edwin L. Artzt led the company's crusade to reduce prices and give consumers better value. "Value pricing" was a fundamental change in long-term strategy for the consumer products giant. The concept involves pricing products at a reasonable "everyday low price," somewhere between the normal retail price and the sale price that is frequently offered. P&G learned through consumer research that up-and-down pricing policies were eroding its brands' perceived value. In other words, consumers began to think that P&G's brands were only worth their discount prices. When P&G discounted products, consumers stocked up and then substituted competitors' products when P&G's products were not on sale.

But the reasons for the switch to value pricing go deeper than consumer perceptions. The fre-

quent promotions were sending costs spiraling within the company. At one point, the company made 55 daily price changes on some 80 brands, which necessitated rework on every third order. Often, special packaging and handling were required. Ordering peaked during the promotions as distributors stockpiled huge quantities of goods (known as forward buying), which resulted in excessive overtime in the factories followed by periods of underutilization. Plants ran at 55 to 60 percent of rated efficiency with huge swings in output. These fluctuations strained the distribution system as well, loading up warehouses during slow periods and overworking the transportation systems at peak times.

With value pricing, demand rates are much smoother. Retailers automatically order products as they sell them. When 100 cases of Cheer detergent leave a retailer's warehouse, a computer orders 100 more. Both P&G and retailers save money. Plant efficiency rates have increased to over 80 percent across the company at the same time that North American inventories have dropped 10 percent.[20]

2. **Order Batching:** To achieve economies of procurement and logistics, firms tend to buy for several months at a time, thereby distorting the true demand for the product. Most purchasing departments place orders with upstream suppliers periodically, ordering a batch that will last several days or weeks, in an attempt to reduce transportation costs or transaction costs. These tactics contribute to larger demand fluctuations further up the chain. Variability buildup due to order batching can be mitigated by reducing transaction costs through various forms of electronic ordering, offering discounts for mixed-load ordering, and using third-party logistics providers to economically combine many small replenishments for/to many suppliers/customers. High-order transaction costs can also be reduced with EDI and computer-aided ordering (CAO). More frequent ordering results in smaller orders and smaller variance.

3. **Price Fluctuation:** Promotions often result in forward buying to benefit from the lower prices. Frequent price changes lead buyers to purchase large quantities when prices are low and to avoid buying when prices are high. A common practice in the grocery industry, this forward buying creates havoc upstream in the supply chain (see the above *OM Practice* box on Procter & Gamble). The best strategy is for sellers to stabilize prices. Activity-based costing systems, which highlight the excessive costs in the supply chain caused by price fluctuations and forward buying, can also provide an incentive for the entire chain to operate with relatively stable prices. Special purchase contracts ("blanket ordering") can be implemented in order to specify ordering at regular intervals to better synchronize delivery and purchase.

4. **Rationing and Shortage Gaming:** During a period of short supply, customers order more than they need, hoping that the partial shipments they receive will be sufficient. Cyclical industries face alternating periods of oversupply and undersupply. When buyers know that a shortage is imminent and rationing will occur, they often

increase the size of their orders to ensure they get the amounts they really need. To counteract this behavior, firms should consider allocating production among customers based on past usage, not on present orders. Encouraging more open sharing of sales, capacity, and inventory data means that buyers are not surprised by shortages. Unrestricted ordering capability can be addressed by reducing the order size flexibility (such as maximum order size) and implementing capacity reservations. For example, a firm can reserve a fixed quantity for a given year and specify the quantity of each order shortly before it is needed, as long as the sum of the order quantities equals the reserved quantity.

7.6 MANAGING SUPPLY CHAINS

Effectively managing a supply chain involves a variety of tasks:

○ *Management of purchasing and supplier relationships,* which includes selecting suppliers and managing the acquisition of purchased parts and components.

○ *Order management,* which includes tasks related to entering and maintaining orders, generating quotations, configuring products, creating and maintaining customer and product/price databases, managing allocations, and managing accounts receivable, credits, collections, and invoicing.

○ *Warehouse and inventory management,* which includes tasks such as picking and packing, creating customer-specific packaging/labeling, consolidating orders, preparing products for shipping, and making replenishment decisions.

○ *Transportation and distribution,* which includes tasks associated with choosing modes of transportation, managing import/export activities, and routing and scheduling shipments.

○ *Information management,* which includes managing the IT infrastructure to support the supply chain.

Although order management and warehouse and inventory management are important, they are relatively routine, so we focus only on the remaining issues.

Purchasing

The **purchasing** (also known as **procurement**) **function** is responsible for acquiring raw materials, component parts, tools, and other items required from outside suppliers. Key activities include receiving purchase requisitions, reviewing and evaluating requisitions, selecting qualified suppliers, aggregating and placing orders, following up on orders, authorizing payments, and maintaining records. In addition, purchasing must continually seek new products and suppliers and evaluate their potential to the company.

Firms have several strategic options for selecting a purchasing approach and for developing a sourcing infrastructure and supplier relationships. The role of purchasing in an organization may range from simply procuring materials at the lowest cost to acting as a true strategic function that can create a significant competitive advantage for the organization. The specific role of the purchasing function depends on (1) the importance of purchasing within the firm and (2) the

OM PRINCIPLE

The principal goal of purchasing is to support its key internal customer: operations. This includes learning the material needs of the organization, selecting suppliers and negotiating price, ensuring delivery, and monitoring cost, quality, and delivery performance. Thus, to support the organization, purchasing must do more than simply buy at the lowest cost.

complexity of the supply market. Whether the importance of purchasing is high or low depends on the percentage of total cost constituted by purchased materials. As for the second dimension, the complexity of the supply market, a supply market is complex if there are few suppliers for critical items of if the level of competition, technology growth, or global sources of materials is continuously changing. Supply markets are considered simple when there are many competing suppliers for materials and no aberrations such as hoarding by suppliers or anticompetitive coalitions. Sometimes even efficient supply markets, such as those in commodities, are considered complex because of the range and complexity of price movements. For example, a firm that makes orange juice may buy oranges in the open market at current prices or purchase commodity futures, creating great uncertainty in the cost of sourcing. Table 7.3 presents a framework, based on these two dimensions, that can be used for developing a purchasing strategy at the component level.

> ## OM PRINCIPLE
>
> The role of purchasing in an organization depends on the importance of purchasing as measured by the percentage of cost that purchased materials represent and the complexity of the supply markets as measured by aberrant conditions such as monopolistic practices, supplier coalitions, futures markets, emerging technology and emerging global suppliers. The more complex the supply markets and the larger the share of total cost represented by materials, the more elevated the role of the purchasing function is likely to be.

Not only does the strategic role of purchasing depend on the importance of purchasing and the complexity of the supply market, but the operations consequences also vary. For example, a purchasing management strategy requires a focus on efficiency and noncritical items. Purchasing standardizes these items and develops simple and efficient processes to acquire them. With a materials management strategy, the focus is on leverage items—large-volume (or large-value) items—and on issues such as vendor selection, product substitution, and the mix of items procured in the spot market and those obtained through long-term contracts. With a sourcing management strategy, the focus is on bottleneck items; these are items that are typically in short supply because of a scarcity of suppliers, frequent breakdowns in the upstream supply chain, or other natural (weather) and unnatural (strike) calamities. With this strategy, purchasing focuses on volume insurance, control of vendors, and backup plans.

| TABLE 7.3 | *Focusing Purchasing Strategy* | | |

Importance of Purchasing	Complexity of Supply Market	Strategic Emphasis	Focus
High	High	Supply management	Integration of supply chain with functional operations
Low	High	Sourcing management	Identification of best global sources for cost, availability, and delivery
High	Low	Materials management	Control of key leverage items; use of multiple, local suppliers
Low	Low	Purchasing management	Functional efficiency and cost minimization

Source: Based on P. Kraljic, "Purchasing Must Become Supply Management," *Harvard Business Review,* September 1983.

Finally, a supply management strategy focuses on strategic items. These are items that change the features of the product or service dramatically, requiring dramatic changes in technology or rapid innovation. To deliver the best features to the market, purchasing must focus on accurate forecasting/market research, long-term supply relationships, risk analysis, and contingency planning in case competitors procure such items.

Managing Supplier Relationships

In business today, operations are often highly decentralized and dispersed around the world. Consequently, managing a complex network of suppliers becomes a critical interorganizational issue. Increasingly, a co-dependent relationship exists between suppliers and their customers. Suppliers are viewed as partners and encouraged to be involved in the product development process. At DaimlerChrysler, for example, suppliers are involved early in the design process.[21] As a result, DaimlerChrysler often finds out about new materials, parts, and technologies before other automakers.

> **OM PRINCIPLE**
>
> Suppliers play a vital role throughout the product development process, from design through distribution. Suppliers can provide technology or production processes not internally available, early design advice, and increased capacity, which can result in lower costs, faster time-to-market, and improved quality for their customers. In turn, they should be assured of stable and long-term business.

A powerful example of supplier partnerships is the response that occurred when a fire destroyed the main source of a crucial $5 brake valve for Toyota.[22] Without it, Toyota had to shut down its 20 plants in Japan. Within hours of the disaster, other suppliers began taking blueprints, improvising tooling systems, and setting up makeshift production lines. Within days, the 36 suppliers, aided by more than 150 other subcontractors, had almost 50 production lines making small batches of the valve. Even a sewing-machine company that had never made car parts spent 500 person-hours refitting a milling machine to make just 40 valves a day. Toyota promised the suppliers a bonus of about $100 million "as a token of our appreciation."

Supplier partnerships offer many other benefits as well. When close relationships are developed, the total number of suppliers can be reduced, since there is no need for competition among suppliers for the same products. With larger contracts, suppliers benefit from economies of scale and customers benefit from volume discounts. Moreover, with long-term contracts, suppliers are more willing to invest in process and system improvements. Many customers even provide assistance in making such improvements. In return, they receive better products and service. For example, the Baldwin Piano & Organ Company set up a 10-year agreement with Southland Marketing, Inc. for piano plates to get "higher quality, more consistent supply, and lower cost."[23] Baldwin helped finance the purchase of the equipment needed to finish the plates and expected to save 10 percent a year on its plate costs as a result of the contract.

> **OM PRINCIPLE**
>
> Effective supplier relationships are treated as an important business process. This includes segmenting suppliers by importance, measuring performance, and providing recognition and feedback.

Many companies are now requiring suppliers to provide evidence, such as quality control charts or test results, showing that their processes are under tight control. The evidence is then used to eliminate or reduce incoming inspections so that items can go directly to production areas for immediate use. A side benefit is the reduction of inventories and associated problems of outdated stocks, deterioration, and scraps or rework if design changes are made.

Many companies segment suppliers into categories based on their importance to the business and manage them accordingly. For example, at Corning, Level 1 suppliers, who provide raw materials, cases, and hardware, are deemed critical to business success and are managed by teams that include representatives from engineering, materials control, purchasing, and the supplier company. Level 2 suppliers provide specialty materials, equipment, and services and are managed by internal customers. Level 3 suppliers provide commodity items and are centrally managed by purchasing.[24]

Measurement plays an important role in supplier management. Texas Instruments measures suppliers' quality performance by parts per million defective, percentage of on-time deliveries, and cost of ownership.[25] An electronic requisitioning system permits a paperless procurement process. More than 800 suppliers are linked to Texas Instruments through an information exchange system. Integrated data systems track the incoming quality and timeliness of deliveries as materials are received. Analytical reports and online data are used to identify material defect trends. Performance reports are sent each month to key suppliers. Joint customer-supplier teams are formed to communicate and improve performance. A supplier management task force of top managers directs current and strategic approaches to improving supplier management practices. Many companies make **supplier certification** the focal point of their supplier management system as a way of measuring performance. Formal programs typically are established to rate and certify suppliers who provide quality materials in a cost-effective and timely manner.

Finally, communication, feedback, and recognition or awards are important in supplier and partnering processes. For instance, the Fastener Supply Corporation, which distributes fasteners, electronic hardware, and other products to over 300 customers, makes frequent contact with its 250 suppliers, invites them to company functions, and shares such information as forecasts of customers' requirements.[26] Feedback should provide timely and actionable information to suppliers to lead to improvement and ensure that suppliers meet the organization's performance requirements.

Transportation and Distribution

Transportation and distribution departments are responsible for selecting transportation carriers, managing company-owned fleets of vehicles, and controlling efficient interplant movement of materials and goods within the supply chain. The critical factors in transportation decisions are speed, accessibility, cost, and capability. Selecting the right transportation modes and carriers can have a significant impact on the bottom line.

> **OM PRINCIPLE**
>
> Transportation and distribution play a key role both externally and internally. Externally, these functions are critical in satisfying customers' needs and expectations. Internally, they lead to efficiency in supply chain performance, enabling the company to operate with lower inventory levels and at lower costs.

The mechanisms used to transport goods are rapidly evolving: breakthroughs like double-stack container trains and computer-aided scheduling, routing, and load assignment assist managers in getting products through the supply chain faster and more efficiently. For example, an important advance in vehicle/logistics systems has been FastShip, a new containership design that is nearly twice as fast as conventional designs. Its developers have coupled ship speed with a new loading/unloading system that rolls strings of containers into and out of the ship's stern, enabling much faster loading/unloading and fast turnaround cycles. In addition, ship operations are integrated with land transportation providers that will transport the containers directly to and from the landside origin/destination with almost no dock dwell time. Another intriguing development is the "Super Blimp," made possible by new blimp technology, propulsion system advances, and advanced navigation and station-keeping systems. These large and speedy (60–100 mph) blimps will pick up huge loads (for example, groups of 40-foot containers) at their origin and deliver them directly to their destinations, without intermediate handling.

Information Technology in Supply Chains

Information technology is vital to supply chain performance. A **business intelligence system (BIS)** helps a company obtain information about all elements of the supply chain. In a BIS, data from different business processes such as marketing, manufacturing, and distribution are consolidated in a large database, called a *data warehouse*, that allows employees to quickly conduct both historical and forward-looking analyses of business patterns. A BIS also extracts key operational data and then "cleans" them (called *data scrubbing*) to remove redundancies, add missing data, and organize the data into consistent formats. All these data are then loaded into a database where employees can access data and make queries. Enterprise resource planning systems, which we describe in the next chapter, are an important form of BIS that support supply chain operations.

Customers are increasingly using the Internet to conduct business. "B2B," or "business to business," relationships have benefited immensely from the Internet. Many companies now allow their business customers to purchase products and collaborate as partners in design and other activities via online systems. Purchasing organizations in particular benefit from the cost savings and productivity gains. Under traditional complex approval procedures, purchase orders typically cost $75 to $150 each to process. Internet purchasing systems drastically reduce costs, speed approvals and delivery, and give buyers more autonomy over the process.

One interesting approach that has gained popularity recently is the reverse auction. In a **reverse auction** an organization asks suppliers to bid on a contract to supply materials. Reverse auctions force suppliers to trim costs and provide the best price, quality, and delivery in order to win the business. Another advantage is that the firm can schedule auctions based on the current needs of the organization, enabling it to better coordinate purchasing activity and monitor it more closely. Many firms are using Web-enabled reverse auctions to encourage supplier competition and save purchasing dollars. During the auction process, suppliers can see the competitors' offerings and have to match those bids to stay in the auction.

7.7 EVOLVING TRENDS IN SUPPLY CHAIN MANAGEMENT

Supply chain management is a rapidly evolving field. What began as a relatively narrow focus on managing inventory and distributing goods has emerged as a vital core business system that can have an impact on a firm's competitive advantage. The following are some of the many technical and conceptual developments that are occurring in SCM:

> **OM PRINCIPLE**
>
> New approaches in supply chain design and strategy are helping firms to rationalize supply chain configuration, increase responsiveness, reduce costs, and exploit global diversity by hedging country-specific risks and exploring new markets.

- *Push versus pull strategies* allow firms to choose between efficiency and responsiveness.

- With *cross-docking,* firms can eliminate storing products in a warehouse and deliver products faster to customers.

- Through *strategic alliances,* firms are integrating customers and suppliers as true partners.

- *Postponement* allows firms to delay product differentiation until the customer needs it, thereby providing for efficiency and quick delivery simultaneously.

- *"Design for Logistics"* enables firms to design effective supply chains through systematic analysis.

- *New information technologies* such as wireless communications are allowing firms to better plan and coordinate the flow of goods and information and to track the progress of products in the supply chain.

- *Business intelligence* and *decision support systems* allow firms to make rapid, more accurate assessments of tradeoffs in the supply chain, resulting in more effective decisions.

In addition, we are seeing some dramatic new ideas in SCM. For example, Xerox and several other companies now operate their supply chain as a closed loop, recycling used equipment, parts, and packaging for refurbishment, reuse, or sale as raw material. In fact, Xerox already generates significant revenue and profit from this initiative. Another developing concept is dynamic supply chain configuration. Most supply chains are designed for static business conditions. A supply chain designed for one set of conditions, however, almost surely is not ideal for another. As the business environment changes, supply chain configuration should be revised. Thus, supply chains should be designed to adapt to environmental changes.

A third relatively new concept is **vendor-managed inventory (VMI)**. With VMI, the vendor (a consumer goods manufacturer, for example) monitors and manages inventory for the customer (a grocery store, for example). Some industries refer to VMI as *just-in-time distribution (JITD)* or *efficient consumer response (ECR)*. For example, the grocery and apparel industries tend to use ECR, whereas the automobile industry tends to use VMI and JITD.

VMI centralizes the supply decision upstream in the supply chain. Although VMI reduces the complexity of the supply chain and the fluctuations that occur because of the bullwhip effect, there are concerns that it results in loss of control and exposure to risk on the part of the customer. Nevertheless, many companies have successfully implemented VMI.

SCM is changing from intra-organization to inter-organization or cross-enterprise integration, from monolithic (within one firm) to collaborative and concurrent supply chain design, from mass-market delivery of standard products and services to customized delivery matching the customer's exact requirement, from reactive (how do we supply products and services given the demand?) to proactive management of demand, and from improving supply chain efficiency to market mediation.[28] As these changes occur, contemporary organizations must address some critical questions:

- How do we coordinate procurement, delivery, and other supply chain improvement initiatives across organizations?

- How do firms in a supply chain collaborate to design the product, process, and supply chain to minimize costs and maximize responsiveness?

- How do we design and coordinate a supply chain to provide customers the exact packages they desire?

- How do we get better demand information, or how can we proactively affect demand?

- How do we minimize the cost of matching the customer's needs with what is provided by an efficient and effective production and delivery system?

These questions can be summarized as: How can we achieve better cross-enterprise coordination for innovation, efficiency, and responsiveness as well as a dramatic shift from reactive supply chain planning to proactive demand and supply management?

Summary of Key Points

- Supply chain management (SCM) is an integrated approach to procuring, producing, and delivering products and services to customers; it includes the management of materials, associated information, and the flow of funds. A supply chain network for a typical manufacturing organization includes the material management functions of receiving and storing raw materials and components; the key processing functions of manufacturing, distribution, and delivery; information-processing and decision-making functions; and functions related to managing transfer of funds.

- Modern supply chains are viewed as integrated systems across the entire value chain and managed as such. Four basic functions of managing a supply chain are planning, sourcing, making products and services, and delivering them. Supply chains can be a significant source of competitive advantage.

- A supply chain can also be viewed from the customer's perspective, resulting in a concept known as the demand chain. A demand chain focuses on a demand-driven "pull" model of operation, rather than a supply-driven "push" model.

- Inventories support the supply chain by providing materials and goods where and when they are needed. Firms carry inventory for four primary reasons: economies of scale, production and capacity smoothing, protection against supply disruptions and demand surges, and profit from price changes. High inventories are often a symptom of ineffective business practices.

- Three primary decisions must be made for inventory management: (1) how to monitor inventory, (2) how much should be ordered, and (3) when orders should be placed.

- ○ Inventory is often classified into five categories: operating, surplus, excess, obsolete, and new product inventory. This classification, along with monitoring inventory-related costs, provides a means for effective performance measurement of inventory systems.
- ○ Supply chain performance can be measured by such metrics as perfect order fulfillment, customer satisfaction, and order fulfillment lead-time; supply chain costs such as order fulfillment costs, total inventory-carrying costs, finance and IT costs, and cash-to-cash cycle time; and aggregate measures such as inventory turnover and response time.
- ○ Two basic ways of structuring a supply chain are based on efficiency and responsiveness. An efficient supply chain is designed for a product whose demand is stable and focuses on minimizing costs of shipping the product from the factory to the customer. A responsive supply chain is designed for products whose demands are unpredictable; it focuses on customer availability and responsive service.
- ○ Strategic design of supply chains involves decisions about the amount of centralization/decentralization in location decisions and the type of planning system to use: a pull distribution system, push distribution system, or base stock system.
- ○ Global networks of facilities offer benefits of increased responsiveness, ease in local customization, and logistical gains afforded by simplification of the distribution network. Accompanying these benefits, however, is the increased managerial complexity associated with planning and operating multiple units.
- ○ The bullwhip effect is the phenomenon of large oscillations of inventory in the supply chain network, triggered by time lags between stages in the supply chain, order batching, price fluctuations, and shortage gaming. Demand variability increases as one moves back up the supply chain away from the retail customer.
- ○ Managing supply chains involves purchasing, order management, warehouse and inventory management, transportation and distribution, and information management.
- ○ Purchasing may be viewed from four different perspectives: low-cost procurement, focus on quality and flexibility as well as cost, integration into design and sourcing decisions, and a strategic function that creates competitive advantage.
- ○ Strong supplier partnerships have many benefits, including higher quality, lower costs, and better delivery. Supplier relationships are treated as an important business process and include segmenting suppliers by importance, measuring performance, and providing recognition and feedback. Certification systems help in this process.
- ○ Transportation and distribution are responsible for selecting transportation carriers, managing company-owned fleets of vehicles, and controlling efficient interplant movement of materials and goods within the supply chain; they play a key role in satisfying customer needs as well as improving internal performance.
- ○ Information technology is vital to supply chain performance. Business intelligence systems, e-commerce, and reverse auctions are among the modern approaches that support supply chain effectiveness.
- ○ The discipline of SCM is continually changing with technological advances; nevertheless, some basic questions related to coordination, collaboration, design, information, and value will continue to drive improvements.

Questions for Review and Discussion

1. What is a supply chain? Why is it important? How does it differ from the concept of a value chain we introduced in Chapter 1?
2. How does SCM relate to traditional inventory management and logistics activities?
3. Describe the key activities associated with supply chains and SCM. How do these tie into a firm's strategic focus?

4. What is the SCOR model? How can it help operations managers who are involved in SCM?

5. What is disintermediation, and what impact does it have on supply chain performance?

6. How can supply chains enhance competitive advantage for a firm?

7. How does a demand chain differ from a supply chain?

8. Define the different types of inventory found in a typical manufacturing firm. Why are inventories important? Why can they be a disadvantage?

9. Discuss the key decisions that must be made with respect to inventory management. How do these decisions affect costs?

10. Discuss different ways in which firms can measure inventory performance. How are these metrics useful to functional managers throughout the firm?

11. Define the different categories of inventory costs. How can these be measured from a practical perspective?

12. Why are broad supply chain metrics important? Discuss different types of supply chain metrics and explain how they might be used in a decision-making context.

13. What impact does reducing lead-time have on supply chains?

14. Explain the difference between functional and innovative products. What are the implications of this difference for supply chain design and strategy?

15. Contrast efficient supply chains and responsive supply chains. How can a firm decide which route to follow in designing its supply chain?

16. What are the two principal issues that must be addressed in designing supply chains? What specific choices do firms have to make within each of these categories?

17. Explain the differences between pull and push distribution systems. When is one system preferable to the other?

18. How are global facilities networks changing the focus of supply chains?

19. Explain the bullwhip effect. What factors contribute to it? How might they be mitigated?

20. What tasks are involved in managing supply chains?

21. Explain the elements of the purchasing function. What are some of the strategic issues that a firm must consider in evaluating its purchasing function?

22. Why are supplier relationships important? What types of approaches and policies are companies using to manage supplier relationships?

23. Discuss some of the major issues involved in transportation and distribution management. How do these affect overall supply chain performance?

24. How do information technology and business intelligence systems affect supply chains? Find some examples of companies that rely heavily on IT for effective supply chain management.

25. Discuss current trends in SCM and their implications for managers.

Internet Projects

To find Web links to carry out each of the following projects, go to the text's Web site at **http://raturi_evans.swlearning.com.**

1. This project involves a location modeling tool at Professor David Simchi-Levi's Web site. On the map of New England, you will see two manufacturing sites, represented by building pictures, and 25 retailers represented by diamonds. The tool allows several parameters to be specified. For the example problem, you may view them by selecting "*parameters*" under the "*optimize*" menu:

     a. **Number locations** specifies how many retailers are involved.

     b. **Number manufacturers** specifies how many manufacturing sites there are in the problem.

c. **Number of depots** specifies how many warehouses the user wishes to build.

d. **Number of product families** specifies how many different products are being manufactured and distributed.

e. **Maximum depot capacity** specifies the storage limits, in terms of product families, of each warehouse.

f. **Maximum distance to depot** specifies how far a warehouse can be from any retailer it serves.

Solve the example problem and comment on your results.

2. For this project, you will be provided with a comprehensive listing of supply chain sites from LogLink's Supply Chain Site Web site. Review the News section and summarize five key trends in supply chain management that affect your firm (or a firm that you know of).

3. Review the summary of a survey about distribution software that you can link to from the text Web site. What are some key features of a distribution software package?

4. The Internet introduces many options for working online with trading partners. Many companies already connect to partners' extranets (such as Wal-Mart's Retail Link) to review sales, inventory, promotions, and supply chain performance data. In this dynamic environment of Internet trading relationships, what is the right approach to Collaborative Planning, Forecasting, and Replenishment (CPFR): Be a spoke on a partner's hub? Join an exchange? Build a hub?

Review the outline of the pros and cons of alternative models of supply chain coordination at the Techexchange.com Web site and provide examples of each form of coordination.

5. The Reverse Logistics Executive Council hosts several firms that are interested in reverse logistics issues. Explore their Web site and summarize the concept of "reverse logistics" as well as five key initiatives in this area.

EXPERIENCE OM

Understanding Supply Chain Variability Using the Beer Game

In this chapter we discussed the bullwhip effect and variability in supply chains. The Beer Game is a well-known SCM simulation that provides a "live" experience of these issues and illustrates the following:

○ Order times, lead-times, buffers, and discounts are costly to the supply chain.

○ Variance is amplified the closer one is to the start of the supply chain.

○ The less one link of the chain knows about the demand faced by the following links, the worse its forecasting is. On the other hand, if the supplier at the furthest end of the chain can access data from the link closest to the end consumer, more money will be saved throughout the chain.

To play the game, go to the text Web site at **http://raturi_evans.swlearning.com,** where you will find links to the game description and an interactive version. We provide an Excel-based version. The guide to the game by Michael Li and David Simchi-Levi gives helpful hints on playing the game.

The beer supply chain is simple: the retailer meets the customer demand and places orders with the wholesaler who then places orders with the distributor who places orders with the factory. There is a lag from the time an order is placed until the time it is received at each node in the supply chain.

The spreadsheet *beergame.xls* in the Bonus Materials folder on the CD-ROM is built on the following assumptions:

○ Demand at the retailer is uniformly distributed between 2 and 11 units.

○ Each link in the supply chain starts with 10 kegs and orders 10 kegs by default. After the first week, the order quantity is computed as the current week's demand less ending inventory. Beginning inventory is calculated as the ending inventory plus the order quantity four weeks previously, because of a two-week lag in ordering and a two-week lag in delivery.

○ The shortage cost for demand not met is $1.00 per case, and the inventory cost for excess kegs is $0.50 per case.

Exercises

1. Run the model and find the total order overage/shortage costs at each link in the supply chain. (If you press the F9 key, you will repeat the simulation using different random numbers; however, the relative results will not vary significantly.) Examine the chart for the overage/shortage amount over time. How would you interpret these results?

2. The current cost of inventory is modeled as $0.50 per case, and the cost of shortage is modeled as $1.00 per case. How much worse off are you if the shortage cost is $2.00 per case?

3. If the ordering policy at any one node in the supply chain is changed to a fixed order quantity, what is the impact on overall cost? You might want to try different order quantities in order to arrive at conclusions here.

4. Increase the lag from order placement to order receipt at any node in the supply chain. How does it affect your results?

5. What steps might you take to reduce the variability in the supply chain?

Inventory Management and Enterprise Planning Systems

Inventory, as we noted in Chapter 7, is an essential element of supply chains and a key strategic asset of many firms. Managing inventories to meet the demands of customers and the needs of operations further up the supply chain is one of the basic activities of operations management. Although inventory management systems have been around for quite a while, they have evolved into powerful, information-technology-driven planning systems that cut across all facets of organizations. *Enterprise resource planning (ERP)* is the result of over 40 years of evolution of traditional inventory management and manufacturing planning and execution systems that allow today's firms to meet the global challenges of flexibly responding to customer needs through integrated information systems. ERP facilitates the identification and implementation of best practices designed to achieve operational excellence and maintain smooth operations of critical business processes. ERP represents a maturing of narrow manufacturing planning systems that were historically isolated from the broader scope of business planning. With today's sophisticated information technology, ERP has become a feasible means for achieving a true systems perspective of business processes and their relationship with traditional operations. Although ERP has become very widespread, many smaller firms still rely on its predecessor technologies; thus, a solid understanding of these is important.

In this chapter we examine the evolution of ERP and the major approaches that comprise and support it. Specifically, we address:
- The evolution of ERP (*Section 8.1*).
- Traditional inventory management and aggregate planning (*Section 8.2*).
- Planning and scheduling techniques using material requirements planning (*Section 8.3*).
- Manufacturing resource planning systems and operations scheduling (*Section 8.4*).
- Characteristics of ERP systems and implementation issues (*Section 8.5*).

Material on the CD-ROM discusses some useful tools and techniques for inventory management and ERP.

15. Quantitative Inventory Models
17. Scheduling and Sequencing
2. Linear Optimization

8.1 EVOLUTION OF ENTERPRISE RESOURCE PLANNING

OM PRINCIPLE

To achieve strategic and competitive objectives of delivery performance, short lead-times, and improved efficiency and effectiveness, firms need efficient planning and control systems that synchronize all the key processes within the organization.

Achieving synchronization across any enterprise requires a systems perspective that links planning with associated business processes. This was the essence of the process view of operations management that we presented back in Chapter 1 (Figure 1.1). Collaborating with customers and supply chain partners enables operations management functions not only to achieve unprecedented levels of customer service but also to do it with fewer resources, such as inventory. One example of the importance of accurate planning and execution is the airline industry. Airline operations performance has long been a source of irritation for consumers (see the *OM Practice* box). Achieving an on-time flight requires careful coordination and synchronization among a variety of processes, such as crew planning and scheduling, food service delivery, fueling, gate assignment, and other airport operations.

OM PRACTICE

"Truth in Scheduling" in the Airline Industry
Operations requires real-time information and an ability to quickly adapt to any process upsets that might occur.

In the mid-1990s, the Transportation Department began requiring airlines to disclose the times that each flight left the runway and touched down. Its monthly consumer report began including information about how long airlines keep planes sitting on the runway and how many flights each airline cancels. Also added to the report was information about delays caused by mechanical problems, which had previously been excluded because the department feared that airlines might fly potentially unsafe planes to help preserve a good on-time record. The department also proposed raising the limit on compensation travelers could collect for lost or damaged baggage. At the time, these were the first major changes to the government's on-time performance reports in seven years. Some airlines touted the reports prominently in their advertisements, but others called them misleading.

The purpose of the monitoring was to spur airlines to better plan and execute their operations. "I think what they have done is give the airlines more incentive to engage in truthful scheduling," said Cornish Hitchcock, an aviation specialist for Public Citizen. Many airlines, however, blamed weather and airport congestion for most flight delays, and some consumer advocates said the reports had less impact than the Transportation Department had hoped. Today, the numbers continue to vary widely depending on the route and time of day, and few travelers realize they can ask a reservation agent for the on-time performance of a particular flight.[1]

Modern planning systems began in manufacturing, as the craft method of production gave way to assembly lines that required a high level of coordination for smooth operations. The earliest forms of manufacturing planning used throughout the first half of the twentieth century were simple reorder point systems, such as the economic order quantity and safety stock determination, and basic tools such as Gantt charts, bills of materials (the product structure of an item), and work and purchase orders. Reorder point systems used historical data to forecast future demand and plan inventory levels. These were easy to implement manually, and were automated on commercial mainframe computers in the 1950s and early 1960s. As computer technology developed, aggregate planning approaches emerged, focused on minimizing costs associated with inventory and production decisions that fed into more detailed material planning systems.

Reorder point approaches, though generally appropriate for managing finished products, were not appropriate for managing raw materials, components, and work-in-process. In the 1960s, IBM developed a more forward-looking and demand-based approach to materials planning that was aided greatly by advances in information technology (IT). **Material Requirements Planning (MRP)** systems began to replace reorder point systems.[2] MRP was an approach for ensuring that materials and all the right parts and subassemblies were available in the right quantities at the right time so that finished products could be completed as scheduled to meet forecast demands. Though MRP proved to be a very good technique for managing materials, it did not take into account other manufacturing resources such as tools, operators, and machine capacity. In the 1970s, an extension of MRP, known as **Manufacturing Resource Planning (MRP II),** was developed that integrated capacity and financial planning and shop floor control along with the materials planning function. It employed a common database so that manufacturing data could be easily converted into financial data, and its simulation capabilities could be used to evaluate alternative policies and answer "What if?" questions about alternative planning scenarios.

Nonetheless, MRP II also had its limitations. For example, it assumed that lead-times were fixed and that capacity was infinite. Furthermore, MRP II did not integrate other new computer-driven systems such as computer-aided design (CAD), computer-aided manufacturing(CAM), or computer-integrated manufacturing (CIM). As the focus extended beyond the boundaries of manufacturing, planning and control systems clearly began to assume an "enterprise" perspective, which led to **Enterprise Resource Planning (ERP).** ERP considers all relevant enterprise resources beyond the manufacturing realm, such as distribution, warehousing, human resource functions, and financial management. Most firms that adopted ERP systems also saw them as a convenient way to redefine obsolete and ossified busi-

> **OM PRINCIPLE**
>
> ERP provides the means to integrate and synchronize what are typically isolated functions like order processing, purchasing, and production into streamlined business processes.

ness processes. Using IT as a key enabler, these systems integrate disparate business information into a consolidated database, allowing for better access and decision making.

Introducing ERP into an organization, however, requires significant reorganization and change in workers' perceptions and behaviors, making implementation a significant challenge. The advent of the Internet has provided new capabilities for increasing flexibility and speed in dealing with customers and suppliers within the broader context of the supply chain. New initiatives such as Customer Relationship Management (CRM) and Supply Chain Management (SCM) are extending the capabilities of ERP. Figure 8.1 summarizes the evolution of ERP into Enterprise Resource Management (ERM).

8.2 PLANNING APPROACHES

Early planning tools developed at the beginning of the 20th century helped to foster the industrialization of many countries. These consisted of simple tools such as work-order boards and Gantt charts (described in Chapter 10), and evolved into more powerful approaches such as inventory management systems and aggregate planning.

Inventory Management Systems

There are two basic types of systems for managing inventory: **continuous-review systems** and **periodic-review systems.** In a continuous-review system, the inventory position is continuously monitored. **Inventory position** is defined as the amount on hand plus any

FIGURE 8.1 | *Evolution of Enterprise Resource Planning Systems*

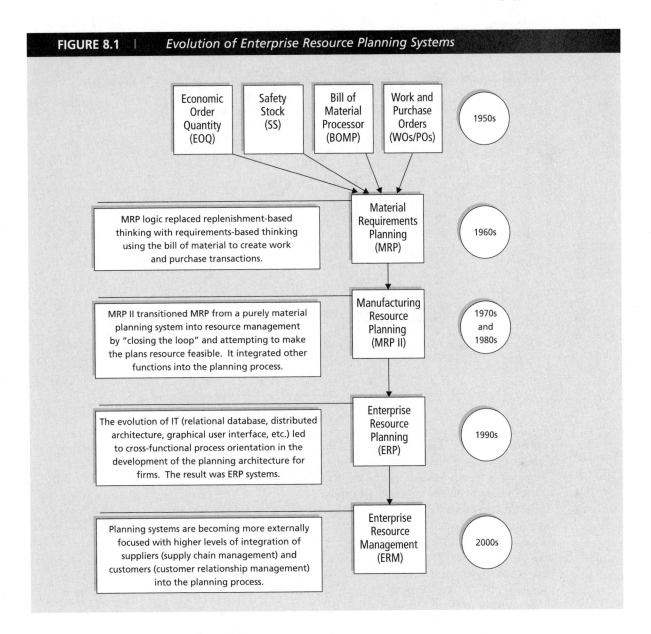

amount on order but not yet received minus backorders. Whenever the inventory position falls to or below a level *r*, called the **reorder point,** an order for Q units is placed (see Figure 8.2). Values for Q and *r* are determined in advance; such a system is often called an **(r, Q) inventory system.** If the reorder decision were based solely on the on-hand inventory level, orders would be placed continuously as the stock fell below *r*. This would clearly be incorrect; that is why inventory position is used to trigger orders. The time until an order arrives is the **lead-time,** as illustrated in the figure.

Most retail stores today have point-of-sale data entry systems that are linked to a continuous-review system. When the clerk enters or scans the item code number, the computer automatically reduces the inventory position for that unit by one and checks to see if the reorder point has been reached. If so, it signals that a purchase order should be initiated to

FIGURE 8.2 | *Continuous Review Inventory System*

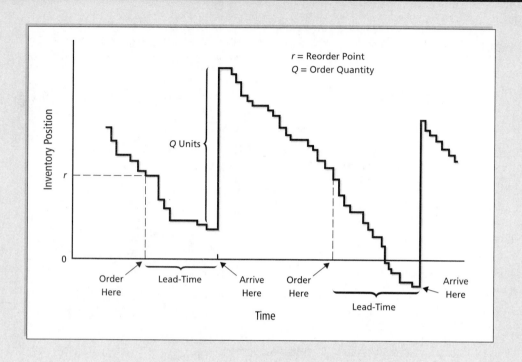

replenish the stock. Without computers, some form of manual system is needed to monitor daily usage and see if the reorder point has been reached. Since this requires substantial clerical effort and commitment by the users to fill out the proper forms when items are used, manual systems are often a source of errors.

An alternative to a continuous-review system is a *periodic-review system*, in which the inventory position is checked only at fixed intervals. If the inventory position is at or below the reorder point, r, when checked, an order is placed for sufficient stock to bring the inventory position up to R, the **reorder level**. This is termed an **(r, R) system**. With such systems, stock clerks usually make the rounds and physically check inventory levels. A tag on the shelf indicates the reorder point for each item, and the stock clerk needs only to compare it to the number of items remaining.

The choice of which system to use depends on a variety of factors. Continuous-review systems require that accurate records of inventory positions be maintained. With today's computer systems, this is usually easy to do; in some situations, however, it is not economical to monitor inventory continuously when manual records must be updated.

The fundamental decisions for continuous-review systems are determining the best values for the reorder quantity, Q, and the reorder point, r. The choice is generally made to optimize overall inventory costs; that is, to balance the cost of ordering against the cost of holding inventory. The classic economic order quantity (EOQ) model can be used to make this deci-

OM PRINCIPLE

Continuous-review systems offer tighter control of inventoried items because orders can be placed to minimize stockout risks. Periodic-review systems are useful when a large number of items can be ordered from the same supplier, since individual orders will be placed at the same time. Thus, shipments can be consolidated, resulting in lower freight rates.

sion and is developed in the Tools and Techniques supplement on the CD-ROM. Similar models have been developed for the (r, R) system, and these models can be extended to address uncertainty in demand from a probabilistic perspective and identify appropriate safety stock levels.

Aggregate Planning

Aggregate planning focuses on overall capacity; it is concerned with product groups as opposed to individual products. Aggregate-capacity measures—barrels per month, units per month, passenger seat miles (in the airline industry), patient bed-days, labor hours per month, and so on—are used in specifying the plan. For instance, a sport-shoe manufacturer might consider broad product lines such as tennis shoes, cross-training shoes, and basketball shoes in developing an aggregate production plan. Individual styles, colors, and sizes are not considered at this level.

If demand is relatively constant, developing a production plan is not difficult. First, we must determine a time horizon, typically one year, and obtain a sales forecast over that period. Next, minimum inventory levels must be established to provide desired levels of customer service. The desirable inventory levels at the beginning and end of the planning horizon must be determined. The total production required over the planning horizon is the total sales forecast plus or minus any desired change in inventory. The required monthly or weekly production rates are then easily determined. For example, suppose an automotive parts company has a current inventory of air filters of 80,000 and wants to reduce the level to 50,000 over the next year. The demand forecast calls for sales of 500,000 filters. The total production required is then 500,000 less 30,000 (the net change in inventory level), or 470,000. Thus, the company needs to manufacture an average of about 39,167 (470,000 divided by 12) filters per month. Producing a constant amount each month is an acceptable strategy provided that demand is also relatively constant. When demand is seasonal or fluctuates significantly over the planning period, production must be planned more carefully lest shortages and/or high inventory levels result.

There are four major ways to respond to fluctuating demand by altering intermediate-range capacity in aggregate planning: production rate changes, workforce changes, inventory smoothing, and demand shifting. These can broadly be classified into three principal strategies:

1. *Level production strategy*—produce the same in each period, while relying on inventory smoothing or demand shifting to enable production to meet demand;
2. *Chase demand strategy*—produce the same amount as the demand forecast each month, using production rate or workforce changes to respond to demand changes; and
3. *Mixed strategy*—use a combination of the above two approaches.

The choice of strategy depends on corporate policies, practical limitations, and cost and competitive factors.

Production-Rate Changes

One of the most common means of increasing the production rate without changing existing resources is through planned overtime. Generally, this requires wage premiums to be paid. Alternatively, hours can be reduced during slow periods, but the reduced pay can seriously affect employee morale. Subcontracting during periods of peak demand may also alter the production rate. This alternative would probably not be feasible for some companies, but it is effective in industries that manufacture a large portion of their own parts, such as the machine-tool industry. When business is brisk, components can be subcontracted; when business is slow, the firm may act as a subcontractor to other industries that may be working at capacity. In that way, a stable workforce is maintained.

Workforce Changes

Changing the size of the workforce is usually accomplished through hiring and layoffs. Both have disadvantages. Hiring additional labor usually results in higher costs for the human resources department and for training. Layoffs result in severance pay and additional unemployment insurance costs, as well as low employee morale. Also, seniority "bumping" practices can change the skills mix of the workforce and result in inefficient production. A stable workforce may be obtained by staffing the plant for peak production levels, but then many workers may be idle during low-demand periods.

In many industries, changing workforce levels is not a feasible alternative. In firms that consist primarily of assembly operations with low skill requirements, however, it may be cost-effective. The toy industry is a good example. Accurate forecasts for the winter holiday season cannot be made until wholesale buyers have placed orders, usually around midyear. Toy companies maintain a minimal number of employees until production is increased for the holidays. Then they hire a large number of part-time workers in order to operate at maximum capacity. As another example, the U.S. Postal Service hires extra mail carriers during the holiday season to increase its capacity. In general, service facilities must meet demand through workforce changes, because other alternatives are simply not feasible.

Inventory Smoothing

Inventory is often built up during slack periods and held for peak periods, though this increases inventory-carrying costs and necessitates increased warehouse space. For some products, such as perishable commodities, this alternative cannot be considered. A related strategy is to carry back orders or to tolerate lost sales during peak demand periods. But this may be unacceptable if profit margins are low and competition is high.

Another typical strategy for smoothing inventory is to make products whose seasonal peaks are opposite. Companies that produce home-heating equipment are usually in the air-conditioning business as well. Thus, marketing and product mix have a direct impact on the decisions involved in aggregate planning.

Demand Shifting

Various marketing strategies can be employed to influence demand. Commonly used in services, higher prices can be charged to reduce peak demand, whereas low prices, coupons, and increased advertising can be used to reduce inventories and increase demand during slack times (such as the winter months for lawn mowers and garden items).

The Experience OM exercise at the end of this chapter guides you through some of the modeling and quantitative solution issues related to aggregate planning. Once an aggregate plan is formulated, it must then be disaggregated into more detailed production requirements. A time-phased plan is called a *master schedule* and usually specifies weekly requirements over a 6- to 12-month time horizon. This schedule is further broken down into demands and requirements for individual components and parts so that the entire production process can be smoothly controlled. This is the role of MRP, discussed next.

8.3 PLANNING AND SCHEDULING WITH MRP

MRP requires five inputs to its planning process:

1. A **bill of material (BOM)** for each end product. A BOM defines the number and type of components that are needed to make each product.

OM PRINCIPLE

MRP is a data-intensive backward-scheduling system. It is driven by due dates for final products or customer orders and schedules materials and resource plans by planning backwards in time from these dates.

2. A **master production schedule (MPS)** that specifies the firm's requirements for final products by time period. These time periods are called **time buckets**, which may be days, production shifts, or weeks.
3. **Planned lead-times** for each process. A planned lead-time is not the amount of time an operation will require; rather, it is the amount of time allowed to perform the task.
4. Accurate information relating to the status of all final product and component **inventory on hand.**
5. Accurate information on the status of all **outstanding orders.**

Based on this information, MRP determines a detailed, time-phased schedule of material requirements, purchase orders, and production orders.

MRP can be applied to a variety of service operations in addition to manufacturing. Consider, for example, an airline. A bill of materials for an airline flight might include the type of plane, number and type of crew members, other staffing resources (mechanics, baggage handlers), consumables (fuel, food, supplies), and physical resources (gates, check-in counters). The airline can create a master schedule that shows the routes flown on a daily basis. Inventory might represent physical items such as food and fuel, as well as availability of crew members and flight attendants in different cities. Examples of lead-times would be the time required to deliver and load food, or to transport a crew into the right city. A schedule that coordinates all the resources necessary to get a flight off the ground would be the output of the MRP process.

Although the logic behind MRP is simple, it did not become feasible until the advent of computers with the capability of processing the immense number of calculations required. MRP was an astounding success in reducing inventory and production lead-times, making customer commitments more realistic, and improving the use of a firm's resources.

The bill of material sets the stage for scheduling. Figure 8.3 shows two examples of bills of material for a bicycle. A *single-level bill of material* shows the basic components or subassemblies that go into making the product. The bill of material on the right is called an *indented (or multilevel) bill of material.* This is essentially a multilevel outline describing the individual parts that are needed to make each of the components or subassemblies. Thus, in Figure 8.3, we see that the front wheel assembly consists of a rim, hoop, spokes, and wire. Finished goods are called Level 0 items; the components that are used in them are called Level 1 items and so forth. Thus, in this example, the bicycle is a Level 0 item; the bicycle frame, handlebars, wheel assemblies, and seats are Level 1 items; and the components used in the front wheel assembly are Level 2 items. Note that the demand for lower-level (higher-numbered) items depends on the demand for higher-level (lower-numbered or "parent") items. In this way, demand, or inventory requirements, for all lower-level items can be derived from the number of higher-level items that are scheduled to be produced. We typically call this a **dependent demand** situation. For example, if we want to produce 50 bicycles, then we know we need exactly 50 frames, seats, brake kits, and front wheel assemblies and, consequently, 50 rims and hoops, $50(36) = 1,800$ spokes, and $50(10) = 500$ inches of wire. It is clear that independent demand models, such as the EOQ, would not be appropriate for managing the lower-level components.

The bills of material define what must be produced; the Master Production Schedule (MPS) defines how much and when. It is a statement of the planned quantities of each item along with their scheduled order release times that are derived from demand forecasts. The planning horizon for an MPS consists of a fixed number of time buckets. Figure 8.4 shows an example of an eight-week MPS for the bicycle.

FIGURE 8.3 | Sample Bills of Materials

Single Level Bill of Material	Indented Bill of Material
Bicycle Model A	Bicycle Model A
1 Frame	1 Frame
1 Seat	1 Seat
1 Brake Kit	1 Brake Kit
1 Front Wheel Assembly	1 Front Wheel Assembly
	1 Rim
	1 Hoop
	36 Spokes
	10-Inch Wire
1 Rear Wheel Assembly	1 Rear Wheel Assembly

FIGURE 8.4 | Example of a Master Production Schedule for Bicycle Model A

	Time Period							
	1	**2**	**3**	**4**	**5**	**6**	**7**	**8**
Gross Requirements	35	35	40	50	50	50	50	40

Gross requirements must be adjusted by inventory that may already be available or planned. This process is called "netting." An example is shown in Figure 8.5. "Gross requirements" refers to the amount of the product or component that is needed to meet demand; "on hand" refers to inventory that is currently available; and "scheduled receipts" refers to outstanding orders that are awaiting completion of delivery. Thus, net requirements = gross requirements − on hand − scheduled receipts.

FIGURE 8.5 | Calculating Net Requirements in the MPS for Bicycle Model A with 50 Units on Hand

	Time Period							
	1	**2**	**3**	**4**	**5**	**6**	**7**	**8**
Gross Requirements	35	35	40	50	50	50	50	40
On Hand	50							
Scheduled Receipts	50							
Net Requirements	0	0	10	50	50	50	50	40

Of all the elements of MRP, the master scheduling process is the most important. The person responsible for master scheduling serves as an information buffer between the demands of marketing to satisfy customer orders and the operations that process them. Figure 8.6 illustrates the market and operational considerations in creating an MPS. The MPS process seeks to achieve the best possible schedule by looking at the resources available before promising marketing when each order will be produced. If inventory, machine capacity, or human resources are not available in sufficient quantities, then it is the responsibility of the master production scheduler to either secure the additional resources or to scale back the obligations of the master schedule.

Although the bills of material and MPS will tell the total number of each part needed, they do not tell *when* the parts are needed. Prior to MRP, it was not uncommon for firms to secure all parts needed to support a full quarter's build schedule at the start of the quarter. The procedure resulted in unnecessarily high inventory levels and holding costs. MRP reduces inventory requirements by scheduling lower-level requirements as needed by specifying *planned lead-times*. A planned lead-time is the time interval allocated to performing a task, such as the final assembly. To understand this, examine Figure 8.7, which shows the planned lead-time for each task in the bicycle assembly. If we want to complete this order by the end of the ninth week, we need to start making the wire stems at the start of the first week; however, all components need not be available at this time. By applying this logic to each time bucket in the master production schedule, MRP creates a time-phased schedule for production or purchase of each individual component. You can now understand the need for a computer-based process for a large and complex assembly.

Given the due date for the final product, MRP schedules backward in time. Thus, a bicycle needed in week 17 must be started in week 8 if the assembly lead-time is 9 weeks. Though highly responsive to customer demand, this backward-

FIGURE 8.6 | *The Master Production Scheduling Process*

FIGURE 8.7 | *A Partial Gantt Chart of Bicycle Manufacturing*

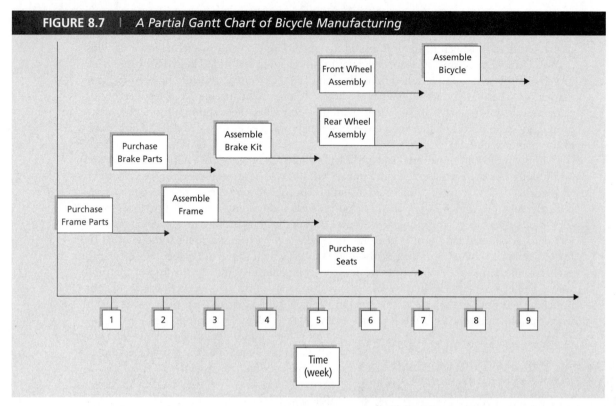

scheduling process effectively ignores resource capacity constraints. Because it assumes that infinite capacity is available, MRP is sometimes referred to as an **infinite scheduling system.** Consequently, when the MPS is compared with actual resource availability, there may be capacity shortages as shown in Figure 8.8a. This, of course, creates a problem for the master scheduler, who must now either provide the extra capacity to meet customer due dates or else delay and/or expedite some orders in order to work within the resource constraints. An alternative is **forward scheduling,** which creates a feasible schedule that works within resource constraints but may not guarantee meeting customer due dates (see Figure 8.8b).

It is generally advantageous to group MRP-specified requirements into smaller production lots—called **lot sizing**—to minimize total cost by better balancing setup costs with inventory-holding costs. Lot sizing is also necessary when several different items or products are produced on common equipment and must be produced in discrete batches. For example, suppose the requirements are as shown below:

> **O M P R I N C I P L E**
>
> MRP-specified requirements for each time period do not consider the economics of production. Consequently, lot sizing—grouping requirements into smaller production lots—is generally used to minimize total cost.

Period	1	2	3	4	5	6	7	8
Requirement	30	40	45	40	50	30	45	40

A simple lot sizing algorithm, called the *periodic order quantity*, groups requirements into regular time intervals such as two-week requirements, as shown below:

Period	1	2	3	4	5	6	7	8
Requirement	30	40	45	40	50	30	45	40
Order Size	70	—	85	—	80	—	95	—

FIGURE 8.8 | *Resource Implications of Backward and Forward Scheduling*

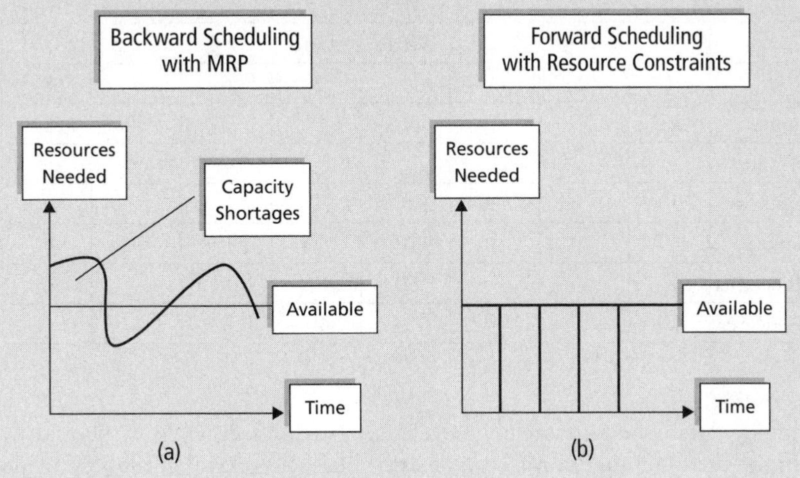

Under this scheme there is only an excess of supply for one week, and demand and supply balance at the end of the two weeks. How does a firm decide on the proper lot sizes? Various algorithms exist to minimize the total cost associated with the lot sizes. The Tools and Techniques supplement on the CD-ROM discusses various techniques for lot sizing.

After a lot sizing technique is applied to the net requirements, the firm has effectively specified the Planned Order Receipts which specify the planned quantities and time periods when orders must be received or completed. Figure 8.9, which continues the bicycle example from earlier in the chapter, shows an example.

Planned Order Receipts generate work orders for production or purchase orders for suppliers. By backing up from the receipt dates by the lead-time for processing these orders, we can schedule Planned Order Releases. Figure 8.10 shows an example with a lead-time of three weeks.

FIGURE 8.9 | *Adding Lot Sizing Results to the MPS for Bicycle Model A with 50 Units on Hand Using a Periodic Order Quality (POQ) Policy of Two Periods*

	Time Period							
	1	2	3	4	5	6	7	8
Gross Requirements	35	35	40	50	50	50	50	40
On Hand 50								
Scheduled Receipts	50							
Net Requirements	0	0	10	50	50	50	50	40
Planned Order Receipts			60		100			90

FIGURE 8.10 | *Determining Planned Order Releases for Bicycle Model A with 50 Units on Hand Using a POQ Policy of Two Periods and a Three-Week Lead-Time*

	Time Period							
	1	**2**	**3**	**4**	**5**	**6**	**7**	**8**
Gross Requirements	35	35	40	50	50	50	50	40
On Hand 50								
Scheduled Receipts	50								
Net Requirements	0	0	0	10	50	50	50	40
Planned Order Receipts				60		100		40
Planned Order Releases	60		100		40			

Having now established how many bicycles are needed and when we should start assembling them, we turn our attention to the subassemblies and parts that must be made available before final assembly begins. The next step in the MRP process is to translate Planned Order Releases for bicycles into requirements for the subassemblies and parts. This process is called "explosion." For example, the Gross Requirements for the Front Wheel Assembly result from the Planned Order Releases for the bicycle (its parent item). Figure 8.11 shows the time-phased requirements for this item. Note that because of the on-hand inventory and scheduled receipts, only one lot of 100 front wheel assemblies needs to be scheduled and made available in period 5.

Moving down to the next level, we see that to support the Planned Order Release of 100 Front Wheel Assemblies in period 3, we would need 3,600 spokes available in period 3. Thus, the schedule for spokes is as shown in Figure 8.12, and an order for a shipment of 5,000 spokes must be placed with the supplier in period 2.

We would continue cascading these calculations down through all levels of the bill of material to generate all of the potential work and purchase orders needed. The earliest ones will be released to become actual orders, and these will appear in the next MRP computation as Scheduled Receipts. The others remain in the system as planned or potential orders.

FIGURE 8.11 | *Time-Phased Requirements for Front Wheel Assembly with Lot Size = 100, Lead-Time = Two Weeks*

Front Wheel Assembly	Time Period							
	1	**2**	**3**	**4**	**5**	**6**	**7**	**8**
Gross Requirements	60		100		40			
On Hand 100								
Scheduled Receipts	70								
Net Requirements	0	0	0	0	30	0	0	0
Planned Order Receipts					100			
Planned Order Releases			100					

FIGURE 8.12	Time-Phased Requirements for Spokes (36 Needed per One Front Wheel Assembly) with Lot Size = 5,000, Lead-Time = One Week

	Time Period							
Spokes	**1**	**2**	**3**	**4**	**5**	**6**	**7**	**8**
Gross Requirements	0	0	3,600	0	0	0	0	0
On Hand 2,400								
Scheduled Receipts	0							
Net Requirements	0	0	1,200	0	0	0	0	0
Planned Order Receipts			5,000					
Planned Order Releases		5,000						

As work orders are completed or purchase orders are received, on-hand inventory will be updated.

When the calculations are completed, if an order is scheduled before week 1, it means that the order is late. In this case, insufficient inventory exists to assemble all items planned for in the master production schedule. It may still be possible to execute the plan, but some activities may need to be expedited. **Expediting** refers to speeding up some downstream operation to perform a task in less than its planned lead-time. If lateness is severe in either time or quantity, the master scheduling process may need to adjust the workload or increase the factory capacity temporarily. Often this is done through the use of overtime and/or by subcontracting out some of the work. Because MRP reports by exception, managers need respond only to exceptions and conditions outside the norm.

One critical issue in creating an MRP schedule is creating a stable schedule. Small changes in the master production schedule or inventory data can sometimes translate into large changes in the schedule for procured parts and subassemblies. This is similar to the "bullwhip" effect in supply chains discussed in Chapter 7 and is referred to as **system nervousness.** The best route to schedule stability is "freezing" the MPS.[3] This means that no changes are made to the MPS within a preset time fence. Typically, this time fence is the manufacturing lead-time for the product since any changes within the lead-time are likely to cause changes to orders that have already been released or are to be released very soon. Creating the discipline of freezing the master schedule is difficult in many firms as the promise of a new customer order means more business and typically it is hard to ask the customer to wait. Nonetheless, one must recognize that a lack of such discipline will oftentimes result in schedule disruptions, poor quality, rework, and overtime costs as the factory is asked to deviate from existing plans on very short notice.

OM PRINCIPLE

Successful implementation of an MRP system costs money and requires discipline. However, an effective MRP implementation will quickly return the initial financial investment and improve overall cash flow. Benefits include improved customer service, better on-time delivery, reduced inventory, higher productivity, revenue growth, and improved profit.

For an interesting analogy to this link between discipline and flexibility, consider this question: Are you more flexible with or without a personal digital assistant like a Palm Pilot? Are you more flexible when you adhere to strict rules when entering data into your PDA or when you don't? If flexibility is defined as your ability to respond to customer requests for your time, you will no doubt agree that a disciplined approach to a Palm Pilot creates maximum flexibility. Similarly, if flexibility of an organization is construed as a market construct—its ability to respond to customer requests—then a disciplined, data-intensive, schedule-driven approach as provided by an MRP system provides the most effective response.

In most MRP implementations, the master production schedule is created differently in make-to-stock (MTS), assemble-to-order (ATO), and make-to-order (MTO) environments. In MTS production, such as soap and toothpaste, an item-level forecast drives the MPS. Sometimes, a "phantom" bill of material may be used to forecast the number of items required (such as total quantity of toothpaste) and ratios or percentages of aggregate forecasts used to assess how many individual units (such as tubes of toothpaste by different sizes) are needed. The organization assumes that the product mix ratio used in the "phantom" bill of material is fairly constant over time; forecasting aggregate sales is statistically less error-prone than forecasting each item in the product mix. In an ATO environment, such as Dell's process of assembling computers in different configurations to specific customer orders, the main variable to satisfy is accurate order promise dates. This implies that the organization should maintain a stable MPS by using time fencing and related methods discussed before. In MTO environments, such as the assembly of recreational vehicles, it is important that the status of customer orders be visible throughout the production process.

In repetitive industries, MRP has been superseded by just-in-time, or JIT (discussed in the next chapter), because the work and purchase order generation capabilities of MRP are not required. JIT organizes a *continuous flow* of incoming materials so the discrete orders of MRP are not needed; the result is much shorter lead-times and lower inventory levels. MRP is still a valuable technique in nonrepetitive industries, however, particularly defense and pharmaceuticals where lot control is critical.

8.4 MANUFACTURING RESOURCE PLANNING

After the development of formalized MRP systems, it became evident that the MRP concept needed to look beyond the planning of materials. Because capacity was not explicitly considered in MRP, numerous problems began to surface, including warehouses full of materials and components, high levels of overtime and subcontracting, failure to produce orders to meet customer due dates, and cash flow problems that even led to bankruptcies. Managers began to expand the concept to include other manufacturing resources allocated to production, particularly financial resources, since production is often measured in terms of dollars. The use of an MRP-based system to plan all the resources of a manufacturing company became known as *Manufacturing Resource Planning (MRP II)*.[4] It involves the broader functions of purchasing, capacity planning, and master scheduling in addition to inventory, production, and strategic financial planning. Because of the competitive pressures to increase quality and shorten lead-times, MRP II became an important element of computer-integrated manufacturing.

> ## OM PRINCIPLE
>
> As a tool for managing, predicting, and controlling a company's resources and operating investments, MRP II, in essence, converts a marketing statement of demand into a workable production plan.

MRP II systems accrue the benefits of ordinary MRP systems, including reduced manufacturing inventories, fewer stockouts, and improved delivery.[5] In addition, several features distinguish MRP II from a pure MRP system:

1. It is a *top-down system*, translating strategic business plans into functional strategies.
2. It uses a *common database*. Manufacturing data can be converted into financial data, allowing individuals throughout the organization to use the data.

3. *What-if simulation capabilities* are routinely used to evaluate alternative plans.
4. It is *user-transparent*. Users at all levels are able to understand the system because of its integration with other facets of the business.

One of the key elements of MRP II is a focus on capacity requirements. As we noted, MRP ignores capacity in creating its schedule. Thus, a capacity reconciliation scheme is needed to ensure that the plan is realistic. Capacity is frequently expressed in a unit that is common to all work centers—standard hours. Several techniques are used:

- **Rough Cut Capacity Planning** converts the master production schedule into capacity needs for key resources and then determines whether the MPS is feasible with respect to capacity limitations. If not, then the master scheduler must revise the MPS to stay within capacity constraints. This process is often iterative and may require several trials before a feasible master schedule is constructed.

- **Capacity Requirements Planning (CRP)** is the process of determining the amount of labor and machine resources required to accomplish all the tasks of production on a more detailed level, taking into account all component parts and end items in the materials plan. CRP requires detailed inputs for all components and subassemblies, including MRP-planned order releases, on-hand quantities, current status of shop orders, routing data, and time standards.

- **Finite Capacity Scheduling (FCS)** is a forward-scheduling technique that tries to match the work content of orders and the capacity of competing resources (discussed in the next section)

Operations Scheduling

Any plan is only as good as its execution. Scheduling serves the important function of ensuring that the plan is executed effectively. **Scheduling** refers to the assignment of priorities to customers and/or manufacturing orders and the allocation of work to specific work centers and/or resources. A schedule specifies the timing and sequence of production and the amount of work to be completed at any work center during any time period. **Production (operations) control** provides data and information to supervisors—customers in queue, work-in-process, manufacturing-order status, actual output, and measures of efficiency, utilization and productivity—to enable them to ensure that materials and tools are available when needed, track progress against planned requirements, and make short-term adjustments when necessary.

Master schedules and MRP plans need to be operationalized on the factory floor. *Finite capacity scheduling (FCS)* matches the work to be done against the available resources. The result is a schedule that never exceeds available capacity and is always feasible to implement on the factory floor. Once the schedule is implemented, of course, managers and supervisors must control progress and may need to make adjustments for machine breakdowns or other problems. The complexity of FCS generally requires sophisticated computer software to integrate and process the variety of data needed to produce a useful schedule. Key inputs into any scheduling system include the types of jobs that can be processed by different resources; specific process routings; processing, setup, and changeover times; due dates or shipping dates; resource availability, such as the number of shifts; and downtime and planned maintenance.

OM PRINCIPLE

Scheduling approaches depend on precise information from the factory floor; thus, accurate data are vital to success.

Many computer-based scheduling systems perform *schedule evaluation*, *schedule generation*, and *automated scheduling*. In schedule evaluation, the schedules are generated manually and then assessed by the computer to determine feasibility and to estimate performance measures. In schedule generation, the computer produces the schedules, which are then reviewed manually. The human scheduler uses his or her judgment and experience to improve the schedule. At the highest level of sophistication—automated scheduling—the computer can generate a schedule, identify problems, and create new schedules.

In selecting a specific approach for FCS, a manager must first consider the criteria for evaluating schedules. These criteria are often classified into three categories: shop-performance, due-date, and cost-based criteria. The applicability of the various criteria depends on the availability of data.

Shop-performance criteria pertain only to information about the start and end times of jobs and focus on shop performance such as machine utilization and work-in-process (WIP) inventory. Two common measures are **makespan,** the time needed to process a given set of jobs, and **flow time,** the amount of time a job spends in the shop.

> **OM PRINCIPLE**
>
> A short makespan aims to achieve high equipment utilization and resources by getting all jobs out of the shop quickly. Low flow times reduce WIP inventory.

Due-date criteria pertain to customers' required due dates or internally determined shipping dates. Two common measures are **tardiness,** the amount of time by which the completion time exceeds the due date (tardiness is defined as zero if the job is completed before the due date), and **lateness,** the difference between the completion time and the due date (either positive or negative). Another common measure is the number of tardy or late jobs. In contrast to shop-performance criteria, these measures focus externally on customer satisfaction. Table 8.1 summarizes shop-performance and due-date criteria.

Cost-based criteria might seem to be the most obvious criteria, but it is often difficult to identify the relevant cost components and obtain accurate estimates of their values. In most cases, costs are considered implicitly in shop-performance and due-date criteria.

Several approaches can be used for FCS. They include optimization-based approaches, dispatching rules, and simulation-driven approaches. Optimization approaches seek to develop an "optimal" schedule to minimize or maximize some scheduling criterion. Many optimization approaches are based on complex linear or integer programming models. An advantage of these approaches is that the scheduling criteria and resource capacity can be considered

TABLE 8.1 *Common Scheduling Criteria*

Criterion	Definition	Objective
Makespan	The time to process a set of jobs	Minimize makespan
Flow time	The time a job spends in the shop	Minimize average flow time
Tardiness	The amount by which completion time exceeds the job's due date	Minimize number of tardy jobs or the maximum tardiness
Lateness	The difference between completion time and due date	Minimize average lateness or the maximum lateness

explicitly in the optimization model. Disadvantages are that objectives must be precisely quantified and a considerable amount of computer processing may be necessary to find a solution. The Tools and Techniques supplement on the CD-ROM describes several simple optimization approaches used in scheduling.

One of the major difficulties of optimization-based approaches is that many real-life problems are too large and complex for them to handle effectively. In the most general job shop situation, we must sequence n jobs on m machines, and each job may have a unique routing. If so, there are up to $(n!)^m$ possible schedules. For example, when $n = 5$ and $m = 4$, there are more than 200 million schedules! These problems are too difficult to solve optimally, and heuristic methods must be used.

Another problem with optimization-based approaches is that they assume a static situation in which all jobs are available at the same time and no new jobs are created during processing. In real manufacturing environments, scheduling is dynamic—jobs are continually being created, eliminated, and changed, and unforeseen events such as machine breakdowns occur that invalidate previously developed schedules. Hence, scheduling decisions must be made over time. Simulation-based approaches apply one or more dispatching rules to rank the order of jobs waiting to be processed at a machine in order to use available capacity effectively. Simulation modeling enables a manager to experiment with a model of the production system to choose the best **dispatching rule** for a particular set of criteria and shop conditions. Examples of typical dispatching rules are given in Table 8.2.

Over 100 different finite scheduling packages are available to companies. The benefits that most companies find in using such software include on-time delivery, higher quality, better customer relations, more realistic schedules, and faster response. Many practitioners, however, feel that scheduling software needs better interfaces with other plant systems, such as forecasting, order entry, and raw material planning.[6]

TABLE 8.2 | *Common Dispatching Rules*

Rule	Description
Static Priorities	
1. Earliest release date	Time job is released to the shop
2. Shortest processing time	Processing time of operation for which job is waiting
3. Total work	Sum of all processing times
4. Earliest due date	Due date of job
5. Least work remaining	Sum of processing times for all operations not yet performed
6. Fewest operations remaining	Number of operations yet to be performed
Dynamic Priorities	
7. Work in next queue	Amount of work awaiting the next machine in a job's processing sequence
8. Slack time	Time remaining until due date *minus* remaining processing time
9. Slack/remaining operations	Slack time *divided* by the number of operations remaining
10. Critical ratio	Time remaining until due date *divided* by days required to complete job

8.5 ENTERPRISE RESOURCE PLANNING

ERP, which is built on the premise that the whole is greater than the sum of its parts, represents the next level of integration from MRP II.

Traditional management systems had generally treated each transaction separately and were built around the strong boundaries of specific functions. Each department typically had its own computer system that was optimized for the particular ways that the department did its work. For example, even though MRP II integrated some portions of a business, its focus was primarily on

> ### OM PRINCIPLE
> Different business functions need to communicate with one another. Order information needs to be integrated with production, production schedules with human resource requirements, purchasing with production scheduling, sales with availability, and so on.

manufacturing planning. Such plans could be coordinated with marketing initiatives, such as an advertising campaign, but this had to be done manually. ERP removed the possibility of human error (such as the operations group not being aware of a marketing promotion and not adjusting their schedule accordingly) by improving the flow of information. Automation of the flow of information from one department to another in any organization became the vehicle for improving effectiveness of plans—this has been the marketing mantra of ERP vendors in the last decade.

ERP systems integrate all aspects of a business—accounting, customer relationship management, supply chain management, manufacturing, sales, human resources—into a unified information system that can be used by multiple users, for multiple purposes, and at multiple locations to provide more timely analysis and reporting of sales, customer, inventory, manufacturing, human resource, and accounting data. This allows a firm to better coordinate supply and demand and to identify critical business issues and address them quickly. A key feature of an ERP system is its flexibility: it can respond to the changing needs of a business by adding or subtracting whatever modules the business needs (see the modules list under Implementing ERP Systems below). ERP systems help organizations to streamline their processes, optimize their resources, and control them on a real-time basis.[7]

Consider a customer order, for example. Typically, an order begins a mostly paper-based journey from in-basket to in-basket around the company, often being keyed and rekeyed into different departments' computer systems along the way. Such a process causes delays and lost orders and is prone to data entry errors. Meanwhile, no one in the company can determine the true status of the order at any given point in time. A sales representative, for example, is typically unable to access the warehouse's computer system to see whether an order has been shipped.

ERP takes a process orientation. Order processing, manufacturing, shipping, and billing are treated as one process. With ERP, a customer service representative has access to all the necessary information to complete the order (the customer's credit rating and order history, current inventory levels, and shipping schedules). So does everyone else in the company. When one department finishes its processing activities, the order is automatically routed to the next department via the ERP

> ### OM PRINCIPLE
> ERP provides the basis to change product features, product mix, and other business variables more rapidly and to respond quickly to changes in demand, competition, and new market opportunities. As business information is distributed throughout a firm quickly and with greater accuracy, higher-quality decisions can be made.

system. As a result, customers get their orders faster and with fewer errors.

Whatever the reasons, ERP is being implemented in all types of industries and organizations. Some examples include aerospace, defense, automotive, banking, insurance, chemicals, pharmaceuticals, consumer goods, health care, electronics, heavy construction, public administration, education, telecommunications, and utilities.

ERP Architecture

Most business planning systems are nothing more than data manipulation tools that store data, process them, and present them in the appropriate form whenever requested by the user. Thus, the key enabler of ERP is a sophisticated information technology infrastructure. It is said that ERP is the finest expression of the inseparability of business and IT. The incremental improvement in IT and the drastic reduction in the prices of computers have made it possible for even a small organization to think about ERP systems. Early ERP systems were built to work only with large mainframe computers, but with the advent of the personal computer, client server technology, and scalable relational database management systems (RDBMS), ERP systems have become widely available.

Most ERP systems exploit the power of *three-tier client server architecture*. In a client server environment, the server stores the data, maintaining its integrity and consistency, and processes the requests of the user from the client desktops. The three-tier architecture adds a middle echelon, embodying all application logic and the business rules that are not part of the application and enforcing appropriate validation checks. Because many organizations that use ERP have multiple locations, online data transfer is important. To facilitate these transactions, other enabling technologies including various IT systems, such as GroupWare, electronic data interchange (EDI), the Internet, intranet, and data warehousing, are used with ERP systems.

Implementing ERP Systems

The three most prominent vendors for ERP software are SAP, Oracle, and PeopleSoft. Although their products have slightly different features, they all provide the same major modules. SAP's R/3 system, which is the market leader, offers the following modules:

- Financial Accounting
- Treasury
- Controlling
- Enterprise Controlling
- Investment Management
- Production Planning
- Materials Management
- Plant Maintenance & Service Management
- Quality Management
- Project System
- Sales & Distribution
- Human Resources Management
- Business Information Warehouse

The modular approach allows firms to add information processing capability incrementally, making it easier to transition to a full ERP implementation. For example, a firm may choose to implement what it perceives are the more important modules for its business first, deferring the more sophisticated applications until after those modules are in place and are providing effective information transactions. The modular approach also allows the software vendors such as SAP to focus on best practices for specific processes in specific industries. For example, quality management practices in pharmaceuticals require *lot tracking*—a firm must be able to trace back and establish exactly when a particular tablet was produced in case there is a problem. Other firms may not need such sophisticated functionality. *Functionality* refers to the specific planning routines chosen as a part of an ERP system. Matching the functionality of the system to the process and planning requirements of the organization is a major challenge. Thus, by using a modular design for the information architecture, SAP is able to design software that meets the need of its customers more precisely without having to deliver a completely customized solution to each organization. SAP's R/3 system also allows mobile and distantly located users to connect through it to the Internet and the business. Other vendors also provide similar functionality in their bundle of products. Some software modules are developed to address the unique requirements of an organization, and are referred to as "bolt-ons." One example is an optimization package for finite scheduling.

The most common reason that companies cancel multimillion-dollar ERP projects is that they discover that the software does not support one of their important business processes. When this happens, they have two choices. They can change their business processes to accommodate the software, which might mean significant changes in long-established ways of doing busi-

> ## OM PRINCIPLE
>
> It is critical for companies to determine if their business processes are compatible with a standard ERP software package before selecting a vendor and trying to implement it.

ness (that often provide competitive advantage) and shake up people's roles and responsibilities (something that few companies are willing to do). Alternatively, they can modify the software to fit the process using bolts-ons, which may slow down the project, introduce errors into the system, and make software upgrades difficult.

Needless to say, implementing an ERP project is costly and time-consuming.[8] Besides direct software costs, firms require data conversion, employee training, integration testing, consulting, and many other expenses. The Meta Group conducted a study of 63 companies of various sizes and found that the total cost of ownership of ERP, including hardware, software, professional services, and internal staff costs, ranged from $400,000 to $300 million; the average cost was $15 million.[9]

Time can also be a major roadblock to ERP implementation. ERP efforts usually take between one to three years, on average, although ERP vendors often suggest a three- or six-month average implementation time in an attempt to sell their products. The important thing is not to focus on how long the process will take, but rather to understand the benefits and how ERP can improve an organization's operations.

The following are the most common approaches to implementing ERP:

1. *Transformation Approach.* Cast off all existing legacy systems at once and implement a new ERP system across the entire company. This is the most ambitious and difficult approach to ERP implementation. Many firms chose this method in the early 1990s, but few attempt it anymore because it calls for the entire company to mobilize and change dramatically. Discarding systems that have been fine-tuned to match the ways people are accustomed to work can be traumatic, and the effort involved is often not worth the risk of failure. Nonetheless, this approach can be effective when the scope of the ERP system is limited to one plant or one department.

2. *Pilot Site Approach.* Install independent ERP systems in each key operation, while linking common processes, such as financial bookkeeping, across the enterprise. Usually, this begins with a pilot installation in one unit where the core business of the firm will not be disrupted if something goes wrong. Once the pilot system is up and run-

ning and all the bugs are worked out, the system can be rolled out to other units. This approach suits large or diverse companies that do not share many common processes across business units. This has emerged as the most common way of implementing ERP, although it does take more time to complete.

3. *Incremental Approach.* Focus on only a few key modules, such as finance, and get the ERP system up and running quickly across the organization. After users have some experience, new modules can be added gradually, expanding the implementation over time. Although this approach is simpler than the other strategies, the payback will be much smaller. It is not a true "enterprise" solution and will not effect much change in employees' behavior. Smaller companies often use this approach.

Modern ERP systems have significantly expanded what they have to offer, and many firms have realized substantial benefits. For example, Timken Steel Company gained 15 percent more output from its current capacity without investing in new plant and equipment.[10] Many others have not yet witnessed the expected results, however. Table 8.3 summarizes the business benefits and challenges associated with ERP systems.

TABLE 8.3	*Benefits and Challenges Associated with ERP*
Benefits	**Challenges**
Multidatabase and multiplatform support	Long implementation times
E-commerce/e-business solutions (online queries)	Massive cost overruns
Wide range of functional business solutions	Stressed relations with software vendor
Internal (supplier) and external (customer) integration	Lack of product support
User defined work flow	Unresolved technical issues
Stable databases	High failure rates (in terms of business benefit)
Consistent source code development and soft coding (easier to change deliverables)	Lack of documentation
Distributed computing	Upgrade problems
Advanced security functions	Massive hardware resources
Easier data sorting and sequencing	Organizational acceptance
Graphical user interface and intuitive report writer generators	Extensive setup and testing

Summary of Key Points

- ○ Efficient planning and control systems are necessary in any organization to synchronize key processes and support the achievement of strategic and competitive objectives. Modern systems have evolved over the years from simple reorder point inventory management approaches to comprehensive business enterprise resource planning systems.

- ○ Inventory management systems consist of continuous-review and periodic-review systems. Continuous-review systems offer tighter control of inventoried items because orders can be placed to minimize stockout risks. Periodic-review systems are useful when a large number of items can be ordered from the same supplier, since individual orders will be placed at the same time.

○ Aggregate planning focuses on developing production plans that balance cost against overall capacity; it is concerned with product groups as opposed to individual products. Four major types of aggregate planning strategies are production-rate changes, workforce changes, inventory smoothing, and demand shifting.

○ Material requirements planning (MRP) is a technique used to plan for and control manufacturing inventories in a dependent demand environment. The key inputs are the bill of materials, master production schedule, planned lead-times, on-hand inventory, and outstanding orders. The output of the process is a schedule for obtaining resources needed to produce the end items.

○ A major disadvantage of MRP is its inability to include capacity constraints in the calculations. This can be addressed by capacity requirements planning techniques, however.

○ Lot sizing is the process of grouping requirements into smaller production lots to better balance changeover costs with inventory-holding costs.

○ Manufacturing resource planning (MRP II) involves the broader functions of purchasing, capacity planning, and master scheduling in addition to inventory, production, and strategic financial planning. It provides simulation capabilities and a better link to functional strategies.

○ Scheduling refers to the assignment of priorities to customers and/or manufacturing orders and the allocation of work to specific work centers and/or resources. A schedule specifies the timing and sequence of production and the amount of work to be completed at any work center during any time period.

○ Common measures for evaluating the merits of a schedule are makespan, which is the time needed to process a set of jobs, and flow time, which is the amount of time a job spends in the shop. Other criteria that relate to customer due dates are tardiness (the amount of time by which the completion time exceeds the due date) and lateness (the difference between the completion time and the due date).

○ Enterprise resource planning (ERP) grew out of narrow manufacturing planning and control systems—reorder point systems, material requirements planning, and manufacturing resource planning—to integrate and synchronize business functions across the organization. ERP systems integrate all aspects of a business—accounting, customer relationship management, supply chain management, manufacturing, sales, human resources—into a unified information system that can be used by multiple users, for multiple purposes, and at multiple locations to provide more timely analysis and reporting of sales, customer, inventory, manufacturing, human resource, and accounting data.

○ The complexity of ERP systems requires costly and time-consuming implementation. Approaches for implementation include casting off all existing legacy systems at once and implementing ERP across the entire company; installing independent ERP systems in each key operation, while linking common processes, such as financial bookkeeping, across the enterprise; and focusing on only a few key modules, such as finance, and getting the ERP system up and running quickly across the organization.

Questions for Review and Discussion

1. Trace the evolution of manufacturing planning systems into organization-wide enterprise systems. What were the characteristics of each major phase of development?
2. What are the key inputs to MRP? How are they used to create a plan?
3. Explain the concept of dependent demand. How does it relate to MRP versus reorder point systems?
4. Why is MRP often referred to as an "infinite scheduling system"?
5. Explain the concept of lot sizing. Why is it necessary after MRP calculations have been completed?

6. How does MRP II differ from MRP?

7. How does ERP differ from its predecessor technologies? What advantages does ERP offer that MRP II could not provide?

8. What issues do firms face when implementing ERP? Identify the principal strategies that have been used to implement ERP, and discuss their advantages and disadvantages.

9. Why are scheduling and production control approaches important? Describe the different scheduling criteria that are used to evaluate schedule performance.

10. What are dispatching rules, and how do they differ from scheduling?

11. An electrical appliance, A, consists of three major subassemblies: B, C, and D. One unit of A consists of two units of B, one unit of C, and three units of D. Subassembly B consists of two units of D, one unit of E, and one unit of F. Subassembly C consists of two units of E. Subassembly D consists of one unit of E and one unit of F. A second major appliance, G, consists of three units of D and four units of F.

   a. Draw the bill of material for products A and G.

   b. If 50 units of A and 25 units of G are required for the month of May, compute the requirements for all components and subassemblies.

   c. Suppose that 100 units of A and 50 units of G are required for the month of June and that at the end of May, this is the stock on hand:

Item	A	G	B	C	D	E	F
Stock on hand	50	25	50	20	350	0	175

   Calculate the requirements for all components and subassemblies.

12. The parts used in manufacturing a yo-yo are shown in Figure 8.13. One thousand yo-yos are needed by week 10. Current inventory levels and lead-times are shown below.

Part	Inventory (units)	Lead–Time (weeks)
Wooden peg	100	1
String	500	1
Sides	200	5
Cartons	—	3

   It is known that 200 sides have already been ordered and will arrive at week 6. When all the parts are available, it takes one week to assemble 1,000 yo-yos.

   a. Determine the net requirements for all components.

   b. Use time phasing to determine an overall schedule.

FIGURE 8.13 | *Bill of Material for Question 12*

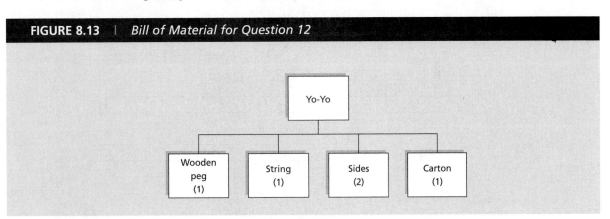

FIGURE 8.14 | *Bill of Material for Question 13*

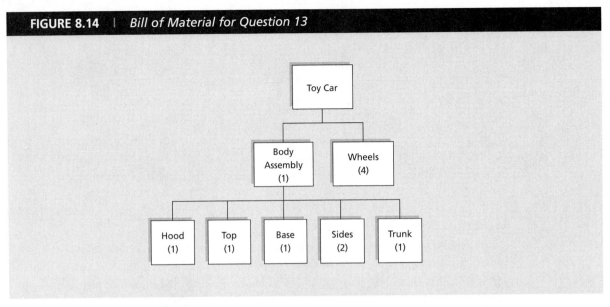

13. The parts used in manufacturing a toy car are shown in Figure 8.14. Five hundred toy cars are needed by week 12. Current inventory levels and lead-times are given below.

Item	Inventory (units)	Lead-Time (weeks)
Toy car	100	2
Body assembly	125	5
Hood	—	3
Top	100	2
Base	175	4
Sides	200	3
Trunk	300	2
Wheels	800	3

a. Determine the net requirements for all components.

b. Use time phasing to determine an overall schedule.

14. The bill of material for a pair of in-line skates is shown in Figure 8.15. Given the information below, determine net requirements for all components and an ordering schedule. Assume that 500 pairs of skates are needed by week 10.

Item	Inventory (units)	Lead-Time (weeks)
Pairs of skates	50	1
Wheel assembly	100	2
Outer shell	25 pairs	3
Inner liner	0 pairs	3
Wheels	1,500	1
Bearings	3,000	1
Wheel frame	600	2
Buckles	5,000	1

FIGURE 8.15 | *Bill of Material for Question 14*

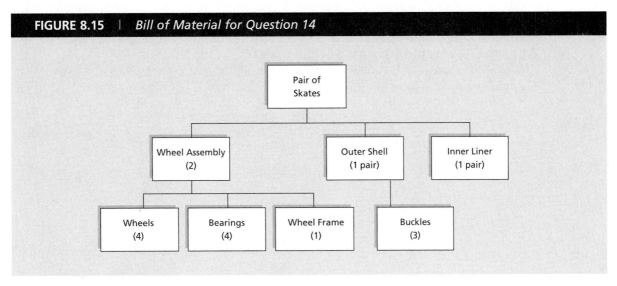

Internet Projects

To find Web links to carry out each of the following projects, go to the text's Web site at **http://raturi_evans.swlearning.com.**

1. ERPCentral provides the latest news for ERP vendors and markets from various sources. Review and summarize one article from its list.

2. Many services for assessing the functionality of ERP systems are now available through the Web. Review the information at the link on the text Web site. What are some models for assessing the compatibility of ERP software with an organization? What are some attributes that a firm should look for in selecting an ERP package? How should it choose between two competing packages?

3. ERP vendors continue to upgrade their software packages. It has been estimated that ERP customers should plan on spending 15 percent of the project's original implementation cost every year to keep their ERP systems up to date. That means keeping up with current releases of the software as well as moving along with changing business conditions. Outline the release history of one of the following ERP systems by gathering information from each of these vendor's Web sites:

   a. SAP

   b. PeopleSoft

   c. Baan

   d. Oracle

4. Many ERP vendors have moved into nonmanufacturing areas such as retail, utilities, health care, and the public sector. Can you find any evidence of this? Use the Web sites for the following organizations or publications.

   a. InformationWeek.com

   b. AMRResearch.com

   c. ComputerWorld

   d. Datamation

   e. CIO Magazine

EXPERIENCE OM

Aggregate Planning Using Spreadsheets

The marketing and sales group has forecast the demand for beer in the forthcoming year at Golden Breweries. Golden faces a seasonal demand that has the following pattern:

Month	Demand
January	1,500
February	1,000
March	1,900
April	2,600
May	2,800
June	3,100
July	3,200
August	3,000
September	2,000
October	1,000
November	1,800
December	2,200

At the beginning of January, 1,000 barrels (bbl) are in inventory. Operating currently at a rate of 2,200 bbl per month, Golden wants to explore several possibilities for setting up the production schedule. The cost structure for beer production allows Golden to change the production level anytime for $5 per bbl change from the previous month irrespective of whether the level is increased or decreased. Once Golden establishes the level of production, not utilizing this capacity costs the company $3 per bbl (undertime cost). If Golden sets the production level lower than what it wants to produce in a given month, it incurs a cost of $6.50 per bbl. Any inventory left over at the end of the month is charged a fixed rate (2 percent of its production cost or $0.02 \times \$70 = \$1.40$) for that month. Not meeting demand results in an opportunity loss of $90 per bbl. This has been assessed as the margin lost on the product not sold as well as goodwill losses for displeasing the customer. Golden's cost structure is summarized below.

Production cost ($/bbl)	$70.00
Inventory-holding cost ($/bbl)	$ 1.40
Lost sales cost ($/bbl)	$90.00
Overtime cost ($/bbl)	$ 6.50
Undertime cost ($/bbl)	$ 3.00
Rate change cost ($/bbl)	$ 5.00
Normal production rate	2,200

A spreadsheet for modeling this scenario is available in the Excel files, Golden Breweris.xls on the CD-ROM, and is shown in Figure 8.16. The spreadsheet is designed to allow you to enter values for production in each month and calculate the cost of the resulting production plan. With such a spreadsheet, it is easy to perform what-if analyses of alternative aggregate planning strategies. To calculate the ending inventory level each month in column F, note that

FIGURE 8.16 | *Aggregate Planning Spreadsheet*

	A	B	C	D	E	F	G
1	Golden Breweries						
2							
3	Production cost ($/bbl)			$ 70.00			
4	Inventory holding cost ($/bbl)			$ 1.40			
5	Lost sales cost ($/bbl)			$ 90.00			
6	Overtime cost ($/bbl)			$ 6.50			
7	Undertime cost ($/bbl)			$ 3.00			
8	Rate change cost ($/bbl)			$ 5.00			
9	Normal production rate			2,200			
10							
11					Cumulative		
12			Cumulative		Product	Ending	Lost
13	Month	Demand	Demand	Production	Availability	Inventory	Sales
14						1,000	
15	January	1,500	1,500	2,200	3,200	1,700	0
16	February	1,000	2,500	2,200	5,400	2,900	0
17	March	1,900	4,400	2,200	7,600	3,200	0
18	April	2,600	7,000	2,200	9,800	2,800	0
19	May	2,800	9,800	2,200	12,000	2,200	0
20	June	3,100	12,900	2,200	14,200	1,300	0
21	July	3,200	16,100	2,200	16,400	300	0
22	August	3,000	19,100	2,200	18,600	0	500
23	September	2,000	21,100	2,200	21,300	200	0
24	October	1,000	22,100	2,200	23,500	1,400	0
25	November	1,800	23,900	2,200	25,700	1,800	0
26	December	2,200	26,100	2,200	27,900	1,800	0
27							
28		Production	Inventory	Lost Sales	Overtime	Undertime	Rate Change
29	Month	Cost	Cost	Cost	Cost	Cost	Cost
30							
31	January	$ 154,000	$ 2,380	$ -	$ -	$ -	$ -
32	February	$ 154,000	$ 4,060	$ -	$ -	$ -	$ -
33	March	$ 154,000	$ 4,480	$ -	$ -	$ -	$ -
34	April	$ 154,000	$ 3,920	$ -	$ -	$ -	$ -
35	May	$ 154,000	$ 3,080	$ -	$ -	$ -	$ -
36	June	$ 154,000	$ 1,820	$ -	$ -	$ -	$ -
37	July	$ 154,000	$ 420	$ -	$ -	$ -	$ -
38	August	$ 154,000	$ -	$ 45,000	$ -	$ -	$ -
39	September	$ 154,000	$ 280	$ -	$ -	$ -	$ -
40	October	$ 154,000	$ 1,960	$ -	$ -	$ -	$ -
41	November	$ 154,000	$ 2,520	$ -	$ -	$ -	$ -
42	December	$ 154,000	$ 2,520	$ -	$ -	$ -	$ -
43		$1,848,000	$ 27,440	$ 45,000	$ -	$ -	$ -
44							
45	Total cost	$1,920,440					

Beginning inventory + production − demand = ending inventory

The formula for Cumulative Product Availability is adjusted for lost sales. Because there are no backorders, the inventory level cannot become negative. Thus, in Figure 8.16 for September, we essentially begin anew with zero inventory. If lost sales occur, we must add them to the cumulative production to maintain the correct relationship:

Cumulative production − cumulative demand = current inventory level

If backorders were allowed, then inventory values could be negative (representing units back-ordered), and we would not have to make any adjustments.

The production plan in Figure 8.16 is an example of a *level production strategy*; that is, production is the same in each period. Such a strategy avoids rate changes but, as is evident, can result in excessive inventories and possibly lost sales. For example, in February we have

$$1,700 + 2,200 - 1,000 = 2,900$$

At this constant production rate, Golden Breweries will build up an inventory of 3,200 barrels in March and suffer lost sales of 500 barrels in August, one of the peak demand months for beer. Incurring shortages and carrying high inventories may not be a good business policy.

1. Does the solution (in terms of how much you produce each month) to the level production strategy in Figure 8.16 change significantly if 100 bbl of initial inventory are dubbed low quality and thrown away (that is, your starting inventory is 900 bbl)? Comment on the changes as well as the role of accurate inventory information in creating production plans.

2. Does your solution change significantly if a 100 bbl consignment on the way to the customer is returned (that is, your starting inventory is 1,100 bbl)? Discuss the counterintuitive result that it is optimal to incur a lost sale when you start with more inventory (as here) as opposed to less inventory.

3. The warehouse manager alerts you that since the current maximum capacity of the warehouse is 3,000 bbl, the level production plan in Figure 8.16 is not feasible. You decide to recalculate the level production rate by setting the monthly production level as (total demand − initial inventory)/12. What changes do you see in your schedule? Does this plan satisfy the warehouse manager's concern? Do you save any money by doing this?

4. The purchasing managers argue that suppliers have a very difficult time meeting Golden's needs during the peak months of June, July, and August using the level strategy in Figure 8.16 because all other breweries are also ordering more during those periods. They also agree that any "lost sales"—such as those that you incurred with the level strategy—are bad for business. So they suggest that production levels at Golden should be anchored to levels that avoid all stockouts. How much would Golden Breweries have to produce with a level production strategy to avoid all lost sales? How much more would this cost than the current plan?

5. The solution that the purchasing managers suggested in question 4 results in excessive inventories for which there is no space. In addition, working capital and line of credit requirements are excessive. The controller suggests that working capital requirements would be reduced if Golden followed a two-level production strategy: use a high production level until the end of peak months (August) and then cut back production to a level that satisfies the remaining demand. How would you rate the performance of such an approach?

6. The production manager believes that better two-level strategies are possible such as operating at a high level in the peak months (June, July, August) and a low level in the other months. How does this "mixed" strategy perform?

7. The sales manager argues that using level production strategies is counterintuitive to her thinking since a firm must respond to the demand from the market on a "when needed" basis. Level strategies don't satisfy this intuition, and they also create unnecessary inventories in low demand periods, resulting in excessive costs. An alternative to a level production strategy is a *chase-demand strategy*—that is, produce the same amount as the demand forecast each month. While inventories will be reduced and lost sales will be

eliminated, many rate changes will generally occur. How does this approach compare with the level strategy?

8. Ignoring issues of capacity or lost sales, one might be interested in finding the solution that results in a minimum total cost. The spreadsheet can be used to seek an optimal solution. You might begin with a level production strategy and then, through trial and error, try to improve the solution. Graphs of the cumulative demand and product availability often assist in identifying improved solutions. Also, examining individual cost categories can highlight areas where costs can be reduced. For example, if examination of costs indicates that inventory cost is relatively high and backorder cost is relatively low, one might search for periods where the ending inventory is high and adjust the production level for those periods. Use the spreadsheet to find the lowest-cost solution you possibly can, and document your experimental process.

9. Although a trial-and-error approach will probably find a relatively low-cost solution, it is not likely to find the minimum-cost solution. Linear programming can be used for finding the minimum-cost solution, and many large corporations use it for similar types of planning problems. Develop a linear programming model to minimize the total cost while ensuring that material balances are maintained. (Hint: This can be a tricky formulation; you need constraints to ensure the correct calculations of overtime and undertime and production rate changes so that these variables can be used in the objective function.)

9 Lean Thinking and Just-in-Time Operations

The emergence of lean thinking in operations management has had a wide impact on how manufacturing and service business operate. Lean thinking represents a strategic initiative that is holistic in approach and practical in implementation. It attacks waste created by structural and infrastructural elements in operations that do not accomplish the task of delivering value effectively, and streamlines processes to deliver value to the customer. Lean thinking began at Toyota, which championed and demonstrated many of the key principles. Two of the most important approaches in lean thinking are just-in-time, a system for producing and delivering the right parts and components at the right time and in the right amounts, and constraint management, which involves synchronizing operations to enhance performance and throughput. All of these ideas have moved beyond manufacturing into service environments.

This chapter covers the principles of lean thinking in operations. Specifically, we address:
- Concepts of lean production and lean thinking (*Section 9.1*).
- Principles of just-in-time (*Section 9.2*).
- Constraint management as an approach to lean operations (*Section 9.3*).
- The relationships between Six Sigma and lean production (*Section 9.4*).

Material on the CD-ROM discusses some useful tools and techniques related to lean thinking and just-in-time.
11. The Seven QC Tools
12. Poka-Yoke (Mistake-Proofing)
15. Quantitative Inventory Models

9.1 LEAN PRODUCTION

Lean production refers to approaches initially developed by the Toyota Motor Corporation that focus on the elimination of waste in all forms, including defects requiring rework, unnecessary processing steps, unnecessary movement of materials or people, waiting time, excess inventory, and overproduction. It involves identifying and eliminat-

OM PRINCIPLE

Lean production is facilitated by a focus on measurement and continuous improvement, cross-trained workers, efficient machine layout, rapid setup and changeover, realistic work standards, worker empowerment to perform inspections and take corrective action, supplier partnerships, and preventive maintenance. Lean production is also facilitated by JIT as well as constraint management techniques, which we discuss later in this chapter.

ing non-value-added activities throughout the entire value chain to achieve faster customer response, reduced inventories, higher quality, and better human resources. As one article about Toyota observed, to see the Toyota production system in action is to "behold a thing of beauty":

> A Toyota assembly plant fairly hums: Every movement has a purpose, and there is no slack. Tour a typical auto plant, and you see stacks of half-finished parts, assembly lines halted for adjustment, workers standing idle. At Toyota the workers look like dancers in a choreographed production: retrieving parts, installing them, checking the quality, and doing it all in immaculate surroundings.[1]

Some of the benefits claimed by proponents of lean production are 60 percent reduction in cycle times, 40 percent improvement in space utilization, 25 percent greater throughput, 50 percent reduction in work-in-process (WIP) and finished goods inventories, 50 percent improvement in quality, and 20 percent improvements in working capital and worker productivity. As one industry expert observed, however, lean production takes "an incredible amount of detailed planning, discipline, hard work, and painstaking attention to detail."[2]

The elimination of all forms of waste is the principal driver for lean production (see the *OM Practice* box on Porsche). The term *waste* is used here in its broadest sense to mean any activity, material, or operation that does not add value. *Muda* in Japanese means "waste," specifically any human activity that absorbs resources but creates no value. It includes mistakes that require rectification, inventory piled up by overproduction, unnecessary processing steps, purposeless movement of employees and material handling, people in a downstream activity remaining idle due to the failure of an upstream activity to deliver on time, and goods and services that do not meet customers' needs. There are two basic types of *muda*: those that create no value but are required by the product development process (Type I *muda*) and those that create no value and can be eliminated immediately (Type II *muda*). Hence, lean thinking involves identifying all types of *muda* and then eliminating them. Lean thinking is the antidote to *muda*; in short, lean thinking is lean because it provides a way to do more and more with less and less.

The Toyota Motor Corporation classified waste into seven major categories:

1. **Overproduction:** For example, making a batch of 100 when it only had orders for 50 in order to avoid an expensive setup, or making a batch of 52 instead of 50 in case some were rejected. Overproduction ties up production facilities, and excess inventory simply sits idle.
2. **Waiting Time:** For instance, allowing queues to build up between operations, resulting in longer lead-times and higher WIP.
3. **Transportation:** The time and effort spent in moving products around the factory as a result of poor layout.
4. **Processing:** The traditional notion of waste, as exemplified by scrap that often results from poor product or process design.
5. **Inventory:** Waste associated with the expense of idle stock and the extra storage and handling requirements needed to maintain it.
6. **Motion:** As a result of inefficient workplace design and location of tools and materials.
7. **Production Defects:** The result of not performing work correctly the first time.

Lean production can easily be applied to nonmanufacturing environments. Pure service firms such as banks, hospitals, and restaurants have benefited from lean principles. In these contexts, lean production is often called **lean enterprise.** For example, banks require quick

OM PRACTICE

Porsche
German manufacturer takes lean lessons from Japan.

By 1992, Porsche, the maker of high-end German sports cars, found sales falling to 25 percent of their 1986 peak. When Wendelin Wiedeking took over as head of the company, he pushed workers to adopt Japanese-style lean production methods. He hired two Japanese efficiency experts and personally sawed off the top half of a row of shelves with a circular saw to reduce inventories. Along with more flexible, negotiated work rules, Porsche revamped its assembly process so that production of 1997's 911 model took only 60 hours, compared to 120 hours for its predecessor. The time to develop a new model was cut from seven years to three. Porsche now uses 300 parts suppliers, down from nearly 1,000, and a quality control program has helped reduce the number of defective parts by a factor of 10.[3]

response and efficiency to operate on low margins, making many of their processes, such as check sorting and mortgage approval, natural candidates for lean enterprise solutions.[4] The handling of paper checks and credit card slips, for instance, involves a physical process not unlike an assembly line. The faster a bank moves checks through its system, the sooner it can collect its funds and the better its returns on invested capital (see the *OM Practice* box on the banking industry).

OM PRACTICE

Lean Manufacturing Approaches in Banking
Many areas of banking share key characteristics with manufacturing, making lean production techniques advantageous.

One North American financial institution applied lean thinking to its check-processing operations. Managers followed one check as it made its way through the bank's systems, documenting the time spent in actual processing and in waiting, rework, and handling. They found that almost half of the bank's notional processing capacity was consumed by nonprocessing activities such as fixing jams and setting up machines. Further investigation revealed wide variations in productivity between individual operators on a single shift. When the work practices of the least and most productive operators were compared, it became evident that although all were engaged in the same task, differences in the way they performed it were creating huge swings in productivity.

To adopt a lean manufacturing approach, the bank first matched the flow of incoming checks to processing capacity. At the end of each business day, the check-processing operation was swamped with more checks than it could hope to handle; this bottleneck created the false impression that capacity was constrained. The bank applied just-in-time principles to the processing of incoming checks and spread the check flow evenly through the day. A second bottleneck occurred at the beginning of the day; standard practice dictated that all checks presented for morning processing be sorted three times. But doing this meant that the morning check volume could not be processed in time to meet the account-posting deadline. But, many of the checks did not need to be completed by the morning deadline, and once the sorting of these low-priority items was shifted to later in the day when volumes were lower, capacity increased by 122 percent.

By uncovering and freeing up "phantom" capacity that had previously been taken up by waiting time, maintenance, and rework, the bank increased its actual capacity by more than 25 percent without investing in additional equipment. The bank was able both to sell its services to other banks at an attractive price and to expand capacity during the most time-sensitive period of the day, when its services could be priced at a premium. In all, these one-off improvements more than doubled the margin contributed by the operation.[5]

Lean production has evolved into **lean thinking**—a philosophy of applying lean concepts to all business operations. In the words of the authors who started the revolution,

Lean Thinking does not provide a new management program for the one-minute manager. Instead, it offers a new way of thinking, being, and doing for the serious manager—one that will change the world.[6]

Lean thinking focuses on creating value for both the customer and the organization through seamless operations within the value chain—through order, design, processing, and delivery. Creating lean operations requires ignoring traditional boundaries of jobs and functions and rethinking specific work practices to eliminate waste, scrap, and delays so that the value chain operates smoothly and without interruptions, providing goods or services at the right time and in the right amounts. Nevertheless, some firms have misconstrued lean thinking to mean cost reduction and downsizing during an economic crisis. Clearly, this is not the case.

Tools for Lean Production

The following are some of the key tools used in lean production:

- **The 5S's:** The 5S's are derived from Japanese terms: *seiri* (sort), *seiton* (set in order), *seiso* (shine), *seiketsu* (standardize), and *shitsuke* (sustain). They define a system for workplace organization and standardization. *Sort* refers to ensuring that each item in a workplace is in its proper place or identified as unnecessary and removed. *Set in order* means to arrange materials and equipment so that they are easy to find and use. *Shine* refers to a clean work area. Not only is this important for safety, but as the work area is cleaned, maintenance problems such as oil leaks can be identified before they cause problems. *Standardize* means to formalize procedures and practices to create consistency and ensure that all steps are performed correctly. Finally, *sustain* means to keep the process going through training, communication, and organizational structures.

- **Visual Controls:** Visual controls are indicators for tools, parts, and production activities that are placed in plain sight of all workers so that everyone can understand the status of the system at a glance. Thus, if a machine goes down, or a part is defective or delayed, immediate action can be taken.

- **Efficient Layout and Standardized Work:** The layout of equipment and processes is designed according to the best operational sequence, by physically linking and arranging machines and process steps most efficiently, often in a cellular arrangement. Standardizing the individual tasks by clearly specifying the proper method reduces wasted human movement and energy.

- **Pull Production:** This is a system (also described as a *kanban system* or *just-in-time*) in which upstream suppliers do not produce until the downstream customer signals a need for parts.

- **Single-Minute Exchange of Dies (SMED):** SMED refers to rapid changeover of tooling and fixtures in machine shops so that multiple products in smaller batches can be run on the same equipment. Reducing setup time adds value to the operation and facilitates smoother production flow.

- **Total Productive Maintenance:** Total productive maintenance is designed to ensure that equipment is operational and available when needed.

- **Source Inspection:** Inspection and control by process operators ensures that the product passed on to the next production stage conforms to specifications.

- **Continuous Improvement:** Continuous improvement provides the link to quality and Six Sigma. To make lean production work, one must get to the root cause of problems and permanently remove them. Teamwork is an integral part of continuous improvement in lean environments.

Many of these tools and approaches were developed or refined in the context of the Toyota production system and will be discussed further later in this chapter. The next section discusses the backbone of the system—just-in-time (JIT).

9.2 OPERATION OF A JIT SYSTEM

Just-in-time (JIT) was introduced at Toyota during the 1950s and 1960s by Kiichiro Toyoda to address the challenge of coordinating successive production activities. An automobile, for instance, consists of thousands of parts. It is extremely difficult to coordinate the transfer of materials and components between production operations. Most factories use a system of **push production** in which they make parts and then send them to subsequent operations or to storage. Of course, a breakdown of some process or demand fluctuations will create an imbalance of inventory between processes. Toyoda recognized the limitations of Western automobile production, which relied on massive and expensive stamping press lines to produce car panels. The dies in the presses weighed many tons, and specialists needed up to a full day to switch them for a new part. To compensate for long setup times, large lot sizes were produced so that machines could be kept busy while others were being set up.

> **OM PRINCIPLE**
>
> Push production typically results in high WIP inventories and high levels of indirect labor and overhead required to transport inventory and materials between operations, both of which increase cost and decrease productivity.

Even before constructing a new plant at Koromo, Toyoda had formulated a clear mental picture of the system he wanted. Instead of a system based on the production of large lots and maintenance of large inventories, he created a **pull production** system with one key principle: to produce the needed quantity of the required parts each day. Employees at a given operation go to the source of the required parts, such as machining or subassembly, and withdraw the units as they need them. Then just enough new parts are manufactured or procured to replace those withdrawn. Thus, if inventories are needed at all, they are minimized. As the process from which parts were withdrawn replenishes the items it transferred out, it draws on the output of its preceding process and so on. Slips, called kanban cards, are circulated indicating the number of parts that had to be made that day at each operation. A **kanban** is a flag or a piece of paper that contains all relevant information for an order: part number, description, process area used, time of delivery, quantity available, quantity delivered, production quantity, and so on. The type and number of units required by a process are written on kanbans and used to initiate withdrawal and production of items through the production process.

Figure 9.1 shows how the withdrawal kanbans and production-ordering kanbans operate. The carrier of process B goes to the store of process A (step 1) with the withdrawal kanbans and empty pallets after a sufficient number have accumulated. When the necessary number of parts are withdrawn, the worker detaches the production-ordering kanbans that were attached to the inventory and places them at the kanban receiving post, leaving the empty pallets (step 2). For each production-ordering kanban detached, a withdrawal kanban is put in its place (step 3). When these units are used, the withdrawal kanban is placed in the withdrawal kanban post (step 4). In process A, the production-ordering kanbans are collected and placed in the production-ordering kanban post (step 5). These kanbans provide the authority to produce the parts (step 6), and the kanbans move physically with the parts throughout the

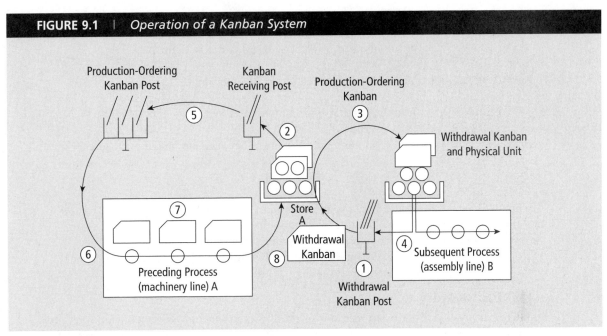

FIGURE 9.1 | *Operation of a Kanban System*

Source: Y. Monden, "What Makes the Toyota Production System Really Tick," *Industrial Engineering*, January 1981, 36–46. Reprinted with the permission of the Institute of Industrial Engineers, 3577 Parkway Lane, Suite 200, Norcross, GA 30092, 770-449-0461. Copyright © 1981.

operations in process A (step 7). The completed parts are placed in inventory, along with their production-ordering kanbans (step 8). In this way, many individual processes are interconnected. Production orders and withdrawal quantities under kanban are approximately 10 percent of the daily demand. With such small lot sizes, it is unnecessary to warehouse WIP inventory, thus minimizing holding costs.

OM PRINCIPLE

The objective of JIT is to create a smooth, rapid flow of all products from the time materials and purchased parts are received until the time the final product is shipped to the customer.

This process begins at final assembly and works backward through all workstations in the production process, continuing even to subcontractors and suppliers. It promotes the production of small lots, minimizes inventories, and reduces storage space requirements. Effective use of a kanban system requires fast and efficient changeovers between parts, a high degree of quality because operations will not be able to reject incoming parts and keep the production line running, and considerable flexibility among workers.

A typical calculation of the number of kanbans in a production system assesses the pipeline and buffer inventory required to sustain the flow of materials through a facility. Suppose that two workstations, A feeding B, are linked with kanban cards and produce at the rate of 10 units per hour. It takes 2 hours to process a kanban container at the feeding work center (A) and 3 hours of wait before this container is processed by B. Then the pipeline inventory between A and B must be:

$$\textbf{Pipeline inventory} = \textbf{demand} \times \textbf{lead-time} = \textbf{10/hour} \times \textbf{(2 hours + 3 hours)} = \\ \textbf{50 units}$$

If a 10 percent buffer is added between these two work centers, then:

$$\text{Buffer inventory} = 10\% \times 50 \text{ units} = 5 \text{ units}$$

Further, if each container with a kanban can hold 11 units, then:

$$\text{Number of containers or kanbans between A and B} = (50 + 5)/11 = 5$$

In general, the calculation of the number of kanbans between any two work centers is:

$$N = d(p + w)(1 + \alpha)/K$$

where d = average demand or throughput rate in units per hour
p = processing time for one kanban or container in hours
w = wait time before a container is processed in hours
α = safety factor that decides the level of buffer inventory for each container
K = size of the container in number of units

JIT Philosophy

There have been various interpretations of the Toyota production system, but until recently, too much attention was paid to operational details, while the overall philosophy was largely ignored. When JIT was first introduced to Western companies, for example, many people thought that it was simply using kanban cards. In reality, Toyoda was inspired by the chapter entitled "Learning from Waste" in *Today and Tomorrow*, a book published by Henry Ford in 1926. As the Japanese production engineering consultant Shigeo Shingo, who was closely involved with the developments at Toyota for many years, observed, "Some people imagine that Toyota has put on a smart new set of clothes, the kanban system, so they go out and purchase the same outfit and try it on. They quickly discover that they are much too fat to wear it! They must eliminate waste and make fundamental improvements in their production system before techniques like kanban can be of any help."[7]

As a result, many attempts to implement what people thought was JIT failed to meet expectations. Shingo defined JIT as "producing what is necessary, when it is necessary, in the amount necessary." In an effort to meet customer needs for rapid response, one often hears the phrase "ship it ASAP," which most people interpret as "ship it *as soon as possible*." In the JIT philosophy, ASAP stands for *Accuracy, Speed, Anxiety*, and

> ## OM PRINCIPLE
>
> Eliminating waste goes far beyond reducing unnecessary WIP inventory. It includes improvements in process design, standardizing operations, reducing setup and changeover times, leveling production, and developing supplier partnerships.

Postponement! Inventory accuracy is essential to good production control, particularly when minimal inventories are kept. Techniques such as cycle counting were used in the Toyota system for keeping inventory records accurate. Speed signifies fast cycle times; techniques for reducing setup time were used to ensure speedy changeovers from one product line to another. Companies should create a sense of anxiety, or urgency, in all activities. *Andon* cords, which allow operators to stop an operation immediately if they detect any quality or operational problem, are used to ensure that problems are quickly resolved. Finally, postponement is the process of delaying commitment of the items in a customer order until the last possible moment. The use of kanban cards avoided unnecessary waste from having the wrong kind of product in the warehouse.

The underlying principles of the JIT philosophy are:

○ Exposing fundamental problems and correcting them with permanent, not temporary, solutions.

○ Striving for simplicity, because simple processes have fewer opportunities for error and are faster to accomplish.

○ Reducing manufacturing throughput times, effectively replacing traditional batch production with continuous processing through the use of small lot sizes, cell manufacturing, and setup reduction.

○ Improving supplier performance to eliminate the need for rework or returns.

○ Improving quality and implementing continuous improvement, because poor quality disrupts the flow and coordination required.

○ Improving labor flexibility through cross-training and increasing empowerment for making decisions on the production line.

Figure 9.2 exhibits a broad framework for JIT. The top portion of the figure shows the linkages between JIT and many of the elements of operations management discussed throughout this book: top management support (leadership), human resources management, quality management, manufacturing strategy, and technology management. All are linked by a company-wide focus on continuous improvement and employee participation, two of the key elements of total quality. The elegance of the system is not in the individual components or techniques, but in the way they link together to facilitate high performance.

The core elements of JIT are classified into seven categories:

1. Production-floor management
2. Scheduling
3. Process and product design
4. Quality improvement
5. Workforce management
6. Supplier management
7. Accounting and information systems

The uniqueness of JIT lies in the specific practices in each category and their relationship with one another, leading to improved manufacturing performance and, ultimately, competitive advantage.

Production-Floor Management

OM PRINCIPLE

Long setup times waste manufacturing resources. Short setup times enable a manufacturer to make short production runs and frequent changeovers, thus achieving high flexibility and product variety.

In addition to pull production and kanban, managing the flow of materials on the production floor in a JIT system focuses on reducing setup times, using small lot sizes, and employing preventive maintenance. For example, Yammar Diesel reduced a machining-line tool setting from 9.3 hours to nine minutes, a U.S. chain-saw manufacturer reduced setup time on a punch press from more than two hours to three minutes, and a midwestern manufacturer was able to cut equipment setup time on a 60-ton press from 45 minutes to one minute. This was accomplished through process improvements such as storing the required tools next to the

FIGURE 9.2 | *JIT Operations Framework*

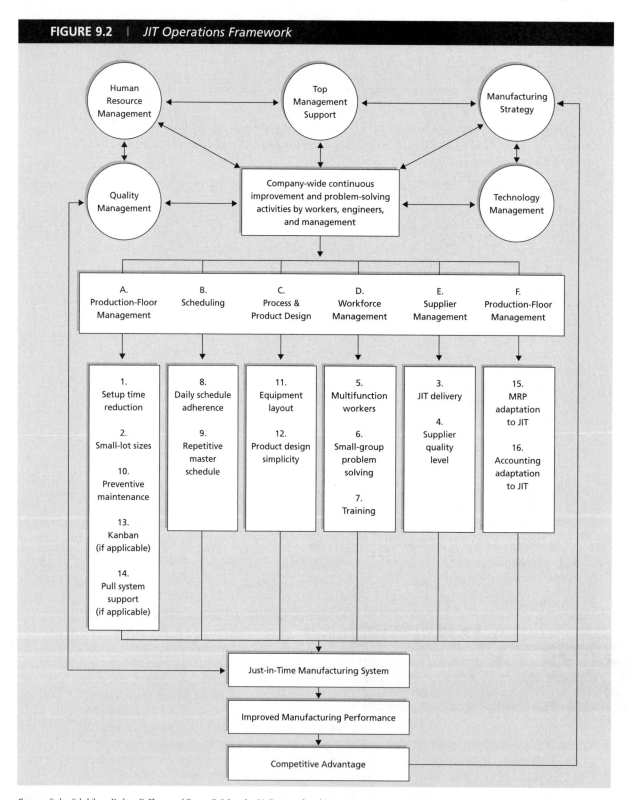

Source: Sadao Sakakibara, Barbara B. Flynn, and Roger G. Schroeder, "A Framework and Measurement Instrument for Just-in-Time Manufacturing," *Production and Operations Management* 2, no. 3 (Summer 1993): 177–194.

machine, using conveyors to move the tools in and out of the machine, and improving the labeling and identification. Previously, the setup tools were poorly identified, poorly organized, and stored far from the machine, requiring a forklift to transport them. Now the machine operator can perform the new changeovers or setups with no indirect assistance.

OM PRACTICE

Harley-Davidson
Simple design changes helped reduce setup time at Harley-Davidson.

After Harley-Davidson's market share fell from a near monopoly to less than 30 percent in the early 1980s, the company embarked on an aggressive strategy for improving quality and manufacturing efficiency. Lean production was an important part of that effort. Simple design changes, in both products and processes, helped it achieve dramatic reductions in setup time. For example, using C-shaped spacing washers instead of O-shaped wash-

ers enabled operators to loosen nuts and slide in the C washers from the side to reposition a machine instead of taking the nuts off and lifting the machine to replace the O washers. Another change involved two crankpins that were similar except for a hole drilled at a 45-degree angle in one and at a 48-degree angle in the other. It took two hours to reposition the machine for the new operation. After engineers designed a common hole angle in the two parts, changeovers could be made by simply inserting or removing a set of spacers on the fixture that held the crankpin for drilling. Setup time was reduced to three minutes.[8]

OM PRINCIPLE

A continuous flow of small lot sizes minimizes unnecessary inventory investment.

Harley-Davidson reduced its setup time by both process and product-part changes, as the *OM Practice* box illustrates.

Using small lots can help to minimize unnecessary inventory. For example, small lots of engine parts can go directly to the assembly line rather than storage. This eliminates materials handling as well as reducing inventory space requirements. Setup costs are usually highly correlated with setup times, since most of the costs of setup are incurred by long setup times and lost production time. Small lots are economical if setup costs are small. This can be seen by examining the EOQ and economic lot-size models (see the Tools and Techniques supplement on the CD-ROM). As the order or setup cost, C_0, decreases, $Q^\star$ clearly decreases, as does the total cost. For purchased materials, establishing long-term relationships with single-source suppliers provides an environment conducive to small, frequent deliveries. Long-term contracts encourage supplier loyalty and reduce the risk of interrupted supplies. A major component of the ordering cost is the cost of receiving, inspecting, and storing material for future use. Small lots can be delivered directly to production, thus eliminating many costly receiving activities. In the past, when suppliers were considered adversaries, safety stock was maintained as insurance against poor supplier performance. Working closely with suppliers on improving quality and establishing a relationship of mutual trust can eliminate the need for inspection, further reducing ordering costs and delays in the production cycle.

Because excess WIP inventory is not available to compensate for equipment breakdowns, production equipment must be highly reliable. This means good preventive maintenance. When machines break down, the root causes must be found and permanent solutions implemented to prevent further breakdowns. Furthermore, preventive maintenance should seek not only to avoid breakdowns, but also to improve the overall capability of processes. **Total productive maintenance** involves the operators themselves in maintenance activities, thereby reducing idle time because operators do not have to wait for maintenance specialists.

Scheduling

Automobiles, appliances, and many other products are mass-produced using "repetitive manufacturing": the same or similar operations are repeated over and over, and an uninterrupted flow of materials goes through the sequence of operations. Although repetitive manufacturing can result in increased productivity and lower costs, careful design and commitment by both managers and workers are required if it is to be effective. The Japanese have recognized this potential in developing the JIT system, which requires a repetitive master schedule that must be rigorously met.

To operate smoothly, a JIT system must minimize fluctuation in production demand. This is accomplished by making finished-product lot sizes as small as possible, ideally one, and having a level master schedule whereby small lots of each product are made every day and even every hour. For example, suppose the production schedule for the next month calls for 600 units of product A, 1,000 units of product B, and 400 units of product C. A typical mass-production plan would be to produce all of product A, then change over to B, and finally to C. During the month, warehouses would be overstocked with product A and have none of product C until the end of the month. A level schedule smoothes production of all products over the month. Assuming that 20 working days are available, the daily production will be 30 units of A, 50 units of B, and 20 units of C. In a JIT environment, this product mix might be smoothed out even further. If 480 minutes are available during the day, the average cycle time per unit would be (480 minutes)/(100 units) = 4.8 minutes/unit. The cycle time for each product is calculated as follows.

Product A: (4.8)(100/30) = 16 minutes/unit
Product B: (4.8)(100/50) = 9.6 minutes/unit
Product C: (4.8)(100/20) = 24 minutes/unit

Production might occur in the following order: B–A–B–C–B–A–B–C–B–A. Such a smooth flow requires rapid changeover and workers who know how to switch from one product to another. A level production schedule also helps smooth demand for tooling, supplies, maintenance, and other activities. Because the pull production entailed in a JIT system requires a high degree of repetitiveness and fixed routings, JIT production is not universally applicable. Nearly all types of production have some degree of repetitiveness, however. In some cases, a small number of products or product families represent a large proportion of production volume. The JIT approach can be effectively applied to these "vital few" products, while the remaining products are controlled by traditional methods.

Process and Product Design

For a JIT system to function effectively, traditional product and process design activities usually have to be modified. In a typical U.S. manufacturing environment, material is transported from a supplier's truck to a warehouse, then later transported from the warehouse to the plant, and finally stored in a holding area or even restocked in another warehouse. In a common process layout, material is often transferred between departments during the manufacturing operations. Consequently, unnecessary costs are incurred in the form of inventory, materials handling, production delays, and so forth.

JIT production requires a smooth flow in which materials introduced at one end of the process move without delay to finished product. Thus, an improved layout would be in a straight line. One innovation that eliminates much unnecessary movement and improves productivity is the use of U-shaped production cells, referred to as a group technology. **Group technology,** or **cellular manufacturing,** combines several machines that perform different tasks into a single work center so that the tasks can be performed without moving large lots of WIP inventories. For example, the pieces of equipment can be placed close together and connected by short roller conveyors. As a result, materials or parts can flow one piece at a time from machine to machine. Inventory is reduced to minimal levels, and operators can move one piece at a time without the need for forklifts or other bulk-materials-handling equipment. In addition, a group layout enables workers to work on more than one machine at a time, thus increasing efficiency. This means that workers must be trained to operate several different machines in a JIT environment. Automation, such as robots, is often used for routine operations in work cells, freeing workers to attend to multiple machines while robots transfer or load parts. This makes it easier to receive immediate feedback on product defects. In addition, several smaller machines are preferred to one large multifunctional machine; this allows rapid setup changes, minimizes bottlenecks, and improves maintenance, causing less disruption to production flow. This type of layout also leads to efficient use of labor. For example, employees are aware of and are allowed to support co-workers who have fallen behind in their production schedule. Production lines set up as a U cell can also be easily rebalanced to compensate for employee absenteeism.

An example of process design that supports JIT and lean production is **SMED (single-minute exchange of dies).** SMED was pioneered by Shigeo Shingo at Toyota and refers to programs that reduce the time required to change machine setups for tooling, materials, and equipment adjustments. Such initiatives were undertaken to reduce unproductive setup time on large stamping dies used to stamp car bodies out of sheets of metal. Starting with changeover times of three to five days that dramatically reduced Toyota's flexibility to change from one model to another, a "stretch goal" of reducing this time to one minute was set initially. The long-term objective is to make instantaneous changeovers that do not impede the continuous flow of operations.

Reducing setup time leads to the following benefits:

○ Batch sizes (and production runs) are smaller, allowing easier scheduling of a diverse product mix.

○ Reduced economies of scale (from large batches) are offset by the reduction in waste and product obsolescence.

○ Decreased setups on bottleneck resources lead to more efficient resource utilization.

○ WIP inventory is reduced as machines are set up with only the raw materials needed to produce the items scheduled.

○ Shop damage to raw materials is reduced because inventory in the production area is minimized.

○ Restocking costs for putting unused materials back into inventory are reduced.

Quality Management
Since lot sizes are small, and there is no safety stock to back up nonconforming items, any quality problem disrupts the flow of materials throughout the plant. In fact, one advantage of small lot sizes is that they reveal quality problems that would have been hidden by large

inventories. Another advantage is that machines are not overworked and can be properly maintained when lot sizes are small. Breakdowns are therefore less likely, and better-conditioned machines improve product quality.

OM PRINCIPLE

JIT cannot function properly if production has a high rate of defective items. Thus, it requires painstakingly careful attention to quality, both in purchasing and in production.

Japanese production workers are their own quality inspectors; knowing that a problem can stop the entire system provides the incentive to produce good-quality parts consistently. Purchased items are not inspected; they are expected to be defect-free when they are received. Japanese manufacturers take great pains to ensure that supplier quality is perfect, even to the extent of helping suppliers solve their own quality problems. The impact of quality in JIT extends down to the housekeeping of the workplace. Cleanliness, simplification, and proper organization promote a safer environment and reduce wasted time, motion, and resources.

Workforce Management

As a result, the JIT concept demands that employees be empowered to make important decisions such as stopping production when a problem is identified. The Japanese call this concept *yo-i-don*. In their companies, an operator who discovers a problem can signal for assistance by activating an *andon*, or yellow warning light. If the problem is

OM PRINCIPLE

People are a critical aspect of total quality control in a JIT environment, in which all employees are regarded as valuable resources; they provide many solutions to problems and ideas for improving performance.

not corrected within, say, one minute, a red light will automatically come on, a siren will sound, and the entire production line will stop. Managers and workers will immediately rush to the scene and try to locate the source of the problem and correct it. As JIT systems in the West apply their versions of the *yo-i-don* concept, management-employee relationships are being forced to change. Managers must respond to criticism from workers and "engage in participative management" if they truly support the JIT approach. Employee motivation depends on an atmosphere of mutual trust and cooperation between managers and nonmanagers. Three key JIT practices based on this type of management-employee relationship are the use of multifunction workers, small-group problem solving, and training.

In many manufacturing and service organizations, there is a high subdivision of labor and strict adherence to union job classifications. For example, union contracts may prohibit a milling machine operator from being assigned to operate a drill press. But to obtain a smooth workflow, workers in group-technology cells must be able to switch from one task to the next and to perform their own setups, maintenance, and inspection. Such multifunction workers help to eliminate inventory between processes, reduce the number of workers required, and give employees a greater sense of involvement and participation in the total production process. Labor unions often balk at the concept, however. Many companies form union-management committees to seek union cooperation.

The JIT philosophy requires that managers invest heavily in training. The Japanese concept of "lifetime training" enables them to take full advantage of the JIT environment. Training is focused on how to perform a job more efficiently and with better quality, use of various problem-solving techniques such as statistical process control, and new skills that increase worker flexibility. In the United States, JIT training has also been aimed at eliminating bad habits formed in tradi-

OM PRINCIPLE

Process improvement depends on the creativity of employees, particularly those working in teams. Small-group problem solving attempts to tap this creativity by encouraging workers to bring production-related problems as well as ideas for improvement to team problem-solving sessions on a regular basis.

tional American manufacturing environments, such as the tendency to assume only limited responsibility and to produce the minimum work possible.

Supplier Management

OM PRINCIPLE

Suppliers must be able to deliver small lot sizes on a continuous basis and with high quality.

Because of the importance of suppliers to the effective operation of JIT, the role of purchasing in JIT is dramatically different from conventional practice. Table 9.1 contrasts JIT purchasing with conventional purchasing practices. Instead of sending one large shipment that must be counted, inspected, and stored before issuance to the production floor, suppliers in a JIT system make smaller deliveries on a daily basis or more frequently to accommodate that day's production schedule. In a true JIT environment, shipments are received in standardized containers, each containing standardized quantities, so that there is no reason to unpack and count all incoming goods. This practice also eliminates the potential for damage through handling and saves space. For that reason, a JIT system functions best when suppliers are located in close geographic proximity to the manufacturer. In North America, where industry is frequently geographically dispersed, transportation delays often make it difficult to achieve this type of vendor support. Saturn Corporation, however, proves it can be done (see the *OM Practice* box).

OM PRACTICE

Saturn

Supplier management is central to Saturn's effectiveness.

Saturn's automobile plant in Spring Hill, Tennessee, manages its suppliers so well that in four years it has had to stop its production line just once "and for only 18 minutes" because the right part was not delivered at the right time. Saturn maintains virtually no inventory. A central computer directs trucks to deliver pre-inspected and presorted parts at precise times to the factory's 56 receiving docks, 21 hours a day, six days a week. Most of Saturn's more than 300 suppliers are not even located near the plant, but are in 39 states and an average of 550 miles away from Spring Hill. Ryder System, the Miami transportation services company, manages the Saturn network. Tractors pulling trailers that are 90 percent full on average arrive daily at a site two miles from Saturn's factory. The drivers uncouple the trailers, which contain bar-coded, reusable plastic containers full of parts, and shuttle tractors deliver them to the plant. Saturn is linked electronically with all its suppliers and reorders parts each time a car comes off the assembly line, an example of a pull production system in action.[9]

JIT purchasing requires that the manufacturer trust the supplier to deliver on time and with zero defects. To build such trusting relationships requires a reduction in the number of suppliers used. All U.S. companies that have implemented JIT systems have reduced the number of suppliers to five or fewer—even to one—for a given part. This way the manufacturer can work more closely with the supplier or suppliers, thus improving design and product quality and reducing costs. In return for the extra effort suppliers make to accommodate JIT manufacturers with more frequent deliveries, standardized shipments, and better quality, suppliers are rewarded with long-term contracts. Hewlett-Packard, for instance, has given its JIT suppliers 18- to 36-month contracts with the potential for renegotiation every 6 to 13 months in exchange for quality improvement or cost reduction.

The tight supply chain required to accomplish JIT, however, incurs significant risk. When a plant making a critical part shuts down, there is virtually no buffer inventory from which to draw. This happened to General Motors when a 17-day labor strike at two part suppliers

TABLE 9.1	*JIT versus Traditional Purchasing*

Conventional Purchasing	Just-in-Time Purchasing
1. Large delivery lot sizes, typically covering several weeks' requirements. Infrequent deliveries.	1. Small delivery lot sizes based on the immediate needs for production usage. Very frequent deliveries; e.g., several times per day.
2. Deliveries timed according to buyer's request date.	2. Deliveries synchronized with buyer's production schedule.
3. Several suppliers used for each part. Multiple sourcing used to maintain adequate quality and competitive pricing.	3. Few suppliers used for each part. Often parts are single-sourced.
4. Inventories typically maintained for parts.	4. Little inventory required because deliveries are expected to be made frequently, on time, and with high-quality parts.
5. Short-term purchasing agreements. Supplies pressured by the threat of withdrawing business.	5. Long-term purchasing agreements. Supplies pressured by the obligation to perform.
6. Products designed with few constraints on number of different purchased components used.	6. Products designed with great effort to use only currently purchased parts. Objective is to maximize commonality of parts.
7. Minimal exchange of information between supplier and buyer.	7. Extensive exchange of information about production schedules, production processes, etc.
8. Purchasing agent as primary focus of communication with supplier.	8. Purchasing agent as facilitator of many points of communication between design engineers, production engineers, etc.
9. Prices established by suppliers.	9. Buyer works with suppliers to reduce supplier's costs and thereby reduce prices.
10. Geographic proximity of supplier not important for supplier-selection decision.	10. Geographic proximity considered very important.

Source: James R. Freeland, "A Survey of Just-in-Time Practices in the United States," DSWP-89-23, The Darden School, University of Virginia, July 1989. Reprinted with permission, The American Production and Inventory Control Society, Falls Church, VA.

forced 22 of 29 North American car and truck plants to close, costing GM between $600 million and $800 million in lost profits.

Accounting and Information Systems

Several traditional cost-accounting practices contribute to the kind of waste that JIT systems are designed to eliminate: tracking and reporting direct labor for purposes of overhead allocation, tracking and reporting machine utilization, using full-absorption costing to determine costs for WIP inventory, and variance reporting.[10] In a JIT environment, small and numerous batches make tracking and reporting direct labor against each production order as in a job-costing system impractical. In addition, increased automation associated with JIT has dramatically reduced direct labor, making it inappropriate to distribute overhead. Machine-utilization tracking encourages managers to produce beyond demand requirements, thus building inventories, which is contrary to JIT goals of inventory reduction. In JIT environments, lead-times are much shorter than in traditional manufacturing systems. Hence, there is little incentive to allocate costs to inventory at any level other than that of finished products. Finally, variance reports are generally not available until the following working day in a traditional manufacturing environment, so any action initiated as a result takes place long after problems have occurred. Such traditional accounting practices have hindered JIT implementation in many companies. Therefore, changes to the accounting system are necessary for effective application of JIT.

Lean Design Principles

It has been argued that the truly innovative aspect of the Toyota production system (TPS) is not the use of kanban, the elimination of WIP inventory, setup reduction, or any other individual practice. Rather, the true innovation involves the processes that Toyota uses to design its production system—that is, how it has innovated and continues to innovate—and the principles guiding these design decisions. The principles of the TPS can be summarized in four basic rules:[11]

> *Work Rule:* All work shall be highly specified as to content, sequence, timing, and outcome.
>
> *Connection Rule:* Every customer-supplier connection must be direct, and there must be an unambiguous yes-or-no way to send requests and receive responses.
>
> *Pathway Rule:* The pathway for every product and service must be simple and direct.
>
> *Improvement Rule:* Any improvement must be made in accordance with the scientific method, under the guidance of a teacher, at the lowest possible level of the organization.

These four rules define processes, work flows, customer interaction, and improvement routines, all of which are vital to lean production.

The **A3 report** is one tool used for problem solving in the course of work. The name "A3" describes the size of paper on which the report is written. The steps of the report include identifying a problem, understanding the current condition, determining the root cause, and developing a target condition, implementation plan, and follow-up plan. These steps are all written and drawn (not typed) on a single piece of A3 paper. The process for A3s begins the application of the four rules to a system. Some ongoing work to apply the TPS model at a small hospital in the Boston area has shown positive evidence that it can effectively "cross over" to nonmanufacturing environments.

After careful study, it has been observed that TPS experts define production systems in terms of "pathways" and "connections." They then redesign the system to streamline pathways and make direct connections with simple, binary communications. The practices so thoroughly documented in the literature are simply some effective ways, proven over time, of streamlining pathways and making connections direct. Furthermore, TPS experts follow a method of implementation that adheres to the principles of testability in Descartes' scientific method. Every piece of the system is predicated on a testable hypothesis of the operation's expected results, such that results different than expected are made readily visible and countermeasures can be taken. This explains why standardized work is so critical to the system. Every time an improvement is proposed, the proposal explicitly states the expected outcome (i.e., an hypothesis), which can be verified or refuted through experimentation. Every employee under TPS is trained in this method of improvement.

JIT in Service Organizations

JIT has had its biggest impact in manufacturing, but service organizations are increasingly finding applications for it. The JIT philosophy supports the reduction of cycle time, which many organizations now regard as a key element of their corporate strategy. From this viewpoint, JIT may even have a greater potential impact in services than in manufacturing (see the *OM Practice* box on its use in the banking industry earlier in this chapter). One overnight package-delivery service saw its inventory investment climb from $16 million to $34 million with conventional inventory management techniques.[12] Implementing JIT reduced its inventory investment, but the company's major objective was to increase profits by providing a 99.9 percent level of service to its customers. Before JIT implementation, its service level, computed by dividing the number of items filled weekly by the number of items requested, was 79 percent. After JIT the level was 99 percent, and the firm looked forward to meeting its goal.

Baxter International is another service company that has experienced the benefits of a JIT system. St. Luke's Episcopal Hospital in Houston has applied JIT to its dispensing of hospital supply products. Most hospitals maintain a large inventory of supplies in a central storeroom and replenish the supplies needed in the various areas of the hospital on a regular basis. St. Luke's adopted a radical strategy; it closed its warehouse and sold its inventory to Baxter International, a major hospital supplier. Baxter has become a partner with the hospital in managing, ordering, and delivering supplies. Baxter fills orders in exact, sometimes small, quantities and delivers them directly to the hospital departments, including operating rooms and nursing floors. The hospital is now saving $350,000 annually due to staff reductions and $162,500 from eliminating its inventory. Its storeroom has been converted to patient care and other productive uses.

CONWIP

Recently, an alternative to kanban has emerged, called **CONWIP**.[13] The idea behind CONWIP (Constant Work-In-Process) is that a new job is introduced to a production line whenever a job is completed. This approach maintains a constant amount of WIP in the line, providing benefits similar to those of a kanban approach, namely, reduced cost and shortened lead-times. Unlike kanban, CONWIP does not deal with specific part numbers, as long as a common measure of WIP exists. For example, many production situations deal with different products of the same generic type, so it is possible to measure WIP in common units of product. An example is keyboards, which might differ only in language.

CONWIP begins with a simple observation about the behavior of operating systems—output levels of any system increase with WIP inventory up to a point. Beyond a critical level of WIP, the output of a system does not increase. Therefore, identifying and maintaining this critical level of WIP is the best approach to managing workflow and schedules.

CONWIP is more flexible than kanban in two respects:

○ Kanban caps WIP at each workstation, whereas CONWIP caps WIP within an entire production line. This can be important when variability exists in a line. For example, if a downstream operation breaks down, under kanban the upstream pipeline is blocked and processing stops, but under CONWIP, upstream stations can still work on all of the orders that have been released. Of course, eventually the line will stop because of lack of order releases, but at least some production continues.

○ In a mixed-product environment CONWIP can be a better alternative than kanban because CONWIP deals with a common measure of the work content.

9.3 CONSTRAINT MANAGEMENT

In Chapter 4 we described concepts of constraint management, or the **Theory of Constraints (TOC),** for process design. The principal objective of the TOC is to establish a process of continuous improvement based on the premise that constraints determine the performance of any system.[14] Here we summarize a TOC-based scheduling method, called drum-buffer-rope, that supports lean thinking.

OM PRINCIPLE
Constraint resources determine the throughput of the facility because they limit a plant's production level to their own capacity; the excess capacity of nonconstraint resources cannot be used.

A **constraint** is any resource lack that prevents a system from achieving continuously higher levels of performance. Limited capacity at work centers, inflexible work rules, inadequate labor skills, and an ineffective management philosophy are all forms of constraints. Since the number of such constraints is typically small, the TOC focuses on identifying them, managing them carefully, linking them to the market to ensure an appropriate product mix, and scheduling the nonconstraint resources to enhance the competitiveness of the production process. In addition to improving throughput, constraint management can help to reduce inventory, lower operating costs, and improve responsiveness. However, constraint management contrasts sharply with JIT in its focus on resources rather than finished product as a basis for scheduling all operations. Firms around the world have achieved significant improvements in bottom-line results, due date performance, lead-time, and quality through the use of the TOC and its five-step process of continuous improvement.

To illustrate the notion of the TOC, we will use a very simple example. A product is manufactured by processing it sequentially through five operations using machines A to E, respectively. The hourly production rates for each machine are as shown in the table below.

Operation:	1	2	3	4	5
Machine:	A	B	C	D	E
Hourly Unit Output Rate:	100	80	40	60	90

It is clear that machine C is the bottleneck, or constraining resource in this process, limiting the maximum output per hour of the product to 40. If the rate on machine B is increased to 90/hour, there is no effect on the output; machine C remains as the system constraint. If the rate on machine C is increased to 50, however, the system could produce an additional 10 units of the product each hour. On the other hand, if the rate on machine C can be increased to 70, only 20 more units of the product can be produced each hour because machine D will become the constraining resource. Furthermore, if the rate of machine B falls to 30 during one hour, we will lose 10 units of product output during that time. Thus, understanding constraints in a system is important.

The **cost per bottleneck minute (C/PB)** ratio and the **contribution margin per bottleneck minute (CMPB)** ratio are performance measures used in the implementation of the TOC. The C/PB ratio is calculated as total facility cost/bottleneck capacity (in minutes). This ratio is useful in a complex production environment with multiple manufacturing facilities, each with its own bottleneck process. The CMPB ratio allows a firm to quickly assess the relative margin generated by alternate products using the bottleneck resource. In the above example, if two products P1 and P2 with margins of $30 per unit and $40 per unit, respectively, were both using the bottleneck resource machine, C, for 10 minutes per unit and 20 minutes per unit, then the organization would prefer to make more of product P1 since it has a higher CMPB ($3 per minute) than P2 ($2 per minute).

The **drum-buffer-rope (DBR)** approach is a finite scheduling mechanism that balances the flow in the system. Recall that material requirements planning (MRP) ignores resource capacities in creating a plan; thus, some adjustments may be required to develop a feasible schedule. DBR plans the flow of materials through the plant by recognizing resource constraints explicitly and is based on the following analogies.[15] The *drum* is a system constraint or other critical resource that sets the pace or "beat" that drives the rest of the schedule. The key idea is to pace all production activities by the production of the drum. The *ropes* are schedules or other signaling methods that tie the release of raw materials and customer promise dates to the production at the drum. *Buffers* are WIP inventories that are maintained just in front of the resource. Although very little WIP inventory is maintained, the buffer inventories help to compensate for unavoidable variations in flow time. The constraint buffer ensures that the drum is always busy; the assembly buffer ensures that parts completed at the drum are not delayed at assembly; and the shipping buffer ensures that customer promise dates can be met. Managing buffers is an important aspect of the DBR approach to ensure that schedules for constraint resources are maintained. Besides being useful for managing the day-to-day operations, the data obtained from monitoring buffers can be used to identify noncritical resources for improvements.

> # OM PRINCIPLE
>
> Any schedule must support market demand while contributing to and being measurable against the organization's goals. It must also be realistic and reflect the limited resources available and be robust in that it must tolerate the inevitable disruptions that will occur.

Returning to the previous example, we would first establish resource C as the limiting constraint. The drumbeat has the same frequency as the capacity of this bottleneck resource, 40 units per hour. The buffer protects throughput from unavoidable disruptions at critical points. Thus, if machine B's output is suddenly reduced from 80 to 30 units per hour, a 10-unit buffer after resource B will protect resource C from this disruption. The rope links the production at each resource to the drum. Thus, if resource B output does fall to 30 units per hour, the rope will be pulled, and the 10-unit buffer will be consumed. It is important that the "gating" operations, such as operation A, be linked very tightly to the resource capacity at C; otherwise the firm will produce a lot of unnecessary (and wasteful) inventory.

DBR scheduling is based on five steps:

1. Identify the system constraint(s).
2. Sequence jobs on the system constraint(s).
3. Decide on the size of the constraint buffers.
4. Decide on the size of the shipping buffers (which forward schedule material from the constraint to shipping and fix the due date to the customer).
5. If, in the previous steps, a constraint has been broken, go back to step 1, but do not allow inertia to create a new constraint.

In effect, this reduces to a single-machine scheduling problem at the constraint. In any facility, there are usually only a few capacity-constrained resources, making it relatively easy to identify and schedule around them. A simple, practical example for scheduling pictures for a junior high school yearbook is given in the *OM Practice* box.

9.4 SIX SIGMA AND LEAN PRODUCTION

In Chapter 6 we introduced the concept of Six Sigma as a quality management framework. Recently, Six Sigma has been recognized as a useful and complementary approach to lean production. For example, a project to reduce cycle time might involve aspects of both. You

OM PRACTICE

School Yearbook Picture Scheduling

DBR streamlines student picture taking.

The basic process for taking yearbook pictures consists of the following steps:

1. All students associated with an organization are assembled and seated in rows.
2. The photographer frames the picture, says "Smile!" and takes the picture.
3. Student names must be associated with the picture.

Under the old system, all students reported to the gymnasium at the same time, resulting in a confusing process of sorting them into groups and deciding which group to photograph next. Identifying students after pictures were developed required many student-classroom hours and was prone to error.

A new process divided the bleachers on the side of the gym into three major sections, A, B, and C, which served as staging areas for specific student groups. A list of student organizations was prepared in advance. Students in the first three organizations were called to the gym over the public-address system. As they arrived, they lined up on the empty section of the bleachers reserved for their group. When all members had arrived, a clipboard was passed down each row for the students to sign. When this was done, the photographer took the group picture, the students returned to class, and the next group was called to the gym. The photographer cycled between each of the three staging areas, and very little time was lost in this changeover activity.

The drum, or critical resource, was the photographer. The ropes, which control the release of material, were not schedules, but rather students who were released to the system by calling the office secretary on a walkie-talkie. The constraint buffer was the assembled students waiting to be photographed. This ensured that the photographer was seldom idle due to lack of readiness of a group. Shipping and assembly buffers were not relevant in this situation.

Twenty organizations were photographed in two hours, about half the time needed with previous methods. Lost class time was minimized, and fewer errors were made in recording names of students in the pictures. In other words, the new system provided lower WIP rates, faster flow times, higher throughput, better quality, and higher productivity than the old method.[16]

---

might apply lean tools to streamline an order entry process and discover that significant rework is occurring because of incorrect addresses, customer numbers, or shipping charges that result in high variation of processing time. Six Sigma tools might then be used to drill down to the root cause of the problems and identify a solution.

Some key differences exist between lean production and Six Sigma. First, they attack different types of problems. Lean production addresses visible problems in processes, for example, inventory, material flow, and safety, while Six Sigma is more concerned with less visible

OM PRINCIPLE

Both lean thinking and Six Sigma are driven by customer requirements and a commitment by senior leadership, focus on real dollar savings and have the ability to make significant financial impacts on the organization, can be used in non-manufacturing environments, and use systematic methodologies.

problems, for example, variation in performance. Another difference is that lean tools are more intuitive and easier to apply by anybody in the workplace, while many Six Sigma tools require advanced training and the expertise of Black Belt or Master Black Belt specialists. For example, the concept of the 5S's is easier to grasp than statistical methods. Despite these differences, they both aim to eliminate waste from the value chain and improve the design and operation of products and processes.

Because of these similarities, many industry training programs and consultants have begun to focus on **Lean Six Sigma,** which draws upon the best practices of both approaches (see the *OM Practice* box on Xerox).

OM PRACTICE

Lean Six Sigma at Xerox

Xerox has renewed the company's focus on quality with a "Lean Six Sigma" initiative.

Throughout the 1990s, Xerox grew at a steady rate. At the turn of the century, however, the technology downturn, coupled with a decreased focus on quality by top corporate management, resulted in a significant drop in the company's stock price and a major management crisis. In 2003, the new corporate leadership, led by CEO Anne Mulcahy, established a new "Lean Six Sigma" thrust, which includes a dedicated infrastructure and resource commitment to focus on key business issues, critical customer opportunities, significant training of employees and "Black Belt" improvement specialists, a value-driven project selection process, and an increased customer focus with a clear linkage to business strategy and objectives.

The key components of Xerox's Lean Six Sigma are as follows:

1. Performance Excellence Process:
   - Supports clearer, simpler alignment of corporate direction to individual objectives.
   - Emphasizes ongoing inspection/assessment of business priorities.
   - Clearly links to Market Trends, Benchmarking, and Xerox Lean Six Sigma.
   - Supports a simplified "Baldrige-type" business assessment model.
2. DMAIC (Define, Measure, Analyze, Improve, Control) Process:
   - Based on industry-proven Six Sigma approach with speed and focus.
   - Four steps support improvement projects and set goals.
   - Used to proactively capture opportunities or solve problems.
   - Includes a full set of Lean and Six Sigma tools.
3. Market Trends and Benchmarking:
   - Reinforces market focus and encourages an external view.
   - Provides a disciplined approach to benchmarking.
   - Establishes a common four-step approach to benchmarking.
   - Encourages all employees to be aware of changing markets.
   - Has strong linkage to Performance Excellence Process and DMAIC.
4. Behaviors and Leadership:
   - Reinforces customer focus.
   - Expands interactive skills to include more team effectiveness.
   - Promotes faster decision making and introduces new meeting tools.
   - Supports leadership skills required for transition and change.

In 2003, Xerox trained over 1,000 senior leaders across the company and communicated this business approach, the key differences from its quality legacy, and its expectations for every employee. The company is rapidly moving Lean Six Sigma concepts from manufacturing and the supply chain into all business areas. It recognizes that full leadership commitment is the key ingredient. As Anne Mulcahy noted, "What I worry most about is how to return Xerox to greatness. . . . Lean Six Sigma is not the only answer, but it's a significant part of the equation."[17]

Summary of Key Points

- Lean production refers to approaches initially developed by the Toyota Motor Corporation that focus on the elimination of waste in all forms, including defects requiring rework, unnecessary processing steps, unnecessary movement of materials or people, waiting time, excess inventory, and overproduction. Two key approaches that support lean production are just-in-time (JIT) and constraint management. Lean production has evolved into lean thinking—a philosophy of applying lean concepts to all business operations.

- Important tools for lean production include the 5S's, visual controls, efficient layout and standardized work, pull production, SMED, total productive maintenance, source inspection, and continuous improvement.

○ JIT is a philosophy for coordinating production activities; its objective is to eliminate all sources of waste, including unnecessary inventory and scrap in production and non-value-added setup time, and thus improve material flow, quality, and productivity. JIT aims to create a smooth, rapid flow of all products from the time materials and purchased parts are received until the time the final product is shipped to the customer.

○ JIT is based on pull production, in which employees at a given operation go to the source of required parts, such as machining or subassembly, and withdraw the units as they need them, as opposed to push production, in which they make parts and then send them to subsequent operations or to storage.

○ Kanban (Japanese for "card") is a card-driven information system often used in JIT to initiate withdrawal and production of items throughout a production process and coordinate independent production activities.

○ JIT is based on seven key components: production-floor management, scheduling, process and product design, quality improvement, workforce management, supplier management, and accounting and information systems. It must be linked to higher-level elements of a company's management.

○ JIT depends on high quality and small lot sizes. Employees are empowered to identify and correct problems at the source. Suppliers support JIT by delivering frequently in standardized containers so as to eliminate intermediate storage.

○ CONWIP, an alternative to kanban, is based on the idea that a new job is introduced to a production line whenever a job is completed. This maintains a constant amount of WIP in the line, providing benefits similar to those of a kanban approach, namely, reduced cost and shortened lead-times.

○ Constraint management, or the Theory of Constraints (TOC), is based on the concept of identifying and managing the vital few constraints in a production system and viewing them as drivers of production. Like JIT, the TOC can improve throughput, reduce inventories, lower costs, and improve responsiveness.

○ The drum-buffer-rope (DBR) approach is a finite scheduling mechanism that balances the flow of the system. The *drum* is a system constraint or other critical resource that sets the pace or "beat" that drives the rest of the schedule. *Buffers* are WIP inventories that are maintained just in front of the resource. The *ropes* are schedules or other signaling methods that tie the release of raw materials and customer promise dates to the production at the drum.

○ Six Sigma has been recognized as a useful and complementary approach to lean production. Nonetheless, some key differences exist between lean production and Six Sigma. Lean manufacturing addresses visible problems in production processes, for example, inventory, material flow, and safety, while Six Sigma is more concerned with less visible problems, for example, variation in performance. Lean tools are more intuitive and easier to apply by anybody in the workplace, while many Six Sigma tools require advanced training and the expertise of Black Belt or Master Black Belt specialists.

Questions for Review and Discussion

1. Explain the principles of lean production and lean thinking.
2. What are some common forms of waste in a manufacturing or service operation? Look around your school and identify some examples.
3. Summarize the tools for lean production.
4. How does pull production differ from push production?
5. Explain the operation of a JIT system. How are kanban cards used?

6. Briefly summarize the underlying philosophy of JIT.
7. List the seven core elements of JIT and explain how each supports lean concepts.
8. What is group technology? What benefits does it offer over traditional process designs?
9. Explain the idea of SMED.
10. What types of "setups" do you perform in your work or school activities? How might you reduce your setup times?
11. What is the role of suppliers in JIT?
12. What is an A3 report, and how is it used?
13. What is the role of "pathways" and "connections" in lean production?
14. How can lean production principles be applied to services?
15. Discuss how JIT might be applied in a fast-food operation. Draw a flowchart to explain your answer.
16. How does CONWIP differ from JIT?
17. Summarize the principles of constraint management.
18. How are C/PB and CMPB performance measures used in implementing the Theory of Constraints?
19. How does the drum-buffer-rope approach work?
20. How does Six Sigma support lean production?

Internet Projects

To find Web links to carry out each of the following projects, go to the text's Web site at **http://raturi_evans.swlearning.com.**

1. Read the article "DaimlerChrysler Corporation's Lean Production Leads Change in Manufacturing and Creates $300 Million in Cost Savings." What are some of the initiatives outlined in this article that led to lean manufacturing?
2. Review the five videos by James Womack (you will need RealPlayer) and summarize the key concepts outlined in the videos.
3. Review the dialogue between Dr. Paul Adler and Dr. Paul Landsbergis on lean production (item 2) and responses to the dialogue (item 3). Summarize the gist of the debate.
4. Twelve practices of lean management include:

    1. Identify and optimize enterprise flow
    2. Assure seamless information flow
    3. Optimize capability and utilization of people
    4. Make decisions at lowest possible level
    5. Implement integrated product and process development
    6. Develop relationships based on mutual trust and commitment
    7. Continuously focus on the customer
    8. Promote lean leadership at all levels
    9. Maintain challenge of existing processes
    10. Nurture a learning environment
    11. Ensure process capability and maturation
    12. Maximize stability in a changing environment

   Summarize specific actions taken in your work environment on four of these practices and then suggest changes that would make them consistent with the lean enterprise model.

EXPERIENCE OM

Understanding Constraints

A firm makes and sells two products, P and Q.[18] Market price, maximum demand, and the operations needed to accomplish production are shown in Figure 9.3. The firm operates with a fixed overhead cost per week of $6,000. This includes all expenses it considers fixed in the planning horizon—wages, utilities, labor costs, and the like. Four different machines, A, B, C, and D, are used in the production process, and the sequence and processing times are also shown in the figure. Currently, the firm has only one of each machine. The plant operates five days a week, eight hours per day.

Using this information, answer the following questions. Clearly explain the rationale for your analysis from the viewpoint of the Theory of Constraints.

1. What would the bill of material for products P and Q look like? (Hint: In a typical firm all purchased parts will be part numbers. Intermediate parts will have part numbers only if they are kept in stock; so theoretically a part number should be created after each process.)

2. Which product will you make more of? Why? (Hint: Develop a master schedule for P and Q that can be produced each week given the capacity constraints for resources A, B, C, and D. This gives you the weekly master production schedule. At this stage do not pay attention to specific sequencing problems that might arise as you move product through the resources. Assume that your goal is to maximize the profit/contribution every week.)

FIGURE 9.3 | *Process Flow for Production of Products P and Q*

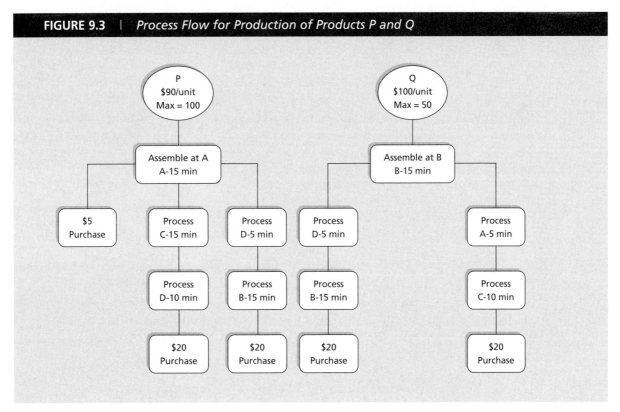

3. An engineer is suggesting a process change that will result in an increase in the total operation time from 20 minutes per part to 21 minutes per part at a cost of $2,000. Should you approve the request? The specific change will increase the time for process D that currently takes 5 minutes for both products to 7 minutes, and decrease the time for B from 15 to 14 minutes (this does not affect assembly).

4. Will you sell product P in Japan for 80 percent of the price? For 90 percent of the price? Why? (Hint: Find out if the quantity of P and Q produced changes given the revised contribution margins for each product at this price.)

5. If you have the money to purchase an additional machine, which one will you buy? Will it change your production strategy?

6. Sequence the master production schedule quantity of P and Q from question 2 taking into account the specific sequence in which work must be performed. Is the master schedule in question 2 feasible? (Hint: You may have to draw a lead-time chart with all activities to check if resources are available for processing a component.)

Projects in Contemporary Organizations

A *project* is a set of tasks that must be performed in a particular sequence, on time, and on budget to achieve a certain result. **Project management** involves all activities associated with planning, organizing, scheduling, controlling, and leading a project to ensure that all tasks are completed and that the project delivers its intended results. The past several decades have been marked by rapid growth in the use of project management as a means by which organizations achieve their objectives.[1] Managing projects efficiently and effectively is a vital skill for managers in all firms, not just project-based businesses, and perhaps is even more important in this new millennium. Many view project management as simply a collection of tools and techniques for planning, implementing, and controlling project activities. As Tom Peters, the well-known management consultant, has noted, however, "having good project management practices in place will no longer suffice; what is required now is excellence in project management if project success is to be the norm."[2] Project management provides a powerful means to marshal an organization's people and resources and accomplish its strategic objectives, particularly in today's highly interdisciplinary business world.

This chapter develops the philosophy and tools of project management. Specifically, we address:
○ The fundamentals of projects and project management *(Section 10.1)*.
○ The project life cycle and project management methodology *(Section 10.2)*.
○ Techniques for project scheduling *(Section 10.3)*.
○ Resource management *(Section 10.4)*.
○ Budgeting and cost control *(Section 10.5)*.

The *Experience OM* exercise at the end of this chapter introduces *Microsoft Project*, one of the most popular commercial software packages for project management.

Material on the CD-ROM discusses some useful tools and techniques for project management.
18. Time-Cost Tradeoffs

10.1 PROJECTS AND PROJECT MANAGEMENT

Project management was first used to manage the U.S. space program. Its practice has expanded rapidly throughout the government, the military, and the corporate world. A **program** is a large, long-range objective that is broken down into a set of projects. The Project Management Institute (PMI) has defined a **project** as "a temporary endeavor undertaken to create a unique

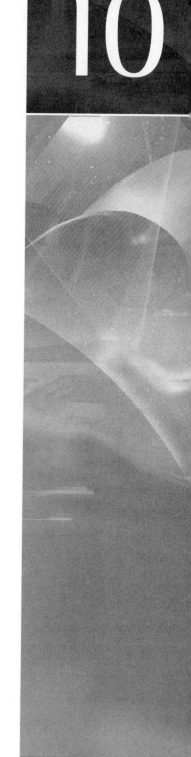

product or service."[3] Thus, a project in the space program might be the development of a Mars exploration vehicle. Projects are divided further into **tasks** or **activities,** which are sometimes also referred to as **work packages.**

Many industries operate on a project basis; the deliverable to the customer is a unique bundle of goods and services. Construction, consulting services, defense contracting, and even home remodeling businesses fall into this category. Firms such as Boeing perform almost all their work on a project basis. In 1997, for example, the Air Force agreed to buy 6 satellites from Boeing and held options for another 27—a $1.3 billion project that was potentially worth hundreds of millions to Boeing.[4] The satellites are used for navigation by military aircraft, ships, land forces, and smart weapons, as well as by civilians to determine locations as part of global positioning systems. Soon afterward, however, the Air Force decided to rebid the contract because it needed to update the satellites with new technologies that had emerged since Boeing was hired to do the work.

Other firms use projects on a short-term or one-time basis to implement new strategies and initiatives (see the *OM Practice* box on Blue Cross/Blue Shield). One example of such a project is the implementation of an enterprise resource planning (ERP) system, as we discussed in the previous chapter. Projects are critical in coordinating the implementation of new information technology (IT) systems. Project managers must continually demonstrate their contribution to the bottom line. This alliance between strategic planning and project management creates an increasingly close but often tense relationship between project and process management.[5]

OM PRACTICE

Implementing Strategy through Projects at Blue Cross/Blue Shield

At Blue Cross/Blue Shield of Louisiana, project management is closely linked to organizational strategy.

Problems often arise because strategic plans are usually developed at the executive level but implemented by middle-level managers who may have only a poor understanding of the organization's capabilities and top management's expectations. On the other hand, when departmental goals and future plans are developed from the bottom up, they invariably lack a vision of the overall company and its competitive strategy.

Blue Cross/Blue Shield (BC/BS) of Louisiana addressed these problems by tying project management activities to organizational strategy. The resulting system provides a set of checks and balances for both BC/BS executives and project man-

agers. Overseeing the system is a newly created Corporate Project Administration Group (CPAG) that helps senior managers translate their strategic goals and objectives into project management performance, budget, and schedule targets. These may include new product development, upgrading information systems, or implementing facility automation systems. The CPAG also works with the project teams to develop their plans, monitoring activities, and reports so that they dovetail with the strategic intentions.

The system offers several important benefits:

- Senior management can select any corporate initiative and determine its status.
- Project managers report progress in a relevant, systematic, timely manner.
- Officers, directors, and managers are able to view the corporate initiatives in terms of the overall strategic plan.
- Senior management can plan, track, and adjust strategy through the use of financial project data captured by the system.[6]

In many cases, ad-hoc projects draw upon resources from core processes within an organization, so failure to manage a key project effectively can be detrimental to the core process. This is particularly true when firms must integrate multiple projects that involve common core processes. The complexity associated with new tasks and objectives, as well as the need to generate and direct resources, creates significant risks in most project environments. To avoid and/or mitigate such risks, it is important to understand the objectives of a project.

OM PRINCIPLE

Projects have several unique characteristics. A project has *well-defined and nonrepetitive objectives*. The objectives may consist of quantifiable performance metrics for the product/service bundle as well as subjective performance indicators such as customer satisfaction. A project has a *definite beginning and end*; it is not a continuous process. A project uses various tools to accomplish and track project tasks and ensure that the project stays within *schedule and cost*. Finally, projects frequently need *resources* such as people, facilities, information, or equipment.

Whether it is a large- or small-scale project, or a long- or short-term project, is not particularly relevant. What is relevant is that the project be viewed as a unique activity consisting of well-defined deliverables to a customer. The following attributes characterize most projects:

1. **Uniqueness:** Every project has some unique elements. For example, no two construction or R&D projects are exactly alike. Projects are generally customized to the customer's needs. In addition to the presence of risk, as noted earlier, this characteristic means that projects, by their nature, cannot be completely reduced to routine.

2. **Complexity and Interdependencies:** Projects are complex enough that the subtasks require careful coordination and control in terms of timing, precedence, cost, and performance. Projects often interact with other projects being carried out simultaneously by their parent organization, and so must be coordinated with other projects. In addition, they always interact with the parent organization's functional operations (marketing, finance, manufacturing, and so on), although such interactions tend to be irregular. Projects often compete with functional departments for resources and personnel.

3. **Life Cycle:** Like organic entities, projects have life cycles. From a slow beginning, they build up in size, then peak, begin a decline, and finally must be terminated. (Also like organic entities, they often resist termination.) Some projects end by being phased into the normal, ongoing operations of the parent organization.

Project Objectives

As we noted in the *OM Principle* above, the two most important objectives for a project are *schedule*—when the project is completed—and *cost*. The ability to successfully manage the schedules and costs of projects can make or break organizations (see the *OM Practice* box on Disney Hall).

Figure 10.1 shows the typical relationship between time and cost in a project. If the duration of the project is too short, it is often necessary to pay premium labor rates to achieve very short completion times. Further, worker errors often increase, resulting in costs for corrections, and productivity often declines. Studies have shown that if a knowledge worker spends 12 hours of overtime on a job, the actual increase in output is equivalent to that normally obtained in 2 hours of regular work. If project work extends beyond an optimum time, costs also increase because people are not working efficiently. Projects in large organizations typically pay an overhead cost to corporate profit and loss statements to sustain the fixed resources on the project. Increased project duration therefore results in increased overhead cost. These trade-offs are project-specific; optimizing on time may be the right thing for one project, and reducing cost (at the expense of time) may be appropriate for another. See the supplement on the CD-ROM for further discussion.

OM PRINCIPLE

The relationship between time and cost in a project is typically not linear. As a rule, there is a project duration that results in optimum cost performance.

OM PRACTICE

Disney Hall: An Almost Unfinished Symphony

The dream of a "world-class" music facility has suffered from project failures.

The 1997 grand opening of Walt Disney Concert Hall, the new home for the Los Angeles Philharmonic, was to be no ordinary night. A new work by American composer John Adams and multimedia staging by director Peter Sellars would launch the Frank O. Gehry–designed building. In the front row would be the guest of honor, Lillian B. Disney, Walt Disney's elderly widow, whose gift of $50 million would have made it all possible. The County of Los Angeles provided the land and additional funding for a parking garage. In 1994, however, the project ran out of funds, and in December 1997, Lillian Disney died at age 98 without seeing her dream fulfilled. It was uncertain that it would ever be completed.

That such a project should flounder remains shocking to all involved. Disney Hall officials said that many factors led to unexpectedly high bids for the project: inflation, escalation of materials' costs, a subcontractors' market affected by the 1994 earthquake and the recession of the mid-1990s, as well as the complexity of Gehry's design. The first cost increases were necessitated by a series of time-consuming redesigns, including an outside firm's acoustical redesign after the competition, as well as two redesigns by Gehry.

Nonetheless, the project seemed to be on track in 1992. But delays and Lillian Disney's deadline forced the parties involved to take a calculated risk that backfired. Using *fast-tracking*, a process in which work on a project begins before a maximum building cost is established, the Disney Hall team and the county agreed to break ground in the hope that the risks of starting early would offset the costs incurred by delaying further. The subcontractors "were working with drawings they did not understand," said one official. "They were not 'bad' drawings. It was a question of the subs not understanding them."[7]

In true Disney tradition, though, all stories have a happy ending. Additional money was raised, including some from other Disney family members, and Walt Disney Concert Hall finally opened in late 2003. You can read more about it from the link at the text Web site at **http://raturi_evans.swlearning.com.**

FIGURE 10.1 | *Typical Relationships between Time and Cost*

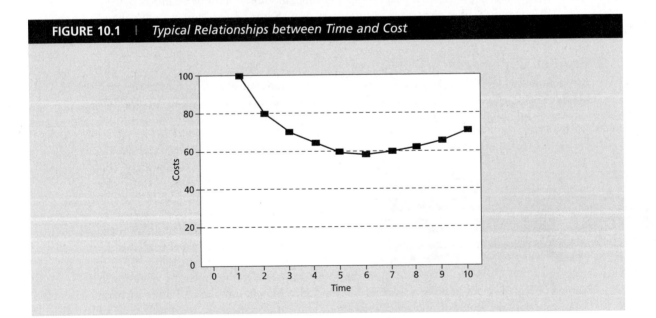

Some managers believe that if enough people are thrown at a project, it can be completed in whatever time is desired. This is simply not true; "Brooks's law," devised by Dr. Fred Brooks based on IBM's system development project experience, contends that adding people to a delayed software project makes it go further behind schedule.[8] Such productivity losses occur for three specific reasons:

1. The learning curve of the new people who join the project.
2. The productivity losses incurred as current project personnel train and orient the new people.
3. The productivity losses due to increased communication linkages between the project team members.

In addition to schedule and cost, a project must meet customer requirements. Meeting customer expectations is often more complex than it seems. Often customers cannot visualize the deliverables early and redefine their expectations as the project progresses—a phenomenon known as "scope creep." They may upgrade their expectations or downgrade them in an effort to have the project delivered faster or cheaper. The problem with scope changes is that they tend to be small and incremental; if a number of them occur, the project budget or schedule may suffer. This is a common cause of project failures. Project managers should advise their customers of the impact of a change in scope so that the customer can make an informed decision. For example, if a customer is told that a requested change will result in a 20 percent increase in project costs, the customer may opt to defer the change. Separating the deliverables into the hard, quantifiable, objective measures of performance (on which legal contracts can be drawn) and the softer, less tangible, customer service–oriented goals is a good idea. The former can be managed through negotiation, courts of law, and "scope" or change control processes. The latter require that the project manager carefully design all customer interactions, paying careful attention to issues such as differences between intended and delivered messages, inconsistency created by multiple points of contact between the client and the project team, and other service breakdowns that may result from poor customer interaction and marketing.

Finally, effective project management should develop organizational learning, that is, improved knowledge about how to conduct projects. This is a less understood but vital objective in every project. Knowledge accumulates over time and over project experience. Both the customers and the organization benefit from such organizational learning. Many large organizations require that project justification proposals include a formal statement of the *business case*—the tangible and intangible value of the project to the organization in terms of patents, learning, and knowledge development.

Project Evaluation and Selection

Many methods exist for selecting projects; they can be broadly classified into financial methods, utility-based methods, risk analysis, and portfolio-based methods (see Table 10.1). Most selection processes in organizations are driven by financial criteria. These methods typically assess the cash outflows and inflows associated with each project, adjust them for depreciation and tax benefits, and calculate a rate of return after discounting the cash flows for financial risk; the result is a rank ordering of projects by financial feasibility. Such methods, however, do not account for the intangible benefits of projects, such as organizational effectiveness and learning. Utility-based methods overcome this shortcoming by evaluating of projects on qualitative criteria. For example, in developing a ranking, a weighted-factor scoring model may consider the value associated with customer benefits, quality improvement, enhanced flexibility, or market share growth.

Risk-based methods incorporate the probability of success or failure into project assessments and allow for assessment of uncertainties in technology or the business environment. Portfolio-based methods, such as project portfolio management (PPM), merge project management with strategic planning and help firms choose projects with the highest potential for achieving overall strategic objectives. They allow simultaneous evaluation of multiple dimensions such as risk, length of project, resources, and funds used for multiple bundles of projects. Balancing the portfolio by including both short-term, low-risk projects and long-term, high-risk projects gives the organization maximum leverage to enhance profitability in the short term and the long term.

The Project Manager and Project Team

Project managers have significant responsibilities (see the *OM Practice* box on Kendle). It is their job

OM PRINCIPLE

The project manager is the focal point in every project and must respond to the needs of three major stakeholders: the organization, the team members, and the customer.

TABLE 10.1   *Methods for Project Evaluation and Selection*

Category	Method	Objective
Financial	Payback period	Evaluate the time in which a project will recover the initial investment.
	Average rate of return	Evaluate the percentage return on the initial investment.
	Net present value	Evaluate the discounted future cash flows of a project.
	Profitability index	Index the future cash flows to the current investment.
	Internal rate of return	Find the discount rate that balances the present value of cash inflows and cash outflows.
	Other profitability methods	Compute profitability while incorporating assumptions of probability of success, total sales, market share growth, and other factors.
Utility-based	Factor scoring models	Assess project feasibility by weighing such attributes as profitability, quality improvement, and cycle time reduction.
	Multi-attribute utility theory	Incorporate the utility function of the decision maker in establishing a ranking of projects.
	Analytic hierarchy process	Understand and assess the hierarchy of objectives of the decision maker using a pair-wise comparison and an ordinal ranking scale.
Risk-based	Simulation	Simulate cash flows to assess financial risk.
	Expected value	Evaluate expected returns or expected net present value by assigning probabilities to alternative risk scenarios.
	Decision tree analysis	View a project as a series of decisions and outcomes to find a series of "best" decisions.
	Real options analysis	Evaluate the option content of the alternatives at each stage of a project as a series of decisions.
Portfolio-based	Project portfolio management	Assess the value and incremental contribution of a project in the context of a portfolio of projects within the firm from a strategic perspective.

to direct and supervise the project from beginning to end. Roles that project managers must perform include the following:

1. Define the project, reduce it to a set of manageable tasks, obtain appropriate and necessary resources, and build a team or teams to perform the project work.
2. Set the final goal for the project and motivate team members to complete the project on time.
3. Provide technical support for financial planning, contract management, managing creative thinking, and problem solving.
4. Learn to adapt to change and act as change agents.
5. Understand and execute the strategy of the firm, especially if the project is large or might change the future direction of the firm.

OM PRACTICE

Kendle International
Project management is central to clinical research trials.

Kendle International, Inc. is a premier provider of quality clinical development services for the pharmaceutical and biotechnology industries. With headquarters in Cincinnati, Ohio, and offices strategically located throughout North America, Europe, and Asia, Kendle provides extensive global monitoring capabilities along with a unique combination of experience and technology to expedite all phases of the clinical development process.

Kendle's project management process includes the following:

○ Preparation of a comprehensive project plan that is reviewed and approved by the sponsor.
○ Deliverable specifications.
○ Time and events schedule.
○ Communication plan.
○ Training requirements.
○ Project-specific operating procedures.
○ Administrative details (drug supply, lab kits, etc.).
○ Regular communication and monitoring to ensure that all operating units at Kendle understand study timelines, budgets, and deliverables.
○ Development/coordination of project-specific training materials/sessions (initial and continuing), as necessary.
○ Regular communication with the sponsor regarding study progress.
○ Proactive approach to identify any issues, internal or external to Kendle, that may negatively affect any project milestone or deliverable and then to develop and implement an appropriate corrective action plan.

Kendle recognizes the critical role that timely and thorough communications play in a project's success. To ensure that each project is completed on time and within budget, no matter what its size or complexity, Kendle has developed a team-style project management system. See their Project Management Wheel in Figure 10.2. This system ensures that comprehensive planning, responsibility definition, communication plans, and action steps are documented in detail by the project team. These planning and tracking systems enable Kendle to meet customers' aggressive timelines for critically important functions, while ensuring that sound clinical practices are followed.

In addition to the project team, each study has a dedicated project manager so that there is a single point of accountability. During the course of the development program, the project manager keeps customers regularly informed about each of the critical project milestones, both with paper and electronic reporting. The project manager is also responsible for the efficient and timely management of project assessments, complete project implementation, and tracking and resolution of any project issues. All project managers receive comprehensive, standardized training in the use of project management tools and tracking systems. All project information is collected in and reported from TrialWatch®, a proprietary suite of software programs that keeps all project staff and the sponsor aware of study progress. TrialWare® enables data to be processed faster by replacing forms with electronic images and utilizing standard database structures to automate workflow, conduct parallel processing, and standardize procedures. In addition, this system also allows Kendle to set and track a variety of study metrics in various areas of clinical development.[9]

continues

FIGURE 10.2 | *Kendle International's "Project Management Wheel"*

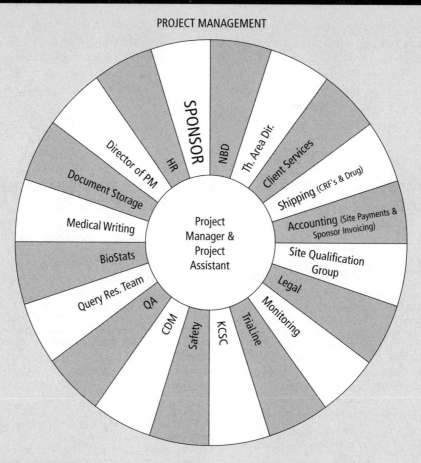

Source: Used with permission from Kendle International.

Although a successful project manager must be a good leader, other members of the project team must also learn to work together. The team members may come from different divisions of the same organization or even from different organizations. Some problems of interaction may arise initially when the team members are unfamiliar with their own roles in the project team, particularly if the project is large and complex. These problems must be resolved quickly in order to develop an effective, functioning team.

Many of the major issues in projects require effective interventions by individuals, groups, and organizations. Behavioral science concepts are helpful in overcoming communication difficulties that block cooperation and coordination. In very large projects, professional behavioral scientists may be necessary to diagnose the problems and advise the personnel working on the project.

OM PRINCIPLE

A fundamental challenge of project management is to enhance communication among individuals, groups, and organizational units in order to remove obstacles that impede interpersonal relations—and the success of the project.

Experienced observers can detect the major symptoms of interpersonal behavior problems that are often the sources of serious communication difficulties among project participants. For example, members of a project team may avoid each other and fail to deal with differences that need to be resolved. They may criticize and blame other individuals or groups when things go wrong. They may resent suggestions for improvement and become defensive to minimize culpability rather than taking the initiative to maximize achievements. All these actions are detrimental to the project.

Although these symptoms can occur with individuals at any organization, they are compounded if the project team includes members from different organizations. Invariably, different organizations have different cultures or modes of operation. Individuals from different groups may not have a common loyalty and may expend their energy in the directions most advantageous to themselves instead of the project team. Therefore, no one should take it for granted that a project team will work together harmoniously just because its members are physically placed together in one location. On the contrary, it must be assumed that good communication can be achieved only through the deliberate effort of the top management of each organization contributing to the project.

Critical Success Factors in Project Management

The inability of project management to deliver on time, within cost, and up to stated performance goals is well documented for software development projects, and such failures occur in other environments as well. The United States spends more than $250 billion each year on some 175,000 IT application development projects.[10] Research by the Standish Group shows that a staggering 31.1 percent of projects will be canceled before completion. Furthermore, 52.7 percent of projects will cost 189 percent of their original estimates. Why is the track record so poor? Many factors contribute to project failure. These include poor planning, personality conflicts, inadequate top management support, and low team morale.

OM PRINCIPLE

Key ingredients for successful projects include well-defined objectives, budgets, and schedules; a planning and control system that allows the project manager to adhere to these over time; and frequent and effective communication, team building, conflict resolution, and the creation of an appropriate environment for group effectiveness.

Several studies have documented the reasons why projects fail or succeed. Table 10.2 provides a summary of these factors, which can be classified as methodical and behavioral. The methodical breakdowns and best practices listed in the first column suggest that successful project management can be summed up as "planning the work and working the plan." The second column suggests that effective project management also depends on effective people management and team-building skills.

A more general framework for assessing performance outcomes considers the roles of four key stakeholders on any project:

1. The project manager.
2. The project team (including third-party vendors of products and services).
3. Senior management.
4. The customer.

While all have the common interest of making the project a success, they may have differing views on what constitutes success (see Figure 10.3). These differing perspectives are bound to result in conflicts that the project manager must reconcile. In general, the perspectives of all four stakeholders must be considered in assessing the outcome of a project.

TABLE 10.2   *Reasons for Project Failures and Successes*

IMPEDIMENTS TO PROJECT SUCCESS

Methodical	Behavioral
Scope of project not clearly defined	Project manager with little leadership ability
Time and resource estimates not correctly established	Weak executive/client sponsorship
No infrastructure for maintenance and control of project activities	Unrealistic expectations of team members or sponsors
Inadequate communications among constituents	Dysfunctional interpersonal dynamics
Ineffective use of project management tools	Project not viewed as an integral part of work
Project manager or team members not selected properly	Team processes not established or agreed upon
Resources not allocated properly	Cross-functional culture clash within the organization
No accountability and/or responsibility for results	Lack of trust among participants in performing required tasks
Customer requirements not clearly defined	Inability to deal with constructive criticism
Tasks lists and work breakdown structure not clearly defined	
Lack of training in project management methodology	
Unreasonable time pressure for completion	

CONTRIBUTORS TO PROJECT SUCCESSES

Methodical	Behavioral
Well-defined goals and objectives	Agreement on goals, objectives, and team processes
Clear task definition and work breakdown structure	High level of team member commitment to achieving results
Clear reporting relationships	Realistic expectations
Effective channels of communication	Effective team-building strategies and processes
Reliable estimates of time, resources, and budgets	Spirit of cooperation among team members
Effective use of project management tools and tracking techniques	Accepting feedback and constructive criticism
Reasonable time frame for project completion	Cooperative intra-organizational culture
	Positive process for conflict resolution

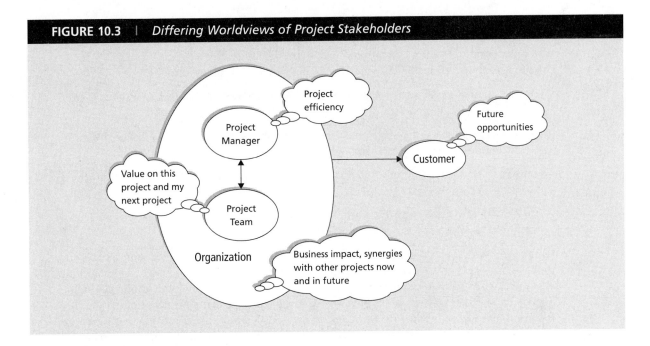

FIGURE 10.3 | *Differing Worldviews of Project Stakeholders*

10.2 PROJECT LIFE CYCLES

Most projects go through similar stages on the path from start to completion. These stages define the **project life cycle:**[11]

- **Define:** This stage focuses on identifying the overall vision, goals, objectives, scope, responsibilities, and deliverables of a project. A common way to capture this information is with a **statement of work,** which delineates this information and is authorized (signed) by all interested parties.

- **Plan:** In this stage, the steps needed to execute the project, determine who will perform them, and identify their start and completion dates are developed. Planning entails activities such as constructing a work breakdown structure and a project schedule.

- **Organize:** This stage focuses on orchestrating the resources so as to execute the plan cost-effectively. Organizing involves activities such as forming a team, allocating resources, calculating costs, assessing risk, preparing project documentation, and ensuring good communications.

- **Control:** This stage assesses how well a project is meeting its goals and objectives and makes adjustments as necessary. Controlling involves collecting and assessing status reports, managing changes to baselines, and responding to circumstances that can negatively affect the project.

- **Close:** Closing a project involves compiling statistics, releasing and/or reassigning people, and preparing "lessons learned."

Top management typically sets the overall policy and selects the appropriate organization to take charge of a project. Management policy also dictates how the project life cycle is accomplished and which professionals should be engaged at different times.

In the early days of project management, the project life cycle was typically portrayed as a sequential process: project managers were to define, plan, organize, control, and close—in that order. Although this made sense on paper, the reality was usually something else. Today, the project life cycle may be characterized by one of several different models:

- In the *waterfall model,* the project is divided into separate stages, and each stage is carried out successively in sequence.

- In the *overlap model,* the stages may be overlapping, such as the use of phased design-construct procedures for fast-track operation.

- In the *spiral model,* each life cycle stage is continuously revisited in order to keep strong control over project risks.

- In the *V-model,* each stage of the life cycle is validated with an external customer (for example, an end user for a software program).

Figure 10.4 shows how these project life cycle approaches can be visualized and outlines the pros and cons of each approach. For example, in today's fast-paced and rapidly changing business environment, there is pressure to accelerate product development without sacrificing quality. The overlap model, also known as "fast-tracking," provides a means of doing this and is commonly used in product development projects as well as in the construction business. As the complexity of projects increases, particularly software development projects, more attention must be paid to customers' requirements. The V-model provides a way of enhancing communication with customers. Similarly, increased uncertainties about technological alternatives and risks result in the use of spiral models, which allow for the creation of multiple prototypes as well as increased levels of internal communication. Most firms have adopted a project life cycle model and often refer to it as their project management methodology (see the *OM Practice* box on Xerox Global Services, Inc.).

> **OM PRINCIPLE**
>
> The choice of a project life cycle model is strategic and depends on such key objectives as time, customer focus, user involvement, level of coordination, and level of control. One model may be more effective than another in different circumstances.

Whatever methodology is used for setting the direction for a project, resource (and cash) consumption follows a familiar pattern through the duration of a project, as shown in Figure 10.5. Every project begins with a "slow" start, followed by an acceleration in momentum, and eventually a slowdown as the project approaches closure. This is valuable information for a project manager, who must control and manage cash and resources throughout the duration of the project.

10.3 STRUCTURING AND SCHEDULING PROJECTS

Projects are successful if they are completed on time, within budget, and to performance requirements. A project manager can draw on a variety of qualitative and quantitative tools for managing the different parts of a project's life cycle: project development, planning and scheduling, managing financial and capital resources, and monitoring progress.

> **OM PRINCIPLE**
>
> The success of a project will always rest on the abilities of the project manager and the team members, not simply on the use of quantitative tools.

Work Breakdown Structure

One of the initial activities a project manager must perform is to define the specific tasks of the project. A **work breakdown structure (WBS)** is a functional decomposition of the

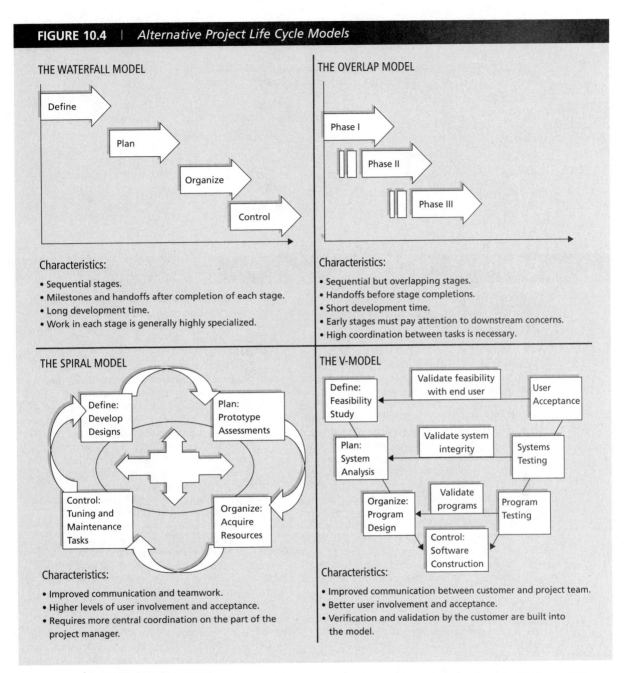

FIGURE 10.4 | *Alternative Project Life Cycle Models*

THE WATERFALL MODEL

Define
Plan
Organize
Control

Characteristics:

- Sequential stages.
- Milestones and handoffs after completion of each stage.
- Long development time.
- Work in each stage is generally highly specialized.

THE OVERLAP MODEL

Phase I
Phase II
Phase III

Characteristics:

- Sequential but overlapping stages.
- Handoffs before stage completions.
- Short development time.
- Early stages must pay attention to downstream concerns.
- High coordination between tasks is necessary.

THE SPIRAL MODEL

Define: Develop Designs
Plan: Prototype Assessments
Control: Tuning and Maintenance Tasks
Organize: Acquire Resources

Characteristics:

- Improved communication and teamwork.
- Higher levels of user involvement and acceptance.
- Requires more central coordination on the part of the project manager.

THE V-MODEL

Define: Feasibility Study
Validate feasibility with end user
User Acceptance
Plan: System Analysis
Validate system integrity
Systems Testing
Organize: Program Design
Validate programs
Program Testing
Control: Software Construction

Characteristics:

- Improved communication between customer and project team.
- Better user involvement and acceptance.
- Verification and validation by the customer are built into the model.

Sources: The V-model is based on B. Boehm, *Software Risk Management* (Washington, DC: IEEE Computer Society Press, 1989); and the spiral model is based on Walker Royce, *Software Project Management—A Unified Approach* (Reading, MA: Addison Wesley Longman, 1999).

tasks that must be accomplished in a project. The tasks may be further subdivided into subtasks and individual work elements. Because it defines the work required to achieve an objective and shows the required interfaces, a WBS is useful for complex projects. A WBS has one drawback, however: it does not show the timing of activities, a topic that we will address later.

FIGURE 10.5 | *Resource and Cash Consumption over the Project Life Cycle*

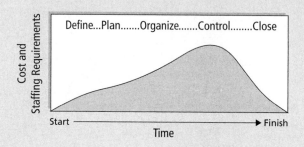

OM PRACTICE

Xerox Global Services, Inc.
Xerox Global Services, Inc. uses a project management life cycle model.

Xerox Global Services, Inc. (XGS, Inc.), a consulting, integration, and outsourcing arm of Xerox Corporation, has a vision: "To provide the most comprehensive, most effective connections between people, knowledge and documents that the world has ever seen." To meet this challenge, it provides a portfolio of services: I/T Managed Services, such as technology deployment, asset management, and procurement; Business Innovation, including knowledge management, application integration, and systems integration; Office Services, including document assessment, asset optimization, and help desk support; and Hosted Services, which include imaging, repository, and document management services. These services are applied at the strategic, process, and infrastructure levels and address not only technology issues, but also people, process, and culture issues.

Central to XGS, Inc.'s delivery of services is project management, which is described by its Client Engagement Process called "X5 Methodology":

1. **Discovery:** There is no such thing as an off-the-shelf solution. Every client is different. Every situation requires a unique response. There may be opportunities to draw on previous solutions, but we never, never start with answers—we start with questions.
2. **Definition:** Define the client's requirements. Define the scope of the project. Define the deliverables. Make everything measurable. Take a "no surprises" approach to every project.

3. **Startup:** Create a detailed project plan based on everything learned in the Discover and Definition phases. Make sure everyone understands it. Stick to it.
4. **Delivery:** Implement according to plan. Follow best practices. Constantly monitor progress. Test as appropriate. Assume nothing. Cut no corners. Work fast, but work smart. If changes are necessary, make sure everyone knows what, why, when, and how. Once the solution is implemented, we provide the support and ongoing management.
5. **Evaluation:** Is the solution meeting or exceeding expectations? How can it be made even better? What about ongoing evaluations management? What has changed since the solution was implemented that must be addressed?

The project manager manages a team that includes technical resource specialists, consultants, and project coordinators. The principal role of the project manager at XGS, Inc. is that of a customer advocate—to ensure that expectations are fully met. This requires careful understanding and documentation of customer expectations such as timeliness, meeting budget, system response, and security. As John Whited, Managing Principal, Project Management Practice, notes, "Most projects fail because user requirements are not understood." These requirements are translated into a detailed work breakdown structure with specific tasks assigned to project team members, as shown in Figure 10.6. This also helps to prepare a budget and monitor progress. Finally, after each project is completed, the team conducts a review of "lessons learned"—What went right? and What went wrong?—to continuously improve the company's ability to meet customer expectations.[12]

FIGURE 10.6 | *Example of Xerox Global Services, Inc.'s Project Work Breakdown Structure*

Acme Grinding Phase II
Requirements Specification Pricing
4/9/02

Activity	SA	Consultant	PM	PCS	PARC	CKM	Extended
Prepare Interview Prep Questions	4						$620.00
Prepare "Service Status" Documentation	1	1					$285.00
Prepare "Applications" Documentation	1	1					$285.00
Prepare "Project Status" Documentation	1	1					$285.00
Prepare "Knowledge Management" Documentation	1	1					$285.00
Prepare "Competitor Information" Documentation	1	1					$285.00
Prepare "Address Book" Documentation	1	1					$285.00
Interview Service team about "Service Status"	2	2	2			2	$1,310.00
Interview Application team about "Applications"	2	2	2			2	$1,310.00
Interview Engineering team about "Project Status"	2	2	2			2	$1,310.00
Interview Service/Application/HR teams about "Knowledge Management"	2	2	2			2	$1,310.00
Interview Marketing/Application teams about "competitor Information"	2	2	2			2	$1,310.00
Interview Sales team about "Address Book"	2	2	2			2	$1,310.00
Interview Sales team about Contact Management Software	2	2	2			2	$1,310.00
Prepare "Contact Management Software" Documentation	1	1					$285.00
Document Users	2						$310.00
Document Goals	4						$620.00

The "Resources" header spans the SA, Consultant, PM, PCS, PARC, and CKM columns.

Source: Used with pemission from Xerox Global Services, Inc.

Consider the tasks associated with implementing an ERP system (see Chapter 8). The system might consist of a product data management (PDM) module, a production order control module, and a master scheduling system that includes materials requirements planning (MRP) and capacity requirements planning (CRP). Each module has to be implemented and tested before the final "Go Live" phase, where all the interfaces between the modules are also tested. A partial list of typical tasks is shown in Table 10.3; in reality, each subtask includes numerous other activities that must be performed. Such a project can be quite complex and daunting, and the project manager needs a way to organize all these activities.

Figure 10.7 illustrates a simple framework to organize work for this project. The project is first decomposed into modules, and tasks for implementing each module are identified below them. Other levels in the WBS could be created based on specific activities for each task.

Gantt Charts

Developed by Harry Gantt in 1916, Gantt charts show a timeline for each project task on a bar chart. They are used for planning project activities and monitoring progress against milestones. For the work breakdown structure in Figure 10.7, the Gantt chart in Figure 10.8 shows when each module of the project is to be conducted and the overall duration of the ERP implementation project.

To create a Gantt chart, we need to determine the start and finish times of each activity. Start times for any activity depend on the interdependencies among the activities in the project. This requires a specification of task dependencies among the activities. A **task dependency** is the relationship between two tasks in which the start or finish of the successor task depends on the predecessor task's start or finish. Specifying dependencies is an essential task of creating a

TABLE 10.3   *Partial Task List for an ERP Project*

- Implement Product Data Management
  - Product definition
  - Financial integration
  - Product definition walkthrough
  - Data management
  - Prepare product costing and routing procedures
  - Pilot testing
- Production Order Control Implementation
  - Review tasks
  - Conduct training
  - Conduct production control walkthrough
  - Determine reporting needs
  - Pilot testing
- Implement Master Scheduling
  - Review master scheduling processes
  - Conduct training
  - Conduct master scheduling walkthrough
  - Prepare master schedule procedures
  - Pilot testing

- Implement MRP/CRP
  - Conduct MRP/CRP training
  - Conduct MRP/CRP walkthrough
  - Prepare MRP/CRP procedures
  - Pilot testing
- Go Live
  - Prepare go live plan
- Schedule and Conduct Training
- Data Management
  - Purchase orders
  - Customer data
  - Inventory and sales orders
- Verify Reporting System and Accuracy
- Verify Costs
- Gather, Review, and Verify Production Inventory Data
- Shut Down Factory
  - Update process data
  - Verify data
- Go Live

FIGURE 10.7   *Example of a Work Breakdown Structure*

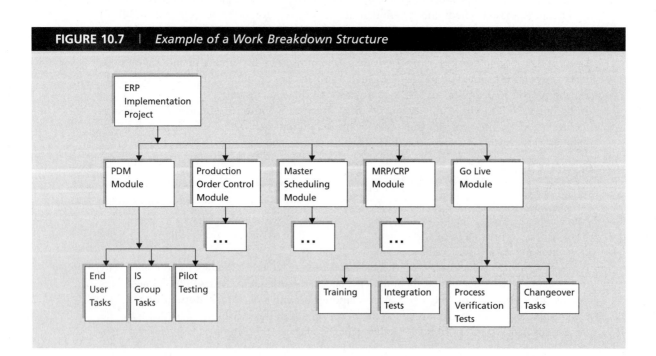

project plan. Task dependencies are reflected in the Gantt chart. For example, in Figure 10.8, Pilot Testing and Production Order Control Implementation cannot start until the PDM module is implemented. Therefore, the start time for these activities will equal the finish time for the Implement PDM activity. The finish times of the activities are then calculated as

Finish time = start time + duration of the activity

There are four basic types of task dependencies (see Table 10.4). The most common dependency is the Finish-to-Start dependency, which describes simple precedence relationships.

Other variations of Gantt charts include *tracking charts* that display task information and the percentage of work completed, *delay charts* that display task schedules and how much tasks can be delayed before the whole project is delayed, *resource charts* that show resource commitments by activity, and *milestone charts* that show key milestone dates. Gantt charts are very useful for quickly sharing project information with team members, project sponsors, subcontractors, and vendors.

FIGURE 10.8 | *Example of a Gantt Chart*

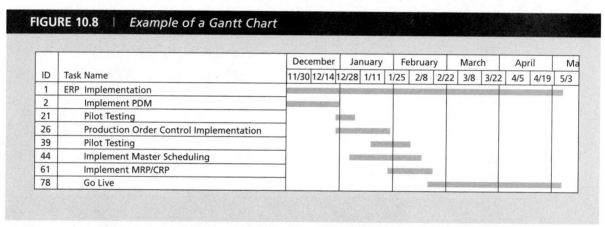

ID	Task Name	December		January		February		March		April		Ma
		11/30	12/14	12/28	1/11	1/25	2/8	2/22	3/8	3/22	4/5	4/19	5/3
1	ERP Implementation												
2	Implement PDM												
21	Pilot Testing												
26	Production Order Control Implementation												
39	Pilot Testing												
44	Implement Master Scheduling												
61	Implement MRP/CRP												
78	Go Live												

TABLE 10.4   *Types of Task Dependencies in Projects*

Task Dependency	Example	Description
Finish-to-Start (FS)	A → B	Task B cannot start until task A finishes. For example, if you have two tasks, "Construct fence" and "Paint fence," "Paint fence" can't start until "Construct fence" finishes. This is the most common type of dependency.
Start-to-Start (SS)	A, B	Task B cannot start until task A starts. For example, if you have two tasks, "Pour foundation" and "Level concrete," then "Level concrete" can't begin until "Pour foundation" begins.
Finish-to-Finish (FF)	A, B	Task B cannot finish until task A finishes. For example, if you have two tasks, "Add wiring" and "Inspect electrical," then "Inspect electrical" can't finish until "Add wiring" finishes.
Start-to-Finish (SF)	A, B	Task B cannot finish until task A starts. This dependency type can be used for just-in-time scheduling up to a milestone or the project finish date, to minimize the risk of a task finishing late if its dependent tasks slip.

Project Networks

Project networks are valuable tools for characterizing the interrelationships of the work breakdown structure of a project graphically and showing the order in which the activities must be performed. Project networks consist of two basic elements: **nodes** (circles or boxes) and **arcs** (arrows). These may be used in two basic ways to characterize a project. In the first approach, called **activity-on-arc,** each arc represents a work task. The nodes establish the precedence relationships among the tasks. In the second approach, nodes represent work tasks and arcs define the precedence relationships. This representation, which is called **activity-on-node,** will be used throughout this chapter. Table 10.5 provides the data showing the key activities for the ERP implementation project, their duration, and the precedence relationships between activities. Figure 10.9 shows the ERP implementation project as an activity-on-node graph.

Critical Path Method

Some of the key questions that a project manager needs to answer are:

○ How long will the entire project take to complete?

○ Which activities determine total project time?

○ Which activity times should be shortened, if possible, to reduce the project duration, and how many resources should be allocated to those activities?

Such questions are addressed using the **critical path method (CPM).** The **critical path** is the sequence of activities that define the total project

> ### OM PRINCIPLE
>
> The critical path is the sequence of activities that takes the longest time and defines the shortest time for project completion. Every project has at least one critical path, but there can be more than one. All the activities on the critical path must be managed carefully; otherwise the entire project may be delayed.

TABLE 10.5 | *Key Activities for the ERP Project*

Activity	Description	Duration	Predecessor
A	Implement PDM and Pilot Testing	10	
B	Production Order Control Implementation and Pilot Testing	14	A
C	Implement Master Scheduling and Pilot Testing	6	A, B
D	Implement MRP/CRP and Pilot Testing	11	B
E	Go Live	8	C, D

FIGURE 10.9 | *Activity-on-Node (AON) Diagram for the ERP Project*

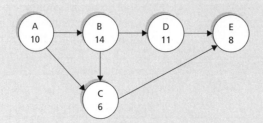

completion time; any delay in a critical activity will delay the entire project. From start to finish in our ERP project example, there are three paths of sequential activities: ACE, with duration of 24 weeks; ABCE, with a duration of 38 weeks; and ABDE, with a duration of 43 weeks. ABDE is the "bottleneck," or critical path; that is, it is the longest path that prevents us from finishing the project in less than 43 weeks. Thus, any delay in activities A, B, D, or E will result in delays to the entire project.

Noncritical activities have **slack,** which is the length of time an activity can be delayed without extending completion of the project beyond the critical path duration. For example, activity C can take up to 5 weeks longer before the length of path ABCE equals 43; if the duration of activity C exceeds 11 weeks, then ABCE will become critical, and the project completion time will exceed 43 weeks. Activities on the critical path (ABDE) have no slack time. Slack times are useful to project managers in several ways. For example, in negotiating delivery dates with a subcontractor, a manager may be less strict with a vendor who delivers to noncritical activities than with one who delivers to critical activities. Additionally, activities with slack give the project manager leeway to better schedule resources, to improve the quality of the task (since there is more time to inspect performance), and to manage cash flows better. Starting slack activities at the latest possible time also delays the financial commitments for some cash flows associated with these activities.

Finding the Critical Path

Finding the critical path by enumerating all possible paths generally is not feasible. To calculate the critical path in a project network, we first compute the **earliest start (ES)** time and **earliest finish (EF)** time for each activity. The earliest start time for all initial activities (those that do not have any predecessors) is zero. The earliest start time for any other activity is the largest of the earliest finish times for all immediate predecessor activities. The earliest finish time is computed as

$$EF = earliest\ start + duration$$

Figure 10.10 shows the ES/EF schedule for the ERP project. The earliest finish time for the terminal activity represents the minimum project duration (and length of the critical path).

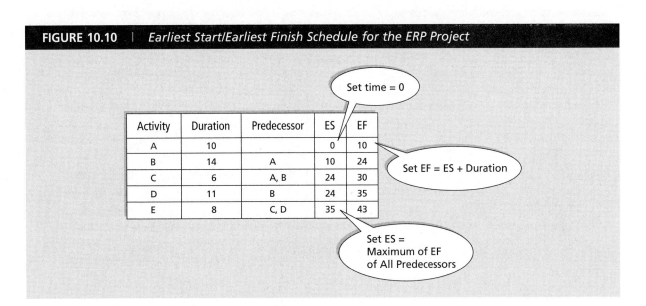

FIGURE 10.10 | *Earliest Start/Earliest Finish Schedule for the ERP Project*

Activity	Duration	Predecessor	ES	EF
A	10		0	10
B	14	A	10	24
C	6	A, B	24	30
D	11	B	24	35
E	8	C, D	35	43

Set time = 0

Set EF = ES + Duration

Set ES = Maximum of EF of All Predecessors

When an activity has multiple predecessors (for example activity E with predecessors C and D), then the earliest start time of that activity is given as the maximum of the earliest finish of all predecessors. In this example, ES(activity E) = Max {EF(activity C), EF(activity D)} = Max {30, 35} = 35.

Next, we compute **latest start (LS)** and **latest finish (LF)** times based on the total project duration (43 weeks in this example). Do this by working from the end of the project back to the beginning. Begin by setting the latest finish times for all ending activities as the total project duration. For any other activity, the latest finish time equals the smallest of the latest start times for all successor activities. Then, the latest start time is computed by the formula:

$$LS = LF - \text{duration}$$

In establishing the latest finish time of an activity with multiple successors (for example, activity B), choose the minimum of the latest start times of all successors (in this case, C and D). Thus, LF(activity B) = Min {LS(activity C), LS(activity D)} = Min {29, 24} = 24. These calculations are summarized in Figure 10.11.

Once the schedule information is computed, slack values can be found. These are calculated as the difference between the earliest start and latest start times, or the difference between the earliest finish and latest finish times, as shown in Table 10.6.

An alternative to the critical path methodology is the *critical chain* approach to project management.[13] Developed by applying the Theory of Constraints to projects, critical chain scheduling shifts the focus from ensuring that intermediate milestones are achieved to ensuring the only date that matters—the promised due date for the project. Critical chain methodology develops a latest start schedule for all activities using conservative time estimates for activity durations. It incorporates task uncertainty and resource constraints to add buffers to the overall project schedule. In contrast to the critical path approach, it tries to set up a project schedule that guarantees that the project will be completed by the promised due date. Shorter project lead-times, improved reliability of project due dates, and increased capacity of the organization to take on more projects have been observed in a number of organizations that have used this approach in a variety of industries.[14]

FIGURE 10.11 | *Latest Start/Latest Finish Schedule for the ERP Project*

Activity	Duration	Predecessor	ES	EF	LS	LF
A	10		0	10	0	10
B	14	A	10	24	10	24
C	6	A, B	24	30	29	35
D	11	B	24	35	24	35
E	8	C, D	35	43	35	43

Set LF = Maximum of LS of All Successors

Set LF = 43

Calculated as LS = LF – Duration

TABLE 10.6		*Complete Schedule Calculations for the ERP Project*					
Activity	**Duration**	**Predecessor**	**ES**	**EF**	**LS**	**LF**	**Slack**
A	10		0	10	0	10	0
B	14		10	24	10	24	0
C	6	A, B	24	30	29	35	5
D	11	B	24	35	24	35	0
E	8	C, D	35	43	35	43	0

10.4 MANAGING PROJECT RESOURCES

OM PRINCIPLE

When resources are involved, there are two objectives for scheduling projects.
1. *Time limited:* The project must be finished by a certain time, using as few resources as possible.
2. *Resource limited*: The project must be finished as soon as possible, but without exceeding some specific level of resource usage or some general resource constraint.

In the project scheduling examples we have considered thus far, we assumed that any resources required to perform the activities were readily available. In the real world, nearly all projects have limited resources available to complete the project in the scheduled time. These include labor, capital, materials and tools, and support services. When these must be allocated among tasks that are scheduled to occur at the same time, sufficient resources may not be available, causing some critical activities to wait until resources are freed up, and resulting in a longer expected project completion time. When project managers deal with multiple projects, each demanding scarce resources at the same time, the problem becomes even more difficult to manage.

Project managers often assume that throwing more resources at a project will improve its performance or avoid delays. Although adding resources to activities can reduce their duration up to a point—at a cost, of course—and thus reduce project completion time, this is not always the case. Earlier we mentioned "Brooks's law," which contends that adding personnel to a delayed software project makes the delay even worse. This "law" can apply to projects in other industries where individuals have highly specialized knowledge. In software development, many tasks are sequential in nature, requiring one person to do them effectively; others only get in the way. In addition, software development requires a great deal of training and communication between team members, resulting in more unproductive time as the team size increases. One of the reasons that software development managers underestimate development time is their failure to understand the learning curve (see Chapter 5). In planning these projects, a common mistake is to base the benchmark on an experienced employee.

In many situations, though, the duration of an activity is normally a function of the amount of resources applied. By understanding this relationship, we can treat the activity duration as a variable and adjust the resource requirements based upon the scheduled activity time.

The first step in considering resources is to specify the amount of resources *available* to the project along with the amount *required* by each activity. Resources available are typically measured by multiplying the number of people available by the amount of time they work. Thus, two persons working for 40 hours each week is equivalent to 80 labor-hours per week or 10 person-days/week. Project managers (or project management software) then attempt to schedule work so that all tasks are scheduled within the constraints of the available resources.

If we have enough resources available at each stage of the project, then the project schedule is driven by time, and the tools we discussed in the previous section can be used to create a feasible schedule. When the rate of resource consumption exceeds available levels, we must resort to other approaches. There are three approaches for managing resources in projects: *resource leveling, effort-driven scheduling,* and *resource-limited scheduling.*

Resource Leveling

Resource leveling (also called *resource smoothing*) attempts to minimize the fluctuations in requirements for resources across the project without extending the project schedule beyond the required completion time. Many project management packages such as *Microsoft Project* have routines for doing this. However, such scheduling is typically performed on an all-or-nothing basis. For example, if a half-time person is available, but the activity requires a full-time person, most project management software packages would delay the task until a full-time person is available. This is obviously not an effective allocation of resources, and most project managers would start the activity using the part-time person.

Resource loading specifies the amounts of resources that an existing schedule requires during specific time periods and provides a general understanding of the demands a project or set of projects will make on a firm's resources. Usually, the earliest start schedule is used to define the initial resource requirements. Based on the resource profile over time, resource leveling seeks to minimize period-by-period variations in resource requirements by shifting tasks within their slack allowances.

To illustrate, consider the project and schedule shown in Table 10.7 (note that this is a different example from the ERP example used earlier). The critical path and total project duration is 5. Task C has two days of slack in the schedule—it can be started on day 2 and finished on day 3, or it can be started on day 4 and finished on day 5.

By shifting the scheduled time for activity C to its latest start, we obtain the schedule shown in Table 10.8. We have effectively reduced the peak resource requirements on the project from 20 to 15 and also smoothed out the resources to a constant level throughout the duration of the project.

| **TABLE 10.7** | *Example of Resource Loading for an Earliest Start Schedule* |

Task	Predecessor	Duration	ES	EF	LS	LF	Slack	Resources	Gantt Chart (by day)				
A	—	1	0	1	0	1	0	15	■				
B	A	2	1	3	1	3	0	15		■	■		
C	A	2	1	3	3	5	2	5		■	■		
D	B	2	3	5	3	5	0	5				■	■
E	B	2	3	5	4	5	0	5				■	■
Resource loads by day									15	20	20	10	10

TABLE 10.8   *Revised Resource Loading*

Task	Predecessor	Duration	ES	EF	LS	LF	Slack	Resources	Gantt Chart (by day)				
A	—	1	0	1	0	1	0	15					
B	A	2	1	3	1	3	0	15					
C	A	2	1	3	3	5	2	5					
D	B	2	3	5	3	5	0	5					
E	B	2	3	5	4	5	0	5					
Resource loads by day									15	15	15	15	15

Effort-Driven Scheduling

In **effort-driven scheduling,** we assume that time and resources are proportionately related; by changing resource levels of activities, we can change the duration of their activity times. For example, if an activity takes 10 days with 3 people, it can be rescheduled for 5 days with 6 people or 3 days with 10 people, at least within some allowable range. This provides the flexibility of smoothing resources and/or changing the project duration by redistributing resources among activities.

Consider the example in Table 10.7. Is there a way to reallocate resources to keep the same project duration without shifting the start time for activity C and still not exceed the resource limitation of 15 people per time period? Activities B and C together require 20 people. To schedule both of these activities together with a total of 15 people would require lengthening the activity times. The key formula is

$$\text{Activity duration} = \text{total person-days required/resource availability}$$

The total person-days required to complete activities B and C (using the original data) is $15 \times 2 + 5 \times 2 = 40$. With a total of 15 people assigned to these tasks together, the task times will have to be $40/15 = 2.67$ days. Applying the formula for each activity individually, we have

Activity B: $2.67 = 30/\text{resource availability}$, or resource availability $= 30/2.67 = 11.23$
Activity C: $2.67 = 10/\text{resource availability}$, or resource availability $= 10/2.67 = 3.74$

Note that the total resources needed for activities B and C together add up to 15. Similarly, activities D and E will be scheduled for $(5 \times 2 + 5 \times 2)/15 = 1.33$ days. The entire project can therefore be completed in 5 days with a constant resource requirement of 15 each day, as summarized in Table 10.9. Clearly, this approach assumes that fractional amounts of resources can be applied, which may not be practical in reality. Also, the assumption that each of the 15 people can work equally effectively on all activities is not applicable in many situations.

Resource-Limited Scheduling

Resource-limited scheduling is a method for minimizing the project duration when the number or amount of available resources is fixed and cannot be exceeded. This method extends the project completion time if necessary in order to keep within the resource limits.

TABLE 10.9	Example of Effort-Driven Scheduling

Task	Predecessor	Original Duration (days)	Resources Required	Work (person-days)	Revised Duration (days)	Gantt Chart (by day)				
A	—	1	15	15	1	▓				
B	A	2	15	30	2.67		▓	▓		
C	A	2	5	10	2.67		▓	▓		
D	B	2	5	10	1.33				▓	
	B	2	5	10	1.33					▓
Resource loads by day						15	15	15	15	15

Consider the example in Table 10.10, and assume that only 10 people are available for the project. For the schedule shown, 15 people are required on days 2 and 3; thus, the schedule must be adjusted to stay within the 10-person resource limitation.

If we simply delay activity C by 2 days, the resource profile becomes 5–10–10–15–15. Clearly, this does not solve the problem. The only option for the project manager in this situation is to extend the project duration by delaying the start date for certain activities. But which activity should be delayed? A good heuristic is to look at the first period of resource overallocation (in this case, day 2), and delay the start of some activity that makes the schedule feasible. Generally, there are many choices; one can delay the activity with the maximum slack or the minimum number of successors. Suppose we choose the activity with the minimum number of successors. Activity B has 2 successors, while activity C has only one. If we push activity C forward by 2 days, we will have reduced the resource requirements in days 2 and 3 to 10, but will have increased the requirements in days 4 and 5 to 15. Now we must delay activity D or E. Since neither has any successors, the choice is arbitrary. If we select E, we have the schedule shown in Table 10.11, which is 7 days long.

TABLE 10.10	Example of Resource-Limited Scheduling

Task	Predecessor	Duration	Resources	Gantt Chart (by day)					
A	—	1	10	▓					0
B	A	2	10		▓	▓			0
C	A	2	5		▓	▓			2
D	B	2	5				▓	▓	0
E	B	2	5				▓	▓	0
Resource loads by day				10	15	15	10	10	

| TABLE 10.11 | | | | *Gantt Chart for Resource-Limited Project Schedule* | | | | | | |

Task	Predecessor	Duration	Resources	Gantt Chart (by day)						
A	—	1	10	▓						
B	A	2	10		▓	▓				
C	A	2	5				▓	▓		
D	B	2	5						▓	
E	B	2	5						▓	▓
Resource loads by day				10	10	10	10	10	5	5

10.5 PROJECT BUDGETING AND EARNED VALUE ANALYSIS

OM PRINCIPLE

The underlying framework for all project accounting is the project schedule. Project budgets can be created based on schedules and resource loadings.

In practice, there are several alternatives for assessing budgets over time. Fixed costs may be expensed at the start of the activity (for example, equipment purchases) or at the end of the activity (e.g., paying a consultant). Variable costs may be expensed based on the project schedule or on the employee's calendar (for example, payroll). Consider Table 10.12, which now includes the costs associated with the activities in the example in Tables 10.7 through 10.11. In Table 10.12, we assume that variable costs are incurred in proportion to the activity duration; thus, for instance, the cost for task B is spread out over the 2 days the task is scheduled. The resulting cost schedule is referred to as the **Budgeted Cost of Work Scheduled (BCWS)** and is calculated by adding all the costs on each day of the project as shown in the last two lines of the table.

By accurately tracking actual costs versus budgeted costs, the project manager can obtain a better idea of the amount of managerial flexibility available. Thus, BCWS information is very useful for the project manager for controlling the project. For example, if by day 4 the project costs have exceeded $12,510, then the project manager might wish to control future expenses more carefully, renegotiate the contract with the customer, and/or

| TABLE 10.12 | | | | *Project Budgeting Example* | | | | |

Task	Predecessor	Duration	Cost	Gantt Chart (by day)				
A	—	1	$1,500	$1,500				
B	A	2	$3,510		$1,755	$1,755		
C	A	2	$5,000		$2,500	$2,500		
D	B	2	$2,000				$1,000	$1,000
E	B	2	$3,000				$1,500	$1,500
Total project budget			$15,010	$1,500	$4,255	$4,255	$2,500	$2,500
Cumulative project budget				$1,500	$5,755	$10,010	$12,510	$15,010

try to get more funds in order to complete the project. Similarly, if the project incurs less cost by day 4, this might indicate that the project is behind schedule and the pace of work needs to pick up. But how can a manager tell whether a cost overrun is due to greater expense than expected or to the work being completed faster than expected? Earned value analysis resolves this dilemma.

OM PRINCIPLE

A project manager's ability to influence the total cost of the project decreases as the project progresses and as irreversible commitments are made over time.

Earned value analysis is an approach for monitoring project costs and expenses. It involves specifying, on a periodic basis, how far each activity has progressed (% complete) and deriving the value of work completed from this information. Value is "earned" as activities are completed. The cumulative value of work completed on any day is then compared to actual costs incurred in completing that work and the amount of work budgeted for completion. Earned value is a uniform unit of measure and thus provides a consistent method for analyzing project progress and performance.

Establishing an earned value analysis system involves the following steps:

1. Establish the work breakdown structure (WBS) to divide the project into manageable portions.
2. Identify the activities to be scheduled.
3. Allocate the costs to be expended on each activity.
4. Schedule the activities over time and assess percent completion.
5. Tabulate, plot, and analyze the data to confirm that the plan is acceptable.

In our example, suppose that on day 4, a manager assesses the actual costs and % complete for each activity as shown in Table 10.13.

The earned value is calculated by multiplying the budgeted cost of the activity by the % complete and then adding the result over all activities. For instance, on day 4, the status of the project is:

○ Budgeted Cost of Work Scheduled (BCWS) = $12,510

○ Actual Cost of Work Performed (ACWP) = $11,400

○ Budgeted Cost of Work Performed (BCWP) = $10,510

TABLE 10.13   *Example of a Gantt Chart with Earned Value Data*

Task	Predecessor	Duration	Budgeted Cost	Actual Cost	% Complete	Earned Value = Budgeted Cost × % Complete	Allocated Cost				
A	—	1	$1,500	$1,600	100	$1,500	$1,500				
B	A	2	$3,510	$3,700	100	$3,510		$1,755	$1,755		
C	A	2	$5,000	$4,600	80	$4,000		$2,500	$2,500		
D	B	2	$2,000	$1,000	60	$1,200				$1,000	$1,000
E	B	2	$3,000	$500	10	$300				$1,500	$1,500
Total costs			$15,010	$11,400		$10,510	$1,500	$4,255	$4,255	$2,500	$2,500
Cumulative costs by period							$1,500	$5,755	$10,010	$12,510	$15,010

The distinction between the BCWS and the BCWP is that the former represents the budget of the activities that were planned to be completed, and the latter represents the budget of the activities that actually were completed. BCWP is often referred to as *earned value*. In this case, the good news is that actual costs are less then planned costs (see Figure 10.12); however, the bad news is that work accomplished on the project is less than anticipated. For example, activity C should have been finished but is only 80 percent complete.

Forecasting Project Parameters Using Earned Value Methodology

Earned value methodology can be used for forecasting the estimated completion time and costs of a project given the current status of the project. To distinguish between cost slippage and schedule slippage on the project, we define

$$\text{Schedule variance (SV)} = \text{BCWP} - \text{BCWS}$$
$$\text{Cost variance (CV)} = \text{BCWP} - \text{ACWP}$$

In our example project at day 4, we compute SV = $10,510 - $12,510 = ($2,000) and CV = $10,510 - $11,400 = ($890). The value of SV indicates that the project is severely behind schedule, and CV indicates that we are also overspending on the project because work with a value of $10,510 was done by actually spending $11,400.

We can forecast that, given the pace of work, the project is going to take longer than 5 days, and with the unfavorable cost variance, it is going to cost more than $15,010. These forecasts can be made by calculating performance indices. The Schedule Performance Index (SPI) is the earned value divided by the planned value (BCWP/BCWS). The Cost Performance Index (CPI) is the earned value divided by the actual cost (BCWP/ACWP). The Estimate At Completion (EAC) value is a number of great interest each update cycle. It indicates where the project cost is heading. Calculating a new EAC is one of the benefits of earned value.

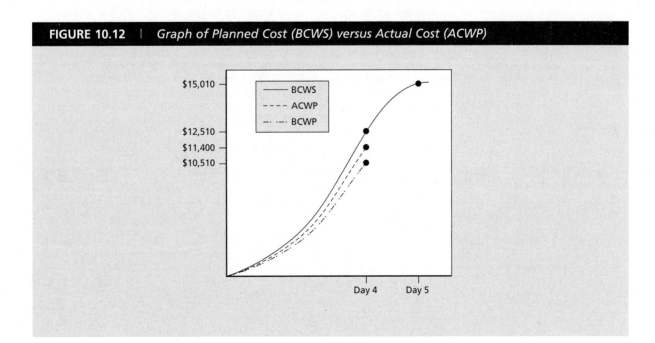

FIGURE 10.12 | *Graph of Planned Cost (BCWS) versus Actual Cost (ACWP)*

However, the actual formula to use for this calculation is a matter of much discussion. One simple way to do this is

$$\text{EAC} = (\text{BAC} - \text{BCWP})/\text{CPI} + \text{ACWP}$$

where BAC = budget at completion, the initial budget for the project.

This formula determines the unfinished or unearned work (BAC − BCWP) and divides it by the CPI. To that is added the sunk cost, or the cost of the completed work (ACWP). From this we can see that poor cost performance, a CPI less than 1, would result in an EAC that is greater than the BAC. More complex formulas factor the CPI to give it more or less influence on the EAC. For our example project, these calculations are

$$\text{SPI} = \$10,510/\$12,510 = 0.84$$
$$\text{CPI} = \$10,510/\$11,400 = 0.92$$
$$\text{EAC} = (\$15,010 - \$10,510)/0.92 + \$11,400 = \$4,891.07 + \$11,400 = \$16,291.07$$

A similar forecast can be made for the project duration using the SPI; if work progresses at the current pace (84% schedule efficiency), then the time to complete the project would be

$$\text{Time to complete the project (TT)} =$$
$$\text{original project duration/SPI} = 5/0.84 = 5.95 \text{ days}$$

OM PRACTICE

The U.S. Navy's A–12 Project
Lack of clear cost data results in project cancellation.

The A–12, a stealth-based Navy aircraft, was the U.S. Navy's premier aviation project. In January 1991, Secretary of Defense Dick Cheney canceled the project, complaining that no one could tell him what the final cost of the project would be. In fact, there were many EACs, some more credible than others. Unfortunately, the more credible EACs were not reported on the summary reports sent to the Office of the Secretary of Defense. A Navy investigation of the A–12 cancellation revealed that adverse information about the A–12 may have been suppressed by the Navy Program Office. The Navy's "inquiry officer" on the cancellation of the A–12 program, C. P. Beach, Jr., concluded that the schedule and cost goals for the A–12 were too optimistic and should not have been supported by government managers in the contract and program offices. Table 10.14 shows the April 1990 cost performance data for the A–12, six months before the project was canceled. Table 10.15 shows four popular performance factors (CPI, SPI, 0.8 CPI + 0.2 SPI, CPI × SPI) and the resulting EACs using the A–12 data. If this range of EACs is considered reasonable, the $4,400 million EAC reported by the contractors was clearly understated.[15]

TABLE 10.14	*Cost Performance Data for A–12 Project (April 1990, Millions of Dollars)*							
Month	**BCWS**	**BCWP**	**ACWP**	**SV**	**CV**	**BAC**	**EAC**	**VAC**
April	2,080	1,491	1,950	(589)	(459)	4,046	4,400	(354)

(Note: VAC = variance at completion = EAC − BAC)

continues

TABLE 10.15	A Range of Estimates at Completion for the A–12 (Derived from the Cumulative Performance Data in Table 10.14)	
Performance Factor	**Performance Factor Value**	**EAC (millions)**
CPI × SPI	0.5481	$6,612
SPI	0.7168	$5,514
.8 CPI × .2 SPI	0.7551	$5,334
CPI	0.7646	$5,292

Summary of Key Points

- Projects—temporary ventures to create a unique product or service—are important in most organizations. Projects have a well-defined schedule and cost objectives, have a clear beginning and end, and use resources to accomplish tasks associated with the project. Project management is the function of coordinating activities and resources to meet the objectives.

- Project managers must often deal with tradeoffs between time and cost; they should realize that adding resources to projects may actually be detrimental. In addition, customer expectations may change during the course of a project, making its management more difficult.

- Project managers must deal with three stakeholders: the organization, team members, and customers. Their responsibilities include project definition, team motivation, technical support, acting as change agents, and ensuring that projects support a firm's strategy.

- Projects succeed or fail because of a host of methodical and behavioral factors. Understanding these factors is crucial to successful project management. Managing the people element and ensuring effective communication among constituencies are critical.

- The project life cycle generally includes defining, planning, organizing, controlling and closing the project. A project debrief seeking to understand "lessons learned" is important for continuously improving project management performance.

- Project management models include the standard sequential approach (the waterfall model), the overlap model, the spiral model, and the V-model. Each has unique benefits and disadvantages. The choice depends on time, customer focus, user involvement, the level of coordination needed, and the level of control required.

- Several tools are available to help project managers in the project life cycle. These include work breakdown structure to assist in defining and documenting complex projects, Gantt charts for developing and monitoring timelines, and project networks for scheduling and sequencing activities.

- The critical path method (CPM) is a tool for identifying the minimum project completion time and the "bottleneck" activities in the project. The critical path is calculated by (1) drawing the project network, (2) calculating the earliest start and earliest finish times for all activities, (3) calculating the latest start and latest finish times for all activities, and (4) calculating the slack, the difference between the earliest start and latest start time for each activity. Activities with zero slack define the critical path.

- ○ Resource-constrained project scheduling involves determining the fewest resources possible to complete a project within a certain time, or to complete the project as soon as possible without exceeding some specific level of resource usage or some general resource constraint. Tools for doing this include resource leveling, effort-driven scheduling, and resource-limited scheduling.
- ○ Budgets for projects can be derived from project schedules and resource loadings. Earned value analysis is a good methodology to keep track of project progress and monitor performance on an ongoing basis.

Questions for Review and Discussion

1. Explain the difference between a program and a project. Why are projects important in business?
2. What are the key characteristics of projects?
3. Explain the typical relationship between time and cost in a project. What challenges does this present for managing a project?
4. What is "Brooks's Law," and why does it occur?
5. Why are "lessons learned" an important activity at the close of a project?
6. Discuss the roles of a project manager in managing projects. What key personal characteristics should such a person have?
7. Explain the reasons for project success and failure. What can organizations do to improve the chances for project success?
8. Describe the important factors that affect interpersonal behavior in project environments and discuss how to deal with them.
9. Describe the typical project life cycle.
10. Explain the four different models for characterizing the project life cycle. How do they differ, and in what circumstances might each be useful?
11. How does a work breakdown structure assist in project management?
12. What is the role of a Gantt chart?
13. Describe the procedure for finding the critical path in a project network.
14. Explain the different approaches used to manage resources in projects.
15. What is earned value analysis? How does it help a project manager monitor progress?
16. The Alaska Pipeline Project was the largest, most expensive private construction project in the 1970s.[16] It encompassed 800 miles, thousands of employees, and $10 billion. At the planning stage, the owner (a consortium) employed a Construction Management Contractor (CMC) to direct the pipeline portion, but retained centralized decision making to assure single direction and to integrate the effort of the CMC with the pump stations and the terminals constructed by another contractor. The CMC also centralized its decision making in directing over 400 subcontractors and thousands of vendors. Because there were 19 different construction camps and hundreds of different construction sites, this centralization caused delays in decision making. At about the 15% point of physical completion, the owner decided to reorganize the decision-making process and change the role of the CMC. The new organization was a combination of owner and CMC personnel assigned within an integrated organization. The objective was to develop a single project team to be responsible for controlling all subcontractors. Instead of having nine tiers of organization from the General Manager of the CMC to the subcontractors, the new organization had only four tiers from the Senior Project Manager of the owner to the subcontractors. Besides providing unified direction and coordination, this reduction in tiers of organization greatly improved communications and the ability to make and implement decisions. The new organization also allowed decentralization of decision making by treating five sections of the pipeline at different geographic locations as separate projects, with a section manager responsible for all functions of the section as a profit center.

At about the 98% point of physical completion, all remaining activities were to be consolidated to identify single bottom-line responsibility, reduce duplication in management staff, and unify coordination of remaining work. Thus, the project was first handled by separate organizations but later was run by an integrated organization with decentralized profit centers. Finally, the organization in effect became small and was ready to be phased out of operation. Find additional information about this project and write a brief commentary on whether you consider this project to be successful. Use the critical success factors listed in the chapter to arrive at your conclusion.

17. The underground railroad tunnel from Britain to France, commonly called the Channel Tunnel or Chunnel, was built by tunneling from each side. Starting in 1987, the tunnels had a breakthrough in 1990. Management turmoil dogged the project from the start. In 1989, seven of the eight top people in the construction organization left. There was a built-in conflict between the contractors and government overseers: "The fundamental thing wrong is that the contractors own less than 6% of Eurotunnel. Their interest is to build and sell the project at a profit. [Eurotunnel's] interest is for it to operate economically, safely and reliably for the next 50 years." (Alastair Morton, Eurotunnel CEO, quoted in *ENR*, December 10, 1990, 56) Find additional articles or materials about this project to assess the views of the major stakeholders.

Problems

1. Construct a project network for a project with the activities shown below. The project is completed when activities F and G are both completed.

Activity	Predecessors
A	—
B	—
C	A
D	A
E	C, B
F	C, B
G	D, E

2. The Mohawk Discount Store chain is designing a management-training program for individuals at its corporate headquarters. The company would like to design the program so that the trainees can complete it as quickly as possible. Important precedence relationships must be maintained between assignments or activities in the program. For example, a trainee cannot serve as an assistant store manager until after she or he has had experience in the credit department and at least one sales department. The following table shows the activity assignments that must be completed by each trainee:

Activity	Predecessors
A	—
B	—
C	A
D	A, B
E	A, B
F	C
G	D, F
H	E, G

Construct a project network for this problem. Do not attempt to perform any further analysis.

3. The following data pertain to a project of launching a new drug.

Activity	Predecessors	Duration	ES	EF	LS	LF	Slack
A	—	5					
B	A	9					
C	A	10					
D	A	7					
E	B	6					
F	C	6					
G	D	6					
H	D	7					
I	G	7					
J	H	10					
K	E, F, I	5					
L	I, J	8					
M	K, L	6					

   a. Complete the table above.

   b. Draw an activity-on-node (AON) diagram for this project.

   c. Interpret the value of slack on all the activities.

4. Maffei Manufacturing Company is planning to install a new flexible manufacturing system. The activities that must be performed, their predecessors, and estimated activity times are shown in the following table. Draw the project network and find the critical path.

Activity	Description	Predecessors	Estimated Activity Time (days)
A	Analyze current performance	—	3
B	Identify goals	A	1
C	Conduct study of existing operation	A	6
D	Define new system capabilities	B	7
E	Study existing technologies	—	2
F	Determine specifications	D	9
G	Conduct equipment analyses	C, F	10
H	Identify implementation activities	C	3
I	Determine organizational impacts	H	4
J	Prepare report	E, G, I	2
K	Establish audit procedure	H	1

5. Colonial State College is considering building a new athletic complex on campus. The complex would provide a new gymnasium for intercollegiate basketball games, expanded office space, classrooms, and intramural facilities. The activities that would have to be completed before beginning construction are listed in the following table.

Activity	Description	Predecessors	Time (weeks)
A	Survey building site	—	6
B	Develop initial design	—	8
C	Obtain board approval	A, B	12
D	Select architect	C	4
E	Establish budget	C	6
F	Finalize design	D, E	15
G	Obtain financing	E	12
H	Hire contractor	F, G	8

a. Develop a project network for this project.

b. Identify the critical path.

c. Develop a detailed schedule for all activities in the project.

d. Does it appear reasonable that construction could begin one year after the decision to begin the project? What is the project completion time?

6. Consider the following data on a resource-constrained network.

Activity	Predecessors	Duration	Resources
A	—	7	2
B	—	1	1
C	—	4	4
D	A	3	1
E	A	8	4
F	B	2	2
G	C	3	1
H	E, F, G	2	3
I	E, F, G	5	1
J	D, H	2	1

a. Construct a Gantt chart of the activities using the earliest start schedule and develop the resource load profile using the template below.

Activity	1	2	3	4	5	6	7	8	9	10	11	12	13	14	15	16	17	18	19	20	21	22	23	24	25	26		
A																												
B																												
C																												
D																												
E																												
F																												
G																												
H																												
I																												
J																												
Resources																												

b. Which activities are the best candidates for leveling?

c. Construct a revised load profile that is leveled (it need not be the best solution).

Activity	1	2	3	4	5	6	7	8	9	10	11	12	13	14	15	16	17	18	19	20	21	22	23	24	25	26		
A																												
B																												
C																												
D																												
E																												
F																												
G																												
H																												
I																												
J																												
Resources																												

7. For the data shown in the table below, construct the project network and develop a total-cost budget based on both an earliest start and a latest start schedule.

Activity	Predecessors	Duration	Expected Cost (thousands of $)
A	—	3	90
B	—	8	16
C	A	1	3
D	A	5	100
E	A	3	6
F	C	1	2
G	D	5	60
H	B, E	4	20
I	H	4	4
J	F, G, I	2	2

8. The total budget for the following project is $100,000. The estimates on % of work completed and actual cost in week 15 are also given.

Activity	Predecessors	Duration	Estimated Cost	% Complete	Actual Cost
A	—	6	$18,000	100	$20,000
B	—	12	2,400	100	2,000
C	A	8	3,200	50	2,000
D	A	10	40,000	80	35,000
E	C	6	3,000	0	0
F	B, D	7	28,000	10	2,000
G	E, F	7	5,400	0	0

a. Compute the BCWS for the project for the first 15 days assuming an earliest start schedule. (Assume costs are incurred linearly through an activity duration.)

b. Compute the BCWP given the current status.

c. Compute the CPI for the project and comment on it.

d. Compute the SPI for the project and comment on it.

e. How would you evaluate the performance on each activity?

f. How many days would you expect the project to take given the performance to date (give both an optimistic and a pessimistic forecast)?

g. What would you expect the project to cost given the performance to date (give both an optimistic and a pessimistic forecast)?

Internet Projects

To find Web links to carry out each of the following projects, go to the text's Web site at **http://raturi_evans.swlearning.com.**

1. Review the tutorial on critical path methods for project scheduling and resource allocation and summarize five lessons learned.

2. Find a local chapter of the Project Management Institute that is close to you and report on its activities. For example, the Southwest Ohio Chapter PMI offers a variety of opportunities for project managers.

3. Download a free copy of "A Guide to the Project Management Body of Knowledge" from the link provided on the text Web site. Summarize how this chapter relates to the information discussed in the article.

EXPERIENCE OM

Experiment with *Microsoft Project*

Microsoft Project is a software program to help you create project plans, communicate them to others, and manage changes as they occur. You will find a link to download a 60-day trial version of *Microsoft Project 2002* from the text's Web site at **http://raturi_evans.swlearning. com.** This tutorial will demonstrate how to create a small project plan and schedule. Complete details are provided in the Bonus Materials folder on the CD-ROM.

Emerging Challenges in Operations Management

The world is changing at a pace that was impossible to predict at the time most of us were born. For businesses to succeed, operations management (OM) principles must be integrated into all business functions. This will require a deep understanding of the process of organizational transformation and the role that OM plays in the process.

This chapter addresses some emerging challenges in OM. Specifically, we address:
○ Performance metrics and their relationship with OM (*Section 11.1*).
○ The changing landscape of business and society (*Section 11.2*).
○ Emerging challenges and opportunities in OM, drawing upon the topics in the previous chapters (*Section 11.3*).
○ A dynamic perspective of OM (*Section 11.4*).

11.1 OPERATIONS MANAGEMENT AND BUSINESS PERFORMANCE

The operations management function touches nearly every aspect of an organization; this was evident in our discussion of structure and infrastructure in Chapter 1, which defined the organization of the text. Let us review the principal drivers of business performance from the operations perspective, which are summarized in Table 11.1. In examining this broad spectrum of metrics, we see a clear theme: creation and improvement of value for all stakeholders throughout the value chain— from customers to shareholders. At the same time, such a large and diverse set of metrics makes it dif-

> **OM PRINCIPLE**
>
> Depending on the industry or the positioning of the organization within its industry, the primary metrics that the organization uses can be vastly different from those of its competitors or other similar enterprises.

ficult for an organization to clearly define and focus on its most vital competitive priorities. Many organizations struggle with this decision or are essentially clueless. Further, what builds long-lasting, sustainable value for the firm can often be an odd mix. Consider Disney, a firm known for its product design and innovation—it is steadfast in its pursuit of creating shareholder value through land acquisitions.[1] Another example is Southwest Airlines, which positions itself with high customer service and low fares, but does so by simplifying operations, for example, flying only one type of aircraft.

TABLE 11.1	Summary of Performance Metrics to the Decision Areas	
OM Focus Area	**Primary Metrics**	**Secondary Metrics**
Strategy	Achieving organizational vision	Accomplishment of action plans
Product and service design	Design quality and market requirements	Product development lead-time; product cost
Process design	Lead time; flexibility	Fixed and variable cost per unit; efficiency
Facilities and capacity	Throughput time; utilization	Fixed and variable cost per unit
Quality	Customer requirements	Conformance and capability
Supply chain management	Delivery lead-time; availability and responsiveness to customers	Total supply chain cost
Schedule management (ERP)	Time and due date performance	Cost; schedule stability
Project management	Duration; total cost	Resource utilization

The stronger and more complete the operations function is, the better an organization will be able to address this challenge. Table 11.1 also provides generic guidance for focusing goals and objectives on the structural and infrastructural elements of the organization that have the most impact and relevance to those goals and objectives. For example, suppose that the customer is willing to pay more for quick delivery than for customization or flexibility. How does an organization respond and make changes so that it can achieve the quickest delivery? Table 11.1 suggests that process design, facilities, and supply chain management would be the principal areas on which to focus resources and plans. Similarly, a firm that struggles to meet due dates for customers will probably get much more value out of implementing an enterprise resource planning (ERP) system than one that has a fairly good record of delivering when promised. Firms with complex products that are engineered to order would probably derive the greatest benefit from paying close attention to product design and project management. Service firms, with primary goals of meeting customers' quality expectations, would focus more on quality management.

Organizations are actively engaged in all eight of these focus areas, juggling initiatives and trying to create pathways to greater competitiveness. Operations managers face important challenges in each area. The remainder of this chapter reflects on how the future will affect OM, and reviews some initiatives that hold promise for the future.

11.2 THE CHANGING LANDSCAPE OF BUSINESS AND SOCIETY

OM PRINCIPLE

The focus of OM practice, as well as supporting research efforts, must continually respond to changes in the business environment and society at large so that organizations can meet customer expectations and remain competitive.

Operations management is a dynamic field, as we saw in discussing its evolution in Chapter 1 (see Figure 1.3). In Chapter 1 we described some of the trends and challenges that CEOs believe will affect U.S. companies in the future. A study by the American Society for Quality in 2002 concluded that the future will arrive much faster than anyone can predict. Although this study focused on impacts on the Society's future and the quality profession, its observations have some interesting implications for OM in general. The study identified four important trends:

1. **Aging Population:** The population of the developed world is aging, but in developing countries it is exploding. This will further deplete natural resources and strain the health-care systems of these countries. Up to half the population of nations such as Mexico and India is under the age of 20. In 1999, the middle class in China was as large as the entire U.S. population, and as the Chinese population ages, it will shift the economic power of the world.

   With an aging society, new and different products and services are going to be needed. This creates new demands and challenges for OM in many industries including the health-care profession, which currently suffers from inefficiencies and quality issues. The *OM Practice* box describes the impact of aging customers on process design. As we saw in previous chapters OM has embraced such new approaches as design for manufacturability and design for environment; perhaps the next innovation will be "design for aging."

OM PRACTICE

Design for the Older Consumer
Improved process design can benefit older citizens.

Most service operations are designed for customers who see through young eyes and move with young bodies. As customers age, their abilities decline, and the world becomes increasingly difficult for them to navigate. For example, rooms may be too dim to see clearly; print becomes illegible and signs go unnoticed; doors, buttons, and switches require more strength and flexibility; floor plans become confusing and stairs become unsteady.

When seniors take their 163 million annual trips, this is the world that they encounter. Their response can range from annoyance and frustration to a sense of weakness, frailty, and dependency. In these situations, they will be, at a minimum, dissatisfied customers, and should an injury occur because of poor lighting, for instance, a lawsuit will likely follow. To create more satisfaction and safety for senior citizens, organizations need to understand how perceptual, mental, and physical abilities change with age; examine how these changes will affect normal activities; and then design an environment that fits seniors' abilities and meets their needs.[2]

The table below shows some examples of process design changes that address some of these issues.

Issue	Process Design Change
Aging reduces brightness	Improve contrast perception with higher illumination. Use higher brightness contrasts. Make printed material and signs readable. Avoid zones different in brightness. Compensate for color change.
Aging makes the world hard to control	Make controls and switches easy to use. Minimize chances of slipping and falling. Make it easier for people to find their way.

2. **Sustainability of Life on Earth:** We are approaching a golden age of environmental protection and sustainable development. Sustainable development will not only protect the earth's resources, but will also become the preferred stimulus of economic growth. Governments and businesses have a tremendous opportunity to provide the systems that will accelerate progress toward sustainability.

Managing these systems will be a principal responsibility for operations managers. New technologies will require new training and skills, as well as integration with existing systems. Operations management is only beginning to integrate environmental issues into design and production processes. Key benefits to firms include improved environmental performance, lower costs, reduced liability, improved compliance (with regulations set by the Environmental Protection Agency and other agencies), fewer accidents, improved public image, and enhanced customer trust. Table 11.2 summarizes the commonly applicable environmental laws in the United States. By anticipating new requirements and making changes to operations, a firm can avoid some future compliance obligations and their associated costs.

The ISO 14001 standards provide a convenient way for firms to formalize environmental concerns through complete assessments and documentation. Much like

TABLE 11.2 *Commonly Applicable Federal Environmental Laws in the United States*

Clean Air Act (CAA)	Establishes ambient and source emission standards and permit requirements for conventional and hazardous air pollutants.
Clean Water Act (CWA)	Establishes ambient and point source effluent standards and permit requirements for water pollutants, including those discharged directly to a water body and to a public sewer.
Federal Insecticide, Fungicide and Rodenticide Act (FIFRA)	Establishes a program for the review, registration, and control of pesticides.
Resource Conservation and Recovery Act (RCRA)	Establishes regulations and permit requirements for hazardous waste management. Also, creates standards for underground storage tanks holding oil or hazardous substances.
Toxic Substances Control Act (TSCA)	Regulates the use, development, manufacture, distribution, and disposal of chemicals. Certain chemicals (such as PCBs) targeted for specific management standards.
Comprehensive Environmental Response, Compensation, and Liability Act (CERCLA, also known as "Superfund")	Establishes program for cleaning up contaminated sites and establishes liability for cleanup costs. Also, provides reporting requirements for releases of hazardous substances.
Emergency Planning and Community Right-to-Know Act (EPCRA)	Establishes a program to inform the public about the hazardous and toxic chemicals used by industries. Reporting requirements apply to companies using, processing, or storing specific chemicals over specified quantities.
Hazardous Materials Transportation Act (HMTA)	Establishes standards for the safe transportation of hazardous materials.

ISO 9000 for quality policy, ISO 14001 defines the framework, processes, and documentation for a comprehensive environmental management system within a firm. ISO 14001 requires an organization to do the following:[3]

o Develop an environmental policy with a commitment to compliance.

o Have a procedure for identifying and having access to environmental laws and regulations.

o Set objectives and targets that are in line with its environmental policy (which includes a commitment to compliance).

o Establish operational control procedures.

o Establish procedures for emergency preparedness and response.

o Establish a procedure for periodically evaluating compliance.

While these requirements relate directly to an organization's compliance management, each of the 17 elements of the ISO 14001 standard can contribute to enhanced compliance.[4] The ISO 14001 environmental standard is currently only voluntary, and many companies have yet to make progress toward certification. Not all environmental issues relate to pollution control. For example, the U.S. Postal Service examined environmental aspects related to the vehicles it operates, the chemicals it uses to maintain equipment, the solid wastes it generates, and the products (stamps) that it sells.[5] In evaluating environmental impacts of processes, an organization should consider air emissions, solid and hazardous wastes, land contamination, local issues (for example, concerns raised by the community such as noise, odor, dust, traffic, and appearance), water effluents, land use, and raw material and resource use.

3. **Renewable Energy Sources:** Renewable resources such as wind, solar, hydro, geothermal, and biomass gradually will replace fossil fuels and nuclear energy as the primary sources of power generation. As these technologies improve, they will become more affordable, and society will realize that dependence on traditional energy sources is foolhardy. This trend will accelerate as fossil fuel availability is reduced, costs escalate, and supplies become subject to political concerns.

   Designing operations to exploit these new resources will certainly be a challenge to the OM profession. For example, Kraft Foods was considering closing down an old, inefficient Sealtest ice cream plant near Boston. The Massachusetts Office of Energy Resources conducted an extensive energy audit at the plant and recommended $3.6 million in energy-saving projects. With the help of Boston Edison, the local utility that financed several of these improvements, the plant experienced a 10 percent increase in productivity. Energy costs of producing a gallon of ice cream dropped from 7.5 cents to 5.5 cents, and fewer emissions were spewed into the air. The plant remained open and 200 jobs were saved; more jobs have been added since.[6]

4. **Growth in Internet Usage:** Internet usage will continue to grow, with remarkable progress made in the developing world. Internet use in developing countries will help certain educated populations become active consumers, as well as producers, of online education and consumer products. The Internet will finally achieve its potential as a business management and product development tool. However, security threats will have to be overcome if corporations are to trust the Internet for product development, which involves proprietary information. Otherwise, dedicated broadband private services will replace the Internet for all but its mass-marketing capabilities.

As we have seen, the Internet has had a major impact on processes and systems for manufacturing and services. As usage and technology grow, operations managers must provide smooth transitions from existing systems and ensure that the new systems meet the needs of all stakeholders. One of the challenges that operations managers face with any new technology is creating standards. For example, many of the failures associated with electronic data interchange (EDI), designed to build connectivity between firms and their suppliers, are attributed to the lack of standards and protocols for exchanging information. Seamless communication between competing technologies and among nations with different standards will remain a challenge.

11.3 EMERGING CHALLENGES AND OPPORTUNITIES

Business challenges are similar across the world with some minor differences. For example, quality improvement initiatives would provide a much better return in India than in the United States, and workforce training and education may be more relevant in Mexico than in Japan. Nevertheless, no crucial business challenge can be addressed without OM involvement. In some cases, meeting these challenges is merely a matter of survival. Consider the case of Arnhold Holdings in the *OM Practice* box.

OM PRINCIPLE

Successful business strategies are focused on three key objectives: *better, cheaper, faster*. These objectives essentially reflect the scope and purpose of OM.

OM PRACTICE

Operations Challenges at Arnhold

Survival in today's economy can require radical changes.

When Michael Green's construction-supplies firm, Arnhold Holdings, Ltd., was enjoying a robust economy, little attention was paid to operational inefficiency. When one person couldn't do the work, two were hired; if a position was difficult to fill, the pay was doubled. On one occasion, Arnhold flew in 100 bathroom closets from the United States to make up for a wayward shipment, when the missing goods were sitting in a Hong Kong warehouse, a decision that cost tens of thousands of dollars. But when the company was hit hard by the Asian financial crisis in 1998, things had to change. The firm had to do whatever it took to survive and be competitive; this included ending its long tradition of lifetime employment and downsizing 32 percent of its workers.

The Asian recession created pressures to tackle business inefficiency and waste. The new-economy forces of falling market barriers, tougher price competition, and a flight of customers to the Internet made many established companies feel vulnerable. Following the example of many U.S. corporations, businesses ranging from China's state-owned enterprises to Japanese automakers needed to reengineer their way to competitiveness. While reducing its workforce was a big part of Arnhold's strategy, doing so without raising productivity would have simply hurt total output. So the company also focused on training, office automation, and pushing workers harder. In 1999, it increased the average number of containers handled per person in the back office by 21 percent, or equivalently, decreased payroll costs for handling each container by 16 percent.[7]

The increase in competitive intensity is being felt in every industry—from health care to education to manufacturing—around the world. Creating a successful operation is not easy. For example, Webvan conceived of an idea to deliver groceries and household supplies to customers from Internet orders. It raised venture capital and set up a massive operations infrastructure for picking, packing, and delivery. Four years later Webvan filed for bankruptcy. In an industry with razor-thin margins, the concept offered the customer benefits that the company could not afford. As a result, Webvan's investors quickly rejected the strategy. Its demise is now a classic tale of OM gone astray. The examples of both Webvan and Arnhold Holdings suggest that organizations need to recognize and understand the emerging challenges in operations.

The linkage between business decisions and operations is not always evident. For example, the quality and reliability of automobiles used to be an important competitive differentiator; today, many automobiles come with warranties as long as 10 years and 100,000 miles. While such decisions are often driven by marketing, the impacts on operations are substantial. For such warranties to be cost-effective, many changes in product design and manufacturing capability must occur. Although the discipline of OM has been around for a long time, and some of the best minds in the world have studied and refined the theories behind design and execution decisions, and practitioners have successfully put the theories to use, OM must still deal with the minute details of operations. (See the *OM Practice* box on Boeing.)

OM PRACTICE

Fastener Problem Brings Boeing to Its Knees
The consequences of ignoring operational details can be devastating.

In 2000, the Boeing Company reported that it had slowed deliveries of all but one of its commercial jet models in order to replace certain substandard fasteners. The fasteners, manufactured from an alloy that makes them prone to cracking, were installed on a wide range of critical components such as wings, engine nacelles, and portions of the fuselage of every jetliner model Boeing builds at its Seattle-area factories.

The problem did not pose an immediate safety threat, and no reports of fastener failures had been received from airlines. Nevertheless, the need to inspect jetliners in use or in production added to manufacturing complications for Boeing. At the same time, about 18,000 engineers and technical workers were on strike at Boeing's operations in the Seattle area over pay and benefit issues. The strike had significantly slowed jetliner deliveries. More 330,000 of the fasteners had been delivered to Boeing by a unit of Cordant Technologies, Inc. The fasteners involve the use of bolts and "collars" that help secure them, and the propensity for cracking has occurred in the collars. Richard Corbin, chief financial officer for Cordant, confirmed that the company had discovered the problem, reported it to all customers that had taken deliveries, and had made an effort to recall and "quarantine" all the suspect parts.[8]

If anything, the importance of OM is increasing, particularly as organizations become increasingly reliant on information technology (IT) and other forms of advanced technology to drive their operations. Throughout the text, we discussed many of the operations issues that affect the decisions of senior managers, from business strategy to the design of supply chains. Many suggest that process knowledge and expertise can be easily imitated, but we strongly disagree. They must be developed internally by managers and workers involved in the processes. This requires a fundamental understanding and continual improvement of OM capabilities. As business becomes more sophisticated and more global, managers in all functional disciplines must deal with the impacts of the challenges that derive from the operations function.

Table 11.3 summarizes the changing focus of OM for each of the topical themes in the previous chapters of the text and provides examples of related initiatives that address these themes. These initiatives cannot be viewed in isolation. For

OM PRINCIPLE

An organization must examine the portfolio of operations' initiatives it has undertaken in the past, is currently working on, and plans to address in the future. In doing so, it must identify synergies across the various projects and eliminate contradictory messages to customers, employees, and other stakeholders.

TABLE 11.3	The Changing Scope of Operations Management	
Topic	**Transition**	**Initiatives**
Scope of OM	From cost-centric to balanced approaches	o Balanced scorecard o Customer-centric definitions of quality—customer intimacy o Time-based competition o Developing responsiveness
Operations strategy	From syntactic to pragmatic	o Sustainability o Renewable advantage o Responding to hypercompetition (agility) o Simultaneously competitive and cooperative
Product design	From unitary to bundled	o Bundling (goods versus services versus contracts) o Speed o Integrative and disciplined o Knowledge management (e.g., guest workers)
Process design	From inside out to outside in	o Customer-centric definition o If it ain't broke, break it (business process reengineering) o Stages of learning, process innovation versus control o Contingency planning (e.g., safety) o Retain emphasis on cost and cycle time benchmarks
Facility design	From plants to clusters	o Global flexibility o Strategy-driven charters o Demise of economies of scale o Modular and flexible layouts
Quality management	From localized to pervasive	o Quality is everyone's job o Quality is a prerequisite for playing the game o Formal and systematic process (MBQNA, Six Sigma, ISO 9000) o Results driven (balance value for customers and other stakeholders)
Supply chain management	From uncoordinated to integrated	o Global supply chain and sourcing o Flexible with innovations in contracting, pricing, and other coordination mechanisms o Data-intensive (CRM, POS data) with ERP backbone o Disintermediation with Internet, vendor-managed inventories
Schedule management (ERP)	From disciplined to flexible	o Continuous improvement and market flexibility o Distributed architecture with open systems interfaces o Centralized information repository and control o Growth in ERP, CRM, and SCM to create market flexibility

continues

| TABLE 11.3 | *The Changing Scope of Operations Management, continued* |
| | | |

Topic	Transition	Initiatives
Lean enterprise	From disciplined to flexible	○ Simultaneous focus on efficiency and flexibility ○ Quality and productivity improvement through "Lean Six Sigma"
Project management	From orthodox to heretical	○ Pursuit of WOW (Tom Peters) ○ Musical cubicles (Dilbert) ○ Web-enabled, real time ○ Use of contractors and temps ○ Workforce diversity issues

example, a project to integrate customer relationship management (CRM) functionality into an ERP system may well be driven by a desire to create greater customer intimacy without incurring the cost associated with an increased sales force. In another case, a Six Sigma quality management initiative might be linked tightly with an alteration in the process design so that there is greater decision making at the point where work is done.

In one large machine tool firm, for instance, implementation of an ERP system required accurate data on inventory levels. To "protect" the integrity of the data, the system was placed in a locked storeroom. Large structures were erected around the storeroom, and the issuance of materials was carefully controlled, costing a lot of money and incurring a significant amount of lost productive time. Two years later, a just-in-time system was implemented, and all the carefully constructed structures and systems were torn down to make inventory more "visible." Meanwhile, wages were frozen as the firm was in dire straits financially. It was very difficult for the workers to understand these changes in such a short period of time. How could they trust the leadership of a firm that threw away millions of dollars and then froze their wages? This unit went out of business three years later. Most of the managers were assimilated into other divisions; most of the operators lost their jobs.

Scope of OM: From Cost-Centric to Balanced Approaches

A major change in OM thinking is a shift from cost-centric to balanced approaches for viewing operations. There are two different ways to think about balancing such issues as cost versus quality. One set of proponents argues that the essential problem of OM is resolving tradeoffs, essentially dealing with the issue that "you cannot have it both ways."[9] Recent thinking suggests that perhaps such tradeoffs are simply excuses; for example, many firms have found that by improving the quality of their product or service, they also reduce the cost.[10] The "balanced scorecard" approach advocates a similar departure from cost-centric metrics that focus on efficiency to a more balanced assessment of the performance of processes.[11] The scorecard includes metrics related to customer satisfaction and delivery time as well as quality.

> **OM PRINCIPLE**
>
> While cost has driven many operations decisions in the past, firms now face such questions as how to simultaneously decrease cost, improve quality, and reduce delivery time, while also making the product or service available when and where the customer needs it. This requires a much more balanced perspective.

One way to resolve these contradictory opinions is to think of the performance of a process in static and dynamic terms. Given current levels of expertise and technology, and current process capabilities, all processes have inherent tradeoffs. The static interpretation suggests that if we do not change the current system, then improvements on one dimension will result in deterioration on others; for example, reducing time to market in new product development will increase costs (for example, overtime costs) or decrease quality (as processes are rushed). This is shown in Figure 11.1a. On the other hand, perhaps reengineering the process, improving organizational expertise, or using better technology will alter the tradeoff curve itself. This dynamic view of operations, illustrated in Figure 11.1b, suggests that simultaneous improvement in the quality of the product and time to market for new product development is entirely possible.

This perspective requires us to think of the process and associated technology in radically different ways. This argument is similar to that made by business process reengineering (see Chapter 4). During the last decade or so, advances in IT and information management capabilities have forced firms to reassess their processes and start with a clean slate. This dynamic view of the relationship between operations metrics has also been referred to as the *cumulative capabilities model*. The cumulative capabilities model argues that over the last four decades, firms have not simply replaced one capability with another, but have accumulated performance capabilities, beginning with cost reduction, then quality, then time, and finally responsiveness.

Three other issues will affect OM practice in the coming decades. All three of them relate to noncost metrics of operations; each of them has seen increased emphasis over the last decade. First, growth in service-oriented business and service components of the product bundle has resulted in heightened emphasis on "customer intimacy." Many firms today are

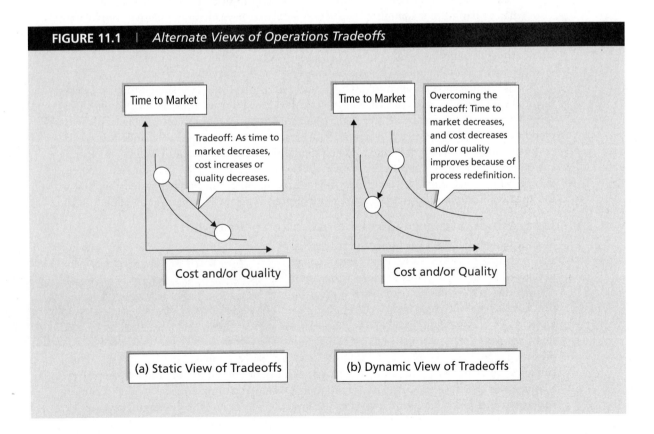

FIGURE 11.1 | *Alternate Views of Operations Tradeoffs*

(a) Static View of Tradeoffs

(b) Dynamic View of Tradeoffs

able to integrate IT effectively into their delivery processes and create high-quality personalized service along with a high level of efficiency. Seven design principles are suggested to accomplish this:[12]

1. Know your customer. Use IT to anticipate customer needs and improve service. The Ritz-Carlton Hotel Company, for example, maintains a database of customer preferences that is available to all employees who interact with customers.
2. Strive for "once-and-done" servicing. Eliminate as many handoffs as possible to complete a transaction. Saks Fifth Avenue has a product locator service that finds out-of-stock products and has them shipped to the customer.
3. Promote value-enhancing self-service. Incorporate customer knowledge into self-service tools. Airline Web sites allow customers to purchase tickets, select seats, confirm flights, and obtain boarding passes.
4. Provide one-stop shopping. Simplify the total service process to create added value. The University of Cincinnati has created a "one-stop" student service center that consolidates registration, financial aid, parking, and so on.
5. Let customers design the product. Offer customers only the services they want and allow them to select those that meet their individual needs. A major bank lets customers select the terms of their loans and home mortgages.
6. Engineer competency into service delivery. Use technology to support service representatives and reduce training needs. USAA call center reps have a wide range of information about products and customers at their fingertips to respond to inquiries and personalize service.
7. Build long-term customer relationships. Develop loyal customers who are willing to pay a premium for a familiar, reliable service. Amazon maintains extensive contact with customers through e-mail with personalized recommendations and incentives.

These principles illustrate some of the OM initiatives that will bring improved customer service through a combination of process redefinition and advanced use of IT.

Second, time-based competition, which emerged in the 1990s as a key customer requirement and source of competitive advantage, continues to be a driving force in consumer decisions. This can only be addressed through sound understanding and improvement of all types of production and business processes. Third, responding to customers' demands for unique products and services will pose increasing challenges. Many products and services today can be customized fairly quickly through initiatives such as mass customization and delayed differentiation. All said and done, the increasing shift from cost- and efficiency-centered thinking in OM toward quality, customer service, time, and responsiveness will be seen across all industries.

Operations Strategy: From Syntactic to Pragmatic

Sustainability is central to defining the strategy of any organization. Not only must the strategy developed be effective in making the organization competitive in the short run, it must also focus on the future. The increased importance given to knowledge management in many organizations stems from the recognition that most artifacts—

> **OM PRINCIPLE**
>
> Knowledge is difficult to copy and/or imitate and is a much more powerful source for creating competitive advantage than processes, technology, systems, and methods.

process, technology, systems, and methods—can be easily copied. For example, if a firm launches a new product with a unique design, despite the protection offered by patent laws, a competitor can "reverse engineer" the product and launch a similar one very quickly. Simply copying such artifacts does not always lead to sustained competitive advantage, however.

Knowledge can be viewed as syntactic, semantic, or pragmatic. **Syntactic knowledge** implies doing the right things, **semantic knowledge** implies recognizing the implications of social interactions and **pragmatic knowledge** implies recognizing all contingencies to deliver the results. Pragmatic knowledge ("street smart" or result orientation) requires that the players intuit what is at stake and work through the political and contested domains effectively to deliver the results. In product development, for instance, syntactic knowledge would imply hiring the right kind of design engineers; semantic knowledge would ensure that they performed well together; and pragmatic knowledge would result in the product development team launching better products more frequently than competitors. To respond to competition in markets such as computers, electronics, and telecommunications, organizations will need more agility in developing and executing strategy and therefore will require a pragmatic perspective. For the operations manager, this might mean sacrificing long-held beliefs about operations, such as the need to maintain control over products and components rather than outsourcing (see the *OM Practice* box on Microsoft's Xbox).

OM PRACTICE

Launching the Xbox

Flextronics has been preaching the benefits of contract manufacturing to consumer electronics companies.

Flextronics operates 80 factories in 28 countries around the world, making cell phones for Ericsson, routers for Cisco, printers for Hewlett-Packard, and PDAs for Palm. On an assembly line in Mexico, workers build the Microsoft Xbox. The company established factories in Guadalajara to take advantage of cheaper labor and relaxed trade between the United States and Mexico. "Microsoft has a ton of money, but if they had to build factories, they wouldn't have done this project," says Flextronics chair and CEO Michael Marks.

The Xbox was a significant change in strategic direction for Microsoft. A company that had never operated a single factory took on the world's leading manufacturer of consumer electronics —Sony. In less than two months, Flextronics set up assembly lines and was able to ship 800,000 units at launch and 700,000 more by the first year's end. To meet those goals, the factory worked continuously 24 hours per day at least a month before the launch date. One tractor-trailer rig full of Xboxes left the facilities every two hours, and one semi full of supplies came in at the same pace.[13]

Another example of pragmatic thinking in operations strategy comes from supply chain transitions in many industries. The growth of strategic alliances between firms in the automotive industry requires them to be simultaneously competitive and cooperative. Large firms that prided themselves on their ability to manage their operations from beginning to end are now systematically dismantling them in order to prosper. Rather than focusing on the scale of operations, they are now focusing on scope—having the right capability. Companies throughout the supply chain are being pulled in two opposing directions: specialization and comprehensiveness. In the auto industry, for example, the big manufacturers have dramatically reduced their base of suppliers. The primary, or "tier one," suppliers are expected to develop more intimate partnerships with the auto companies and meet ever-more-stringent requirements, such as offering a broad range of services for one-stop shopping, while providing high quality at lower cost. To meet these requirements, many suppliers are developing cooperative relationships with competitors while striving to remain focused on their own core competencies.[14]

Market pressures are also forcing small companies to work together in ways that few people could have imagined a decade ago. For example, when a plastics-molding company got a new customer, they felt they were in a bind. They wanted the business but did not have the capabilities to do some of the finishing work that the job would require. They had two choices: tell the customer they can do only half the job and risk losing the business, or work with a competitor to complete the job and possibly risk losing the customer to the competitor. The company opted for the latter, and the two competitors cooperated to produce the part together.[15]

Small firms now routinely share benchmarking information, seek help from one another to achieve better quality and performance, or jointly market their services to customers, even working closely with competitors. This phenomenon occurs not just in manufacturing, but in service businesses such as insurance and retailing as well.

Product Design: From Unitary to Bundled

The "bundling" of products and services is another important trend. This phenomenon is evident in everything from the toys that accompany McDonald's Happy Meals to the next-day, in-home service contracts provided with Dell computers. Conventional goods and services are also being replaced by "offers" or contracts— promises to provide future goods or services for which customers pay a fixed price, usually every

> **OM PRINCIPLE**
>
> The distinction between product and service attributes is increasingly becoming blurred. In other words, both manufacturing and service organizations face the dilemma that customers demand "no product without service" and "no service without product."

month. Such offers include insurance, computer leasing and service, cable television, and DVD rental programs. They extend the time horizon of customer contact, provide a more constant source of revenue, and offer other advantages:

1. **Speed:** Offers usually provide real-time response to customer needs.
2. **Connectivity:** The Internet provides the capability to make offers available online and provide interactivity, allowing the customer to modify delivery attributes in real time, and gives the customer "anyplace" access and response.
3. **Customization:** Offers allow customers to learn, filter, customize, and upgrade their selections on a real-time basis.

Firms that are shifting to offers instead of traditional goods and services face many operational challenges in the form of designing them, providing call center support, and deploying customer service. Their choices on bundling the appropriate benefits for the customer and designing the appropriate delivery platform become more critical. This requires that conventional modes of thinking about operations change. Consider, for example, the shift in health care from fee-for-service to "subscription" pricing with HMOs. Instead of encouraging patients to stay in the hospital for longer periods (which would generate more revenue in a fee-for-service model), HMOs systematically try to minimize the average length of stay and insist on preventive care so that they see as few customers as possible. Since the patient is going to pay a subscription fee anyway, it makes sense to encourage behaviors that minimize the use of resources.

As products become more bundled, the focus shifts from standard and custom designs to "learning-oriented" designs and community building. The best example is perhaps found in software development—most firms in this industry pay a lot of attention to choosing the right platform from the beginning, offering upgradable options periodically, providing learning opportunities for users through sophisticated Web sites, and building communities (for example, the extensive community of programmers built by game developers such as Nintendo, Sega, and Microsoft).

Process Design: From Inside Out to Outside In

The field of industrial engineering (IE) grew rapidly in the twentieth century, drawing upon Taylor's principles of scientific management, and focusing on a simple theme: study the process and make it better. This was also the focus of most business process reengineering (BPR) projects during the 1990s, many of which failed. [16] These traditional approaches left many questions unanswered: Who are the "customers" for improvements? How do improved process designs address customers, rather than simply cost and productivity? Such questions suggest that process design should be driven from the "outside in" to generate stronger competitive advantage.

Such efforts would include positioning BPR more strategically. The availability of new IT has enabled most large organizations to effectively integrate customers, process, and information. The following are five types of organizational transformation enabled by IT:[17]

1. Localized implementation
2. Internal integration
3. Business process redesign (reengineering)
4. Business network redesign
5. Business scope redefinition

Work barriers between functions can be broken down through internal integration—the sharing of data or the use of common databases, the standardization of applications, and the standardization of computer hardware and networks. This increased flow of relevant and useful information between functions leaves activities unchanged but better coordinated and managed. Over time, the increased transparency resulting from internal integration helps the organization identify activities that add no value and new ways of carrying out a particular process—the focus of BPR. Business network redesign is the extension of BPR to the network of relationships that exist among an organization and all the other organizations and individuals who collectively support its processes. [18] For instance, one organization might have competence in logistics management and might perform this function for the whole network. [19] Finally business scope redefinition involves a transformation of an organization's understanding of itself and the way it adds value for its stakeholders. For example, Reuters transformed itself from a wire news service provider into a provider of targeted financial information and analysis. Thus, as firms elevate the strategic role of their BPR efforts toward business scope redefinition, they must shift their process thinking from an "inside out" approach to an "outside in" approach.

OM PRINCIPLE

Questions about the external impacts of the process design are paramount for the future operations manager, and tools and methods for studying the interfaces of process with customers, partners, competitors, communities, and environments are vital for success.

BPR is but one example of a broad range of inter- and intra-organizational changes that include increased democratization of the workplace, employee empowerment, and customer focus. An organization must explore and understand the environment it has created through BPR before embarking on further change.

Facility Design: From Plants to Clusters

The historical example of the textile industry in Prato, Italy, illustrates the changes in facility design.[20] The artisans of the fourteenth century who dyed, spun, and wove textiles created an economic backbone for this region. Over the years, advances in technology allowed the firms to become larger and more vertically integrated, but they were not profitable. The markets wanted increasing variety, but the firms' facilities had become an impediment. Meanwhile, new dyeing and finishing techniques had emerged, and new technology had made smaller-scale weaving and spinning affordable. Some mill owners decided to split up their facilities and emphasize small-scale, flexible manufacturing networks. One by one, they succeeded until by 1980, all but one of the Prato mills had undergone similar disintegration, turning a sluggish, threatened industry into a thriving community of innovative, flexible companies, each a world class competitor.

The modern-day *impannatori* are the key to the success of the Prato system; as in the Middle Ages, these agents provide central brokerage for the firms in the network. About 20,000 firms employing some 70,000 people use several hundred such brokers. The brokers' thorough knowledge of the capacity, capability, and loading of each of the producers enables them to source production for customers, find customers for spare production capacity, and serve as intermediaries in the negotiations. Effective management of this complex information set, trustworthiness, and honesty are the hallmarks of the successful *impannatori*.

Small-scale facilities have also succeeded in other industries. In the steel industry, for instance, small scale drives innovation and market responsiveness as demonstrated by the mini-mills that have moved into more profitable market niches. Small beer producers (micro-breweries and pub-breweries) discovered that a subset of consumers like nonstandard, often nonpasteurized beers and make their choice of beer a personal statement. Specialized equipment producers such as Micropub Systems developed equipment to profitably serve this market. Recent developments in the airline industry challenge scale-driven operations with a point-to-point air taxi service. For short-haul business travel, employees waste enormous amounts of time trav-

> ## OM PRINCIPLE
>
> In many industries, scale economies restrict opportunities for innovation, responsiveness to customers, employee development, and sensitivity to industry and environmental changes.

eling to and from airports. As a result of delays and limited connections, they often arrive late or have to leave prematurely to get to their destinations on time.[21] The logic of air taxi services is simple: commercial air travel uses only 3.5 percent of the 5,736 public airfields in the United States and Canada. While only 22 percent of the U.S. population live within 30 minutes of a major hub airport, 93 percent live 30 minutes from a public airfield that can be utilized for point-to-point air taxi service.

With smaller facilities, as is common in the service sector, comes the challenge of developing and coordinating the cluster of facilities that emerges to meet customer demand for products and services. Such clusters commonly develop facility charters that define the role of specific facilities in a global network of plants.[22] Multinational firms with globally dispersed operations face immense challenges in rationalizing the plant charters for their facilities as well as coordinating the distribution of goods and services globally, particularly with highly uncertain financial markets and exchange rates. For example, some firms set up distribution centers in emerging markets and gradually move processes to these centers to provide increasing levels of service to local customers. Many of these decisions are based on short-term incremental and opportunistic thinking, however, rather than being made from a strategic planning perspective. Strategy-driven charters that provide a systematic rationalization of the role of every facility in the cluster can deliver great benefits to the organization.[23]

The principal strategic reasons for selecting a particular facility location are access to low-cost inputs, use of local technology, or proximity to markets.[24] A plant that may have originally been located close to customer markets may, over time, invest in technical knowledge, build a more sophisticated supplier base, or develop special technical adaptations that may deliver value on a global scale; thus, its original role may change, and a new location may be more appropriate.[25] By investigating the charters of the facilities in its cluster, an organization can reposition facilities, increase the transfer of knowledge, and develop a cohesive strategy for the entire cluster. This clarification of roles also makes it possible to assess the performance of the managers of these facilities more appropriately: for example, an offshore plant in the Maquiladora region in Mexico will not be unnecessarily burdened with issues related to product development and/or customer responsiveness; its agenda in the grand scheme of things is focused on low cost delivery.[26]

One advantage of optimizing a system of plants is that individual plants can specialize.[27] To derive the benefits of specialization, plants must be managed to integrate material flows, management skills, product/process developments, or other knowledge among plants. Plants then develop roles and have distinct management systems in place to transfer the benefits of the specialization back to the other plants in the network.

Developing global flexibility in clusters of facilities spread throughout the world will remain the most imposing challenge for operations managers. Even when they resolve the strategic inconsistencies they inherit from piecemeal decisions about where and when to set up facilities, they still have to manage the global coordination of people, processes, and information and material flows.

Quality Management: From Localized to Pervasive

Many of the emerging initiatives in quality management focus on making quality improvement an organization-wide initiative in which every employee participates. Several alternatives for focusing an organization around a quality theme exist. The Malcolm Baldrige National Quality Program Criteria for Performance Excellence (see Chapter 6) is generally recognized as the standard for high-quality practice. Similarly, the ISO 9000 standards are used throughout the world as a framework for establishing a quality system. The Six Sigma process, which we also briefly discussed in Chapter 6, has gained considerable momentum among many organizations (see the *OM Practice* box). Six Sigma's focus on measurable bottom line results, a disciplined statistical approach to problem solving, rapid project completion, and organizational infrastructure make it a powerful methodology for improvement.

> **OM PRINCIPLE**
>
> Quality is a necessary prerequisite for competing in today's competitive environment. Most organizations will continue to develop and implement formal processes for ensuring quality in their goods and services as well as in their management practices.

In many ways, Six Sigma is the realization of many fundamental concepts of "total quality management" (TQM), notably, the integration of human and process elements of improvement.[28] Human issues include management leadership, a sense of urgency, focus on results and customers, team processes, and culture change; process issues include the use of process management techniques, analysis of variation and statistical methods, a disciplined problem-solving approach, and management of fact. Nonetheless, Six Sigma is more than simply a repackaging of older quality approaches, such as traditional TQM. They differ in several ways including the following:

○ TQM is based largely on worker empowerment and teams; Six Sigma is owned by business leader champions.

○ TQM activities generally occur within a function, process, or individual workplace; Six Sigma projects are truly cross-functional.

○ TQM training is generally limited to simple improvement tools and concepts; Six Sigma focuses on a more rigorous and advanced set of statistical and other tools.

○ TQM is focused on improvement with little financial accountability; Six Sigma requires a verifiable return on investment.

Six Sigma has become an important factor in strategic planning and strategy deployment. For example, Motorola's "second generation" Six Sigma is an overall high-performance

OM PRACTICE

GE's Six Sigma Journey
Six Sigma transforms General Electric.

At GE's annual operating manager meeting in January 1998, 25 business leaders from around the globe excitedly described how Six Sigma was transforming the way their businesses worked. They shared what they had learned from projects such as streamlining the back room of a credit card operation, or improving turnaround time in a jet engine overhaul shop, or "hit-rate" improvements in commercial financial transactions. Most of the presenters focused on how their process improvements were making their customers more competitive and productive.

○ GE's Medical Systems division described how Six Sigma designs produced a tenfold increase in the life of CT scanner X-ray tubes, increasing the "uptime" of these machines and the profitability and level of patient care given by hospitals and other health-care providers.

○ Superabrasives, GE's industrial diamond business, described how Six Sigma quadrupled its return on investment and gave it a full decade's worth of capacity despite growing volume—without spending a nickel on plant and equipment capacity.

○ The railcar leasing business described how it reduced turnaround time by 62 percent at its repair shops, making it three times faster than its nearest rival. Black Belts and Green Belts (employees specially trained in statistics and quality improvement methods) worked with their teams to redesign the overhaul process, resulting in a 50 percent further reduction in cycle time.

○ The plastics business, through rigorous Six Sigma process work, added 300 million pounds of new capacity (equivalent to a "free plant"), saved $400 million in investment, and had plans to save another $400 million). "Six Sigma, even at this relatively early stage, delivered more than $300 million to our 1997 operating income," said the report.

Six Sigma training has become a prerequisite for promotion to any professional or managerial position at GE—and a requirement for any award of stock options. Six Sigma has permeated every GE business, energizing and exciting its employees and moving the company closer to its goal: to become a "global enterprise with the agility, customer focus, and fire in the belly of a small company."[29]

system that executes business strategy.[30] Its results are evident in Motorola's Commercial, Government, and Industrial Solutions Sector division, which received a Baldrige Award in 2002. Motorola's new approach to Six Sigma is based on the following four steps:

1. *Align executives with the right objectives and targets.* This means creating a balanced scorecard of strategic goals, metrics, and initiatives to identify the improvements that will have the most impact on the bottom line. Projects are not limited to traditional product and service domains but extend to market share improvements, better cash flow, and improved human resource processes.

2. *Mobilize improvement teams around appropriate metrics.* Teams use a structured problem-solving process to drive fact-based decisions; however, the focus on defects and dpmo (defects per million opportunities) sigma levels is less important, particularly in human-intensive processes such as marketing and human resources. For example, the definition of a defect as "employee performance that falls below a certain level" can be controversial and easily manipulated. Continuous measures such as invoice delivery time or credit approval response time are replacing count-based measures such as the number of overdue invoices or the percentage of dissatisfied customers.

3. *Accelerate results.* Motorola uses an action learning framework methodology that combines formal education with real-time project work and coaching to quickly take employees from learning to doing. Project teams receive support from coaches on a just-in-time basis. Projects are driven to be accomplished quickly, rather than over a long period of time. Finally, a campaign management approach helps integrate various project teams so that the cumulative impact on the organization is, in fact, accelerated.

4. *Govern sustained improvement.* Leaders actively and visibly sponsor the key improvement projects required to execute business strategy and review them in the context of outcome goals. An important step is for leaders to actively share best practices and knowledge about improvements with other parts of the organization that can benefit.

Six Sigma continues to be Motorola's tool of choice for driving bottom line improvements. More efforts will be focused on product design that enhances the overall customer experience across the value chain. As such, Six Sigma projects increasingly involve key customers, suppliers, and other business partners.

Supply Chain Management: From Uncoordinated to Integrated

Integration of supply chain activities to deliver value to the customer remains the most important and lucrative challenge for operations managers. The last decade saw the development of many new mechanisms to coordinate activities between buyers and suppliers of industrial and consumer products and services. These developments, along with the growth in global supply chain and sourcing, have allowed many organizations to deliver value to the customer through better integration of their activities with those of their suppliers and their distributors. The following are examples of these coordination mechanisms, some of which were discussed in Chapter 7:

> **OM PRINCIPLE**
>
> Innovations in contracting, pricing, and other coordination mechanisms such as Internet-based exchanges will continue to add flexibility to the process of conducting transactions in the supply chain.

- Reverse auctions.

- Vendor-managed inventory.

- Just-in-time distribution (JITD), in which organizations decide and allocate orders to distributors, as opposed to distributors deciding how much and when to order.

- Contract price protection and buyback policies, in which manufacturers reduce risks for retailers and distributors.

- Discount pricing for early orders, in which manufacturers gives discounts to retailers.

- JIT II programs, in which a supplier's employee is provided an office at the customer's facility to assess the customer's needs, perform procedural tasks associated with purchasing and delivery, and ensure customer satisfaction.

Information technology will continue to refine supply chain management (see the *OM Practice* box on Internet auctions). Most organizations have a well-established ERP backbone; harnessing the power of the data available to ERP systems for effective supply chain management will be a key focus in the future. For example, CRM systems will allow assessment of customer segments through data mining or cookies that track Internet orders. These data can be related to such ERP information as specific transactions, order sizes, profitability levels, quality requirements, and credit and financing data. Together, these applications provide synergy in answering such questions as: Which segments are more profitable? What goods or services bundle best in a given market segment? How much and what kind of advertising should we use?

Schedule Management: From Disciplined to Flexible

Information technology is a complex, dynamic managerial asset, but incorporating IT with the "physical" world of operations will continue to be a challenging task. Consider the dilemma faced by retail organizations that sell goods through traditional retail outlets as well

OM PRACTICE

Internet Auctions in the Auto Industry
Suppliers and automakers benefit from Internet auctions.

When the Big Three automakers announced that they had joined forces to form a single online marketplace, parts suppliers were glad that they would no longer have to manage relationships with each manufacturer, but they worried that the centralized system might force them to cut their prices and reduce profits.

Earlier, when General Motors and Ford Motor Company announced plans to set up rival Internet exchanges for their suppliers, parts makers were wary. They feared that these online auctions would increase costs, not cut them, as the automakers insisted would happen. GM was also leaning on suppliers to move all their business to the GM site, a difficult proposition for the numerous companies that supply both automakers.

The agreement by GM, Ford, and DaimlerChrysler AG to create a single Internet marketplace appeared likely to benefit the largest suppliers and help them become more efficient. Auto executives insisted that there would be plenty of offsetting benefits for suppliers, including deeper discounts for the parts and supplies they buy and huge savings from reduced inventories because the system would give them instant access to production plans down the supply chain. They also assured suppliers that the system would be fully confidential. So far the automakers seem to be benefiting. A recent auction on GM's site, for example, saw price reductions of 10 percent for tires and 40 percent for rubber hoses.[31]

---

as the Internet. The task of planning inventories, developing shipment schedules, and conforming to customers' expectations is much more complex in this environment. Those that do it well (for example, FedEx) can achieve a powerful operations-based competitive advantage. At the same time many, such as Webvan, have failed. Nonetheless, the possibility of combining IT with operations expertise to build businesses that have never existed before or to revolutionize existing businesses presents a huge opportunity.

Many organizations have implemented sophisticated ERP systems to match the process and information flows associated with all the transactions of the organization. As they have done so, they have created more consistent operations and processes. For example, returned merchandise is handled exactly the same way by every warehouse of Amazon.com. Roger Schmenner of Indiana University cites an interesting paradox that governs organizational thinking when it comes to ERP implementation: The planning and scheduling discipline created by ERP systems is exactly what allows them to respond more flexibly to varying market conditions. ERP is a tool that allows organizations to move from chaos to control, from disorder to discipline; control and discipline are prerequisites to continuous improvement.

This principle is illustrated in Figure 11.2. ERP systems create a controlled and disciplined environment, which is a prerequisite to continuous improvement. Improvement is either not sustained or is mistargeted in chaotic environments. Since basic rules that govern processes and transactions are unclear in chaotic environments, it is hard to tell whether an improvement idea is

OM PRINCIPLE

ERP provides the means to supply vital information to managers so that they can make informed decisions and guide improvement tasks in the right direction.

aimed in the right direction or whether the organization will be able to sustain it. Consider a firm that believes that customers and product development engineers impose an excessive amount of engineering change orders on the process, making it inefficient and wasteful. (Engineering change orders make the inventory associated with old designs obsolete and disrupt the production schedule.) Without a good information system, such as ERP, that allows the firm to assess the "real" cost of a change order, any action by managers is suspect. If they reduce the number of change orders released to operations, they don't know whether they

FIGURE 11.2 | *The 3C Model for ERP Implementation*

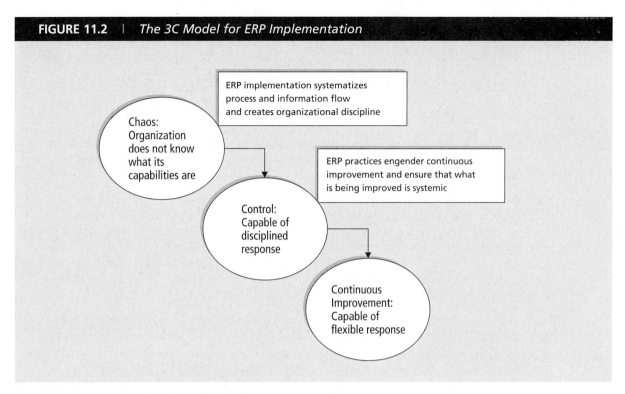

have improved the system (through cost reduction) or made it worse (the product is not innovative or does not meet customer's needs).

Using ERP effectively means that firms will engage in new activities to customize specific deliverables from the ERP system to their advantage. For a consumer products firm, for instance, this might mean developing middleware that allows it to use point of sale (POS) data effectively to guide manufacturing schedules.

Project Management: From Orthodox to Heretical

Conventional project management has been centered on getting the task done to the customer's specification within time and budget constraints. It typically uses a linear model of process flow (as in critical path thinking from the 1950s) and assumes that the project's success is derived primarily from customer satisfaction and a monetary return to the organization. It develops process heuristics that are simple, but not always effective; for example, if a project is behind schedule, add more resources to it.

Heretical thinking in project management builds on these orthodox themes and adapts them to contemporary challenges. The classic Dilbert cartoons are the best examples of heretical thinking in project management. In creating a caricature of the "musical cubicles" game created by projects in many engineering firms, Scott Adams questions many of the traditionally held beliefs in project management. Similarly, on the one hand, the work of Tom Peters puts project management on a pedestal and argues about its pervasive influence in organizations; on the other, it advocates more ad hoc thinking in finding project management solutions. Some of the issues raised about the role of the project manager include:

○ **Activities versus Achievements:** Activities are the means to an end; achievements are the desired end results. Project managers who can drive projects from an achievement perspective instead of an activity perspective have some notable advantages.

○ **Avoiding the Activity Trap:** Instead of thinking strategically to define the measurable results the project should achieve, the project manager and sponsor often focus on the unimportant bells and whistles of the project's tasks. The project manager must ask tough questions of the project sponsor and stakeholders: How will you measure success at the end of this project? What do you really want to buy for all this money we're going to spend? Getting answers to these questions forces the kind of conceptual thinking required at the front end of a project and avoids the activity trap.

○ **Communication First, Then Collaboration and Coordination:** While all three are important to project management, communication (upward, lateral, downward) is more important than anything else.

○ **Focus on Uncertainties:** Project management must reconcile two conflicting aspects of projects—the increasingly important need for speed and the equally important need for reliability in delivering the project as promised. Project management must deal with uncertainty in an attempt to deliver project outcomes with certainty. One way of thinking about how to deal with this conflict is to develop strategies to avoid increasing project lead-time while protecting against Murphy's Law. The way we manage for uncertainty in projects is at the core of improvement in project performance.

The transition from linear models (for instance, the "waterfall model" discussed in Chapter 9) to alternate project life cycle paradigms, such as the overlap, spiral, and V-models, represents emerging thinking in project management. Large reductions in cycle time can be realized by applying "concurrent engineering."[32] Successfully implementing concurrent engineering has proved difficult for many organizations, however. Some implementation failures and challenges have been linked to the increased coordination required among development team members by the overlapping of activities.[33] In another case, applying concurrent engineering actually increased cycle times because of unsuccessful cross-functional teams, the primary coordinating structure in this approach.[34] Alternatives such as the critical chain method are already being deployed at firms such as Procter & Gamble for managing new product development projects.[35] Similarly many process heuristics are being re-evaluated in software development projects.

> **OM PRINCIPLE**
>
> If projects are to be a key source of innovation in organizations, then the linear thinking embedded in the critical path method (CPM) and all software packages derived from this building block will need to be revisited.

Many project management software packages today are Web-enabled, and provide real-time data to project managers for effective control of people, time, and cost. They also allow for easier and more effective communication. Finally, the use of contractors and temporary workers from across the globe on projects and issues related to managing diversity on a project team will also pose important challenges for project managers in the future.

11.4 OPERATIONS MANAGEMENT IN A DYNAMIC WORLD

When he coined the term *scientific management* in the 1900s, Frederick W. Taylor started the field of industrial engineering, from which emerged operations management.[36] Over the years many new tools, methods, techniques, and paradigms for managing operations for competitive advantage have emerged. The assumptions, models, and thought patterns of "Taylorism," which were influential in the successful development of American mass production, persist to this day. One assumption was that there is "one best way" to undertake each task, regardless of its human and social aspects. We have come a long way from that mode of thinking. Taylor's assumptions were based on the beliefs that the environment, the goals, the process, and the technology are known, and that managers think of new methods and workers implement them.

The assumption that the world is complex, but fully specified, creates many problems in an era when change is the only constant phenomenon. The days when operations managers would select rigid procedures for workers, then monitor the process to ensure their compliance, are over. This static view of OM undervalues the key contributions made by the people who perform the tasks. In quality management and process change, the most important and difficult task of the operations manager is to involve people who will make choices that benefit the organization in the long run. Ultimately, this is the most challenging aspect of OM.

In the emerging view of OM, three elements are critical for effectively analyzing dynamic situations:[37]

1. **Knowledge and Learning:** Knowledge is an explicit input to every process, and knowledge of the best ways to produce or serve is always incomplete. Relevant knowledge includes how processes should be done, the sources and types of common problems, and how those problems should be resolved. In the future, firms that manage, exploit, and augment their knowledge base across the organization will have a significant competitive advantage over other firms. Since knowledge is always incomplete, organizational learning and preservation of knowledge assume great importance in factories, service outlets, and all units within an organization where work gets done. Some have argued that all factories (workplaces) in an organization are best viewed as learning laboratories designed and operated to enhance the rate of learning.

2. **Contingencies:** Contingencies (also known as problems) arise due to gaps in knowledge; typically, they happen when a realized event does not match an anticipated event. Contingencies must be considered explicitly during the design of processes and operating methods. The Avis program for car rentals is a good lesson in planning for contingencies—by anticipating every possible action by the customer, Avis has designed a fail-safe process. Avis analyzed more than 130 possible actions by the customer during the rental process and then designed the process for every possible state the business transaction could "accidentally" fall into.

3. **Problem Solving:** Every operations manager must identify unfavorable contingencies and solve them on an ongoing basis. Using the "problem instances" as learning experiences is the most valuable OM principle in the entire text. If a problem is neglected or performed on an ad hoc basis, no real learning results for the organization. This will significantly diminish the organization's performance over the short run and the long run.

These factors lead to our final principle:

OM PRINCIPLE

The success of the operations manager in the future will be defined by his or her competencies as reflected by knowledge and learning, contingencies, and problem solving. The most important principle for the operations manager is to use process "problems" to an advantage—solve them in the short term to please the customer and retain the learning about the contingency within the organization in the long run.

Questions for Review and Discussion

1. Discuss the role of metrics in each focus area of OM. How does a focus on metrics provide guidance for operations managers in making critical business decisions?

2. Summarize the impacts of the following aspects of the changing business and societal landscape on OM: aging population, sustainability of life, renewable energy sources, and growth in Internet usage. How might they affect each OM focus area?

3. Scan recent issues of business periodicals (*Fortune*, *BusinessWeek*, and the like) to find examples that address each of the challenges discussed here. Write three brief essays about examples similar to the *OM Practice* boxes in the text.

4. Interview one or two operations managers in a local company for their perspectives on how the profession is changing and the challenges they face now and expect to face in the future.

Internet Projects

To find Web links to carry out each of the following projects, go to the text's Web site at **http://raturi_evans.swlearning.com.**

1. A best manufacturing practices survey at the Department of Navy Web site documents a number of facilities that have benchmarked themselves for effective practices in operations. Download one of the reports and summarize the best practices outlined in the report.

2. In the course of an average business day, managers face a steady stream of problems. Taking them on one by one is often described as "fire fighting" or "crisis management." In 1999–2000, various study committees and development teams at the Center for Quality Management undertook to develop new methods, or to adapt existing methods, to address four sources of business complexity (see Figure 10.3). They developed four methods—the Enterprise Model, the SCORE process, the ARMED process, and the Four Gears. Each method addressed two of the sources of complexity. Review the articles from the Spring 2002 (Volume 11, number 1) issue of the Center for Quality Management online magazine and summarize your key findings about making organizational change.

3. Out-of-the-box thinking requires that organizations preparing for the future pay greater attention to knowledge management: building and harnessing the knowledge power of their employees. Review an article or a discussion thread at the Web link provided and draw five key conclusions about how operations managers can prepare their organizations for more effective knowledge management in the future.

4. Visit the operations management page at "The Manager" Web site and list five additional emerging issues in OM that were not discussed here.

End Notes

Chapter 1

1. John E. Ettlie, "BMW: Believing the Banner," *Automotive Manufacturing and Production,* April 2001, 38.

2. Fred Vogelstein, "Mighty Amazon," *Fortune,* May 26, 2003, 60–74.

3. David Woodruff, "Porsche Is Back—and Then Some," *BusinessWeek,* September 15, 1997, 57.

4. Steven Goldman, Roger Nagel, and Kenneth Preiss, *Agile Competitors and Virtual Organization* (New York: Van Nostrand Rheinhold, 1995), 61.

5. Alex Taylor III, "Crunch Time for Jac," *Fortune,* June 25, 2001, 34–36.

6. "Can the Nordstroms Find the Right Style?" *BusinessWeek,* July 30, 2001.

7. Philip Siekman, "The Big Myth about U.S. Manufacturing," *Fortune,* October 2, 2000, 244[C]–244[E].

8. Stewart Deck, "Fine Line," *CIO,* February 1, 2000. http://www.cio.com/archive/020100/dell.html.

9. Sandra Vandermerwe, *From Tin Soldiers to Russian Dolls: Creating Added Value through Services* (Oxford: Butterworth-Heinemann, 1993), 68–69.

10. Ronald Henkoff, "Service Is Everybody's Business," *Fortune,* June 27, 1994, 48–60.

11. This example is from Stan Davis and Christopher Meyer, *Blur: The Speed of Change in the Connected Economy* (Boulder, CO: Perseus Books, 1998).

12. Michael Porter, *Competitive Advantage: Creating and Sustaining Superior Performance* (New York: The Free Press, 1998).

13. Deck, "Fine Line."

14. Ravi Venkatesan, "Strategic Sourcing: To Make or Not Make," *Harvard Business Review,* November–December 1992, 98–107.

15. B. P. Shapiro, "Staple Yourself to an Order," *Harvard Business Review,* 70, no. 4, July–August 1992, 113.

16. Justin Martin, "Ignore Your Customer," *Fortune,* May 1, 1995, 121.

17. Ram Ganeshan and Terry P. Harrison, "An Introduction to Supply Chain Management" (Department of Management Science and Information Systems, Penn State University, May 22, 1995, working paper).

18. Marshall Fisher, "What Is the Right Supply Chain for Your Product?" *Harvard Business Review,* March–April 1997, 105–116.

19. George Johnson, "Dear APICS," *Production and Inventory Management Review,* 6, no. 5 (May 1986), 10, 16.

20. Alex Taylor III, "It Worked for Toyota: Can It Work for Toys?" *Fortune,* November 1, 1999, 1, 36.

21. B. Shapiro, "Can Marketing and Manufacturing Coexist?" *Harvard Business Review,* 55 (1997), 104–114.

22. Robert S. Kaplan and David P. Norton, "Using the Balanced Scorecard as a Strategic Management System," *Harvard Business Review,* January–February 1996, 75–85.

23. Funda Sahin, "Manufacturing Competitiveness: Different Systems to Achieve the Same Results," *Production and Inventory Management Journal,* First Quarter 2000, 56–65.

24. Charles H. Fine, Richard St. Clair, John C. Lafrance, and Don Hillebrand, "The U.S. Automobile Manufacturing Industry," U.S. Department of Commerce, Office of Technology Policy, December 1996.

25. "The Nation's CEOs Look to the Future," U.S. Department of Commerce Study No. 818407, July 1998.

26. American Society for Quality, "Foresight 2020: The American Society for Quality Considers the Future," undated report.

27. Scott D. Upham, "Crystal Ball 2010: Shapes of Things to Come," *Automotive Manufacturing and Production,* September 2000, 18–19.

28. Robert J. Heibeler. "Benchmarking Knowledge Management," Strategy and Leadership 24, no. 2 (March–April 1996), as cited in Verna Allee, *The Knowledge Evolution: Expanding Organizational Intelligence* (Boston: Butterworth-Heinemann, 1997), 8.

29. Carla O'Dell and C. Jackson Grayson, "Identifying and Transferring Internal Best Practices," APQC White Paper, 2000. http://www.apqc.org/free/whitepapers/cmifwp/index.htm.

30. Mohamed Zairi and John Whymark, "The Transfer of Best Practices: How to Build a Culture of Benchmarking and Continuous Learning—Part 1," *Benchmarking: An International Journal*, 7, no. 1 (2000), 62–78.

Chapter 2

1. James Brian Quinn, *Strategies for Change: Logical Incrementalism* (Homewood, IL: Richard D. Irwin, 1980).

2. Adapted from Katrina Brooker, "The Nightmare before Christmas," *Fortune*, January 24, 2000, 24–25.

3. Robert Hof, Debra Sparks, Ellen Neuborne, and Wendy Zellner, "Can Amazon Make It?" *BusinessWeek*, July 10, 2000, 38–43.

4. A. Blanton Godfrey, "Planned Failures," *Quality Digest,* March 2000, 16.

5. G. Hamel and C. K. Prahalad, "Strategy as Stretch and Leverage," *Harvard Business Review*, March–April 1993, 75–84.

6. Funda Sahin, "Manufacturing Competitiveness: Different Systems to Achieve the Same Results," *Production and Inventory Management Journal*, First Quarter 2000, 56–65.

7. Detailed information about Shouldice Hospital can be found at http://www.shouldice.com/harvard.htm.

8. Wickham Skinner, "Manufacturing—Missing Link in Corporate Strategy," *Harvard Business Review,* May–June 1969, 136–145; and "The Focused Factory," *Harvard Business Review,* May–June 1974, 113–121.

9. The concept of a continuous production process was the essential feature of the conveyor belts and chutes that Oliver Evans installed in 1784 in his Delaware flourmill. In 1913 Henry Ford used a moving assembly line for manufacturing magnetos, cutting down assembly time from 18 to 5 minutes. By the early twentieth century, the assembly line had become the symbol of modern mass production methods. Henry Ford's logic in designing a more efficient system for production was not based just on the economic incentives of low-cost production. Dealing with immigrants from different countries, Ford designed a system that allowed for uninterrupted production without significant investment in training or a need for communication. Although the assembly line created more wealth than any other singular concept in the twentieth century and Henry Ford was named "Businessman of the Century" by *Fortune* magazine, its attractiveness is diminishing. In 1973, a Department of Health study of the relationship between work and health cited the negative effects of the "dehumanizing" assembly line including alcoholism and drug addiction, high absenteeism, and low productivity. Most firms operating assembly lines today seek to compensate for these effects by providing greater task autonomy and increasing the use of worker teams.

10. Richard B. Chase, "Where Does the Customer Fit in a Service Operation?" *Harvard Business Review*, November–December 1978, 137–142.

11. This becomes a little tricky since the customer's presence itself, such as staying in a hotel room, may not demand any transactions. The modifications suggested to this measure include measuring active contact time, measuring time when value is added, or differentiating the different types of contact (a letter mailed to the customer versus the customer's physical presence in the system). The implications for operations, indeed, vary depending on the interpretation given to the word *contact*.

12. John E. Ettlie, "What the Auto Industry Can Learn from McDonald's," *Automotive Manufacturing and Production,* October 1999, 42; David Stires, "Fallen Arches," *Fortune,* April 29, 2002, 74–76.

13. John Haywood-Farmer, "A Conceptual Model of Service Quality," *International Journal of Operations and Production Management,* 8, no. 6 (1988), 19–29.

14. Roy Wood, "Delta to Add More Kiosks for Check-in," *The Cincinnati Post,* April 4, 2002; Don Baker, "Delta to Rely More on Self-Service Kiosks," *The Cincinnati Post*, February 6, 2003; Lisa Biank Fasig, "Techno Advances Move to Retailers' Selling Floors: Systems Range from Self-Checkouts to Bridal-Registry Orders," *The Cincinnati Enquirer,* July 2, 2000.

15. Marcos Barbalho, Scott Dunn, and Vince Colabello, "The Globalization of Logistics," *Manufacturing Systems,* 16, no. 2 (February 1998), 132–141.

16. "Strategic Planning: What Works . . . And What Doesn't," APQC White Paper. http://www.apqc.org.

17. Bob King, *Hoshin Planning: The Developmental Approach* (Methuen, MA: GOAL/QPC, 1989).

18. The Ernst & Young Quality Improvement Consulting Group, *Total Quality: An Executive's Guide for the 1990s* (Homewood, IL: Dow Jones–Irwin, 1990).

19. Based on Solectron Malcolm Baldrige National Quality Award Application Summary, 1997.

20. Henry Mintzberg, James B. Quinn, and John Voyer, *The Strategy Process* (Upper Saddle River, NJ: Prentice Hall, 1995), 15–17.

21. National Institute of Standards and Technology, 2000 Baldrige National Quality Program Award Winner Profile.

22. Based on W. Briner, M. Geddes, and C. Hastings, *Project Leadership* (Hamshire, UK: Gower Publishing, 1996).

23. Skinner, "Manufacturing—Missing Link in Corporate Strategy."

24. Jerry Useem, "Boeing versus Boeing," *Fortune*, October 2, 2000, 148–160.

25. See the discussion of time in fast-speed industries in Charles H. Fine, *Clockspeed* (Reading, MA: Perseus Books, 1998).

26. Robert M. Grant, R. Krishnan, Abraham B. Shani, and Ron Baer, "Appropriate Manufacturing Technology: A Strategic Approach," *Sloan Management Review* 33, no. 1 (Fall 1991), 43–54.

27. David Upton, "The Management of Manufacturing Flexibility," *California Management Review*, 36, no. 2, Winter 1994, and "What Really Makes Factories Flexible?" *Harvard Business Review*, July–August 1995, 74–84.

28. Thomas A. Stewart, "Brace for Japan's Hot New Strategy," *Fortune*, September 21, 1992, 62–73.

Chapter 3

1. Steven Wheelwright and Kim Clark, *Revolutionizing Product Development* (New York: The Free Press, 1992), 28–29.

2. Michael Treacy and Fred Wiersema, "The Discipline of Product Leaders," in *The Discipline of Market Leaders* (Reading, MA: Addison Wesley, 1995), 83–96.

3. Preston G. Smith and Donald G. Reinertsen, *Developing Products in Half the Time: New Rules, New Tools* (New York: John Wiley & Sons, 1998). An interesting application of this concept is found in Morris A. Cohen and Teck Ho, "Ingersoll-Rand: New Product Development Process and Strategy" (University of Pennsylvania and University of California, Los Angeles, working paper, 1996).

4. W. G. Downey, "Developing Cost Estimating," Report of the Steering Group for the Ministry of Aviation, HMSO, 1969.

5. J. Corbett, "Design for Economics Manufacture," *Annals of C.I.R.P.*, 35 (1986), 93.

6. J. P. Womack, Daniel T. Jones, and Daniel Ross, *The Machine That Changed the World: The Story of Lean Production* (New York: HarperCollins, 1990).

7. Faith Keenan, "Opening the Spigot," *BusinessWeek* e.biz, June 4, 2001, EB17–20.

8. Joanne Muller and Katie Kerwin, "Cruising for Quality," *BusinessWeek*, September 3, 2001, 74–76.

9. Kevin Hendricks and Vinod Singha, "Delays in New Product Introductions and the Market Value of the Firm: The Consequences of Being Late to the Market," *Management Science* 43, no. 4 (April 1997), 422–436.

10. Morris A. Cohen and Tech H. Ho, "A Teaching Note on Tradeoff Analysis and Portfolio Management in New Product Development" (University of Pennsylvania and University of California, Los Angeles, January 1995).

11. C.F. von Braun, "The Acceleration Trap" and "The Acceleration Trap in the Real World," *Sloan Management Review*, Fall 1990, 49–58, and Summer 1991, 43–52.

12. Richard A. D'Aveni and Robert Gunther, *Hypercompetition: Managing the Dynamics of Strategic Maneuvering* (New York: The Free Press, 1994).

13. Muller and Kerwin, "Cruising for Quality."

14. Ames Rubber Corporation, Application Summary for the 1993 Malcolm Baldrige National Quality Award.

15. Peter J. Kolesar, "What Deming Told the Japanese in 1950," *Quality Management Journal*, 2, no. 1 (Fall 1994), 9–24.

16. Justin Martin, "Ignore Your Customer," *Fortune*, May 1, 1995, 121–126.

17. Jennifer Reese, "Starbucks: Inside the Coffee Cult," *Fortune*, December 9, 1996, 190–200.

18. Alan Vonderhaar, "Audi's TT Coupe's Ever So Close," *Cincinnati Enquirer*, November 27, 1999, F1.

19. Robert A. Green, "BMW Drives Safety with Quality," *Quality Digest*, August 2001, 26–29.

20. Wolfgang Schneider, "Test Drive into the Future," *BMW Magazine*, 2 (1997), 74–77.

21. Vincent G. Reuter, "What Good Are Value Analysis Programs?" *Business Horizons*, 29 (March–April 1986), 73–79.

22. John Haywood-Farmer, "A Conceptual Model of Service Quality," *International Journal of Operations and Production Management*, 8, no. 6 (1988), 19–29.

23. Sarah Anne Wright, "Putting Fast-Food to the Test," *Cincinnati Enquirer*, July 9, 2000, F1.

24. Adapted from Douglas Daetz, "The Effect of Product Design on Product Quality and Product Cost," *Quality Progress*, June 1987, 63–67.

25. Brian Dumaine, "Payoff from the New Management," *Fortune*, December 13, 1993, 103–110.

26. Peter Dewhurst, "Product Design for Manufacture: Design for Disassembly," *Industrial Engineering*, September 1993, 26–28.

27. David Pescovitz "Dumping Old Computers—Please Dispose of Properly," *Scientific American*, 282, no. 2 (February 2000), 29. http://www.sciam.com/2000/0200issue/0200techbus2.html.

28. An early discussion of this topic can be found in Bruce Nussbaum and John Templeton, "Built to Last—Until It's Time to Take It Apart," *BusinessWeek*, September 17, 1990, 102–106. A more recent reference is Michael Lenox, Andrew King, and John Ehrenfeld, "An Assessment of Design-for-Environment Practices in Leading US Electronics Firms," *Interfaces*, 30, no. 3 (May–June 2000), 83–94.

29. Nussbaum and Templeton, "Built to Last."

30. Edwin Davies, "Time to Market: How Long Does It Take to Develop a New Biotech Drug," http://www.btinternet.com/~edwindavies/manufacture/manufacture_hgh_tpa_text.htm.

31. P. S. Adler, "Interdepartmental Interdependence and Coordination: The Case of the Design/Manufacturing Interface," *Organizational Science*, March–April 1995, 147–167.

32. "Can This Man Save Chrysler?" *BusinessWeek*, September 17, 2001, 86–94.

33. Geoff Lancaster, "Marketing and Engineering Revisited," *Journal of Business and Industrial Marketing*, 10, no. 1 (1995), 6–15.

34. Don Clausing and Bruce H. Simpson, "Quality by Design," *Quality Progress*, January 1990, 41–44.

35. Gunnar Hedlund and Jonas Ridderstrale, "Toward a Theory of the Self-Renewing MNC," in *International Business: An Emerging Vision*, Brian Toyne and Douglas Nigh (eds.) (Columbia, SC: University of South Carolina Press, 1997).

36. Solar Turbines, "New Product Introduction," BNPI/797/2.5M, 1997.

37. Wheelwright and Clark, *Revolutionizing Product Development*.

38. Michael A. Cusumano and Kentaro Nobeoka, *Thinking beyond Lean* (New York: Free Press, 1998).

Chapter 4

1. *Autoweeks' Official Racing Fan Guide*.

2. Albert H. Segars, Warren J. Harkness, and William J. Kettinger, "Process Management and Supply-Chain Integration at the Bose Corporation," *Interfaces*, 31, no. 3 (May–June 2001), 102–114.

3. See, for example, Bruce Johnson, "A Manager's Understanding of the Primary, Secondary, and Tertiary Effects of Equipment and Process Technology" (Ph.D. diss., University of Cincinnati, 1989).

4. Jon R. Katzenback and Douglas K. Smith, "The Discipline of Teams," *Harvard Business Review*, March–April 1993, 111–120.

5. Adapted from John Noerr, "Benefits for the Back Office, Too," *BusinessWeek*, July 10, 1989, 59.

6. Sometimes a process is not operated at its maximum production rate. In those instances, one must distinguish between the rate at which units can complete the process (the minimum cycle time of the process) and the rate at which they actually do complete the process (the actual cycle time).

7. Jonathan B. Weinbach, "Rushing for Your Flight? Hurry Up and Get in Line," *The Wall Street Journal*, April 21, 2000.

8. The terms *flow time, throughput time,* and *lead-time* are used interchangeably to refer to the time it takes for the customer or the product to go through the system. *Cycle time,* as defined earlier, is the time between two contiguous outputs from a system.

9. Stanley E. Fawcett and John N. Pearson, "Understanding and Applying Constraint Management in Today's Manufacturing Environments," *Production and Inventory Management Journal*, 32, no. 3 (Third Quarter 1991), 410–455.

10. Michael S. Spencer and Samuel Wathen, "Applying the Theory of Constraints' Process Management Technique to an Administrative Function at Stanley Furniture," *National Productivity Review*, 13, no. 3 (Summer 1994), 379–385.

11. Bela Gold, "CAM Sets New Rules for Production," *Harvard Business Review*, November–December 1982, 169.

12. D. Gerwin, "Manufacturing Flexibility: A Strategic Perspective," *Management Science*, 39, no. 4 (Apr 1993), 395–410.

13. "Flexibility Helps Company Cope with Rapid Growth," *Modern Materials Handling*, August 1987, 54–56.

14. "Take 3 People and Build a Motorcycle," *Production*, November 1995, 60–63.

15. Steven Spear and H. Kent Bowen, "Decoding the DNA of the Toyota Production System," *Harvard Business Review*, September–October 1999, 96–106.

16. Andrew E. Serwer, "Michael Dell Turns the PC World Inside Out," *Fortune*, September 8, 1997, 76–86.

17. Steve Lagasse, "Diamond Packaging's Semi-Automatic Carton Line Setup Time Reduction Team," *Target*, 12, no. 4 (September–October 1996), 44–45.

18. Lawrence S. Pryor, "Benchmarking: A Self-Improvement Strategy," *Journal of Business Strategy*, November–December 1989, 28–32.

19. Robert C. Camp, *Benchmarking: The Search for Industry Best Practices That Lead to Superior Performance* (Milwaukee, WI: ASQC Quality Press and UNIPUB/Quality Resources, 1989).

20. Christopher E. Bogan and Michael J. English, "Benchmarking for Best Practices: Winning Through Innovative Adaptation," *Quality Digest*, August 1994, 52–62.

21. John Hackl, "New Beginnings: Change Is Here to Stay," Editorial Comment, *Quality Progress*, February 1998, 5.

22. Michael Hammer and James Champy, *Reengineering the Corporation* (New York: Harper Business, 1993).

23. Bogan and English, "Benchmarking for Best Practices: Winning through Innovative Adaptation."

24. Roger Ballou, "Reengineering at American Express: The Travel Services Group's Work in Progress," *Interfaces*, 25, no. 3 (May–June 1996), 22–29.

25. Adapted from ASQ Quality Auditor Certification Brochure (July 1989).

Chapter 5

1. Richard Boulton, Barry Libert, and Steve Samek, *Cracking the Value Code: How Successful Businesses Are Creating Wealth in the New Economy* (New York: Harper Business, 2000).

2. Ken Zino, "Economies of Scale: Nothing like It Ever Existed Before; Nothing like It Will Ever Exist Again," *Autoweek,* January 9, 1989, 31.

3. Judith Motti, "Schwab Integrates Bricks and Chicks," *InformationWeek*, June 19, 2000.

4. D. A. Garvin, *Operations Strategy: Text and Cases* (Upper Saddle River, NJ: Prentice Hall, 1992).

5. Based on our discussion with the Assistant General Manager, Strategic Quality and Manager Logistics, Toyota Motor Manufacturing, Northern Kentucky.

6. Wickham Skinner, "The Focused Factory," *Harvard Business Review,* May–June 1974, 113–121.

7. Ismini Scouras, "American Power Keeps Its Focus," *Electronic Buyer News,* September 2, 1996, 28.

8. R. W. Schmenner, "Multiplant Manufacturing Strategies among the Fortune 500," *Journal of Operations Management,* 2, no. 2 (1982).

9. M. A. Cohen and H. L. Lee, "Resource Deployment Analysis of Global Manufacturing and Distribution Networks," *Journal of Manufacturing and Operations Management,* 2 (1989), 1–104.

10. E. Dieter, "From Partial to Systemic Globalization: International Production Networks in the Electronics Industry" (working paper 98, Berkeley Roundtable on the International Economy, University of California at Berkeley, 1997).

11. Sean B. McAlindon, "What's the Right Size for an Assembly Plant?" *Automotive Manufacturing and Production*, October 1997, 13–14.

12. William J. Abernathy and Kenneth Wayne, "Limits of the Learning Curve," *Harvard Business Review,* September–October 1974, 109–119.

13. A. Bernstein and W. Zellner, "Outsourced—and Out of Luck," *BusinessWeek*, July 1995, 60–61.

14. F. Bruck, "Make versus Buy: The Wrong Decisions Cost," *The McKinsey Quarterly,* 1 (1995), 28–47.

15. Adapted from Jeffrey D. Camm, Thomas E. Chorman, Franz A. Dill, James R. Evans, Dennis J. Sweeney, and Glenn W. Wegryn, "Blending OR/MS, Judgment, and GIS: Restructuring P&G's Supply Chain," *Interfaces,* 27, no. 1 (January–February 1997), 128–142.

16. Jack Cook, "Hospitals Not in the Bed Business," *Cincinnati Enquirer,* June 24, 1993, A11.

17. See Robert H. Hayes and Steven C. Wheelwright, *Restoring Our Competitive Edge* (New York: John Wiley & Sons, 1984), 52–53.

18. "Now Playing on Screen 29: Megaplexes Are Taking Over, Driving Out the Smaller Chains," *Business Week,* July 7, 1997, 46.

19. Robert Oberwetter, "Building Blockbuster Business: Can Revenue Management Land a Starring Role in the Movie Theater Industry?" *OR/MS Today,* June 2001.

20. Shankar Basu and Roger Schroeder, "Incorporating Judgments in Sales Forecasts: Applying the Delphi Method at American Hoist and Derrick," *Interfaces,* 7, no. 3 (May 1977), 18–27.

21. Based on W. C. Jordan and S. C. Graves, "Principles on the Benefits of Manufacturing Process Flexibility," *Management Science,* 41, no. 4 (1995), 577–594.

Chapter 6

1. Nabil Tamimi and Rose Sebastianelli, "How Firms Define and Measure Quality," *Production and Inventory Management Journal,* 37, no. 3 (Third Quarter 1996), 34–39.

2. David A. Garvin, "What Does Product Quality Really Mean?" *Sloan Management Review,* 26, no. 1 (1984), 25–43.

3. Early history is reported in Delmer C. Dague, "Quality—Historical Perspective," in *Quality Control in Manufacturing* (Warrendale, PA: Society of Automotive Engineers, February 1981); and L. P. Provost and C. L. Norman, "Variation through the Ages," *Quality Progress* 23, no. 12 (December 1990), 39–44. Modern events are discussed in Nancy Karabatsos, "Quality in Transition, Part One: Account of the '80s," *Quality Progress,* 22, no. 12 (December 1989), 22–26; and Joseph M. Juran, "The Upcoming Century of Quality," address to the ASQC Annual Quality Congress, Las Vegas, May 24, 1994. A comprehensive historical account may be found in J. M. Juran, *A History of Managing for Quality* (Milwaukee, WI: ASQC Quality Press, 1995).

4. *The PIMS Letter on Business Strategy,* no. 4 (Cambridge, MA: Strategic Planning Institute, 1986).

5. Kevin B. Hendricks and Vinod R. Singhal, "Does Implementing an Effective TQM Program Actually Improve Operating Performance? Empirical Evidence from Firms That Have Won Quality Awards," *Management Science* 43, no. 9 (September 1997), 1258–1274. The results of this study have appeared in numerous business and trade publications such as *Business Week* and *Fortune.*

6. W. Edwards Deming, *The New Economics for Industry, Government, Education* (Cambridge, MA: MIT Center for Advanced Engineering Study, 1993).

7. Adapted from March Laree Jacques, "Big League Quality," *Quality Progress,* August 2001, 27–34.

8. Paul W. DeBaylo, "Ten Reasons Why the Baldrige Model Works," *Journal for Quality and Participation,* January–February 1999, 1–5.

9. "ISO 9000 Update," *Fortune,* September 30, 1996, 134[J].

10. Astrid L. H. Eckstein and Jaydeep Balakrishnan, "The ISO 9000 Series: Quality Management Systems for the Global Economy," *Production and Inventory Management Journal* 34, no. 4 (Fourth Quarter 1993), 66–71.

11. "Home Builder Constructs Quality with ISO 9000," *Quality Digest,* February 2000, 13.

12. Ronald D. Snee, "Why Should Statisticians Pay Attention to Six Sigma?" *Quality Progress,* September 1999, 100–103.

13. A composite of ideas suggested by Stanley A. Marash, "Six Sigma: Business Results through Innovation," *ASQ's 54th Annual Quality Congress Proceedings* (2000), 627–630; and Dick Smith and Jerry Blakeslee, *Strategic Six Sigma: Best Practices from the Executive Suite* (New York: Wiley, 2002).

14. Ronald D. Snee, "Guest Editorial: Impact of Six Sigma on Quality Engineering," *Quality Engineering,* 12, no. 3 (2000), ix–xiv.

15. "GE Reports Record Earnings with Six Sigma," *Quality Digest,* December 1999, 14.

16. Rochelle Rucker, "Six Sigma at Citibank," *Quality Digest,* December 1999, 28–32.

17. Adapted from Jong-Yong Yun and Richard C. H. Chua, "Samsung Uses Six Sigma to Change Its Image," *Six Sigma Forum Magazine,* 2, no. 1 (November 2002), 13–16.

18. C. M. Creveling, J. L. Slutsky, and D. Antis, Jr., *Design for Six Sigma in Technology and Product Development* (Upper Saddle River, NJ: Prentice Hall, 2003).

19. Ronald D. Snee and Roger W. Hoerl, *Leading Six Sigma* (Upper Saddle River, NJ: Prentice Hall, 2002).

20. The authors are grateful to Joe Sener, Vice President for Business Excellence at Baxter International, for providing this information.

21. "Testing for Conformity: An Inside Job," *Golf Journal,* May 1998, 20–25.

22. "DaimlerChrysler's Quality Practices Pay Off for PT Cruiser," *News and Analysis, Metrologyworld.com,* March 23, 2000.

23. For an interesting, albeit academic, discussion of the psychology of human error and its relationship to mistake-proofing, see Douglas M. Stewart and Richard B. Chase, "The Impact of Human Error on Delivering Service Quality," *Production and Operations Management,* 8, no. 3 (Fall 1999), 240–263; and Douglas M. Stewart and John R. Grout, "The Human Side of Mistake Proofing," *Production and Operations Management,* 10, no. 4 (Winter 2001), 440–459.

24. See *Poka-Yoke: Improving Product Quality by Preventing Defects.* Edited by *NKS/Factory Magazine,* English translation copyright © 1988 by Productivity Press, Inc., P.O. Box 3007, Cambridge, MA 02140, 800-394-6868.

25. Adapted from the Ritz-Carlton Hotel Company's 1992 and 1999 Application Summaries for the Malcolm Baldrige National Quality Award.

26. *Reports of Statistical Application Research,* Japanese Union of Scientists and Engineers, 33, no. 2 (June 1986).

27. This case study was adapted from a Mitsukoshi case published in *A Book of QC Themes.* Toyoki Ikeda (Tokyo, Japan: Chuukei Shuppan, 1990), 334–338.

Chapter 7

1. U.S. Department of Commerce, "Manufacturing and Trade Inventories and Sales," February 14, 2002, CB02-21, at http://www.census.gov/mtis/www/current.html; Calvin Lee, "Demand Chain Optimization: Pitfalls and Key Principles," Nonstop's Supply Chain Management Seminar Series Whitepaper.

2. Mike Aghajanian, director at Pittiglio, Rabin, Todd & McGrath.

3. The Supply-Chain Council was formed in 1996–1997 as a grassroots initiative by several firms including AMR Research; Bayer; Compaq Computer; Pittiglio, Rabin, Todd & McGrath (PRTM); Procter & Gamble; Lockheed Martin; Nortel; Rockwell Semiconductor; and Texas Instruments. See http://www.supply-chain.org/ for information on the Supply-Chain Council and the development of the SCOR model.

4. Joseph C. Andraski, Joseph P. Wisdo, and Rick D. Blasgen, "Dispatches from the Front: The Nabisco Story," *Supply Chain Management Review,* Spring 1997, 22–30.

5. Eryn Brown, "The Push to Streamline Supply Chains," *Fortune,* March 3, 1997.

6. Timothy Van Mieghem, "Lessons Learned from Alexander the Great," *Quality Progress,* January 1998, 41–46.

7. Comment by Bob Runge, chief marketing officer at Pivotal, in "Demand Chain Networks: Maximizing Revenue and Customer Retention," business paper, Pivotal Corporation, at http://www.pivotal.com. This paper was developed from "Chain of Demand" and "Parallel Objectives," *Pivotal Magazine,* April 2001.

8. Adapted from Martin Christopher and Hau Lee, "Supply Chain Confidence: The Key to Effective Supply Chains through Improved Visibility and Reliability" (working paper, Stanford Global Supply Chain Management Forum, November 2001).

9. Hau L. Lee and Seungjin Whang, "Demand Chain Excellence: A Tale of Two Retailers," *Supply Chain Management Review,* 5, no. 2, March–April 2001, 40–47.

10. Tim Minahan, "Supply Chain Key to Growth at Koppers," *Purchasing,* April 17, 1997.

11. James A. G. Krupp, "Measuring Inventory Management Performance," *Production and Inventory Management Journal,* 35, no. 4 (Fourth Quarter 1994), 1–6.

12. "Business Report," *Fortune,* March 19, 1998.

13. The source of this rule of thumb is a firm in Cincinnati that observed such a reduction empirically. We have not validated the legitimacy of this rule ourselves.

14. Marshall L. Fisher, "What Is the Right Supply Chain for Your Product?" *Harvard Business Review,* March–April 1997, 105–116.

15. Tim Laseter, Barrie Berg, and Martha Turner, "What FreshDirect Learned from Dell," *Strategy & Business,* Spring 2003, http://www.strategy-business.com.

16. "Honda Encounters Some Surprises on the Road to Marysville, Ohio," *The Wall Street Journal,* March 22, 1983.

17. Kenichi Ohmae, *Triad Power: The Coming Shape of Global Competition* (New York: Free Press, 1985), 5–6.

18. Much of this discussion is adapted from Kasra Ferdows, "Making the Most of Your Foreign Factories," *Harvard Business Review*, March–April 1997, 73–88.

19. Han Lee, V. Padmanabhan, and Sevgjin Whang, "Information Distortion in a Supply Chain," *Management Science*, 43, no. 4 (April 1997), 546–558.

20. Facts in this box were drawn from Patricia Gallagher, "Value Pricing for Profits," *Cincinnati Enquirer*, December 21, 1992, D-1, D-6; "Procter & Gamble Hits Back," *BusinessWeek*, July 19, 1993, 20–22; Bill Sapority, "Behind the Tumult at P&G," *Fortune,* March 7, 1994, 75–82.

21. Justin Martin, "Are You As Good As You Think You Are?" *Fortune*, September 30, 1996, 142–152.

22. Valerie Reitman, "Toyota's Fast Rebound after Fire at Supplier Shows Why It's Tough," *The Wall Street Journal*, May 8, 1997, 1.

23. Ursula Miller, "Baldwin Finds New Supplier," *Cincinnati Enquirer*, February 9, 1999, B10.

24. Larry Kishpaugh, "Process Management and Business Results," presentation at the 1996 Regional Malcolm Baldrige Award Conference, Boston, Massachusetts.

25. Texas Instruments Defense Systems & Electronics Group, Malcolm Baldrige Application Summary (1992).

26. Hokey Min, "A World-Class Continuous Quality Improvement Program: The Fastener Supply Corporation Case," *Production and Inventory Management Journal*, Fourth Quarter 1998, 10–14.

27. Scott Wooley, "Replacing Inventory with Information," *Forbes*, March 24, 1997, www.forbes.com.

28. Adapted from Laura Kopczak and M. Eric Johnson, "Supply Chain Management: How It Is Changing the Way Managers Think" (working paper, Tuck School of Business, Dartmouth College, February 2003).

Chapter 8

1. Adapted from *The Wall Street Journal*, September 27, 1994, B10. See also "Truth in Scheduling Rule," Aviation Consumer Action Project, http://www.acap1971.org/whatsnew/ITSR.cfm.

2. Joseph Orlicky, *Material Requirements Planning* (New York: McGraw-Hill 1975).

3. S. Kadipasaoglu and V. Sridharan, "Alternative Approaches to Reducing Schedule Instability in Multistage Manufacturing under Demand Uncertainty," *Journal of Operations Management*, 13 (1995), 193–211.

4. T. E. Vollmann, W. L. Berry, and D. C. Whybark, *Manufacturing Planning and Control Systems*, 4th ed. (New York: Irwin/McGraw-Hill, 1997).

5. Tom Wallace, *MRP II: Making It Happen* (New London, NH: Oliver Wight Limited Publications, 1990).

6. R. Lawrence LaForge and Christopher W. Craighead, "Computer-Based Scheduling in Manufacturing Firms: Some Indicators of Successful Practice," *Production and Inventory Management Journal*, First Quarter 2000, 29–34.

7. Mac Exon-Taylor, "Beyond MRP—The Operation of a Modern Scheduling System," *Supply Chain Management,* 2, no. 2 (1997), 43–48.

8. Dorien James and Malcolm Wolf, "A Second Wind for ERP," *McKinsey Quarterly*, 2, no. 2, (2000), 100–107.

9. Christopher Koch, Derek Slater, and E. Baatz, "The ABCs of ERP," at http://www.cio.com.

10. Amal Kumar Naj, "Manufacturing Gets a New Craze from Software: Speed," *The Wall Street Journal*, August 16, 1996.

Chapter 9

1. Alex Taylor III, "How Toyota Defies Gravity," *Fortune*, December 8, 1997, 100–108.

2. D. Dimancescu, *The Lean Enterprise* (New York: AMACOM, 1997); and J.P. Womack and D.T. Jones, *Lean Thinking: Banish Waste and Create Wealth in Your Corporation* (New York: Simon and Schuster, 1996).

3. David Woodruff, "Porsche Is Back—and Then Some," *BusinessWeek*, September 15, 1997, 57.

4. Anthony R. Goland, John Hall, and Devereaux A. Clifford, "First National Toyota," *The McKinsey Quarterly,* 4 (1998), 58–66.

5. Ibid.

6. James P. Womack, Daniel T. Jones, and Daniel Roos, *The Machine That Changed the World* (New York: HarperCollins, 1990).

7. S. Shingo, *A Study of the Toyota Production System from an Industrial Engineering Viewpoint* (Cambridge, MA: Productivity Press, 1989).

8. Jon Van, "Leaks No Longer Strain Harley-Davidson Name," *Chicago Tribune*, November 4, 1991.

9. Ronald Henkoff, "Delivering the Goods," *Fortune*, November 28, 1994, 64–78.

10. See Scott R. Hedin and Gregory R. Russell, "JIT Implementation: Interaction between the Production and Cost-Accounting Functions," *Production and Inventory Management Journal,* 33, no. 3 (Third Quarter 1992), 68–73; B. Maskell, "Management Accounting and Just-in-Time," *Management Accounting,* 68, no. 3 (1986), 32–34.

11. Steven Spear and H. Kent Bowen, "Decoding the DNA of the Toyota Production System," *Harvard Business Review,* 77, no. 5 (September–October 1999), 97–106.

12. R. Inman and S. Mehra, "JIT Implementation within a Service Industry: A Case Study," *International Journal of Service Industry Management,* 1, no. 3 (1990). See also R. Inman and S. Mehra, "JIT Applications for Service Environments," *Production and Inventory Management Journal,* 32, no. 3 (1991), 16–21.

13. Wallace J. Hopp and Mark L. Spearman, *Factory Physics* (Boston: McGraw-Hill, 1996).

14. E. M. Goldratt, *The Haystack Syndrome: Sifting Information Out of the Data Ocean* (Croton-on-Hudson, NY: North River Press, 1990).

15. W. Steven Demmy and Barbara Sue Demmy, "Drum-Buffer-Rope Scheduling and Pictures for the Yearbook," *Production and Inventory Management Journal,* 35, no. 3 (Third Quarter 1994), 45–47.

16. Ibid.

17. Based on Xerox presentation notes, courtesy of George Maszle, Corporate Quality, Xerox Corporation.

18. Based on Eli Goldratt's lecture notes from OPT seminar, University of Arizona, 1986.

Chapter 10

1. J. Meredith and S. Mantel, *Project Management: A Managerial Approach,* 4th ed. (New York: Wiley, 2000).

2. Tom Peters, *The Pursuit of WOW: Every Person's Guide to Topsy Turvy Teams* (New York: Vintage Books, 1995), and *The Project 50 (Reinventing Work), Fifty Ways to Transform Every "Task" into a Project That Matters!* (New York: Knopf, 1999).

3. Project Management Institute, *Project Management Body of Knowledge* (Drexel Hill, PA: PMI, 1987), 167.

4. "Boeing Loses $1.3 Billion Satellite Contract Options," *The Wall Street Journal,* February 19, 2000.

5. Jeffrey L. Whitten, Lonnie D. Bentley, and Kevin C. Dittman, *Systems Analysis and Design Methods,* 5th ed. (New York: McGraw-Hill Irwin, 2000).

6. P. Diab, "Strategic Planning—Project Management Competitive Advantage," *PM Network,* July 1998, 25–28.

7. Diane Haithman, "Disney Hall: Unfinished Symphony?" *Los Angeles Times,* February 27, 1995.

8. See F. P. Brooks, *The Mythical Man Month* (Reading, MA: Addison-Wesley, 1975).

9. Our thanks go to Amy Crawford of Kendle International for providing this information.

10. "Why Projects Fail," The Standish Group, 2000. For more information on project failure and success, visit the Web site for Unfinished Voyages!

11. In some project environments, the life cycle consists of the following five phases. During the *concept phase,* the idea for a project arises, and preliminary cost and schedule estimates are developed at a high level to determine if the project not only is technically feasible but also will have a payback. In the *formulation phase,* the complete project plans are developed. These plans often include a statement of work, a work breakdown structure, and schedules. During the *implementation phase,* the plan is executed. Energy is expended to achieve the goals and objectives of the project in the manner prescribed during the formulation phase. In the *installation phase,* the final product is delivered to the customer. At this point, considerable training and administrative support are provided to "please the customer." The *sustaining phase* covers the time the product, such as a computing system or a building, is under the customer's control and an infrastructure exists to maintain and enhance the product.

12. Our appreciation goes to John Whited of Xerox Global Services, Inc. for providing this example.

13. Eliyahu M. Goldratt, *Critical Chain* (Great Barrington, MA: North River Press, 1997).

14. Dee Jacob, *Introduction to Project Management the TOC Way—A Workshop* (New Haven, CT: The A.Y. Goldratt Institute, 1998).

15. Adapted from Department of Defense data published in *Oversight Hearing on the A–12 Navy Aircraft* (Washington, DC: Ross & Perry, 2002).

16. F. P. Moolin, Jr., and F. A. McCoy, "Managing the Alaska Pipeline Project," *Civil Engineering,* November 1981, 51–54.

Chapter 11

1. Richard Boulton, Barry Libert, and Steve Samek, *Cracking the Value Code* (New York: Harper Business, 2000), 71.

2. Design for Aging Concepts at Ergo Gero: Human Factors Science at http://www.ergogero.com/pages/designforaging.html.

3. International Organization for Standardization, *ISO 14001: Environmental Management Systems—Specification with Guidance for Use* (1996). Tom Tibor, with Ira Feldman, *ISO 14000: A Guide to the New Environmental Management Standards* (Homewood, IL: Irwin Professional Publishing, 1996). International Organization for Standardization, *ISO 14004: Environmental Management Systems—General Guidelines on Principles, Systems, and Supporting Techniques* (1996).

4. Craig P. Diamond, "Voluntary Environmental Management System Standards: Case Studies in Implementation," *Total Quality Environmental Management* (Winter 1995/1996), 9–23.

5. The U.S. Postal Service, *Environmental Resources Handbook* (November 1995).

6. National Association of State Energy Officials, *Energy Efficiency and Renewable Sources: A Primer* (July 1998), at http://www.naseo.org.

7. Jesse Wong, "At Arnhold, Today's Realities Force Produce-or-Else Attitude," *The Wall Street Journal*, February 15, 2000.

8. Andy Pasztor and Jeff Cole, "Boeing Slows Most Deliveries, Cites Glitch with Fasteners," *The Wall Street Journal*, March 7, 2000.

9. W. Skinner, "Manufacturing—The Missing Link in Corporate Strategy," *Harvard Business Review*, 47, no. 3 (1969), 136–145; and *Manufacturing in Corporate Strategy* (New York: John Wiley & Sons, 1978).

10. R. H. Hayes and S. C. Wheelwright, *Restoring Our Competitive Edge: Competing through Manufacturing* (New York: John Wiley & Sons, 1984); R. H. Hayes and G. P. Pisano, "Manufacturing Strategy: At the Intersection of Two Paradigm Shifts," *Production and Operations Management* (Spring 1996), 25–41.

11. The development of the balanced scorecard method can be traced to David Norton, CEO of Nolan Norton, the research arm of the accounting firm KPMG, and Robert Kaplan, Professor of Accounting, Harvard University. Senior managers from 12 corporations shared a belief that exclusive reliance on summary performance measures was hindering the organizations' abilities to create future economic value. The findings were compiled in a book and several articles: for example, R. S. and D. P. Norton, "The Balanced Scorecard-Measures That Drive Performance," *Harvard Business Review* (January–February 1992); "Putting the Balanced Scorecard to Work," *Harvard Business Review* (September–October 1993); "Using the Balanced Scorecard as a Strategic Management System," *Harvard Business Review* (January–February 1996); and *The Balanced Scorecard* (Boston: HBS Press, 1996).

12. Peter Kolesar, Garrett van Rysin, and Wayne Cutler, *Creating Customer Value through Industrialized Intimacy*, at http://www.strategy-business.com/strategy/98304/authors.html.

13. Based on Jeffrey M. O'Brien, "The Making of the Xbox: How Did the World's Largest Software Publisher Become a Hardware Manufacturer Overnight? One Word: Flextronics," *Wired*, issue 9.11 (November 2001).

14. Kenneth Preiss, Steven L. Goldman, and Roger N. Nagel, *Cooperate to Compete: Building Agile Business Relationship* (New York: John Wiley & Sons, 1996).

15. Donna Fenn, "Sleeping with the Enemy," *Inc.* (November 1997), 78.

16. Michael Hammer and Steven A. Stanton, *The Reengineering Revolution* (New York: HarperCollins, 1995), 336.

17. N. Venkatraman, "IT-Enabled Business Transformation: From Automation to Business Scope Redefinition," *Sloan Management Review* (Winter 1994).

18. N. Venkatraman, "IT-Induced Business Reconfiguration," in M. Scott Morton (ed.), *The Corporation of the 1990s* (Oxford: Oxford University Press, 1991), 122–158.

19. J. B. Quinn, *Intelligent Enterprise* (New York: Free Press, 1992).

20. Ramchandran Jaikumar and David M. Upton, "The Coordination of Global Manufacturing," in Stephen P. Bradley, Jerry A. Hausman, and Richard L. Nolan (eds.), *Globalization, Technology and Competition: The Fusion of Computers and Telecommunications* (Boston: Harvard Business School Press, 1993).

21. For an excellent description of what the average airline passenger has to endure, see Henry Mintzberg, *Why I Hate Flying* (New York: Texere Publishing, 2001), at http://www.etexere.com.

22. R. Schmenner, "Multiplant Manufacturing Strategies among the Fortune 500," *Journal of Operations Management*, 2, no. 2 (February 1982), 77–86.

23. A. D. MacCormack, L. J. Newman III, and D. B. Rosenfeld, "The New Dynamics of Global Manufacturing Site Location," *Sloan Management Review* (Summer 1994), 69–80.

24. K. Ferdows, "Making the Most of Foreign Factories," *Harvard Business Review* (March–April 1997), 77–88.

25. T. Flaherty, "Coordinating International Manufacturing and Technology," in Michael Porter (ed.), *Competition in Global Industries* (Boston: Harvard Business School Press, 1986), 83–109.

26. C. Bartlett and S. Ghoshal, *Managing across Borders: The Transnational Solution* (Boston: Harvard Business School Press, 1989).

27. W. Skinner, "The Focused Factory," *Harvard Business Review* (May–June 1974), 113–121.

28. Ronald D. Snee, "Guest Editorial: Impact of Six Sigma on Quality Engineering," *Quality Engineering,* 12, no. 3 (2000), ix–xiv.

29. Adapted from General Electric's 1997 Annual Report.

30. Matt Barney, "Motorola's Second Generation," *Six Sigma Forum Magazine,* 1, no. 3 (May 2002), 13–22.

31. Robert Simison, Fara Warner, and Gregory L. White, "GM, Ford, Daimler Chrysler to Create a Single Firm to Supply Auto Parts," *The Wall Street Journal,* February 28, 2000.

32. C. J. Backhouse and N. J. Brookes, *Concurrent Engineering: What's Working Where* (Brookfield, VT: The Design Group/Gower, 1996).

33. C. J. Haddad, "Operationalizing the Concept of Concurrent Engineering: A Case Study from the US Auto Industry," *IEEE Transactions on Engineering Management,* 43, no. 2 (1996), 124–132.

34. S. C. Wheelwright and K. B. Clark, *Revolutionizing Product Development: Quantum Leaps in Speed, Efficiency, and Quality* (New York: Free Press, 1992).

35. Jeffrey Elton and Justin Roe, "Bringing Discipline to Project Management," *Harvard Business Review* (March–April 1998), 3–7.

36. F. W. Taylor, *Scientific Management (Comprising Shop Management, The Principles of Scientific Management, and Testimony before the Special House Committee)* (New York: Harper & Brothers, 1947).

37. Ramchandran Jaikumar and Roger E. Bohn, "A Dynamic Approach to Operations Management: An Alternative to Static Optimization" (Working paper, March 1992, revised May 1992). Address correspondence and reprint requests to Professor Roger Bohn, IR/PS, UCSD, La Jolla, CA 92093-0519, Rbohn@UCSD.edu.

Index

Note: Italicized page locators indicate tables/figures.

Engineering Data Management (EDM), 88
Enterprise resource planning (ERP), 18, 21, 103, 228, 230, 246–49, 250, 319
  benefits and challenges with, 249
  ERP architecture, 247
  evolution of, 229–30, *231*
  implementing ERP systems, 247–49
Environmental assessment, 33
Environmental Protection Agency, 321
Environmental regulations, and inputs, 9
Environmental sustainability, 24
Environmental uncertainties, delays and, 70
EOQ, 232, 267
Equipment variation, 187
Ergonomics, 106–7
Ernst & Young, 47
ERP. *See* Enterprise resource planning
ERP Project
  activity-on-node diagram for, *300*
  complete schedule calculations for, *303*
  earliest start/earliest finish schedule for, *301*
  key activities for, *300*
  latest start/latest finish schedule for, *302*
  partial task list for, *298*
Errors, preventing, 186
Errors per opportunity, 56
e-tailers, problems with, 33, 34
European Community, 177
EVA, 52
Excess capacity policy, *154*
Excess inventory, 204, 224
Expansionist strategy, 154
Expediting, 241
Experience curve, 156
Explosion, 240
External customers, 11
External failure costs, 172
External suppliers, 10

Facility construction, lead–time for, 153
Facility design: from plants to clusters, 331–33
Facility focus strategies, *140*
Facility layout, 117–19
Fair shares allocation, 211
Fastener Supply Corporation, 220
FastShip, 220
Fast-tracking, 286, 294
FCS, 243–44
Fear, 170
Features, and quality, 164
Federal environmental laws, commonly applicable, in the United States, 321
Federated Department Stores, 46
FedEx, 3, 56, 59, 164, 208
Fee-for-service (FFS), 30
Fill rates, 58, 61
Finance, 19, 28
  costs of, 224
  from design, operations, and marketing to, 85
Financial methods, 287, *288*
Financial perspective, 52
Finished goods inventory, 202
Finite Capacity Scheduling (FCS), 243–44
"Fitness for use," 56, 171
5 S's, for lean production, 261
Flexibility
  measuring, 58, 61
  process design and, 116–19
Flexible manufacturing system (FMS), 103
Flextronics, 329
Florida Power and Light, 47
Flow time, 108, 110, 244, 250
Fluctuation inventory, 202
Fluidity, 66
FMS, 103
Focused facilities, 138–39, 157
Focusing purchasing strategy, *218*
Ford Motor Company, 4, 26, 74, 107, 116, 336
  design for assembly and, 82
  Rouge complex and, 131, 137
Ford, Henry, 58, 110, 121, 131, 167, 264
Forecast cycle, 206
Forecasting, 151–52, 157, 245
Fortune, 4
Forward buying, 216
Forward integration, 10
Forward scheduling, 238
  resource implications of, *239*
France, 5
Freezing, 241
FreshDirect, designing supply chain at, 209
Full-scale production, ramp-up to, 83
Function, process *versus*, *99*
Functionality, 248
Functional products, 208

G

Gantt, Harry, 297
Gantt charts, 229, 297, 299, 311
  example of, *299*
  example of, with earned value data, *308*
  partial, of bicycle manufacturing, *238*
  for resource-limited project schedule, *307*
Garvin, David A., 164
Gehry, Frank O., 286
General Electric, 16, 51, 82, 178, 181
  Six Sigma benchmark and, 180, 334
General Electric Transportation Systems, 199
General Foods, 106
General Mills, 121
General Motors (GM), 4, 26, 68, 82, 106, 271, 336
Georgia Web group, 93
Germany, 5
Global facilities networks, 211–12
Global integration, 26
Globalization, 24, 25–26, 87–77, 91
Global networks of facilities, 224
Globiis (Global Business Integrated Information Systems), 199
GM. *See* General Motors
Goal, The (Goldratt), 115
Goldratt, Eliyahu, 115, 127
Gold Standards, 6
Gold Star Chili, Inc., 100
  organization of, *101*
Golf balls, quality spin on, 183
Goods, 5
  comparisons among services, contracts and, 7
  and services, 3
Goodwill costs, 205
Green, Michael, 323
Group layout, 119, 123
Group technology, 269
GroupWare, 247
Growth phase, in product life cycle, 67, *68*
GTE, 122

H

Hamann, Elise, 134
Hamel, G., 35
Hard technology, 103, 123
Harley-Davidson, 3, 58, 119, 267
Harris, Ford, 197
Harvard Business School, 38, 52, 104
Haywood-Farmer, 44
Headley, Dean, 111
Health-care environment, operational challenges in, 30–31

R

Q